THE
HISTORY OF
CHINA

ADVISORY BOARD

THE HISTORY OF CHINA

Second Edition

David Curtis Wright

The Greenwood Histories of the Modern Nations
Frank W. Thackeray and John E. Findling, Series Editors

AN IMPRINT OF ABC-CLIO, LLC
Santa Barbara, California • Denver, Colorado • Oxford, England

Library of Congress Cataloging-in-Publication Data

Wright, David Curtis, 1960–
   The history of China / David Curtis Wright. — 2nd ed.
     p. cm. — (Greenwood histories of the modern nations)
   Includes bibliographical references and index.
   ISBN 978–0–313–37748–8 (hardcopy : alk. paper) — ISBN 978–0–313–37749–5 (ebook)
1. China—History. I. Title.
DS735.A2W74 2011
951—dc22   2011010866

ISBN 978–0–313–37748–8
EISBN 978–0–313–37749–5

15 14 13   2 3 4 5

This book is also available on the World Wide Web as an eBook.
Visit www.abc-clio.com for details.

Greenwood
An Imprint of ABC-CLIO, LLC

ABC-CLIO, LLC
130 Cremona Drive, P.O. Box 1911
Santa Barbara, California 93116-1911

This book is printed on acid-free paper ∞

Manufactured in the United States of America

To my son Timothy

Contents

Series Foreword

The Greenwood Histories of the Modern Nations series is intended to provide students and interested laypeople with up-to-date, concise, and
analytical histories of many of the nations of the contemporary world.
Not since the 1960s has there been a systematic attempt to publish a
series of national histories, and as series advisors, we believe that this
series will prove to be a valuable contribution to our understanding
of other countries in our increasingly interdependent world.

Some 40 years ago, at the end of the 1960s, the Cold War was an
accepted reality of global politics. The process of decolonization was
still in progress, the idea of a unified Europe with a single currency
was unheard of, the United States was mired in a war in Vietnam,
and the economic boom in Asia was still years in the future. Richard
Nixon was president of the United States, Mao Tse-tung (not yet Mao
Zedong) ruled China, Leonid Brezhnev guided the Soviet Union, and
Harold Wilson was prime minister of the United Kingdom. Authoritarian dictators still controlled most of Latin America, the Middle East
was reeling in the wake of the Six-Day War, and Shah Mohammad
Reza Pahlavi was at the height of his power in Iran.

Since then, the Cold War has ended, the Soviet Union has vanished,
leaving 15 independent republics in its wake, the advent of the

computer age has radically transformed global communications, the rising demand for oil makes the Middle East still a dangerous flash-point, and the rise of new economic powers like the People's Republic of China and India threatens to bring about a new world order. All of these developments have had a dramatic impact on the recent history of every nation of the world.

For this series, which was launched in 1998, we first selected nations whose political, economic, and socio-cultural affairs marked them as among the most important of our time. For each nation, we found an author who was recognized as a specialist in the history of that nation. These authors worked cooperatively with us and with Greenwood Press to produce volumes that reflected current research on their nations and that are interesting and informative to their readers. In the first decade of the series, more than 40 volumes were published, and as of 2008, some are moving into second editions.

The success of the series has encouraged us to broaden our scope to include additional nations, whose histories have had significant effects on their regions, if not on the entire world. In addition, geopolitical changes have elevated other nations into positions of greater impor-tance in world affairs and, so, we have chosen to include them in this series as well. The importance of a series such as this cannot be under-estimated. As a superpower whose influence is felt all over the world, the United States can claim a "special" relationship with almost every other nation. Yet many Americans know very little about the histories of nations with which the United States relates. How did they get to be the way they are? What kind of political systems have evolved there? What kind of influence do they have on their own regions? What are the dominant political, religious, and cultural forces that move their leaders? These and many other questions are answered in the volumes of this series.

The authors who contribute to this series write comprehensive his-tories of their nations, dating back, in some instances, to prehistoric times. Each of them, however, has devoted a significant portion of their book to events of the past 40 years because the modern era has contributed the most to contemporary issues that have an impact on U.S. policy. Authors make every effort to be as up-to-date as possible so that readers can benefit from discussion and analysis of recent events.

In addition to the historical narrative, each volume contains an introductory chapter giving an overview of that country's geography, political institutions, economic structure, and cultural attributes. This is meant to give readers a snapshot of the nation as it exists in the contemporary world. Each history also includes supplementary information following the narrative, which may include a timeline that represents a succinct chronology of the nation's historical evolution, biographical sketches of the nation's most important historical figures, and a glossary of important terms or concepts that are usually expressed in a foreign language. Finally, each author prepares a comprehensive bibliography for readers who wish to pursue the subject further.

Readers of these volumes will find them fascinating and well-written. More importantly, they will come away with a better understanding of the contemporary world and the nations that comprise it. As series advisors, we hope that this series will contribute to a heightened sense of global understanding as we move through the early years of the twenty-first century.

Frank W. Thackeray and John E. Findling
Indiana University Southeast

Preface to the Second Edition

This revised edition contains 30,000 more words than the first and includes new chapters on Taiwan and on mainland China in the twenty-first century. I have also included new material in several of the other chapters as well, particularly eyewitness primary accounts of the Great Leap Forward, the Cultural Revolution (the twin follies of Mao's rule over China), and the Tiananmen Massacre. May China never again have to abide such tragically tumultuous times and the tyrants who cause them.

The bibliography and bibliography essay are expanded, and there is a new section on Internet resources about China.

Thanks are due Kaitlin Ciarmiello at Greenwood Press/ABC-Clio for her patience and forbearance as I completed this revised edition during a move from one residence to another.

My oldest son Timothy will soon will soon be married, and I dedicate this revised edition to him and the new life adventure on which he is about to embark.

Calgary
22 February 2010

Timeline of Historical Events

B.C.

1300s	Decimal system understood and used
1384	Shang establishes last capital, near Anyang
1122?	Shang overthrown; Zhou established
800s	Decline of Western Zhou
770	Eastern Zhou founded
ca. 600–300	Hundred Schools
551	Birth of Confucius
500s	Iron plows used
300s	Compass invented, trace harness developed and used, and drilling for natural gas
336	First use of crossbow on the battlefield
200s	Farmers plant crops in straight rows Concept similar to Newton's First Law of Motion understood

221	Eastern Zhou overthrown; China unified under Qin Shihuang and the Qin dynasty
213	Qin Shihuang has almost all non-Legalist books burned
206	Qin dynasty overthrown
206–202	Civil war
202	Liu Bang founds Han dynasty
100s	Circulation of blood in the body understood, paper invented, and parachutes used
165	First government examination held for prospective civil servants
147	Han Wudi enthroned
133	Han Wudi abolishes intermarriage system with Xiongnu as a prelude to war
90	Detente between Xiongnu and Han
54	Xiongnu submit to Han
25	First suspension bridge built
A.D. 9	Wang Mang usurps Han throne 23 Wang Mang overthrown; Han reestablished as Eastern Han
31	Waterwheel invented and used
40	Xiongnu civil war
ca. 100	Majority of Northern Xiongnu submit to Han; minority flee "to parts unknown"
100s	Seismograph invented and used
200s	Stirrups first used
220	Fall of Han
280	Brief and shaky reunification of China under (Western) Jin 304–589 North-South Division; barbarian regimes in north, Chinese dynasties in south
500s	China thoroughly converted to Buddhism; Hanggliding in China
589	China reunified under Sui dynasty
618	Sui overthrown, Tang founded

620s	Tang emperor Taizong twice challenges Turkic khans to personal combat
630	Turks submit to Taizong, who reigns as Emperor over the Chinese and Heavenly Khan over the Turks
649	Taizong's death; Turks become restless
680	Turks gain independence from China
712–756	Tang China reaches greatest height during Xuanzong's reign
744	Turks conquered by Uighurs
755	An Lushan rebellion shakes Tang China to its very foundations
763	An Lushan rebellion and aftermath quelled, with help of Uighurs
868	First complete printed book
879	Huang Chao rebellion; Huang Chao slaughters thousands of Christians, Jews, and Muslims in Canton (Guangzhou)
907	Fall of Tang, Five Dynasties period
960	Last of Five Dynasties overthrown, Song founded by Zhao Kuangyin, or Song Taizu
976	Death of Song Taizu
1000s	Formula for gunpowder published, Mercator-style map projections used, and inoculation against smallpox
1004	War between Song and Kitan Liao
1005	Shanyuan Treaty concluded between Song and Liao
1092	First mechanical clock invented in Kaifeng, which kept good time until 1126, when the Jurchens overran the city
1115	Jurchen Jin dynasty founded
1127	Southern Song founded
1140s	Song patriot general Yue Fei recalled from war with Jurchens by capitulationist imperial counsellor Qin Gui; Yue Fei dies in prison; Song accepts humiliating "vassal" status vis-à-vis the Jurchen Jin; First use of movable type
1160s	Renewed fighting between Song and Jin; Song's vassal status canceled

1206	Temujin proclaimed Chinggis Khan (Genghis Khan)
1227	Chinggis Khan dies
1234	Jurchen Jin destroyed by Mongol conquerors
1251	Mongol conqueror Möngke enthroned, launches all-out assault on Southern Song
1259	Möngke Khan dies without conquering Southern Song
1260	Khubilai Khan, brother of Möngke, enthroned; continues campaign against Southern Song
1279	All of China conquered by Mongols; Yuan dynasty begins
1294	Khubilai Khan dies
1360s	Widespread rebellion against Mongol rule in China
1368	Mongol Yuan dynasty overthrown by Zhu Yuanzhang; Ming founded
1403	Third Ming emperor, Yongle, moves capital from Nanjing to Beijing; sends navigator Zheng He (Cheng Ho) on several voyages
1449	Western Mongol forces reach Beijing and take Ming emperor prisoner
1500s (to 1570)	Frequent Eastern Mongol raids on Ming China
1570	Formal peace treaty between Ming and Eastern Mongols; Mongol conversion to Buddhism and subsequent reduction of Mongols' martial ardor
ca. 1600	Manchus emerging in Manchuria as a new threat to Ming China
1630s	Widespread peasant rebellion throughout China
1644	Ming overthrown by rebel peasant leader Li Zicheng; Manchus enter Beijing this same year, overthrow Li, and found Qing dynasty
1662–1723	Sixty-year reign of Kangxi, the Qing's first great emperor
1683	Qing emperor Kangxi conquers Taiwan and soon formally incorporates it into Chinese territory
1736–1796	Sixty-year reign of Qianlong, the Qing's second great emperor

1793	British diplomat Lord Macartney's mission to the Qianlong emperor for diplomatic representation and trade concessions ends in frustration and failure
1816	British diplomat Lord Amherst's mission to the Qing, with purposes similar to Lord Macartney's mission, also fails
1830s	Opium addiction becomes a widespread problem in southern China; Qing government decides to interdict opium
1834	British diplomat Lord Napier's blustering confrontation with the Qing authorities fizzles out
1839	Imperial Commissioner Lin Zexu confronts the British over the opium trafficking; British opium seized and destroyed
1839–1842	Opium War between Britain and China
1840	Britain declares war on China
1840s	Hong Xiuquan encounters Christianity and begins the Taiping Rebellion, a pseudo-Christian revolt against the Manchu Qing government
1842	Treaty of Nanking signed, which provided for cession of Hong Kong to the British Crown
1844	China concludes Treaty of Wanghsia with the Americans and Treaty of Whampoa with the French
1850s	Renewed friction between China and Britain over treaty ports
1853	Hong Xiuquan and his Taiping rebels capture Nanjing and make it the seat of a pseudo-Christian theocracy bent on overthrowing the Qing
1854	Zeng Guofan begins his long military struggle against the Taiping Rebellion
1857–1858	Britain once again at war with China
1858	Treaty of Tientsin signed between China and Britain; provided for residential diplomats in Beijing
1859–1860	Renewed friction and war between China and Britain; Lord Elgin, former Governor General of Canada, invades Beijing and burns the Manchu Summer Palace (Yuanming Yuan)

1860	Convention of Peking concluded between China and Britain; provided for cession of Kowloon Peninsula, opposite Hong Kong
1861–1895	China's Self-Strengthening Movement, a halfhearted reform program
1862	Zeng Guofan begins his massive attack on Nanjing, the stronghold of the Taiping Rebellion
1864	Zeng Guofan recaptures Nanjing after defeating the Taiping forces
1894–1895	First Sino-Japanese War; Qing defeat and Japanese victory
1895	Treaty of Shimonoseki signed between China and Japan; provided for cession of Taiwan to Japan
1898	Abortive Hundred Days Reforms of Kang Youwei; "scramble for concessions"; several Western nations wring more privileges and territorial concessions from the Qing government
1900	Boxer Rebellion and subsequent quelling by allied Japanese, European, and American forces
1901	Boxer Protocol signed; imposed onerous indemnities on Qing
1911	Qing overthrown by republican revolutionaries inspired by Dr. Sun Yat-sen; Republic of China founded
1914	Yuan Shikai, a former Qing general, betrays the new republic and attempts to have himself crowned emperor of a new dynasty; dies in 1916
1916–1927	Warlord period
1917–1921	May Fourth Movement
1919	May 4 and later, nationwide protest movements against Japanese annexation of Shandong province
1921	Founding of the Chinese Communist Party in Shanghai
1925	Sun Yat-sen dies; period of cooperation between his Nationalist party and the Chinese Communists ends
1926	Chiang Kai-shek begins Northern Expedition to break the power of the warlords and unify China

1927	Northern Expedition nominally unifies China; Chiang Kai-shek turns on the Chinese Communists in bloody crackdowns; Communists go underground in cities while a group under Mao retreats to the countryside
1931	Japanese seize Manchuria
1932	Japanese establish a puppet government and nation called Manchukuo
1934	Chinese Communists begin the Long March
1936	Decimated Chinese Communist forces reestablished in Yan'an; Xi'an Incident; Chiang Kai-shek kidnapped and forced to call off the civil war with the Chinese Communists and fight the Japanese invaders
1937	Japan launches all-out war against China; Rape of Nanking: Japanese troops murder 300,000 unarmed men, women, and children in Nanjing
1945	Defeat of Japan and end of World War II
1945–1947	American diplomats attempt unsuccessfully to broker a peace agreement between the Chinese Nationalists and the Communists
1947	February 28 Incident on Taiwan: thousands of anti-Nationalist demonstrators hunted down and murdered by Nationalist troops and police
1948	Land reform on Taiwan begins
1949	Chinese Communists win the civil war and take over the mainland; remnants of Chiang Kai-shek's defeated forces and government flee to Taiwan; In Beijing, Mao declares the founding of the People's Republic of China (PRC)
1950	June: North Korean forces invade South Korea September: Allied forces land in Inchon and put North Korean aggressors to flight November: Chinese Communists enter the war
1953	Truce ends the Korean War China's first Soviet-style five-year plan
1957	Hundred Flowers Campaign launched; Great Leap Forward begins
1959–1962	Mass starvation in China; an estimated 20–40 million perish

1961   Play *Hai Rui Dismissed from Office* obliquely criticizes Mao
                for the disastrous Great Leap Forward

1965   France diplomatically recognizes the People's Republic of
                China

1966   Mao launches Cultural Revolution

1967   Anarchy in China

1968   Cultural Revolution largely reined in

1970   Canada diplomatically recognizes the PRC

1971   Richard Nixon visits China; Flight and death of Lin Biao;
                Chiang Kai-shek's Nationalist regime expelled from the
                United Nations and replaced by representatives from the
                People's Republic of China

1975   Death of Chiang Kai-shek on Taiwan

1976   January: Death of Zhou Enlai September: Death of Mao
                Zedong; Tiananmen Incident; Gang of Four arrested

1977   Deng Xiaoping's political comeback

1978   Democracy Wall briefly permitted; Chiang Ching-kuo
                becomes President of the Republic of China on Taiwan

1979   Deng Xiaoping visits America; China invades Vietnam;
                United States cuts ties with the Republic of China on
                Taiwan and diplomatically recognizes the People's Republic
                of China on the mainland

                U.S. Congress passes the Taiwan Relations Act

                Kaohsiung Incident in Taiwan

1980   Lin Family Murders in Taiwan

1981   Professor Chen Wen-chen murdered in Taiwan by rogue
                Kuomintang agents in Taiwan's Garrison Command

1983   Anti–spiritual pollution campaign

1984   Chinese-American writer Henry Liu (Liu Yiliang/Jiangnan)
                murdered in California by organized crime gangsters hired
                by the fascist wing of the Kuomintang.

1987   Martial law and White Terror in Taiwan end

1987–1988   Anti–bourgeois liberalization campaign

1988	Death of Chiang Ching-kuo on Taiwan
1989	April–May: Student protest movement June 4: Tiananmen Square Massacre; Dismissal and house arrest of Zhao Ziyang; Jiang Zemin becomes Deng's protégé´
1991	Jiang Zemin poised to be Deng's heir-apparent
1995	With Deng in ill health, Jiang Zemin effectively runs the country; Lee Teng-hui, president of the Republic of China on Taiwan, delivers a speech at Cornell, much to the anger of the Chinese Communists
1996	First open and democratic presidential elections held in Taiwan; Lee Teng-hui becomes the first democratically elected Chinese leader in history
1997	February: Deng Xiaoping dies; Jiang's formal transition to power uneventful; July: Hong Kong reverts to Chinese control, ending Britain's colonial rule
1999	April: Falun Gong protestors personally offend Jiang Zemin; May: NATO bombing of Chinese embassy in Belgrade; anti-NATO riots in several Chinese cities; American embassy in Beijing vandalized by mobs; June: Tenth anniversary of the Tiananmen Square Massacre passes unobserved and uncommemorated; President Lee Teng-hui insists that the Republic of China on Taiwan will negotiate with the People's Republic of China on the mainland only on the basis of equal, "government-to-government" relations, which greatly angers the Chinese Communists
2000	Y2K computer bug hoax fizzles in China, as everywhere else in the world; February: Mainland China makes new threats on Taiwan as new conditions for its invasion of the island are announced; March: Presidential elections in Taiwan; Chen Shuibian, a known supporter of Taiwan independence and the candidate least favored by Beijing, is elected with 39 percent of the popular vote
2001	January: *The Tiananmen Papers* published in the United States
2004	Publication (and subsequent banning) of "Investigations into the Chinese Peasantry" [*Zhongguo nongmin diaocha*] in China; Hu Jintao completes consolidating his political and military succession to Jiang Zemin; Chen Shuibian narrowly reelected to the presidency in Taiwan

2006   Construction of Three Gorges Dam completed

                     Shih Ming-teh in Taiwan launches unsuccessful popular
                     protest movement to depose President Chen Shuibian for
                     corruption

2007   China surpasses the United States as the world's top emit-
                     ter of greenhouse gasses

2008   Beijing Summer Olympics. Boyang dies on Taiwan

2009   Chinese Communists announce they will not allow multi-
                     party parliamentary democracy in China

2010   Google publicly chafes at China's Internet search engine
                     censorship requirements

1

Geography, Government, Population, and Early History

GEOGRAPHY

Geographical Orientations

Geographically, China was and still is an isolated civilization. A brief glance at a map will show that of the ancient world's four great early civilizations (Mesopotamia, Egypt, the Indus River valley in Pakistan, and the Yellow River on the North China Plain), China is by far the most remote. China is bounded to the east and south by the Pacific Ocean, to the southwest and west by the massive Himalaya and Pamir mountain ranges, and to the north by steppe lands and the desolate terrains of Siberia.

It would, however, be a mistake to conclude that China's geography cut it off completely from contact with the rest of the world. People could and did travel to China via overland routes, such as the famous Silk Road, and on the seas. But such travel was hazardous and very time consuming, and throughout much of history China has been somewhat "mysterious" and fascinating to the outside world.

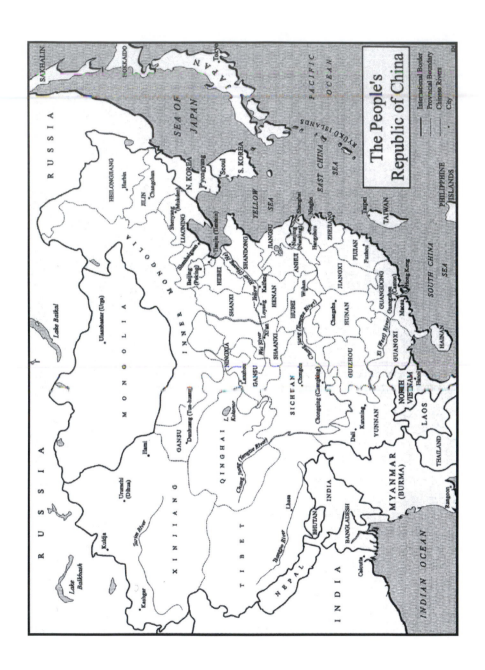

The People's Republic of China

International Border
Provincial Boundary
Chinese River
City

Northern China

Two major geographical realities in China are the Yellow and Yangtze (Yangzi) Rivers. The Yellow River flows through northern China from the Qinghai and Tibetan Plateaus, gradually winding its way down into Inner Mongolia and northern China, through the North China Plain, and thence to the Yellow Sea. The Yellow River gets its name from the rich, yellowish-brown soil called loess that it carries in suspension along its course. This fertile soil is deposited on the North China Plain, making it an eminently suitable place for agriculture. The North China Plain is, in fact, the birthplace of Chinese civilization.

The Yellow River is both a blessing and a curse to China. Its greatest benefit is, of course, the water and fertile soil it carries. At the same time, the very loess that makes agriculture possible also creates its own hazards. It is so abundant and heavy that the river is constantly depositing. Over thousands of years the Yellow River has created its own beds and channels on the accumulated loess, and these are often higher than the surrounding countryside. The loess banks at the edges of the river form natural dikes that hold the river in its course. These dikes, however, are weak and historically have broken every few decades, and the resultant floodwaters have inundated millions of acres of prime farmland. Historically the floods continued until the river created another channel for itself. Yellow River course changes have been so dramatic that the river has flowed into the Yellow Sea from both the northern and the southern sides of the Shandong Peninsula. Whenever the dikes break, hundreds of thousands of people are literally flooded out of house and home, and famine and pestilence are the usual results. For over 2,000 years, Chinese governments have been concerned with shoring up and repairing these dikes so that they do not break and disrupt the agricultural cycle. In premodern or "imperial" China the competence of some governments was measured in part by how well they maintained the Yellow River's dikes. In addition to these hazards, the Yellow River is not navigable by large boats because it is too shallow, swift, and full of sandbars. It is also not a particularly attractive or picturesque river. For all of these reasons, the Yellow is sometimes known as "China's Sorrow." Like the Tigris and Euphrates Rivers in Mesopotamia, the Yellow seems poised to bring both abundance and calamity. Today, however, that calamity is largely one of scarcity, not overabundance. For the past few years the waters of the Yellow River have been completely utilized by agricultural and industry before the river empties into the sea!

Northern China has a climate not unlike the Great Basin in Utah and Nevada: scorchingly hot in the summer and sometimes bitterly cold in the winter. Northern China is usually relatively dry, especially in comparison with the south, because there is not abundant rainfall. The landscape is mostly dry and brown. Dry crops grow best here: barley, millet, and wheat. There is usually only one crop a year.

Southern China

Many Westerners visualize the Chinese countryside as lush, green rice paddies on terraced mountainsides peopled by hardworking peasants in conical banana-leaf hats toiling away at their tasks, sometimes using a pole balanced across their shoulders to carry baskets suspended on twines from both ends. Tea bushes and perhaps some towering green mountains surrounded by lingering clouds complete the picture. This image is not necessarily inaccurate or unreasonable; there *are* in fact such picturesque areas in China every bit as beautiful, if not more so, than the photographs and traditional Chinese scroll paintings we have all seen. But we must remember that such images pertain very much to *southern* China, where the climate is warm and humid and rainfall is abundant.

The traditional demarcation between northern and southern China is the Qinling mountain range, equivalent to the Continental Divide in North America. The Qinling divides much of China into two great drainage systems. Water in northern China eventually flows into the Yellow River, whereas rivers and streams in southern China eventually flow into the Yangtze River. The Qinling range also demarcates important climatic and ecological differences between northern and southern China. Some areas of southern China are so warm and receive so much rainfall that two and even three crops a year are common. Even so, however, crops grown in southern China cannot usually rely on rainfall alone. This is especially true of rice, which must grow in warm climates and under constant submersion. For this reason, rice is grown in paddies, which are essentially large, shallow ponds with earth bottoms. The water depth in paddies must be maintained at a depth of a few inches all the time rice is growing. At the beginning of the planting season, rice seedlings are inserted, often still by hand, into flooded and prepared paddies. They then grow for a few months until the rice stocks are mature, after which the paddy is drained and the stocks are allowed to dry out for a few days before harvesting. After this, the paddy is prepared for the next crop.

All of this is, in comparison with the dry cropping in the north, a relatively complex form of agriculture, one that requires extensive manpower and labor organization, widespread irrigation networks, and constant attention to maintaining the water levels. The technology and seeds for this wet rice cultivation, which were introduced into southern China from Southeast Asia relatively late in Chinese history, around A.D. 200, produced a population explosion. Rice cultivation is arduous, but the large agricultural yields justify the hard work. An acre of rice can feed many times the number of people that an acre of barley or millet can. The large rice harvests sustained a much larger population than northern agriculture could, and gradually the population in southern China grew, through both natural increase and net immigration to the region. By around A.D. 1100 the majority of China's population was living in southern China, a situation that continues today.

It is important to remember that even though it has a much smaller population than southern China has today, northern China is where it all began. The north, and not the south, is the cradle of Chinese civilization.

The Yangtze River, which flows through southern China, is one of the most striking geographical features of the region. It has its origins in the Tibetan mountain ranges, but unlike the Yellow it does not pick up a large amount of loess or other sediment as it flows westward through the Sichuan Basin and ultimately into the Pacific Ocean. In contrast with the Yellow River, the Yangtze is deep and navigable for much of its distance, although some cataracts do interrupt its course. Although the Yangtze does flood with disastrous consequences at times, these floods are more often the result of excessive rainfall rather than the collapse of its natural dikes. As catastrophic as Yangtze floods can be, they do not compare with the magnitude of destruction and devastation that follows a change of course in the Yellow River.

GOVERNMENT

The government of China is a one-party, authoritarian Communist dictatorship that allows no significant political opposition to its policies or criticism of them. The Chinese Communist Party (CCP) runs the country and controls all political and administrative machinery, although eight tiny, token parties tightly controlled by the CCP are allowed to exist as long as they behave themselves and do not question government policies or the party line.

Freedom of expression is severely restricted in China, but theft of intellectual property is extremely widespread, and virtually everything is for sale, including pirated CDs, pirated computer software, counterfeit luxury goods, illicit drugs, and the sexual services of prostitutes. The Chinese government sees and openly encourages the widespread pursuit of wealth as a way of distracting the Chinese people from demanding political reforms and democracy. The Chinese Communists seem often to turn a blind eye to social vices but clamp down swiftly and completely on any movement designed to secure popular political sovereignty for the Chinese people. The government, when it wishes, is able to exert complete control over all newspapers, magazines, book publishers, and television and radio stations. The Chinese Communists are currently attempting to control the flow of information over the Internet and now block the websites of such distinguished newspapers as the *New York Times*, the *Washington Post*, and other news sites critical of China's political repression and human rights abuses. (The ever-resourceful Chinese people, however, easily circumvent these restrictions by having friends outside China forward articles to them from these sites as electronic mail.) Censorship is mostly political but occasionally can assume a puritanical streak and be directed against the overtly sexual written word. In May 2000 the Chinese Communists banned the novel *Shanghai Baby* (*Shanghai Baobei*) because of its striking depictions of sexuality and drug abuse in Shanghai. The novel sold 80,000 copies before it was banned, but underground copies of it were widely available to anyone, including curious foreigners, who wanted to read what the government had proscribed and confiscated.

China's government is technically divided into executive, legislative, and judicial branches, but in reality the executive branch wields all significant political power. In the executive branch, China's heads of state are the president and vice president who are "elected" to five-year terms by the National People's Congress, China's unicameral rubber-stamp parliament. The heads of government, on the other hand, are the premier and several vice premiers. Members of the cabinet, a body called the State Council, are appointed by the National People's Congress. The Chinese people themselves have little to do with the selection of their national leaders and must remain passive observers of the power struggles between various factions of the Chinese Communist party and the Chinese government it controls.

China's nominal legislative branch is the National People's Congress. Its nearly 3,000 members are "elected" to five-year terms by municipal, regional, and provincial people's congresses, which bodies themselves are tightly controlled by one-party rule of the Chinese Communists. The National People's Congress is a deliberative and advisory body, but it has little real legislative power or policy-making authority. Very few of its members dare to vote against CCP directives. The Chinese Communists view with suspicion and horror any attempts to transform the National People's Congress into a genuinely independent policy-making body.

China's judiciary branch is headed up by the Supreme People's Court, members of which are appointed by the National People's Congress. The judiciary is far from independent and frequently bows to the wishes of the CCP and the executive branch. In China, the rule of man still largely prevails over the rule of law, although recently there have been some hopeful indications that the judiciary may be moving toward a more independent posture.

There are four basic levels of the Chinese government, and these are based closely on precedents dating back to China's dynastic or imperial era: (1) the central government in Beijing, (2) the provinces (and four large urban areas equivalent to provinces), (3) the counties (*xian*) in rural areas and cities (*shi*) in urban areas, and (4) the work unit (*danwei*). China is currently composed of 23 provinces (22 mainland provinces and the island of Taiwan, which China still considers its 23rd province), 4 major municipalities administratively equivalent to provinces (Beijing, Chongqing, Shanghai, and Tianjin), and 5 "autonomous regions": Tibet, Inner Mongolia, Xinjiang, Ningxia, and Guangxi. China is a unitary state with very little division of powers or federalism. As in imperial China, administrative levels are organs of the central government. Interestingly enough, however, some provinces have recently shown surprising backbone and integrity in resisting some of the *diktat* out of Beijing.

Under Article 116 of Communist China's latest of many constitutions (this one adopted in 1982), the autonomous regions are (in theory at least) free to "enact regulations on the exercise of autonomy and other separate regulations in the light of the political, economic, and cultural characteristics of the nationality or nationalities in the areas concerned." But, according to this same Article 116, the National People's Congress (itself a rubber-stamp parliament manipulated by the CCP) still has final say over any policies and regulations. Thus, the CCP regularly overrules any meaningful political and religious freedom for Tibet. The supposedly autonomous regions are powerless to prevent the Han Chinese from flooding into their regions and diluting their cultural integrity. Inner Mongolia is now more than 90 percent Han Chinese and is "Mongolian" mostly in name only. Xinjiang's population is now close to 50 percent Han Chinese, and garrisons of Han Chinese troops are stationed all over Tibet.

Roughly paralleling the structure of the government is the CCP itself, which controls the appointments of all important Chinese leaders and dictates policy direction to the government. The most important central levels of the CCP (which nationwide claims more than 50 million members) are, in ascending order of power, the Party Congress, the Central Committee, the Politburo, and a small group within the Politburo called the Standing Committee, which is the core clique of China's dictatorship. As with the highest levels of government, appointments to the Politburo and the Standing Committee are matters of factional struggles, political infighting, and personal relationships rather than democratic election.

The Chinese Communists claim to have achieved a revolution in China in 1949, but many aspects of their rule are quite reminiscent of imperial Chinese governance. As outlined above, the structure of their government is essentially based on imperial models. Like the Ming and Qing dynasty emperors, the Chinese Communists have made Beijing their capital, and it is certainly no accident that some of their most important government offices are right next to the Forbidden City of the Ming and Qing dynasties. Until his death in 1976, Mao Zedong was essentially the emperor of China, and millions of Chinese grew up making obeisance before his portrait and wishing him "ten thousand years" (wansui) every day. As Kenneth Lieberthal has pointed out, both the imperial system and the Communist system, which the Chinese learned from the Soviets, "utilized ideology to buttress the legitimacy of the system, and held that the leaders embodied the correct ideology, leaving no room for private, individual interests or for organized opposition to the state" (Lieberthal 1995, 157). Like their Confucian predecessors from the dynastic era, the Chinese Communists today claim that their ideology and their books obviate any need for their subjects to enjoy authentic, participatory democracy. They are convinced that they, and not the Chinese people, know what is best for China. Just as the gentry of late imperial times secured social elite status by studying for and passing examinations on the official national orthodoxy (Cheng-Zhu Neo-Confucianism), today's elites, the cadres (Communist functionaries), secure their status because of their familiarity with, and adherence to, state orthodoxy (now Marxism-Leninism Mao Zedong Thought and the Thought of Deng Xiaoping and Jiang Zemin). Instead of reading the Four Books and the Five Classics, China's elites are now required to read and regurgitate the works of Marx, Lenin, Mao, Deng Xiaoping, and Jiang Zemin.

Truly, in China, the more things change, the more they remain the same.

Reasonable and rational people everywhere recognize that China is not a free country. Freedom House, a distinguished nonprofit, non-partisan organization based in New York City and Washington, D.C., which has promoted democracy, political rights, and civil liberties worldwide for over 60 years, has ranked China as "Non-Free" (NF) since it first began publishing its ranks of countries in 1972. China now lags behind many of its neighboring East Asian nations in terms of basic human freedoms. Japan, for instance, has always been rated as completely free by Freedom House. Taiwan progressed from NF to PF (Partly Free) in 1976 and to F (Free) in 1996. South Korea progressed from PF to F in 1988. Mongolia's transition to freedom was quick and dramatic, progressing from NF in 1990 to F in 1991. (Mongolia was the first and thus far the only Asian nation to overthrow Communist dictatorship and establish a democracy.) Thailand and the Philippines have been inconsistently ranked PF and F since the 1980s; since 1972 Singapore has consistently been rated PF.

POPULATION AND DEMOGRAPHICS

In the year 2010, China's population was approximately 1,319,000,000, or between a fourth and a fifth of humankind. China remains the most populous nation on earth, although India will likely surpass China for this dubious distinction sometime during the next decade. China is still a rural country, with slightly more than half of its population living in the countryside. (China today is more urban than it has ever been before, and urbanization is expected to continue.) Approximately 67 percent of the population is between the ages of 15 and 64; those below the age of 14 account for 28 percent, and the elderly above age 65 represent the remaining 5 percent.

China officially recognizes 56 "nationalities" or ethnic groups within its borders. Of these, by far the largest group is the Han (sometimes simply called "the Chinese"), who compose roughly 92 percent of the nation's population. The other 55 ethnic groups make up the remaining 8 percent of China's population. Some of the better known of these minority groups include Tibetans, Mongols, Hui (Muslims), Uighurs, Manchus, Zhuang, Koreans, Kazaks, Ozbeks, Tatars, and even Russians! The largest ethnic minority, the Zhuang, includes about 14 million people; the smallest group has fewer than 2,500. All of these people, according to a political theory currently fashionable in China, are Chinese (*Zhongguo ren*). The Han are undeniably the majority among the Chinese as thus defined, but other minority peoples such as Mongols, Zhuang, and Tibetans are as Chinese as the Han are. This is Beijing's version of demographic political correctness, and Westerners who dare refer to the Han as Chinese and to the non-Han as non-Chinese are often shrilly denounced in Chinese newspapers and press conferences and in the frenetic writings of Chinese ultranationalists.

In addition to overpopulation, China suffers from a serious demographic imbalance because of traditional notions that favor sons over daughters. In 1990, China's population was 51.6 percent male and 48.4 percent female. Although this disparity was already bad, it has and will continue to worsen. By 2015, China will have 40 to 60 million fewer women than it would under normal, natural circumstances. Selective abortion of female fetuses in many cities is widespread, and female infanticide is widely practiced in some regions, especially in the more backward areas of the interior provinces of China Proper. In the year 2000 there were already over 40 million more men than women in China, and by 2009 there were already 32 million more men *under the age of 20* than women. The natural ratio of baby boys to baby girls is around 107 to 100, but in some areas of China selective abortion of female fetuses has led to a spectacularly unnatural ratio of 120 boys to 100 girls. In jurisdictions where the Chinese allow a second child to be born if the first is a girl, the ratio is even more unnaturally distorted: 143 to 100. This disastrous disproportionality will only worsen as the twenty-first century unfolds. In the future, tens of millions of Chinese men will be unable to find wives. A huge surfeit of single and angry young men could, if mixed with the xenophobia and antiforeignism periodically fanned by the Chinese Communists to shore up and guarantee their political power, produce a toxic nationalistic brew with frightful implications for East Asian and world security.

The vast majority of the Chinese live in what is sometimes called "China Proper" (a term Beijing finds distasteful), a region that encompasses approximately half of China's territory and the majority of its Han population, or the provinces of Anhui, Fujian, Guangdong, Guizhou, Hebei, Henan, Hubei, Hunan, Jiangsu, Jiangxi, Shaanxi, Shandong, Shanxi, Sichuan, Yunnan, and Zhejiang. China Proper, an area about half the size of the continental United States, has one of the highest population densities in the world. It is home to more than 1,319,000,000 people, or slightly more than four times the entire American population! China is, as the Chinese themselves say, packed with "mountains and seas of people." The Chinese government today rules over massive numbers of people without precedent in human history.

These numbers and proportions, which may seem both astronomical and abstract in their statistical forms, have real-world manifestations and represent vast challenges and liabilities for China. China is in fact a grossly overpopulated country, and its major cities team and overflow with people, bicycles, taxis, and buses. The high population density seems to have an adverse effect on courtesy and social manners. When a city bus arrives at a stop, waiting throngs stampede and pack into it like sardines. People waiting for an elevator crowd into it before those already inside have had a chance to get out. The Chinese have no concept of lining or queuing up in an orderly manner for any purchase or service, and people who crowd and push the most aggressively and obnoxiously are usually the first to obtain the service or item they wish to purchase. Retail stores are cramped and narrow because space is always at a premium. Traffic on city streets is unimaginably chaotic by Western standards, and in some major cities electronic timer displays at stoplights remind impatient taxi and bus drivers of how much time remains before it is their turn to proceed. Municipal refuse removal services are largely inadequate, and public garbage receptacles are few and far between. Garbage and organic refuse litters the streets, and parked bicycles, motorcycles, and crates of commercial goods clog the sidewalks, making them all but impassable. In the hot and humid summer months, the city air is filled with the odor of rotting refuse and stagnant, polluted water in streetside ditches. No Western traveler to East Asia can help but note that the filth and disorder of Chinese cities stands in marked contrast with the cleanliness and order of cities in Japan. Unfortunately, the scruffiness and litter of Chinese cities even seems to characterize some of the Chinatowns in North America and Europe.

EARLY HISTORY

Earliest China: Xia and Shang, to 1122 B.C.

China is the world's oldest living civilization. Such an assertion may seem startling at first, but it is true. The Sumerian and Egyptian civilizations are older, but they are now dead. The Chinese today are quite justified in feeling a more direct and continuous connection with their heritage than Europeans can claim from their Roman, Teutonic, Slavic, Celtic, or Jewish pasts.

Mythology and Archaeology

In traditional accounts, several cultural heroes are credited with major contributions to Chinese civilization. Some of the most important of them are listed below.

Cang Jie invented Chinese characters, or the written Chinese language.
Shen Nong invented agriculture.
Sui Ren discovered the use of flint to produce and use fire.
The Yellow Emperor (Huangdi) invented boats and the bow and arrow.
His wife discovered the secret for making silk.
You Chao shi invented houses and shelters.
Yao, a descendant of the Yellow Emperor, was the first great sage king. He perfected a calendar and the means for tracking the movements of the planets and stars. He eventually chose a competent government minister named Shun, rather than his own son, as his successor.
Shun, as king, perfected the government bureaucracy and spelled out the four classic punishments for criminals (fines, beatings, banishment, and death). He struggled with a catastrophic flood that befell China during his reign.
Yu, also known as Yu the Great, was chosen by Shun to deal with the flood-waters. Unlike a previous minister, who failed at the task by attempting to *contain* the floodwaters, Yu decided to *channel* them away through a network of ditches and canals. Utterly dedicated to this task, he was ultimately successful at it. Shun was so impressed that he made Yu his heir. Yu was the founder of the Xia dynasty (2205 B.C.?–1766 B.C.?), and with his reign we enter into the realm of credible recorded history.

These accounts of early cultural heroes are interesting because they reveal what many Chinese historically have thought were most important about their past: these cultural heroes introduced developments that enabled people to live differently from the beasts.

Archaeologists look for evidence of the origins of government. The most important clues for this question are, of course, written records. In their absence, archaeologists and early historians can also consider physical objects that suggest the presence of organization and hierarchy in society. Such evidence might include burial patterns and practices as well as armor and weaponry.

Archaeologists and early historians also consider the question of writing and its origins. When indeed did writing first appear in China? This is a fascinating and perplexing question. The earliest known specimens of writing in China date to the Shang dynasty (1766 B.C.?–1122 B.C.?). These earliest Chinese documents are inscribed on, of all things, tortoiseshells and the shoulder blades of cattle.

The question of the reasons for and uses of such peculiar documents or artifacts takes us directly into recorded Chinese history. The first Chinese dynasty noted in Chinese records is the Xia, but its existence has yet to be conclusively corroborated by archaeological evidence. The Shang is the first dynasty for which there is a massive amount of corroborating archaeological evidence.

How and why Shang archaeological artifacts first came to light is a fascinating story. In the late 1800s a Chinese farmer near Anyang (in northern China) quite accidentally discovered some tightly sealed earthenware jars buried in his field. Inside these jars were several carefully preserved bones with recognizably Chinese characters inscribed on them. Subsequent investigation revealed that these bones were, in fact, verification of the Shang dynasty. Thousands of them were eventually unearthed and stored for scholarly investigation. Further digs in the area uncovered cemeteries and the foundations of ancient buildings. An entire ancient civilization had been discovered in northern China, and it was an exciting time.

Scholars who poured over the bones soon discovered that they could read many of the inscriptions, which seem to have been phrased in question form and answerable with a simple "yes" or "no." The questions often concerned weather prognostications, the reasons for natural disasters, and queries about the outcomes of upcoming battles. As scholars began to read these questions they found that they frequently mentioned supernatural beings. Nature gods, deceased ancestors, and a sort of head or chief god named "Di" (pronounced "dee") often figured into them. In fact, the questions seem to have been directed to one or more of them. The bones also very often were bored with small holes that had cracks emanating from them. Just to make matters more mysterious and compelling, digs in Shang cemeteries often turned up exquisitely crafted bronze vessels, evidence of a highly militaristic society, and mass burials of people who suffered violent and untimely ends.

What did all this mean? Scholars gradually pieced together the pieces of this mystery until they concluded that the inscribed bones, sometimes called "oracle bones," were used in *divination*, or in posing questions to supernatural entities and receiving answers to them. The questions were the inscriptions on the bones, and the answers came in the form of cracks on the bones. The cracks were created by applying a red-hot awl or poker in a hole bored into the bone, and the shape and orientation of the cracks indicated the supernatural order's answers. Questions were most frequently directed to the ancestors of the Shang royal clan. The assumption was probably that they were more approachable and comprehensible than the nature gods or the high god Di. A special priestly class was probably in charge of this entire system of divination.

But why did the supernatural order bother to respond to the questions in the first place? This is where the bronze vessels and the mass burials come in: The gods and ancestors probably responded because they were *paid* to do so, sometimes with blood libations or offerings. There is compelling evidence that the Shang practiced human sacrifice. Blood offerings were often made with bronze vessels by the living, and the presence of bronze vessels in burials also suggests that the Shang Chinese believed they would be needed in the afterlife to receive the offerings. (Many bronze vessels were also used for practical, nonritual purposes such as cooking.) But it would obviously be against the Shang's self-interest to murder its own population for these blood offerings, and this might explain the Shang's warlike nature. Because the Shang needed a steady stream of sacrificial victims, it was constantly on a war footing. Prisoners of war were likely transported back to the Shang kingdom and there maintained and murdered as needed. These non-Shang sacrificial victims kept the entire divinatory system functioning.

Ruling over the Shang's religious society was a king, and his relatives served as noblemen who administered areas of his kingdom on his behalf. Other than this we know relatively little of the political history of the Shang except for the succession of its kings, whose names are found inscribed on oracle bones. We also have relatively little information about the Shang's social or economic history. We know the most about Shang religious life because the only documents the Shang leaders thought worthy of careful preservation were the oracle bones, not the details of their day-to-day administration or the lives of their subjects. Only the king had the right to conduct the divination ceremonies, and most Shang Chinese probably believed that only the ancestors of the noblemen were entitled to an afterlife. The Shang government, therefore, had excellent motivation to keep this entire system functioning. If the Shang royal house and government were ever overthrown, there would be no more Shang royal priestly class to make the offerings and pose the questions and read the cracks. The communicative link with the supernatural order would be lost, and the universe would seem chaotic and incomprehensible. Things such as the weather, diseases, natural disasters, and defeats in battle would happen for no apparent or discernible reason, and this the Shang Chinese government found unthinkable. It felt compelled to maintain and safeguard the ancestral cult at all costs.

The unthinkable eventually did happen, however, and the Shang dynasty was overthrown. Chinese tradition tells us that the last leader of the Shang was such a tyrannical megalomaniac that he took to calling himself Di. If we are to believe Chinese tradition and the accounts written centuries later by Chinese historians who might have had some knowledge of Shang political history, Di's government was so harsh that the people of the Shang were left with no option other than rebellion. They were well aware that this was an enormous step to take, and how they justified their rebellion is discussed in the next chapter.

2

Pre-Imperial China: ca. 1122–221 B.C.

FEUDAL UNITY: WESTERN ZHOU

Early Chinese historical records, written mostly by a historian in the second century B.C., tell us that the last years of the Shang were full of tyranny and misery. The last Shang king in particular was a megalomaniac who exploited his subjects in outrageous ways, forcing them to work and fight in battles to the breaking point. Things got so bad that eventually a western region of the Shang named Zhou began planning and launching the unthinkable: armed uprising. In the years leading up to the uprising, Zhou was led by King Wen (*wen* means "cultured" or "lettered"), one of ancient China's major cultural heroes. The people of Zhou were culturally and linguistically Chinese, although there is some evidence that they had once allied themselves with a "barbarian" or nonagricultural, proto-Tibetan people called Qiang (which literally means "goats").

King Wen led his people in armed rebellion against tyranny, but he did not live long enough to see the Shang completely overthrown. Zhou victory over Shang was achieved by King Wu (*wu* means

"martial" or "military"), King Wen's son. King Wu made his own
capital city in Zhou and then launched an all-out attack against Shang
around 1122 B.C. As he approached the Shang's capital city, he was
greeted by throngs of Shang slaves who were eager to be liberated from
Shang servitude. They joined King Wu's armies gladly and attacked the
Shang capital city with him. The result was an overwhelming defeat for
the Shang, and the last Shang king committed suicide. The triumphant
King Wu then returned to his own region of Zhou, and his new dynasty
eventually ruled over all Chinese civilization.

The Zhou knew that its revolution against Shang would be controversial, even shocking, to many people. The Shang had ruled and practiced
its ancestral cult for so many centuries that many Chinese could
not imagine a world without it. After all, if the Shang royal house were
overthrown, how would people understand the cosmos? The religious
idea that the Shang house alone was entitled to communicate with the
supernatural order probably made them willing to put up with tyranny
for as long as they did. The Zhou rulers formulated a justification
or explanation for their actions called the Mandate of Heaven. The mandate theory, which was simple and basic in its essential elements, held
that the high god Di was disgusted with late Shang tyranny and oppression. Di could tolerate the Shang no longer and looked around China for
a righteous ruler, eventually deciding on the good King Wen, upon
whom he bestowed his "mandate" or approval.

Thus there was a change in the supernatural order's approval of the
ruling regime. This was a new and revolutionary concept; it meant that
no government could ever claim the right to eternal rule. "Heaven," a
Zhou term for the supernatural order, would approve and sustain a
government only as long as it ruled righteously and did not oppress
its people. If and when a government turned into a tyranny, the mandate would be withdrawn and the Chinese people would be justified
in rising up and overthrowing it. After the Zhou's conquest of the
Shang there were, in fact, about a dozen major changes of dynasty
until the entire dynastic system was overthrown in A.D. 1911.

The theory of the Mandate of Heaven eventually held that Heaven
would indicate its displeasure with the ruling government through a
series of abnormal events in nature: floods, famines, droughts, earthquakes, and so on. For this reason, throughout most of their history,
the Chinese people have been keenly interested in natural disasters
and what they might portend for the future of the current government.
Even astronomy could indicate that the time was right to rebel. When
King Wen's astronomers observed an alignment of five planets, they
considered it a portent approving his plans for an uprising.

There was an important and subtle shift in religious attitude here. In taking careful note of the position and alignment of planets, King Wen was paying attention to the cosmos or nature and the way it functions. He was looking more to the world of nature for guidance than to any god. The word the Zhou Chinese used for nature and its functions (on earth as well as in the skies) was "Heaven." He and many Zhou Chinese seem to have concluded that the world of the dead and the gods was not exclusively worthy of human attention. Heaven itself had its own standards and ways of communicating with people, and perhaps they could understand Heaven as much by observing it as by offering prayers and sacrifices to the gods and ancestors. A more rational contemplation and observation of Heaven became increasingly popular during the Zhou, and it marked a step away from the more directly "religious" approach of the Shang Chinese. In fact, Zhou kings called themselves "Sons of Heaven" because they believed they were doing the will of Heaven and conforming to its standards. (The term "emperor" [*huangdi*] did not come into widespread use until the third century B.C.)

While this more rational approach to understanding the cosmos overshadowed the cult of the dead, it never eclipsed it. It would be quite a mistake to conclude that the Chinese discarded ancestral veneration after the Shang. They did not, and veneration of the ancestors is a Chinese religious custom that continues right up to the present, especially in Hong Kong and Taiwan. The cult of the dead lost some of its supreme central importance to the Chinese people and government but was never fully forgotten.

King Wu eventually set up a new government in China. His government was a feudalism, meaning that it had a central headquarters and capital city but divided up China into semi-independent regions called *guo*, or "states," which were ruled over by noblemen, or members of the Zhou royal family. (The Zhou instituted a system of five ranks for these noblemen.)

What happened to the old Shang royal family? King Wu did not completely exterminate it but allowed it to continue offering sacrifices to its ancestors. These rituals, however, were now private family functions and no longer held significance for the central government. The Shang royal family was not satisfied with this arrangement, and after King Wu died it rebelled against the Zhou. Because King Wu's son and successor was much too young to deal with this rebellion, King Wu's brother, known to history as the Duke of Zhou, was assigned as a regent or temporary ruler to act on behalf of the young king. The Duke of Zhou is another of ancient China's greatest cultural heroes, and Confucius (born hundreds of years after these events) greatly admired him. After quelling the Shang rebellion, many people expected the Duke of Zhou to assume power himself. It is, after all, rare for people to relinquish power once they have gained it. The good duke, however, willingly stepped down as soon as King Wu's successor was old enough to rule on his own, and thereafter lectured him on how to govern effectively. For this action the Duke of Zhou is remembered in Chinese history as a paragon of public virtue and selflessness.

DISINTEGRATION: EASTERN ZHOU

As with the fall of the Roman Empire, the fall of the Zhou seems to have resulted from a combination of internal decay and external aggression. Internally, many of the feudal lords had begun to disregard the directives of the Zhou kings during the 800s B.C. Internal division and weakness likely made the Zhou a tempting target for all of the "barbarians" who lived out on the outskirts of the Central States of the Zhou.

These barbarian peoples weakened the Zhou, and at the beginning of the eighth century B.C. they successfully attacked and sacked the Zhou's capital city. The Zhou government had to flee far to the east and set up another capital city, from which it ruled over a territory smaller than the original Zhou. This defeat marks the distinction between the early Zhou, sometimes called the "Western Zhou," and the later, weakened Zhou, which is known to history as the "Eastern Zhou."

The Eastern Zhou was only a shadow of the Western Zhou. During the Eastern Zhou the power and authority of the Zhou king was drastically reduced, so much so that he eventually became little more than a figurehead. The feudal domains supposedly under his control became more or less independent states and were often at war with one another, and feudal lords more often than not gave him nothing but lip service. The fighting between the states eventually became so bad that the Zhou fell in the third century B.C. One of the many states, the Qin, eventually prevailed against all the others and unified China (the area once occupied by the Zhou's Central States) in 221 B.C.

CONFUCIANISM

The Eastern Zhou was a time of chaos and moral decline. Accompanying the fighting between states was a decline in public order. Some young people no longer respected their elders, and crime was on the rise. Even the feudal lords who contributed to this disintegration usually claimed to be doing so for the eventual good and reunification of China. They and their commanding generals probably thought they held the key to making China orderly again, but inevitably there were also people who believed that the key to reunification and recovering the past glories of the early Zhou lay not in fighting, but in a moral or philosophical regeneration. Confucius was one of many who thought of ways to reform China. Because his particular school of thought prevailed over all the others and was made China's official state ideology in the second century B.C., he is well known worldwide. During the Eastern Zhou, China was so full of philosophers and thinkers who thought they knew how to right all of China's wrongs that the Chinese have called long segments of the Eastern Zhou the "Hundred Schools" period. This general period lasted from the sixth through fourth centuries B.C.

Confucius was confident he had the correct answer. There is nothing mysterious or mythical about Confucius; he was born in the state of Lu, in what is now the province of Shandong, around 551 B.C. to a minor aristocratic family. As a child he was precocious and bookish, and like many of his contemporaries he began to idealize the past as the world around him was crumbling. He imagined that the early days of the Western Zhou were the lost golden age and should be recovered. As a young man he was so confident that he knew the secret of the early Zhou's success that he began seeking employment with any government that would listen to him and apply his ideas. Confucius eventually had a midlife crisis and abandoned his search for government employment, but he did not forsake his ideals. Instead, he began gathering pupils who listened to his ideas and explored their implications with him. Confucius's hope was that a few of his star pupils might eventually obtain government jobs and apply his ideas for the good of China. He remained an idealist throughout his life.

Like many idealists, Confucius was frustrated with the world around him. He wanted to change the world, to bridge the gap between what is and what ought to be. Current society was not as it should be, and in his imagination early Zhou society was largely perfect. Certain qualities in the early Zhou had been lost, and the entire thrust of his teachings was toward their recovery. He spoke mainly of two things: *li* and *ren*.

Li means "ritual" or "ceremony" and, in a broader or more extended sense, "propriety." Confucius believed that careful attention to the ceremony or ritual of major life events (such as marriages and funerals) was enormously important. If the conventions and functions of these rituals were performed attentively and properly, he argued, their performers eventually would be trained to abide by the broader conventions of public morality. Ritual performance was an important key to ethical behavior and social order. Just as a ritual occasion has certain positions and functions for its performers, so a moral society had expectations of its members, and fastidious attention to the former would lead to moral regeneration in the latter. In other words, ritual performances were microcosms of society and the world; they were miniaturized training grounds for living and functioning in the world and bettering it. If one performed ritual often enough that one could do it effortlessly, almost as second nature, an ethical and moral life would also become second nature in one's life in society.

Confucius, then, emphasized ritual. He believed that ritual had something important to teach people and that this had been well understood during the early Zhou. Somehow this vision or understanding had been lost and now had to be recovered. In order to grasp the essential importance of ritual, another quality was necessary, and this he called *ren*. The basic meaning of *ren* is something like "benevolence" or "humaneness" or "consummate humanity." Confucius regarded *ren* as an inward quality, a state of mind or heart that would enable people to understand completely the importance of ritual performance and apply it in their lives in society. He understood this inward quality as encompassing kindness, compassion, mercy, humanity, and perhaps many of the other virtuous, qualities we today tend to identify in good, kindhearted people. For Confucius *ren* was more than simple niceness or sentimentality. It was a profound wisdom that would produce understanding of ritual and also become the fundamental wellspring of the other virtues he often regarded highly: loyalty, uprightness, frugality, and filial piety, or loving respect for one's parents.

Without this *ren*, ritual performance could be largely pointless or meaningless. People could, after all, go through the motions of ritual or ceremony but not have their hearts in it, and they might even laugh at it or find it pompous. The overall thrust of Confucius's teachings concerned *ren* and its importance in ritual and ultimately in society. *Ren*, and *li* closely associated with it, were the keys to restoring order in China. But for all the importance he attached to it, Confucius never really defined *ren*. Perhaps this was because he believed that ultimately it was beyond words. Boiling *ren* down to a conceptual definition has been left to Western scholars. According to Harvard's Benjamin Schwartz, it "embraces all the social virtues and the capacity to perform the *li* in the proper spirit" and is the "capacity to make the individual act well in all the encounters of social life" (Schwartz 1985, 75–76).

Confucius. (Sofiaworld/Dreamstime.com)

Furthermore, Confucius did not tell his disciples how to get *ren*. He dwelled on its importance and sometimes linked it with *li*, but he never assigned a specific cause-and-effect relationship between the two. At one point in the *Analects* (an incomplete record of Confucius's discussions with his disciples), he indicates that proper performance of *li* will lead to *ren*, but in other places he seems to say that *ren* is necessary in the first instance for *li* to teach its performers what they need to know about their roles in society. Confucius may well have viewed *li* and *ren* as so interrelated, so much the parts of an organic whole, that any attempt to divide or define them or assign causal priority to one over the other might have seemed artificial or contrived. Any man who thoroughly grasped the interrelationship between the two and knew their importance for social and political order he called a *junzi*, which has been translated variously as "gentleman" or "princeling" or "evolved man." His ultimate aim was to have many *junzi* in the world who would transform it and recover the lost golden age of the early Zhou.

Confucius sincerely believed in the superiority of antiquity over the present. He harked back to the lost golden age rather than looking forward to a new age on earth. He refused to think of himself as an innovator. He insisted all of his life that his purpose was not to introduce anything new into Chinese society, but to restore what was good about antiquity. Confucius was ultimately a practical, this-worldly philosopher. His program for reforming China probably impressed many people as impractical, and indeed it may have been, but his ultimate concerns were with the here-and-now rather than the there-and-then. He wanted to restore order and morality to China more than he wanted to speculate about the world's creation or the disposition of the gods or what happens to us when we die. His answer to queries about these topics are classic. When asked about death, Confucius replied, "Never having understood life, how can we know about death?" He had no taste for discussing supernatural or paranormal phenomena; the *Analects* record that "the Master did not speak of strange phenomena, feats of strength, chaos, or gods." Spirits and gods may have existed; in fact, there is some evidence that he may have been a theist. More important for him than the question of the existence or nonexistence of the spirits and gods was the question of what to do with them: "Pay your respect to the spirits and gods but keep them at a distance." What good did it serve to speculate at length about them or to be preoccupied with them? There were enough pressing concerns in this life to occupy all of a person's time.

Although Confucius was not religious in the sense that he set aside questions about the divine and the afterlife, he did have a reverence for Heaven that seems to border on something approaching the fervor of religious devotion. For him, Heaven was not as much the abode of a divine being or immortal souls as it was the embodiment of nature or the cosmos. For him, Heaven or nature displayed the order, rhythm, and predictability that he wanted to replicate in the social order. Heaven was trying to speak with us and had something to teach us if we could just hear it. We as human beings should observe and learn the well-ordered regularity and constancy of Heaven and be impressed by it—we had only to see how the seasons come and go in an orderly manner, how the seasons change in order, how the agricultural cycle begins and ends every year, and so on.

Mencius (c. 380–289 B.C.)

Confucius had many successors or continuators, not all of whom were distinguished. Eventually two thinkers, born well after his death, emerged as representing two distinct strands or varieties of Confucian thought: Mencius and Xunzi.

Among Mencius's interests was the question of the nature of man. Was man naturally and innately predisposed to good or bad behavior? Mencius insisted that man is innately good and that he becomes bad as he loses track of his innate goodness. This innate goodness he equated with Confucius's *ren* and argued that every human being possesses *ren* at birth, but many lose track of it as they grow older and confront the pressing exigencies of life. But there are certain focused or critical moments when our innately good nature can make itself powerfully known. To illustrate his point, he asked his listeners to imagine a baby crawling up to the mouth of a well and teetering on the brink, about to fall in. Do we feel something when we imagine this? Of course we do: we are horrified at the possibility of the baby falling in and would do everything within our power to save it. These spontaneous feelings show that the seeds of *ren* are still inherently within us even though long obscured. To recover and cultivate this sense of *ren*, we simply have to discover and be true to our authentic selves. One might call Mencius a *ren* philosopher.

Xunzi (c. 300–237 B.C.)

Xunzi disagreed with this position. He was acquainted with Mencius's thoughts on the nature of man and rejected them. He argued that man was innately bad and that the Confucian virtue of *ren* was obtainable not through discovery of the authentic self, but through the *defeat* of the authentic self by means of strictures and conventions of rightness. These restrictions he equated with *li* and argued that *li* is a necessary prescription to help man overcome his innately bad nature. So *ren* came not through spontaneous self-discovery but through repeated performance of, and submission to, *li*. One might call Xunzi a *li* philosopher.

Ultimately the vast majority of Chinese concluded that Mencius was right about this question and that Xunzi was wrong. Nevertheless, Xunzi was and still is respected for wrestling with this most vexing and pressing philosophical question.

TAOISM

Not everyone accepted Confucius's ideas. In fact, some Chinese adamantly rejected them. The Taoists, in particular, regarded much of Confucianism as suffocating and restrictive. Taoists were free-spirited souls who saw in nature itself, rather than in any ritual or inward human quality, the ultimate curative powers for political and social ills. Taoists often used the term *tao* (pronounced "dow" or "dau") in speaking or writing about their ideas. The primary meaning of *tao* is "way," while some of its secondary meanings include "path" or "road." As a verb, it can mean "to walk" or, interestingly enough, "to talk."

Taoism is a fairly diverse school of thought in Chinese intellectual history, but its most important and authoritative work is the *Tao-te ching*. (*Daode Jing* is the spelling system now preferred in mainland China; the title means "The Text on the Power of the *Tao*" or, as Arthur Waley has translated it, "The Classic of the Way and Its Power.") A small gem of a book written a few centuries B.C., it delivers its ideas in a terse and epigrammatic but utterly profound style. (The best translations are not wordy but preserve and reflect the compactness and tremendous expressiveness of the original.) The relative simplicity of the book's language can be deceptive because it makes a few words go a long way and because some of its passages are amenable to more than one interpretation. The *Tao-te ching* is easy to read but hard to understand.

The historical origins of the *Tao-te ching* are somewhat murky. The traditional account attributes its authorship to a philosopher with the title of Lao-tzu (Laozi in the spelling system currently preferred in mainland China), which means something like "old master" or "venerable philosopher." According to this account, Lao-tzu (whose surname was Li) worked as an archivist for the Zhou government sometime during Eastern Zhou times. As he grew older he concluded that China had lost its way, and upon his retirement from public life he determined to leave China forever and depart for the great white north to live in the uncivilized natural grandeur of Central Asia. As he rode out to the final frontier pass, a guardsman begged him to stay a while and write down his wisdom for the benefit of future generations. This he did, according to the account, and the result is the text of the *Tao-te ching* as we have it today.

Modern textual critics question this account and instead attribute the authorship of the *Tao-te ching* to several philosophers whose wise and pithy sayings were eventually assembled into a compendium or anthology that was later named *Tao-te ching*. Regardless of its authorship, it is the beauty and appeal of the book itself that concern us here. The *Tao-te ching* is, next only to the Bible, the most translated book in the world. This is at least in part because its simple, expressive language and mysterious, paradoxical images are quite appealing and engaging to many people. The book is conventionally divided into two main sections; the former contains some of the more mysterious or paradoxical passages, and the latter details its indictments of the chaotic present and its vision of a perfect society. One famous paradox

Huge statue in Fujian province of Laozi, traditionally regarded as the founder of Taoism. (Bbbar/Dreamstime.com)

concerns the ability of water, the softest known substance in nature, to wear down and erode rock, nature's hardest substance:

> The softest [substance] under Heaven
> Gallops like a horse right on through the hardest [substance] under
>   Heaven
> Only nothingness penetrates spacelessness
> Therefore I know the benefit of non-action
> And the instructional value of not speaking.
> The benefit of non-action:
> Nothing else under Heaven can equal it!

In a passage reminiscent of Ecclesiastes 12:12, the *Tao-te ching* urges that running about in pursuit of knowledge is ultimately futile and useless:

> Go not out your door,
> And you can know all under Heaven;

Look not out your window,
And you can see the *tao* of Heaven.
The farther you leave [in pursuit of knowledge],
The slighter your knowledge will be.
Therefore, the sage
Travels not, yet knows
Sees not, yet understands
Acts not, yet accomplishes.

What is the point of all this? These paradoxes and observations are interesting and compelling in and of themselves, but there is a larger purpose behind them, an epistemological purpose. (Epistemology refers to the study of knowledge and how it is obtained, or simpler yet, it is the study of how we know what we know.) The intent was not simply to delight and perplex readers, but to convince them that another way of learning was available to them: they could get in touch with their feelings and apply them to understanding the *tao*. There were real limits to what their intellects alone could comprehend; if they applied only their intellects in their observations of the world, they would eventually come up against these types of paradoxes. The larger point of these passages was perhaps to point out that a deeper, more profound type of knowledge and understanding was available, one that involved the heart and intuition and feeling. It was precisely this type of intuitive approach that would enable one to grasp the *tao* in its fullest and most profound sense. The *tao* was somewhat mysterious and was not to be understood simply through intellectual means because it was much greater than our finite powers of reasoning. We must grasp the entire meaning of the *tao* with our feelings and our hearts, rather than just with our minds. Intuition rather than intellection was the most important key to comprehending the *tao* of the universe. The *tao* was to be taken directly into the heart or soul and appreciated there rather than being dissected and analyzed in the intellect. Ultimately, there was a real and practical purpose for introducing this new epistemology; if people could learn to learn this way, their fuller understanding of the *tao* would change their lives. That would lead to a reordering of society and governance, and, in turn, lead to the peace and tranquility craved by the Eastern Zhou Chinese. There was plan and purpose in the seeming madness and mystery of the *Tao-te ching*.

Once people understood the *tao* they would not talk or write much about it, because they would know that it was beyond words. They would, nevertheless, be able to act well and within the guidelines of the *tao*, which held the key to ordering the world. Thus, a Taoist would not rob or kill or destroy not because there were man-made regulations against such behavior, but simply because he would feel or know intuitively that such actions were against the dictates of the *tao*. For Taoists, man-made laws and standards of behavior were undesirable because they obscured or overlooked the *tao*. In fact, the appearance of such laws and the moral and ethical teachings that inevitably accompanied them were indications that the *tao* had already been lost. Taoists believed that humankind had once understood the *tao* and had lived in accordance with it, but had taken a wrong turn somewhere in the course of history and lost track of it. Their hearts no longer felt the *tao*, so they were left to their own intellectual devices, which produced the chaos deplored by Taoists. Taoists longed to return to the golden age of simplicity and harmony with nature and its *tao*.

What was this Taoist golden age? It was a time in human experience right after people had discovered agriculture and lived in small, isolated agricultural settlements. People lived in contentment with primitive forms of agricultural technology and their unadorned homes. Because they were simple and rustic and therefore in intuitive touch with the *tao*, they were content with their lives and took no thought of doing unnatural things like building large cities or raising huge armies. Their countries (*guo*) were no larger than villages.

Just when and why did things go wrong? We might blame one thing: ambition. Ambitious leaders lost track of the *tao* and this agrarian simplicity and began to imagine how grand it would be if these small villages and their populations could be gathered into greater geopolitical units. Transportation and communication networks soon brought people into greater numbers that were, for Taoists, unnatural and contrary to the *tao*. As this trend continued, towns and cities appeared, with their attendant needs for walled defenses, standing armies, marketplaces, continuous food sources from the countryside, and, perhaps most horrifying for a Taoist, man-made laws and ethical teachings.

The Taoists, then, had a problem with nothing less than civilization itself. For them, life in the cities, along with all of the artificiality and obtuseness of intuition it implied, was the beginning of the end. Humankind could never live in peace until it got back in touch with the *tao* and returned to unadorned simplicity. As people were unnaturally combined into progressively larger units, they began paying more attention to each other than to the *tao*. As a result the *tao* was gradually abandoned, and in its place appeared Confucian moral teachings. For Taoists, any serious discussion of Confucian virtues and ethical conventions was prima facie evidence that humankind had already lost its "way," or the *tao*. The way back to order and tranquility was not a matter of adhering to these virtues, but of abandoning them:

Sever "sageness," forsake "wisdom,"
And the people shall benefit an hundredfold.
Sever "ren," forsake "justice,"
And the people shall again be filial and compassionate.
Sever cunning, forsake profit,
And there shall be no brigands or thieves.
[But as mere] words, these three [measures] are insufficient;
Hence there are more instructions:
Show plain white silk,
Embrace the uncarved block,[*]
Lessen selfishness,
Bereave the appetites.

The *Tao-te ching* delivers one of its most stinging indictments of Confucian thought and moral virtues in the following passage:

After the great *tao* was abandoned
There was "ren" and "justice."
After "wisdom" appeared,
There was enormous pretension.
After the six human relationships fell into disharmony,
There was "filial piety" and "compassion."
After the nation slid into turmoil and chaos,
There were "loyal ministers."

For Taoists, the "sage" or wise ruler clearly foresees this tragic state of moral affairs as a terrifying possibility and seeks to avoid it. For the most part he can do this simply by doing *nothing*: he follows the Taoist path of nonaction, which politically means blunting his ambitions and remaining content. Because he actually does little if anything, his population is unaware or only vaguely aware of his very existence:

The greatest ruler
Is unknown to his people.
The next best, the people love and honor,
The next they dread,
And the next they revile.

---

*"Plain white silk" (*su*) and "the uncarved block" (*pu*) are Taoist images for naturally unadorned, unspoiled simplicity.

There are times, however, when the Taoist sage must act in some ways. He must endeavor to keep vanity, greed, envy, and sophistry at bay for his population. He takes action only if his pristine utopia of loosely associated agricultural communities is threatened by ambitious nation-builders or teachers spreading dangerous, fallacious ideas:

> Exalt not the wise,
> And the people shall not contend.
> Prize not rare objects,
> And the people shall not steal.
> See not desirable things,
> And the people's hearts shall not be disturbed.
> Hence, in his government the sage
>> Empties their minds
>> And fills their bellies,
>> Weakens their ambitions
>> And strengthens their bones.
> He ever makes the minds and hearts of his people
> Devoid of knowledge and devoid of longings
> So that the "wise ones" will not dare interfere.
> In acting through nonaction,
> There is nothing he does not govern well.

Lack of contentment leads to an unnatural striving for larger accomplishments and greater heights, and this the Taoists deplore. They also warn against the danger of overdoing things and striving for the utmost. They would not like all of the modern talk of "striving for excellence" or "reaching for the stars." For them, this striving would smack of an anxiousness born of alienation from the *tao*. They would rather muddle along in mediocrity. Hold back a little, stay content, live long, be happy.

Preserving or recovering the Taoist paradise is, then, primarily a matter not of acting but of refraining from action. The wisest ruler refrains from doing too much. Doing too much is, after all, what ruined the Taoist agrarian paradise of small, scattered agricultural communities and combined them into larger, unnatural units.

Taoism is, then, a mystical and intuitive contemplation of the nature of the universe. Its essence is, however, quite applicable to practical, worldly affairs. As a political ideology, Taoism idealizes the era before the rise of civilization and its attendant problems. Taoists did, obviously, realize that civilization was here to stay and that there could probably be no literal return to the lost Taoist paradise and its atomized pattern of isolated agricultural settlements. It was still possible, however, to appreciate Taoism as stripped down to its essential points and to apply it in broad, analogical terms to everyday practical situations and problems. Thus, in the age of civilization, Taoism as a political philosophy became a laissez-faire ideology that embraced a minimalist, conservative approach in government, gently encouraged a renewed awareness of the nature of the universe, and anticipated the behavioral changes that would result from this awareness.

But Taoism was much more than just a political ideology and could be applied in many other directions. Throughout Chinese history Taoist thinkers have come up with seemingly endless applications of Taoist ideas. These applications have, for instance, included Taoist ways for interpersonal relations, artistic expression and military campaigns. In interpersonal relations, ideas extended from basic Taoist concepts encourage us not to be high-profile and confrontational. Have no enemies and you will have no conflicts. Avoid the temptation to assume powerful positions of leadership that will expose you to great vulnerabilities. Doing a little is better than doing a lot, especially when it comes to dealing with dangerous or potentially volatile situations.

As far as artistry is concerned, many Chinese have concluded that a Taoist awareness can foster and spur the creative impulses by setting the individual free. Once artists understand the *tao*, their artistic uniqueness or voice approach will take care of itself. The *tao* will help artists be their own best selves and realize their own best potentials and perspectives.

It may seem surprising that Taoist thinkers would apply their philosophy to military conflict. To be sure, the *Tao-te-ching* does not approve of military conflict, but more specifically it speaks of not glorying in military might and of avoiding conflict if at all possible. But if there *is* to be a fight, ideas extended from Taoism hold that the warrior should conserve as much of his energy as possible while at the same time sapping the enemy of theirs. He should assume a low profile in fighting and not launch massive frontal assaults on fortified enemy positions or engage in positional warfare. The classic Taoist style of combat is guerilla warfare. If you must fight, do not assemble huge armies with banners and drums and fanfare. In modern Western military terms, do not form large units such as brigades and divisions as your fundamental fighting unit, but rather form small fire teams of three or four men who come together only briefly for combat and then disperse quickly, thus making them more difficult targets for the enemy. Appear seemingly from out of nowhere and return to nowhere as soon as possible. Linger about the enemy's flanks and do not assemble your forces; your enemy will then have no idea of your over-all strength. Emerge from behind the scenes and hit the enemy hard, then quickly evaporate back into the woods. Continue this pattern for some time and you will gradually frustrate the enemy and rob him of his vitality and will to fight, while preserving your own. Do not fight the enemy on his own terms but on yours, which will likely be strange and aggravating to him. This style of warfare enabled the Americans to prevail against the British and the United Empire Loyalists in the American Revolution. (Ironically enough, it is also the strategy the Viet Cong used to defeat the Americans in Vietnam.)

CONFUCIANISM AND TAOISM

Confucians and Taoists had decidedly different views of the world; Taoist attitudes might smack of irresponsibility to Confucians, but Confucian moral teachings might strike Taoists as pretentious and foolishly off-center. Nevertheless, the great majority of Chinese came to see Taoism and Confucianism not as exclusive but as complementary. People could subscribe to Confucianism as a public, governmental ideology while embracing Taoism in their personal lives. Thus, after Confucian thought was made China's official state ideology in the second century B.C., a busy and worried Confucian government bureaucrat could go home at night and be more of a Taoist. Taoism reminded him not to take worldly concerns too seriously and to relax every once in a while. Taoism helped him prepare for his pressing duties the next day. It lent balance and sanity to his life. Taoist ideas might not have been directly applicable to the task of governing in the age of civilization, but Taoism, which was much too appealing and compelling to disappear entirely, acted as a tonic, a corrective content to remain in the shadows and behind the scenes, where the *tao* belongs.

This Confucian-Taoist synthesis was not always a completely comfortable one, but it became part of Chinese culture and the Chinese consciousness. Most of China's greatest emperors and dutiful government officials were essentially Confucianists at heart; most of the great poets and painters were, on balance, more Taoist. Thus, a cultured Confucian gentleman might not always be pleased with the antics of a free-spirited Taoist poet, but he would often tolerate them because the Taoist pole of his consciousness would gently remind him that great creative geniuses do not always completely subscribe to Confucian conventions of politeness and decorum.

As different as Taoism and Confucianism may seem at first and even second glances, they share several characteristics. First, both systems of thought seek ultimately to cure practical, this-worldly maladies. Both want to remedy the problems of the Eastern Zhou. Neither seeks to speculate on the origins of the world or humankind or to discuss at length humankind's relations with the divine. Taoism, more mystical in its appreciation of the universe, dwells on the benefits for the here-and-now that this appreciation would bring. Second, both Confucianism and Taoism share the common conviction that humankind once lived as it should, with good governments and orderly societies. For Confucians, this lost golden age was during the early years of the Zhou; for Taoists, it occurred when humankind first began living agriculturally. Third, both Confucians and Taoists regard nature as having something important to teach humankind. Confucians, who label nature "Heaven," are in awe of the orderliness and cyclical, predictable rhythms they observe in it. In nature, or Heaven, everything has its place and functions and behaves accordingly. Confucians strive to apply their intellects in analyzing and understanding this order with their minds, with the ultimate objective of replicating the order of Heaven in the social and political order. Taoists also revere nature and see much instructional value in it, but for them the *tao* of nature and the universe are much more accessible through humankind's intuitive capacities than through their intellects. Finally, both Confucianism and Taoism make the *individual* the key focal point for beginning the reform of society and government. For Confucius, a society of individuals who possessed the quality of *ren* and knew the importance of *li* in its broader social applications would be an orderly and livable society. For Taoists, grasping the *tao* was an intensely individual process, and a society full of people who understood the *tao* would spontaneously right itself.

LEGALISM

Legalism (sometimes also called Realism) was another school of thought in Eastern Zhou times, and in some important ways it was quite unique. In fact, it would probably be wrong to call Legalism a philosophy; it was more of a statecraft or *realpolitik*, a technique for keeping a ruler in power, his nation strong, and his population obedient and submissive. Legalism sought to accomplish these objectives through a simple recipe of rewards and punishments specified by laws. There was no abstract consideration of right and wrong; right was simply what the ruler wanted, and wrong was what he did not want. Legalism was a straightforward, anti-intellectual approach to governance. Legalists had very little patience for Confucian or Taoist ideas; for them, talk of *li* or *ren* or the *tao* was all mumbo jumbo and vain imagining. Legalists thought people were to be motivated not by any of these amorphous philosophical considerations, but by fear of punishment and longing for reward. Taking their cue from the Confucian philosopher Xunzi, Legalists insisted that humankind was stupid and predisposed toward evil. The followers of Xunzi soon parted company with Legalism when Legalists refused to believe in any possible perfectibility of human beings. (Xunzi taught that people could indeed overcome their innately evil natures and gain *ren* if they submitted to *li* and allowed it to change them.) Legalists insisted that people were unreformable and had to be constantly controlled through laws specifying punishments and rewards for every conceivable behavior.

Legalists heartily disagreed with Confucianists and Taoists who harked back to a lost golden age. For many Legalists, there never was a golden age in the first place. They were out to create an ideal society and state here and now, for the first time in history. Some Legalists argued that even if there had been a golden age in the past, it would be impossible to restore or replicate it now because the times had changed drastically; yesterday's methods were incapable of solving today's problems.

Legalist thinkers formulated their ideas over two or three centuries. Various Legalist ideas and governmental techniques were eventually synthesized by a Legalist named Han Fei, who died in 233 B.C. His book, *Han Feizi* (Master Han Fei), was a compendium of administrative technique, law, and criticisms of Confucianism, Taoism, and other minor schools of thought. The teachings of the book might well be characterized as ruthless and brutal. Han Fei spells out, among other things, his contention that the methods of the golden ages imagined by Confucians and Taoists were utterly inapplicable to the current situation. In his most famous passage, he uses a parable to illustrate his point:

> If somebody in this present age should praise the ways of Yao and Shun . . . he would certainly be ridiculed by contemporary [Legalist] sages. Hence the sage does not seek to follow the ways of the ancients, nor does he regard precedents as the rule. He examines the circumstances of his own time and plans his course of action accordingly.
>
> There was once a man of Sung who tilled his field. In the midst of his field stood the stump of a tree, and one day a hare, running at full speed, bumped into the stump, broke its neck, and died. Thereupon the man left his plow and kept watch at the stump, hoping that he would get another hare. But he never caught another hare, and was only ridiculed

by the people of Sung. Now those who try to rule the people of the
present age with the conduct of government of the early kings are all
doing exactly the same thing as that fellow who kept watch by the
stump. (de Bary et al. 1960, 130)

The Legalist ruler is not to be benevolent or loving or practice *ren* in
dealing with his subjects because this will only spoil and ruin them; people are motivated to act only by threat of force and by laws specifying
rewards and punishments. Li Si, another Legalist who continued in this
vein, urged the application of extremely harsh punishments for intellectuals who would not conform to the wishes and programs of the state.

Legalism was, then, completely amoral and highly unphilosophical.
It eventually became the official ideology of the state of Qin, which
defeated all other states and unified China under its rule in 221 B.C.
It assumed that people could not be taught but only compelled or
enticed. Legalist law was not natural law; that is, it did not claim to
be modeled after the world of nature. Nor was it divine law, because
it did not pretend to derive of divine sources or dispensations.
Unabashedly man-made, it made no references to unchanging standards of right and wrong. People were recruited into government service not on the basis of their moral qualities or broad learning but their
proven administrative expertise. Officials who accomplished what the
government wanted were promoted and rewarded; those who did not
were demoted and punished.

If Legalism can be called the rule of law, it certainly was not a democracy. Laws came from the whims of the ruler, not from the consent of the
governed or the expressed popular will. Legalists held a very dim view
of their subjects; they could not trust a populace they regarded as stupid
and self-serving to formulate their own laws. Taoists deplored this
viewpoint because laws are in and of themselves indications that the
government had lost its "way." Confucian scholars also found Legalism
particularly revolting because the laws often seemed coldly arbitrary
and did not accommodate any moral or ethical considerations. They
concluded that the rule of law was not nearly as good as government
by benevolent men who understood *li* and possessed *ren*.

MINOR SCHOOLS OF THOUGHT

Confucianism, Taoism, and Legalism are commonly (and correctly)
thought of as the most important of the Eastern Zhou schools of
thought. There were, however, other schools as well, and the reasons
the Chinese rejected them are interesting and illuminating.

Mo-ism, or the school of Mo Di (fl. 479–438 B.C.), was a manifestly religious system of thought. Confucianism, Taoism, and even Legalism had one thing in common: they were not very religious. Its major figure, Mo Di, is known in Chinese intellectual history as Mozi, or "Master Mo." Mozi was a devoutly religious man who argued that the ills of the Eastern Zhou time came from not being religious enough. He argued forcefully that "ghosts and spirits" do exist and that human beings owe them acknowledgement and respect:

> The people give themselves up to evil, violence, thievery, and rebellion, using weapons, knives, poison, fire, and water to assault innocent persons on the roads and byways and seize their carriages and horses, robes and furs, for their own benefit. All of these conditions come about for the same reason, and as a result the world is in disorder.
>
> Now why do we have this state of affairs? It all comes about because people are in doubt as to whether ghosts and spirits exist or not, and do not realize that ghosts and spirits have the power to reward the worthy and punish the wicked. If we could only make all the people in the world believe that the ghosts and spirits have the power to reward the worthy and punish the wicked, then how could there be any disorder in the world? (Watson 1963, 94)

Although Mozi was not opposed to ritual per se, he deplored ritual extravagance and excess and often associated it with Confucianism. He also had a great reverence for Heaven and believed that it did intervene in human affairs. For him, however, Heaven was more personal than it was for the Confucians or Taoists. It was not a mere abstraction or operative principle of the universe. He also preached a teaching he called "universal love," or love applied equally to all human beings without regard to hierarchy or familial relation. According to Mozi, people should love other people's parents, families, and countries as much as their own. He argued at considerable length that if people really did love everyone equally, there would be no crime or aggression or campaigns against other states:

> Great states attacking small ones, great families overthrowing small ones, the strong oppressing the weak, the many harrying the few, the cunning deceiving the stupid, the eminent lording it over the humble—these are harmful to the world . . .
>
> When we inquire into the cause of these various harms, what do we find has produced them? Do they come about from loving others and trying to benefit them? Surely not! They come rather from hating others

and trying to injure them. And when we set out to classify and describe those men who hate and injure others, shall we say that their actions are motivated by universality or partiality? Surely we must answer, by partiality, and it is this partiality in their dealings with one another that gives rise to all the great harms in the world. Therefore we know that partiality is wrong. (Watson 1963, 39)

The teaching of universal love shocked Confucianists, particularly Mencius, who constantly railed against it and upheld a strict social and familial hierarchy as essential to social stability and political order.

Mo-ism eventually failed in China, perhaps because the polemics of Mencius and Zhuangzi (Master Zhuang, a Taoist philosopher who explained Taoist teachings through wit, parody, and parable) against it were so effective. Mozi's teachings were, according to Frederick W. Mote, "distinct from all others ever enunciated by any philosopher or teacher in Chinese history" (Mote 1971, 88). Perhaps this explains its demise in China: Mo-ism was simply too strange, too much at variance with Eastern Zhou experience and observation:

We must conclude that the most aberrant feature of Moism within the intellectual and cultural milieu of early China was its failure to accommodate to some basic psychological factors. It displayed no awareness of natural human feelings and their influence on the way societies work. In the ancient anti-Mo-ist critiques of most telling significance, Moism was "contrary to the hearts of all men," as Chuang-tzu [Zhuangzi] put it. (Mote 1971, 90)

Logicians

Ancient China had a tight system of logic and finely distinguished analytical categories, but the Chinese of the Eastern Zhou were not impressed with it and dismissed it as trivial and unimportant. One school called the "Logicians" (sometimes also called "Dialecticians" or "Nominalists") seem to have approximated Western standards of logic and hair-splitting ontological distinctions.

By far the most famous passage from a Logician philosopher concerns definitions and conceptualizations. It comes from the *Gongsun Longzi*, a book written by the Logician Gongsun Long. Imagine Gongsun Long riding a horse and approaching a gate guarded by a gatekeeper. "Horses are not allowed beyond this gate," the gatekeeper informs him. "This is not a horse but a white horse," Gongsun Long replies and then rides brazenly through. The point? "Horseness," "whiteness," and "white horseness" are distinct and exclusive categories.

A: "Is it correct to say that a white horse is not a horse?"

B: "It is."

A: "Why?"

B: "Because 'horse' denotes the form and 'white' denotes the color. What denotes the color does not denote the form. Therefore we say that a white horse is not a horse."

A: "There being a horse, one cannot say that there is no horse. If one cannot say that there is no horse, then isn't [it] a horse? Since there being a white horse means that there is a horse, why does being white make it not a horse?"

B: "Ask for a horse, and either a yellow or a black one may answer. Ask for a white horse, and neither the yellow horse nor the black one may answer. If a white horse were a horse, then what is asked in both cases would be the same. If what is asked is the same, then a white horse would be no different from a horse. If what is asked is no different, then why is it that yellow and black horses may yet answer in the one case but not in the other? Clearly the two cases are incompatible. Now the yellow horse and the black horse remain the same. And yet they answer to a horse but not to a white horse. Obviously a white horse is not a horse." (Chan 1963, 235–36)

If the meticulous sophistry of this irritating passage tries the patience of the modern Western reader, he or she can imagine what the Eastern Zhou Chinese would have thought of it. To them it seemed the height of indulgence, irresponsibility, and frivolous extravagance. Here was the Eastern Zhou facing all manner of social, political, and military challenges, and all Gongsun Long and his ilk could do was discuss whether or not a white horse is a horse. What discernible relevance did this gobbledygook have to the task of righting the world? True philosophers should concern themselves with human affairs and not with vacuous pedantry. The Taoist philosopher Zhuangzi said of the Logicians and their contrived arguments that they might outdebate people but that they could never convince them that they "turned men's minds and altered their ideas," and that they "were able to subdue people's tongues but not to win their hearts" (deBary 1960, 84). The Chinese had too much common sense and too many better things to do than spend their time on this kind of sophistry.

TECHNOLOGICAL INNOVATIONS

Pre-imperial China, and the Eastern Zhou era in particular, will probably always be best known for the rise and fall of its feudal political structure and its cultural and intellectual efflorescence. There were, however, several quite astounding technological and scientific innovations during this period, and interestingly and ironically enough, many of them date to the fourth century B.C., a time during the Eastern Zhou called the "Warring States" when warfare between states had reached its most intense level. Only during the past few decades have Western scholars begun to realize just how advanced premodern Chinese technology and science really were. ("Premodern China" refers to China before 1840 or so.) The late great British China specialist Joseph Needham and his team of researchers at Cambridge University worked on the history of Chinese technology and science since the 1950s. Together they produced a monumental, multivolume work entitled *Science and Civilisation in China*, a project that is still ongoing despite Needham's recent death. In this continuing work, Needham and others have presented a bewildering array of overwhelming evidence showing that premodern China was quite advanced in engineering, agriculture, industry, medicine, warfare, transportation, mathematics, and the physical sciences. The results of their research prove conclusively that many inventions, discoveries, and innovations long thought to have been accomplished by Europeans actually originated in China several hundred years before they were known in the West. Throughout this book, we will be discussing Chinese "firsts" in scientific and technological innovations.

One supremely important innovation in pre-imperial China was the trace harness. This invention, which dates to the fourth century B.C., revolutionized agriculture. Prior to the advent of the trace harness, farm animals that pulled plows were harnessed around their necks and stomachs with something called a throat-and-girth harness. This was, of course, inefficient and cruel because it choked the poor beast when it pulled any significant burden. There is evidence that in the fourth century B.C., the Chinese began placing a yoke across the animal's chest, from which traces or shafts connected it to a carriage. This simple and ingenious innovation placed the burden not on the neck of the animal but on the chest, which was much more able to withstand the strain of pulling loads. Astonishingly, this simple innovation was unknown in the ancient Middle East or the Roman Empire, and it did not emerge in medieval Europe until the eighth century A.D., about nine hundred years after it was first used in China.

By the sixth century B.C., at the very latest, the Chinese were using iron plows. Chinese designs of the plow included a remarkably efficient one that used a plowshare to cut the soil and a moldboard to turn the soil over as the plow was pulled forward. This type of plow, which was finally introduced into Europe during the seventeenth century, contributed greatly to the European agricultural revolution. By the third century B.C., the Chinese also understood the importance of planting crops in long, straight lines. Plants placed in straight lines usually do not interfere with each other's growth and allow winds to pass through without causing extensive crop damage. Straight-line cropping was not widely practiced in Europe until well into the eighteenth century A.D.

Ancient Chinese medical knowledge was also advanced. By the second century B.C., at the very latest, Chinese medical practitioners had discovered that blood circulates throughout the body and understood fully that the heart pumped the blood. Chinese medical instructors actually constructed elaborate pumps and circulatory networks to use as teaching aids for their students. Today, many Westerners still believe that the circulation of the blood was discovered by William Harvey in the early seventeenth century A.D. This knowledge, which seems so very commonplace to us today, spread to Europe from the Arabs, who obtained it from China.

By the fourth century B.C. the Chinese were drilling for natural gas and using it as a heat source, thus preceding Western natural gas drilling efforts by about 2,300 years. Natural gas seems to have been discovered accidentally by workers who were drilling in the earth for brine, or water saturated with salt from salt deposits in the earth's crust. When they found both brine and natural gas together, the ingenious and practical Chinese used the natural gas to boil vats of the brine, thus removing the water and leaving the salt behind. Some drilled wells yielded only natural gas, and the Chinese called these "fire wells." Later innovations facilitated the transport of natural gas through bamboo pipelines and even the use of portable tanks to carry it.

The innovations and discoveries listed above had practical applications. It would be wrong to suggest that the Chinese were interested in mere technology and did not generate purely scientific insights. Something very close to Newton's First Law of Motion was known to the Chinese by the fourth century B.C. Newton's First Law states that "every body continues in its state of rest, or of uniform motion in a right line, unless it is compelled to change that state by forces impressed upon it." A Mo-ist book dating to the fourth or third century B.C. states, "The cessation of motion is due to the opposing force . . . if there is no opposing force . . . the motion will never stop. This is as true as that an ox is not a horse" (Temple 1986, 161). The Mo-ists, in fact, were quite scientific in their thought. Mo-ist writings also accurately and conceptually defined a circle as a body of points that are all equidistant from a centrally located point.

The ancient Chinese were also mathematically sophisticated. They used the decimal system as early as the fourteenth century B.C., during the Shang dynasty, an astonishing 2,300 years before the first known use of the decimal system in European mathematics. The Chinese were also the very first people in the world to use a place for zero in mathematical calculation. On Chinese counting boards, a blank space indicated the place for zero. The Chinese may not have invented the actual symbol for zero, but this is largely insignificant, given their knowledge of its importance and their use of a literally empty place holder to indicate it.

One invention Westerners have tended to credit to the Chinese is the compass. Both the Europeans and the Chinese seem to have made the first use of the compass in navigation during the twelfth century A.D., but the Europeans obtained the compass itself from China, where it had been known since the fourth century B.C. The compasses used in twelfth-century navigation involved the use of magnetized needles, but the earliest Chinese versions of the compass seem to have been spoons or other objects fashioned from naturally magnetic lodestone. The earliest mention of a simple lodestone compass occurs in a fourth-century B.C. Chinese source, but a more detailed description dates to the *Han Fei-tzu*, the third-century B.C. work on Legalism. The Chinese term for compass is "south-pointer" or "south-pointing needle" because the ancient Chinese thought of south, not north, as the cardinal direction.

The fourth century B.C. was the height of the Warring States period in Chinese history, so it should not be too surprising to find that the Chinese were busily creating new and more effective ways of killing each other. During this period, the Chinese were the first in the world to invent and use the crossbow on the battlefield. The crossbow incorporates a small, powerful bow onto a stock that is steadied against the body or shoulder and releases the bowstring with a mechanical trigger device. The trigger device was important because it enabled the shooter to hold the crossbow steady and devote his efforts to aiming the weapon, not struggling to keep the string drawn back with one of his hands. This generally gave the crossbow more accuracy than the conventional longbow. The earliest textual reference to the crossbow dates to the middle of the fourth century in the famous *Art of War* by Sun-tzu (also spelled Sunzi). One of Sun-tzu's descendants recorded the first known use of crossbows on the battlefield in 336 B.C. For more than two thousand years thereafter, the Chinese perfected the crossbow and it strategic use. It was finally eclipsed in the late nineteenth century by modern gunpowder weaponry. Despite the ancient Chinese efforts to prevent the export of the crossbow, it quickly spread around the world. The Chinese of the Warring States period of the Eastern Zhou were also the first in the world to use chemical and especially poison gas weapons on the battlefield. Mo ist writings record the use of poison gas as a defensive measure against enemy troops who were digging tunnels into besieged cities. This was over two thousand years before mustard gas was used against entrenched positions in Europe during World War I. For centuries after this, Chinese militarists perfected ways of making and delivering tear gas and chemical bombs into the ranks of their enemies, especially after the Chinese invention of gunpowder in the ninth century A.D.

3

Early Imperial China: 221 B.C.–A.D. 589

UNIFICATION AND LONGEVITY: QIN AND HAN, 221 B.C.–A.D. 220

China during the Eastern Zhou period was chaotic and divided. Ultimately, a rival state named Qin (pronounced "cheen") prevailed militarily over all other states and unified China under its rule in 221 B.C. The Qin then imposed its name on the rest of China, and it is from "Qin" that we get our term "China" in English and also the various pronunciations of "China" in many other European languages.

Several factors contributed to the Qin victory. Geography played an important role; the Qin was relatively isolated in western China from the rest of the states. The Qin was a rugged, semifrontier region located in the very fertile valley of the Wei River, a tributary of the Yellow. The Qin's natural geography made it easy to defend but very difficult to capture, which also worked to the Qin's advantage. Because most of the great battles during the Eastern Zhou were fought in other areas of China, the Qin escaped with its economy and polity relatively unscathed.

The Qin government was also an aggressive recruiter of administrative and military talent. The Qin early on saw the value of Legalists and the political ideology they espoused and promoted, and the Qin more than any other state in China actively recruited them into government service. Legalist advisors helped the Qin transform itself from a feudal government to a highly centralized, unitary state. The Qin stripped feudal lords of their land and allowed common peasants to use it. This may seem like a positive and progressive step for the Qin to take, but the Qin, of course, did not do it for completely altruistic reasons. Like the feudal governments it was dismantling, the Qin government financed itself largely through agricultural taxation. What distinguished the Qin from feudal governments was that the Qin wanted *all* of the tax revenue from agriculture and was unwilling to share a portion of it with any feudal hierarchy.

Legalist advisors reduced all formerly feudal regional and local governments to levels of the central government. The Qin largely abolished the system of hereditary nobility because it considered it a potential threat, and in its place it instituted an administrative system staffed by people who had proven their fitness for leadership by their tangible accomplishments. Commoners who proved themselves competent in civilian or military spheres were promoted and rewarded; incompetent aristocrats in military or civilian leadership were dismissed from their posts and deprived of their salaries. What mattered to the Qin was individual merit, not family background or bloodline. In other words, the Qin transformed itself from an aristocracy to a meritocracy. To protect this new centralized meritocracy from challenges from within, the Qin accepted the Legalists' advice and instituted a system of mutual surveillance and responsibility on the local level. It also handsomely rewarded informers.

One of the Qin emperors, known to history as Qin Shihuang, was destined to emerge victorious against all other states and unify China under an imperial system. Upon his success in 221 B.C. he imposed new standards of uniformity on the Chinese. First of all, he standardized ideology by making Legalism the Qin's guiding thought and outlawing all other schools of thought. His adamantly anti-intellectual state regarded Taoists and Confucians as subversive. In 213 B.C. he had most non-Legalist books burned, and the next year he buried alive more than 400 intellectuals who would not recant their beliefs in non-Legalist thought. He also imposed on China the Chinese script and the Qin's standards for coinage, weights, measures, and even the axle lengths of carts. An enormously ambitious program of construction projects also fit into his plans for China, as did a huge palace complex for himself and a large network of roadways to many parts of China. For these projects he pressed hundreds of thousands of laborers into work and brutally killed or tortured those who resisted performing their assigned duties.

Qin Shihuang was, in short, a great emperor who accomplished the unification of China, but he was enormously brutal and despotic. A tyrant and a megalomaniac, he took upon himself the title of *huangdi*, a title composed of two Chinese characters that together mean something like "magnificent ruler" or perhaps even "magnificent god." (The chief deity in the Shang pantheon was called "Di," which is the same character in the compound *huangdi*.) For better or worse, all subsequent emperors in Chinese history were called by this title, but none of them equaled his record of ruthless despotism and brutality. Many Chinese today have a love-hate attitude toward Qin Shihuang. Almost all applaud him for unifying China, for imposing standards of uniformity (in areas other than ideology), and for constructing, with the help of Legalist advisors, the basic model for governmental administration that China would follow for more than 2,000 years into the future. Against these accomplishments and contributions, the vast majority of Chinese weigh the negatives of his reign: despotism, anti-intellectualism, and cruelty.

The Great Wall of China: Mostly Myth

Almost every discussion of Qin Shihuang's reign includes the one accomplishment that seems to typify both the positive and negative aspects of his reign: the Great Wall of China. According to the typical account, Qin Shihuang completed earlier Zhou wall construction projects by connecting them all up to form the Great Wall, which he built to protect China from the savage and warlike Xiongnu or "Huns" on China's northern border. He may even have punished laborers who did not work hard enough on the project by executing them and having their bodies buried within the Great Wall. When finished, this Great Wall supposedly extended all the way across China, effectively dividing the Chinese civilization on the south from the world of the barbarians, or pastoral nomadic peoples, of the northern steppe lands. There it remained until the present in one state of repair or another, periodically undergoing renovation projects. Today it stands as monumental and artifactual testament to the industry of the Chinese people and the despotic, boundless ambition of Qin Shihuang. It is such a magnificent structure that it is the only man-made object on the earth that can be seen from orbit or, by some accounts, the moon.

All of this makes tantalizing copy for travel brochures and grist for the publishing mills that endlessly crank out glossy, coffee-table picture books about China. There is, however, one major problem with this standard and sensationalized description of the Great Wall: it is wrong in its entirety. Historian Arthur Waldron has exploded hoary legends and proven conclusively that much of what we once thought we knew about the Great Wall is pure myth. First of all, the Great Wall of China is not ancient but was built during the Ming dynasty (A.D. 1368–1644). Many traditionally minded historians of China have long maintained that although the Great Wall as it stands today was last renovated during the Ming, the site of the wall itself goes all the way back to Qin Shihuang's day. Waldron, however, has shown that there is only the flimsiest of evidence to support this notion. Earlier Chinese dynasties, including the Zhou and the Qin, did in fact build walls, but the locations of these walls were scattered throughout many areas of northern China and never constituted the one continuous and fixed wall that Chinese and foreigners recognized as the Great Wall. He points out that Marco Polo, whose travels during the thirteenth century A.D. often took him through areas where the Great Wall supposedly existed, never even mentioned it. Waldron maintains that the Great Wall was built for the first time during the Ming and did not exist in any form before that dynasty. Of course, this is not to say that the Great Wall is not magnificent. It is, as anyone who has traveled to it and stared along its length knows firsthand. All Waldron maintains is that the wall is not *ancient*. Qin Shihuang had nothing to do with its construction.

Another myth concerns the Great Wall's supposed visibility from outer space, either in orbit or on the moon; however, no astronaut has ever claimed to see the Great Wall, either from orbit or from the moon. Waldron verified this by reviewing all NASA voice transcripts for the Apollo and space shuttle flights. (The wall is visible with satellite magnification and imagery, of course, but it is completely invisible to the naked eye.) One of Waldron's earlier articles on the Great Wall even quotes a NASA scientist to the effect that seeing the Great Wall from the moon with the naked eye would be like seeing a Popsicle stick with the naked eye from a height of about 350 kilometers (approximately 217 miles)! He has established that the myth of the wall's visibility from the moon predates manned space flight. Included in his book is a *Ripley's Believe It or Not* cartoon from the 1930s that advances just such a claim.

The Death and Burial of Qin Shihuang

After conquering China and unifying it under his rule, Qin Shihuang began to look for a new challenge. His cruel policies led to many attempts on his life, and in this he found his next challenge: his own mortality. He wanted to live forever, and he became obsessed with discovering an elixir of immortality—some chemical or medicinal compound that would halt or perhaps even somewhat reverse the aging process in his body. He seems to have hit upon mercury, of all things, as a possible candidate for this elixir. Ironically, he died in middle age, possibly as the result of ingesting too much mercury. (Bodily decay does in fact slow down in persons who have died from mercury poisoning, and this observation may have been responsible for his fascination with mercury as a possible elixir of immortality.)

Qin Shihuang was buried in a magnificent tomb complex that thousands of workers had been constructing for him for many years. Sima Qian, a great historian who lived during the Han dynasty, describes the tomb itself as a huge model of the cosmos that contained a domed roof with the constellations painted on it and even a geographical model of China on the floor, complete with rivers of mercury representing China's Yellow and Yangtze Rivers. His casket was supposedly placed floating on an artificial sea of mercury. When the tomb was finished, the workers were killed by sealing them inside the tomb so they would not divulge the magnificence of what they had been working on, and the entrances to the tomb were booby-trapped with crossbows.

Modern archaeologists have located the tomb and have inserted probes deep into it. These probes reveal that there is indeed a high concentration of mercury in the tomb, more than 100 times the naturally occurring rate. Sima Qian's accounts have been verified archaeologically before, and many scholars expect that archaeologists one day will discover a tomb largely matching his description of it.

The exact location of the tomb has not always been precisely known. In fact, it was not discovered until the early 1970s, when a team of Chinese peasants drilling a well accidentally drilled into a portion of the tomb's outer complex, which contained a large contingent of exquisitely made life-sized terra-cotta soldiers. (Terra-cotta is fired but unglazed clay.) Subsequent digs have revealed thousands of such terra-cotta soldiers arrayed in military formations as if to guard the tomb itself, which looks at first glance like a small hill but is in fact a huge, man-made mound. Many of the formations of terra-cotta soldiers and terra-cotta horses are now on public display near Xi'an in

Shaanxi province. Because some of them were spoiled by exposure to oxygen and sunlight, later excavations made better efforts to preserve them. The Chinese today are in no hurry to excavate the gigantic tomb at the center of the burial complex. They know where it is, and when the time is right and the funding is in place, they will excavate it.

The Fall of the Qin

The Qin was undone and overthrown because of the very Legalist ideology that had helped establish it in the first place. In retrospect, it seems that the main contribution of Legalism and the Qin state that applied it was the unification of China and the creation of a structural model for future dynastic governments. Legalism as an ideology was later abandoned during the Han dynasty.

Two great rebel alliances emerged, and by 206 the Qin was deposed and its capital city sacked. China was well rid of a harsh dynasty and totalitarian government. By 210 B.C., the Qin's subjects had been pushed to the limits of their endurance. There followed a four-year civil war between the two rebel alliances, one under the leadership of Xiang Yu, an aristocrat from one of the powerful states before the Qin unification, and Liu Bang, a coarse and unrefined commoner who had risen to military leadership by dint of his native intelligence, resourcefulness, and widespread popular appeal. Liu Bang was originally under Xiang Yu's command but broke away from him because he disagreed with Xiang Yu's military tactics and found him to be unnecessarily cruel and vengeful toward the Qin. The two commanders eventually came into conflict, and in 202 B.C. a dramatic and decisive clash, celebrated ever since in Chinese literature, ended with Liu Bang's triumph and Xiang Yu's suicide.

The Rise of Han

In 202 B.C. Liu Bang became the founding emperor of the Han dynasty, a regime that endured until A.D. 220 with one brief interruption, which occurred during the life of Christ. Liu Bang was one of only two commoners in Chinese history ever to found a major dynasty. (Zhu Yuanzhang, the founder of the Ming dynasty in A.D. 1368, was the only other.) He had the common touch and exuded the common man's sense of decency and fair play, and for this the Chinese have loved him ever since.

Liu Bang is remembered for understanding the importance of relying on competent and educated men for advice and expertise in government and for ameliorating some of the harshest Qin excesses. As a commoner, Liu Bang had considerable instinctive sympathy for the ordinary peasant and took measures to relieve his plight. He reduced the agricultural tax rate from over one-half the crop to one-fifteenth and also reduced the number of capital offenses. General peace and prosperity characterized his reign and the reigns of his immediate successors, and the Chinese people were finally able to rest after centuries of turmoil and suffering. China's population exploded between 200 and 150 B.C., and the economy grew by leaps and bounds. A brief domestic revolt broke out in 154 B.C., but it was quickly quelled. These were quiet and content decades.

It is possible to give Liu Bang too much credit for the positive aspects of his reign. After all, he never faced the monumental task of unifying China; the Qin, for all of its totalitarian excesses, had accomplished that. He could well afford to reduce the tax rates because he never had to fund the enormous armies necessary for achieving national unity. Neither did he have to break the power of the feudal ruling class and invent an effective governmental structure and administrative framework; credit for those belongs, once again, to the Qin. The Han was built upon Qin foundations and took much of the credit, and very little of the blame, for what the Qin had accomplished. In retrospect it is quite apparent that the Qin's contributions to China were unity and imperial order. Once this had been accomplished, the dynasty had outlived its usefulness and was ready to be overthrown by a fundamentally different regime. Whereas the Qin was Legalist in its ideology, the Han eventually proclaimed its Confucian orientation. The ideological difference showed up in the different policies pursued by the two dynasties.

Things began to shift from quiescent to active and rambunctious again upon the succession of the Han emperor Wudi in 147 B.C. Wudi, whose reign title means "martial emperor," seems to have concluded, by the middle of the second century B.C., that the Chinese people had rested and prospered for long enough and that it was time to shake things up a bit. Wudi, the greatest Han emperor, was also surely one of the most important emperors in Chinese history. A strong-willed ruler with passionately held opinions, he aggressively pursued his program for increasing China's greatness. Internally, he wanted to break the power of the merchants who were amassing huge fortunes. Fearing that the merchants' enormous wealth might eventually lead to subversive political ambition, he forbade them to purchase land and took other steps to stop their participation in land speculation and landlordism. He established exclusive government rights to the production and distribution of essential commodities such as salt and iron. His official government monopolies over salt and iron enabled him to sell these commodities at artificially high prices, thus driving salt and iron merchants out of business and guaranteeing the government a steady stream of tax revenue. Wudi also launched a very aggressive campaign against the Xiongnu who lived along China's northern borders in the steppes and constantly attacked China for material advantage. His warfare against them led to the expansion of China's borders and to the eventual submission of the Xiongnu, although not during his lifetime. Wudi also ruled during a time of great cultural efflorescence. He was the emperor who made Confucian thought China's official state ideology, and during his reign he sought to foster Confucian education for government employees. The great Chinese historian Sima Qian wrote the first comprehensive history of China during this time.

Han power declined after the death of Wudi, and his successors were mostly mediocre men who lacked vision and the instinct to govern effectively. By the time of Christ, landlordism was rearing its ugly head once again, with wealthy merchants buying up huge tracts of land and charging the peasantry exploitive rents. These huge rents meant that the government had to charge less in taxes, and as government revenue dried up, social chaos ensued. Some became convinced that the Liu family's mandate to rule Han China had finally evaporated, and in A.D. 9 an ambitious and fanatical Confucian literalist named Wang Mang usurped the Han throne and sought to remake China into the literal image of Confucius's vision of the early Zhou period. Wang named his regime the Xin dynasty ("xin" means "new" or "renewal"). In his efforts to make China all over again, he bungled badly, and his attempts to mimic early Zhou feudal institutions only made a bad situation worse. Wang Mang, China's Oliver Cromwell, also created many new problems for China, not the worst of which was a huge wave of internal rebellion. Even nature itself did not cooperate with him: the Yellow River broke through its dikes. Rebellion against his regime had emerged by A.D. 18, and by A.D. 23 he and his government had been overthrown.

A descendant of the Han royal family reestablished the dynasty in A.D. 25, but this time the capital was farther to the east in Loyang, instead of Chang'an, where it had been located during the first half of Han rule. Thus the restored Han dynasty is sometimes called "Later Han" or "Eastern Han." The founders of the late Han virtually played back early Han history, wrestling with greedy merchants and once again subduing the Xiongnu. A long twilight period of Han rule endured until the second century A.D., when landlordism and foreign depredations once again took their toll on Han prestige and power. Incompetent emperors did not help the situation, and by 175 there was widespread rebellion. The dynasty finally fell in 220, and from this time until 589, China experienced chaos and internal division. Indeed, the period of division endured for more than 350 years, longer than the entire national history of the United States. Unlike the Roman Empire, however, China finally pulled itself together again, and it has almost always been unified ever since.

Confucianism as the State Ideology

During the earliest years of the Han, almost all government officials were aristocrats from old-money families. Liu Bang realized the limits of his education and knew he would need bright, educated men in his government. Such men flocked into his government on the basis of glowing letters of recommendation from prominent scholars and officials who attested to their intelligence, industry, and moral reputations.

After a few decades, the Han government was overwhelmed by thousands of such letters praising their candidates to the skies. In 165 B.C. a Han emperor decided that he would administer examinations to assess these candidates' cultural knowledge and their acquaintance with Confucian doctrine—he had taken the first step toward establishing the civil service examination system for aspiring government employees.

Emperor Wudi took another important step toward this system by proclaiming Confucianism the official state ideology and by founding a national university where candidates could study for government service. Wudi inherited the earlier Han emperors' strong distaste for the Qin and its Legalist ideology and greatly preferred the moral teachings of Confucius. Thus, the ideological legacy of this strong-willed emperor endured for 2,000 years, until the last imperial dynasty was overthrown in 1911. But even today, at the dawn of the new millennium, aspects of Confucian thought (namely submission to governmental authority) are still emphasized in the People's Republic of China.

Sima Qian, China's greatest historian, produced his great work *Shiji* (Records of the Grand Historian) during Wudi's reign. A Confucian himself, Sima Qian attended to his writing with tenacious dedication, and Wudi was probably a major cause of this dedication. During one of Wudi's campaigns against the Xiongnu, a Han general was defeated and captured. Wudi insulted his reputation and otherwise belittled his record. Sima Qian had the temerity on this occasion to disagree with Wudi publicly and come to the captured general's moral defense. Wudi was so enraged that he presented Sima Qian with two possible punishments: death or castration. Sima Qian reluctantly chose castration and was thus deprived of the opportunity to produce male offspring to carry on his name. This situation greatly distressed Sima, and he channeled his paternal instincts into his historical writing. He decided that, if he could not have human progeny, his bequest to posterity would be his book of history. The end result was a magnificent history of China from earliest times to his own day. In this work, Sima Qian set forth the facts in a straightforward and fairly objective manner. He held and expressed his own strongly held opinions on Confucian morality and other many historical issues, but he was careful to designate these as such and to separate them from the formal historical record. Much of what we know of China's pre-imperial history comes straight from the pen of Sima Qian, and his book became a model or template for much of subsequent historical writing in China. The man Wudi had meant to disgrace and perhaps even destroy was to become China's model historian for two millennia.

The Xiongnu

As China was unifying itself under the Qin, a great and powerful foe was also emerging in the steppe lands on China's northern borders: the Xiongnu, or the Huns. The Xiongnu were pastoral nomads. They were *pastoral* because they domesticated animals and relied on milk and meat products for their diet, and they were *nomadic* because they moved from place to place in search of naturally occurring grass pasturage. They were skilled equestrians who rode horses while herding their animals (mostly sheep). A highly mobile people, they rejected permanent abodes and elected instead to live in collapsible and portable felt tents traditionally called *yurts*. They occasionally hunted wild animals to supplement their food supply. Because they were good equestrians and skilled riders, they were able to apply their knowhow militarily, and they became formidable mounted warriors who could shoot arrows accurately even while riding at a fast gallop.

The Xiongnu and other groups of pastoral nomads who came after them very often were at war with China. For 2,000 years there was intermittent warfare between the agricultural world of China and the pastoral nomadic world of the grass steppe lands north of China, an area we today call Mongolia. The pastoral nomads were by far and away the Chinese dynasties' greatest foreign policy headache; in fact, for the last thousand years of imperial Chinese history, from about 960 to 1911, these pastoral nomadic peoples conquered and ruled over parts of China, and sometimes all of China, more than 70 percent of the time.

Historians are not content to look at the long and hostile history between China and the pastoral nomads and leave it unexplained. Traditional Chinese historians have usually understood this pattern of conflict to be evidence that the pastoral nomads were barbarians and less than fully human; thus, their depredations and greediness might be understandable. Descriptions of them by Chinese historians were often hostile and uncomplimentary, as in this passage written about the Xiongnu by Sima Qian:

> They move about in search of water and pasture and have no walled cities or fixed dwellings, nor do they engage in any kind of agriculture. Their lands, however, are divided into regions under the control of various leaders. They have no writing, and even promises and agreements are only verbal. The little boys start out by learning to ride sheep and shoot birds and rats with a bow and arrow, and when they get a little older they shoot foxes and hares, which are used for food. Thus all the young men are able to use a bow and act as armed cavalry in time of war. It is their custom to herd their flocks in times of peace and make their living by hunting, but in periods of crisis they take up arms and go off on plundering and marauding expeditions. This seems to be their inborn nature. For long-range weapons they use bows and arrows, and swords and spears at close range. If the battle is going well for them they will advance, but if not, they will retreat, for they do not consider it a disgrace to run away. Their only concern is self-advantage, and they know nothing of propriety or righteousness. (Watson 1993, 129)

More than a millennium later, the Song dynasty (906–1279) Neo-Confucian literatus Ouyang Xiu (1007–1072) launched into a stronger debate against the pastoral nomadic "barbarians" who continued to threaten China's security in his own day. In particular he deplored the Han dynasty's (202 B.C.–A.D. 220) diplomatic practice of marrying princesses off to barbarian leaders, particularly the Xiongnu, in attempts to secure harmonious relationships with them. (Ouyang Xiu's argument along these lines is somewhat surprising, since the Han dynasty fairly quickly gave up this intermarriage system and replaced it with the tributary system, which was far more favorable to Han China symbolically.)

Fine girls from the imperial clan were married in yurts, and good palace
men were consigned to the desert. Sir, offering men, girls, and local
products as tribute is the conduct of vassals and servants! ... *Arrivals*
from the desolate zones are announced, but there should be no talk of
[eminent Chinese] *going* there. ... What are we to make of the Son of
Heaven, in his dignity, entering into alliance with the Xiongnu as
"brothers"? of the emperor's daughter, designated as such, being tamed
as a shrew along with barbarian hags? of steamy mothers embracing
their sons and [eminent Chinese] following their filthy customs? The
difference between China and the barbarians is our distinction between
father and son, man and woman. For the pleasant and seductive beauty
[of these Chinese women] to be destroyed and curtailed among the alien
brood—this is foul disgrace in the extreme! But none of the Han rulers
or ministers were ashamed of it. (Wright 2002, 382)

The same condescending attitude about pastoral nomads is found in
the works of European historians writing about the Huns after the fifth
century A.D., when elements of the Xiongnu had migrated westward
into Hungary, emerged as the Huns of Attila, and threatened the security of the late Roman Empire. Some Chinese today still share these
attitudes about the Huns, Turks, and Mongols, who harried and
threatened their civilization. Traditionally, a significant number of premodern historians in China argued that the moral and cultural influence of Chinese civilization would eventually subdue and assimilate
the pastoral nomad and his animal-like way of life.

For the last century or so, European and modern Chinese historians
have been attempting to find alternate explanations for the Sino-
nomadic conflict. ("Sino" simply means Chinese.) Some scholars have
suggested that famine or drought might have been a cause for the
fighting: when there was little rainfall on the steppe, the pastoral
nomads' animals had little grass to eat and became thin and unable
to give much milk. The pastoral nomads then had little to eat and
were driven by desperation to attack China and other civilized societies for the food they needed. There may be something to this theory,
but it cannot be proven or disproven. Others have argued that power
relationships determined whether the pastoral nomads attacked or
not: when China was strong, the nomads stayed away, and when
China was weak, the pastoral nomads were attracted to it like
vultures and took what they wanted. This theory is not credible,
however, because just the opposite seems to have been true during
much of imperial Chinese history; often when China was strong and
internally unified, a powerful nomadic empire emerged on its
northern borders.

Still other historians and anthropologists have sought to explain Sino-nomadic warfare in ecological terms. That is, they have examined the differing ecologies and economies of pastoral nomadic and civilized, agricultural societies and have concluded that an agricultural economy is much more complex and productive than a pastoral nomadic economy. Certain commodities desired or needed by pastoral nomads can be produced only by civilized societies. When pastoral nomads feel a need or desire for these commodities, they attack. Three scholars have argued along these lines, but with different points of emphasis: Sechin Jagchid, a native of Inner Mongolia; Thomas Barfield, an American anthropologist; and A. M. Khazanov, a Russian anthropologist who emigrated to the United States in the 1980s. Jagchid argues that the pastoral nomads attacked China only when the Chinese refused, for whatever reason, to trade with them in the commodities they desperately needed: metals, textiles, and grain. Barfield's perspective is that the attacks were made mainly for luxury items (not subsistence commodities, as in Jagchid's theory), which were used to finance nomadic empires. Khazanov argues that the nomads simply did whatever they estimated was the easiest: trading or raiding.

The Xiongnu rose to power at about the same time the Qin unified China. After establishing his dynasty, Liu Bang launched an attack on the Xiongnu that turned out disastrously for him; he was badly defeated and barely escaped with his life. For centuries after this, the Han Chinese feared and respected the Xiongnu. Liu Bang decided that the Xiongnu were there to stay, so he and the Xiongnu established a framework called the "intermarriage system" for diplomatic relations between the two states. This system entailed four basic elements:

1. Annual payments of silk, wine, and foodstuffs from Han to Xiongnu
2. Granting the *shanyu* (the leader of the Xiongnu) an imperial Han princess to wife
3. Equality between Han and Xiongnu
4. Defined borders between Han and Xiongnu

Border markets were also established between the two states, but not as formal elements in the intermarriage system. According to Barfield, wine and silk were luxury items and the payment of them to the Xiongnu substantiates his thesis; Jagchid, on the other hand, considers that the presence of border markets and the payments of food to the Xiongnu are favorable to his theoretical perspective.

The intermarriage system of diplomacy is sometimes laconically called the "brides and bribes" policy. Of course, it viewed women, in this case princesses, as mere chattel or pawns for exchange with the great pastoral nomadic empires in Mongolia. Chinese literature is full of melancholy poetry about the sad lots of imperial princesses who left their homelands forever and lived out dreary, lonely lives in the bland, cold felt tents of their barbarian husbands.

The intermarriage policy worked well until the reign of Wudi. Wudi was fed up with the system and, as part of his general program of territorial expansion and military assertion, sought to replace it with a system implying a much more subordinate role for the Xiongnu vis-à-vis the Han: the so-called "tributary system." In 133 B.C. he abolished the intermarriage system altogether and broke off diplomatic relations with the Xiongnu. He then launched a war against the Xiongnu that endured for almost half a century and nearly bankrupted the Han treasury. His military strategy against the Xiongnu had four main objectives:

1. Reoccupying all areas once occupied by the Qin
2. Establishing an entente with the enemies of the Xiongnu
3. Expanding far into Central Asia and controlling the Turkic oasis states there, thus depriving the Xiongnu of their control over them and the protection fees they charged
4. Launching military raids into Mongolia to weaken and divide the Xiongnu

These policies did not work immediately, and the Han realized that defeating the Xiongnu would be no easy matter. When attacked, the Xiongnu often simply packed up and moved, and Wudi's troops exhausted themselves chasing them and were frustrated by their failure to engage the enemy in combat. Wudi also learned that he did not actually have to engage the Xiongnu in combat to weaken them; springtime raids into the steppes of Mongolia kept the Xiongnu on the move and weakened their animals, which had endured wintertime shortages of fodder. A stalemate was in the making, and in spite of some minor victories the Han achieved in 119 and 102, an uneasy detente between the states had developed by 90 B.C.

In the long run, however, the biggest loser turned out to be the Xiongnu. The constant Han raids eventually took their toll, and Xiongnu tribesmen were restless for the material benefits they had enjoyed from China during the era of the intermarriage system. Xiongnu weakness tempted their enemies and led to attacks by non-Xiongnu pastoral nomads. Civil war among the Xiongnu themselves was the last straw, and by 54 B.C., after the death of Wudi, a majority of Xiongnu were indicating their willingness to submit to the Han.

It had taken the Xiongnu several decades to come to this point because they greatly feared one thing: the tributary system that Wudi had insisted the Han would impose on them if and when they decided to submit to Han overlordship. It had three provisions:

1. The Xiongnu, far from receiving a Han princess given in marriage to their *shanyu*, would be required to send a hostage from their imperial family to the Han.
2. The Xiongnu would be required to perform rituals of submission to the Han emperor.
3. The Xiongnu would periodically be required to pay tribute to the Han.

For decades the Xiongnu resisted these provisions because they thought they would entail genuine submission and vassalage to the Han. But once the Xiongnu had accepted them, they were startled and delighted to find that these provisions ultimately were mere *gestures* of submission and did not require any real subjection to China. They were also overjoyed and astonished to learn that, in exchange for these ritual gestures, the Chinese rewarded them quite handsomely in material goods, out of all proportion with the value of the measly items they presented as "tribute" to the Han emperor. Once they had seen through the system, they were quite willing to embrace it. It was all a sham, and the Xiongnu were soon figuring out ways to take advantage of the system. They actually pressured the Han to allow them to come more frequently to perform the rituals of submission and offer their local goods to the Han emperor as tribute.

Even though some Chinese might have known that they were essentially paying for flattery from the Xiongnu, they continued to support the tributary system. As a result, China's relations with the Xiongnu were largely peaceful until A.D. 9, when Wang Mang usurped the Han throne and tried to restore Zhou-style political feudalism. Wang Mang actually tried to make the tributary system entail real (as opposed to ritual or symbolic) submission to China. The Xiongnu balked at this, of course, and soon began to attack China once again. By the end of Wang Mang's reign in A.D. 23, the Xiongnu were once again feeling powerful enough to demand the restoration of the old intermarriage system, but the restored or Eastern Han would hear of none of this. As it turned out, by A.D. 40 the Xiongnu were once again divided against themselves in a civil war, and roughly the southern half of the Xiongnu chose to submit to Han China rather than to the northern Xiongnu.

Around A.D. 100, an allied force of Han Chinese, Xiongnu, and other pastoral nomadic warriors attacked and defeated the northern Xiongnu. After this, most of the northern Xiongnu also submitted to China, but a minority flfled northward and westward "to parts unknown," according to later Han historical documents. These Xiongnu may have migrated across the Eurasian landmass to emerge, 300 years later, as the Huns under Attila, who menaced the Roman Empire. (The phonetic similarity between "Xiongnu" and "Hun" seems to substantiate this equation of the Xiongnu with the Huns known to the later Roman Empire, as also does recent archaeological and documentary evidence. This Xiongnu/Hun equation is, however, still somewhat controversial and is not unanimously accepted in scholarly circles.)

THE FALL OF HAN AND THE PERIOD OF DIVISION, A.D. 220–589

Toward the end of the Eastern Han, the old problems came back to haunt China. Landlordism was once again on the rise, the northern barbarians or pastoral nomads were making hostile movements, tax revenues were down, and regionalism was up. A major uprising called the Yellow Turban Rebellion, which broke out in A.D. 186, nearly succeeded in overthrowing the Han. It was quelled only after a coalition of generals was given almost total discretion and the military power to fight it. After the rebellion was put down, these generals, unwilling to give up military power after they had tasted it, became warlords or regional military strongmen who did whatever they pleased with little regard for what the dynasty thought of their actions. The Han was never the same again, but it limped on until a general accepted the abdication of the last Han emperor in A.D. 220. Thereafter China fell into a period of division and chaos that lasted for more than 350 years. China did, however, finally succeed in reunifying itself again in the 580s.

The first part of the Period of Division is known as the Three Kingdoms period. Three states succeeded the Han and pretended to be working for the eventual reunification of China. This period is highly romanticized in Chinese history, and stories of the alliances, betrayals, and battles between the three states have long been stock themes in Chinese literature. A popular historical novel about this period, called the *Romance of the Three Kingdoms*, is one of China's all-time favorite literary works, and even trained historians are sometimes confused between the historical records about the period and the episodes immortalized in the novel.

Brief and tenuous unity was achieved in A.D. 280 by a state called Western Jin, which tried once again to restore feudalism to China. Like Wang Mang's attempt, this ended in utter failure, and the Jin government lost half its territory to Xiongnu invaders. The Jin government then had to flee from Loyang, its original capital, to Nanjing (Nanking), where it lingered on for a few more decades before being overthrown. Thereafter China was divided along north-south lines, with a series of short-lived native Chinese dynasties in the south with Nanjing as their capital, and an even more abysmal succession of barbarian dynasties in the north. China was a deeply divided and chaotic nation during this time, and the people of northern and southern China began to wonder if their once-great civilization would ever be unified again. Northern and southern Chinese began to develop cultural differences and to develop prejudices toward one another, some of which still exist today.

Life was hard in China during this period. National unity was lost, and the transportation and communication infrastructure of Han times fell into ruins. Money largely went out of circulation and the economy reverted to barter. (Transition from a monetarized economy to a barter system frequently entails a drastic drop in standard of living.) During this period, pastoral nomadic peoples first swept down into China and ruled directly over portions of it. During the Han, the Xiongnu seldom if ever took territory away from China and ruled over it themselves; the Xiongnu and the pastoral nomads of their day were not sophisticated enough to learn the art and science of efficiently governing a sedentary society. During the Period of Division, however, some pastoral nomads learned the Chinese civilizational arts and began competently governing Chinese territories they had conquered. Thus a pattern of "conquest dynasties" developed during this period, and such dynasties were to be very influential and important in the last thousand years of imperial Chinese history.

During the Period of Division, two foreign cultural influences began percolating into China: pastoral nomadic and Buddhistic. Buddhism, from India, was from a unique and manifestly non-Chinese civilization, and the northern barbarian dynasties were run by pastoral nomads, who were different in language, culture, and ecology. Some Chinese feared that these twin cultural influences would dilute or completely overwhelm Chinese civilization, but it never happened. When China was reunified in the 580s, it emerged with its civilization intact. Buddhism and the material culture of the barbarians (musical instruments, chairs, and cuisine) added to the fabric of Chinese culture but did not fundamentally alter it. China was still China after the long and bitter nightmare of the Period of Division had ended.

Buddhism Comes to China

Buddhism first gained a foothold in China during the Period of Division. It came in not directly from India but from Central Asian Buddhist kingdoms that had converted to Buddhism a few centuries earlier. (Some of these kingdoms had originally been founded by the generals of Alexander the Great, and later their populations converted to Buddhism, thus combining *Buddhist* religion with *Greek* culture.) The religion had been known in China since Han times, but it never flourished during that dynasty. This is probably because the basic message of Buddhism, that life is suffering, did not resonate with the Han Chinese. Life was fairly good in Han China, and the majority of Chinese seem to have had little if any desire to alleviate the pain of life with a palliative religion.

Buddhism can be summarized in terms of its "Four Noble Truths." In India, during the sixth century B.C., the Buddha taught four truths:

1. Life is suffering. In life everyone experiences pain and sorrow. We all get sick and eventually die.
2. Suffering is caused by desire.
3. Desire can be eliminated.
4. Desire can be eliminated through the Eightfold Path, a set of eight instructions for minimizing desires and the suffering they create.

Once a person truly succeeds in eliminating all desire, he will have achieved *nirvana*, a state difficult to define but which connotes a state of desireless, and therefore painless, bliss.

One variety of the religion called Mahayana Buddhism taught that because strictly abiding by the Eightfold Path was an extremely difficult or even almost impossible thing to do, merciful beings called *boddhisatvas* who had achieved nirvana themselves had, at the time of their deaths and on the brink of stepping into eternal nirvana, stepped back and turned their compassion and attention to the mortal, suffering world. By having come this close to eternal nirvana and then temporarily backing away from it for the sake of the world, they had accrued to themselves an inexhaustible fund of merit that could be imputed to all people who turned to them in faith and supplication.

Mahayana Buddhism was, then, a type of savior religion, and it appealed deeply to the Chinese of the Period of Division. Life in China at this time *was* rough and entailed much suffering. Buddhism had great appeal in both northern and southern China, among the elite and commoners alike. The rulers of the barbarian conquest dynasties in northern China found the religion attractive precisely because it was not Chinese and because it had come from another great and ancient civilization. But the elite of the native Chinese dynasties in southern China also found Buddhism acceptable because of its art, its more advanced teachings, and its message of possible surcease from suffering. Commoners in both northern and southern China accepted Buddhism because of its message and the beautiful and colorful art the Buddhist missionaries used to explain the fundamentals of the religion. By the 500s, China had been thoroughly converted to Buddhism.

Some Chinese Buddhists were so interested in the religion that they became monks and traveled all the way to India, the land of Buddhism's origins. There some of them even mastered the extremely difficult Sanskrit language in which Buddhist *sutras* (religious writings) were written and translated them into Chinese. Eventually, Buddhism in China took its own peculiar doctrinal turns. The Chan ("Zen" in Japanese) school of the religion became the most well known of these.

During the first wave of Buddhism's entry into China, the Buddhist missionaries and early Chinese converts used Taoist terminology to translate Buddhist terms. This, however, led to conceptual confusion and created misunderstandings. Most Buddhists in China eventually decided to transliterate, rather than translate, Buddhist terms in their full foreignness. That is, they decided not to translate the terms at all, but more or less to spell them out exactly as they sounded in Sanskrit. Many Buddhist terms thus had a very foreign ring to Chinese ears, but this actually added to their mystery and reinforced the point that they were indeed different from Taoist ideas and concepts.

Buddhism fit nicely into the Confucianist-Taoist duo and transformed it into a religious and philosophical trio. The Chinese during this time concluded that Confucianism was applicable to governmental affairs, while Buddhism and Taoism pertained more to an individual's private, inner religious life. But Confucianism during this time seemed somewhat irrelevant because there was no effective central government in China that could seek to apply it. Buddhism and Taoism gave people much more solace and comfort in their lives, and most Chinese, and even many Chinese emperors, more or less preferred them over Confucianism. The Period of Division and the Sui and Tang dynasties that followed it were the heyday of Buddhism in Chinese history. Toward the late 800s and the end of the Tang dynasty, there was finally something of an intellectual rebellion against Buddhism among many of China's intellectuals (see Chapter 4).

Technological Innovations

China saw a staggering number of technological innovations during the Han dynasty and even during the chaotic Period of Division that followed it. The Chinese were the first people in the world to harness the power of rushing water in streams and rivers, and they did so 1,200 years before the Europeans. In A.D. 31 a regional government official invented a waterwheel that transmitted power from a running stream to the large bellows (devices that blow air) of an iron-casting operation. The forced air from the bellows was used to heat up the temperature of charcoal fires until they were hot enough to melt iron. This was, of course, an important innovation in Chinese metallurgy.

The Chinese also built the first suspension bridge in the world, 1,800 years before such bridges were known in the West. (A suspension bridge is a structure that holds a roadway or walkway on ropes or cables.) The first mention in Chinese historical materials of such a bridge, which dates back to Han times in 25 B.C., describes a suspension bridge in the Himalayas. A Chinese Buddhist monk who traveled to India at the end of the fourth century A.D. mentions crossing it along his journey. This was likely a catenary bridge, which means that the planked pathway of the bridge followed the curved contours of the suspended rope and did not constitute a flat passage surface. True non-catenary suspension bridges were made possible by the Chinese when they invented iron-chain suspension techniques. The first such bridge in Europe was not built until the eighteenth century.

Everyone knows that the Chinese invented paper, but it was not the flimsy stuff pounded from wood fibers and shaped into thin sheets like the pages of this book. Paper is actually the substance left behind when any loose and finely pounded fibers are suspended in a container of solution, allowed to settle to the bottom in thin deposits, and then allowed to dry after the solution is drained away. For centuries, paper in Europe was made of linen and was exceptionally strong and enduring, as an inspection of a European book printed the 1600s and 1700s will reveal. (In fact, the pages of these books will outlast their covers and will still be around long after the highly acidic paper used in some early twentieth-century book publishing has literally crumbled and cracked into dust.) The oldest piece of paper in the world, found in China this century, dates back to the second or first century B.C. This paper, made of pounded hemp fibers, is thick and not very smooth. This crude but very strong paper apparently had uses other than as a medium for writing. In fact, early paper in China was so durable that it was sometimes used as clothing and even light body armor.

The oldest paper on which writing survives dates to A.D 110 of Han China and records the rebellion of a frontier tribe. After paper replaced silk and bamboo as the most common material on which to write, the bark of the mulberry tree became the most popular pounded fiber for making paper. But even this wood-fiber paper was so tough that it found use as clothing, curtains, and mosquito nets. The Chinese were also the first in the world to promote and practice the use of paper for reasons of personal hygiene. For centuries the Chinese carefully guarded the secret of papermaking, but eventually it spread to the Near East and still later to Europe. Today it is sometimes supposed that when Arab armies from the Abbasid Caliphate defeated Tang dynasty forces in the eighth century A.D. at the Talas River (near modern Uzbekistan), Chinese prisoners who knew the prized secret of papermaking shared it with their captors in Baghdad.

Stirrups are such commonplace devices today that it is difficult to imagine riding horses without them. Ironically, even though the Chinese were not a great horse-riding people, they were the first in the world to invent stirrups, in the third century A.D. Centuries before this, the great mounted warriors of Alexander the Great and the Romans rode their horses without them and were jostled about on horseback with no platform from which to stand up and stabilize their rides. These warriors had to hang on to the horse's mane to steady themselves, and often they had trouble mounting their horses. Perhaps because they were not great horsemen themselves, the Chinese sought a remedy for these difficulties and eventually devised a very simple and effective one. Chinese stirrups, made of cast metal and thus quite durable, hung in suspension from the saddle and constituted a platform on which the rider could stand and steady himself. Being able to do this greatly increased the rider's stability and enabled him to be much more accurate with a bow and arrow. Thus the stirrup, originally developed for peaceful purposes, quickly found military application and greatly increased the lethality of the mounted archer. Pastoral nomads were quick to note the utility of these simple devices and soon adopted them for their own use. Because the stirrups were made into solid shapes, they did not flex and thus bind the feet of the rider the way some early rope predecessors of the stirrup had done among certain pastoral nomadic tribes. The earliest mention of the stirrup we have in the

Western world is the writings of a Byzantine emperor in the sixth century A.D. Thus, stirrups were apparently known and used in China for about 300 years before they became known to the West. The stirrup was probably transmitted to the West by the Avars, a warlike tribe of pastoral nomads who were also known to the Chinese.

The seismograph, an instrument for detecting earthquakes when no perceptible local earthquake activity is felt, is a Chinese invention. This supposedly modern instrument was actually invented by a scientist and mathematician, Zhang Heng, in the second century A.D. We have only documentary descriptions of it, but apparently Zhang's instrument consisted of a metal urn on the outside of which several metal balls were held in the mouths of cast-metal dragons. Cast-metal frogs with open mouths waited below for the balls to fall, and when a certain ball fell into a frog's mouth, it indicated the direction in which the earthquake occurred. This was important information for a Chinese government to know, since it could launch relief efforts quickly without having to wait for word to arrive from the affected province, a process that might take several days, depending on its distance from the capital city. This seismograph did not measure the intensities of quakes, but even as a direction finder it found use in China more than 1,400 years before it was known in Europe.

The Chinese invented hang gliding and parachuting. A Taoist alchemist of the fourth century A.D. experimented successfully with man-carrying tethered kites, and by the sixth century the Chinese emperor of a minor dynasty was compelling his prisoners and erstwhile enemies to jump from heights while mounted on tetherless kites. One such flight was so successful that its terrified passenger managed to fly for a distance of about two miles. As far as parachutes are concerned, every red-blooded schoolchild knows that Leonardo da Vinci recorded in his notes the concept of parachutes. The Chinese, however, went beyond conceptual sketches of parachutes and actually used them successfully as early as the second century B.C. The great Han historian Sima Qian records in his history a story of how a man fleeing from a pursuer jumped from a height using several large conical straw hats tied together to his body and landed on the ground safely. Another anecdote dating to the thirteenth century A.D. records how a robber jumped from a high tower in southern China with two large umbrellas in his hands and managed to land without injury. Parachutes were not used safely and effectively in Europe until the late 1700s.

4

Middle and Late Imperial China: A.D. 589–ca. 1800

SUI UNIFICATION AND TANG SUCCESSION: 589–907

After over 350 years of internal division, China finally managed to pull itself back together. This was accomplished by the Sui, a short-lived dynasty (589–618) that used, like the Qin before it, extraordinarily harsh measures to achieve unity. Also like the Qin, the Sui was overthrown because of its harsh and totalitarian nature and replaced by a milder, long-lasting dynasty. Just as Han followed Qin, so the Tang (A.D. 618–907) followed the Sui.

The first Sui emperor surveyed Chinese farmlands and, with the power of his new state, confiscated land from wealthy landlords who had been charging outrageous rents for centuries and depriving Chinese governments of their needed revenue. The new taxes he imposed on China's peasants were lower than the former rents had been, so the peasants welcomed this change. He also reestablished the capital at Chang'an, the former Han capital, and began digging the Grand Canal from southern China to Chang'an. This canal eventually became an important waterway linking northern and southern China.

This helped reconnect north and south, which had been separated from each other for a long time and ruled over by different governments.

The first Sui emperor was, unfortunately, succeeded by his megalomaniacal son, Sui Yangdi, who is second only to Qin Shihuang in Chinese history for being a harsh and extravagant despot. He pressed his people to the breaking point and ruined much of that which his father had accomplished, ultimately dooming his dynasty. He wasted money on huge construction projects and built a massive and ostentatious palace for himself. He was obsessively driven to complete the Grand Canal, at enormous expense. He even pressed women into construction work when male laborers were too few. When the canal was finally finished he took a flamboyant tour down it. His power was, for a time, seemingly limitless; his every whim was satisfied. He is notorious in Chinese history for compelling thousands of women to make paper and silk blossoms and paste them on the branches of bare trees in the wintertime, in order to cure his wintertime depression.

Yangdi squandered national resources on huge, unsuccessful military campaigns. He attacked Korea three times during his reign but failed to conquer the peninsula, and his defeats cost the lives of several hundred thousand troops. In 617 he attacked the Turks; this action also ended disastrously for the Sui and almost resulted in Yangdi's capture. All of these military debacles seriously depleted the state budget, and to make up for the shortfall, he required taxes to be paid years in advance. When the peasants could take no more of this and rebelled, he appointed a general named Li Yuan to quell the rebellions. Li Yuan, however, was fed up with Yangdi and soon turned against him. A Sui official assassinated Yangdi in 618, and Li Yuan created his own dynasty, the Tang, which was to last for almost 300 years.

The Tang is one of China's two golden ages. Almost every Chinese points to the Han and the Tang as the two times when Chinese civilization was at its highest and most powerful. The Chinese call themselves "men of Han" after the Han dynasty, and they call overseas Chinese communities and Chinatowns "Streets of Tang People." Like the Han, the Tang had a huge territory that extended in a long arm out along the Silk Road into Central Asia, and, also like the Han, the Tang managed for a time to defeat the northern barbarians and extend their domination over them. In the Han, the barbarians were the Xiongnu or Huns, but during the Tang they were the Turks. This may surprise some modern readers because we usually think of the Turks as living in modern Turkey and other parts of the Middle East, but the earliest known Turk homeland was in the area known as Mongolia today. Eventually, the majority of Turks migrated westward and converted to Islam. In fact, the founding emperors of the Tang dynasty were themselves part Chinese and part Turkish, and they spoke both languages and were familiar with both cultures. Their Turkish heritage was enormously beneficial to them in establishing authority over the Turks.

By the early eighth century, Tang China was the world's wealthiest, most powerful state, and its capital, Chang'an was the largest city in the world and surpassed Constantinople in splendor. Chang'an was the terminus of the Silk Road, the pot of gold at the end of the rainbow, where merchants from all over the Eurasian world gathered to trade and enjoy the amenities of sophisticated urban culture. Tang Chang'an was a very cosmopolitan and multicultural city in which many world cultures and religions flourished. Foreign music, cuisine, dances, and wines were all the rage in Chang'an, and the Tang Chinese had a taste for foreign exotica and foreign objets d'art. Powerful, confident Tang China had no need to fear or despise foreigners or their cultures.

The Tang had a series of competent and energetic emperors, one of whom was a woman, Empress Wu, who usurped the throne at the end of the seventh century and reigned for 23 years over the dynasty, which she renamed Zhou. (Actually, it is technically inaccurate to call her an empress because an empress was only the wife of the ruling emperor.) Empress Wu was the first and only female emperor (*huangdi*) to reign and rule in Chinese history. Traditional Chinese historians have long portrayed her as a ruthless, ambitious, and unprincipled woman who changed the dynasty's name and dealt harshly with her critics and opponents. But she was by no means a failure, and during her rule she did see one accomplishment that had eluded her Sui and Tang predecessors: the submission of Korea to Tang suzerainty.

The Tang eventually overcame Empress Wu's challenge and restored the dynasty's name and ruling royal clan. During the reign of Emperor Xuanzong (r. 712 to 756), the Tang reached its greatest height culturally and militarily. Some of Tang China's greatest poets and painters flourished during his reign. When Xuanzong became enamored of one of his son's concubines, Yang Guifei, he turned significant political and military power over to her. She took advantage of Xuanzong's doting by appointing her relatives to prominent positions of leadership in the government and military. One such appointed relative of hers, An Lushan, came out in open rebellion against the Tang in 755 and plunged China into years of chaos that shook the dynasty to its very foundations. Tang China never fully recovered from this period of rebellion, which was suppressed at length and with great difficulty in 763 with the help of the Uighurs, another warlike pastoral nomadic people who had defeated the Turks in Mongolia a decade or two earlier and were now the masters of the steppe. Tang China entered a long and gradual period of decline. Late Tang China was a melancholy time, and this general national mood is superbly reflected in some of the lyrical poetry of the time.

The Tang dynasty slipped into precipitous decline during the late ninth century when a huge domestic rebellion led by Huang Chao broke out in the drought-stricken North China Plain and quickly spread to other areas. In 879 Huang Chao captured the southern Chinese city of Canton (Guangzhou) and slaughtered thousands of Jewish, Muslim, and Christian merchants there, perhaps because he blamed them in part for China's difficulties. Huang Chao's rebellion was overthrown with the help of the Kirgiz, yet another warlike pastoral nomadic people, but this was a hollow victory. The Tang continued as a shadow of its former greatness until 907, when regional military commanders formerly loyal to Tang decided to end the fiction of the dynasty's power and authority over them. These commanders then became warlords and vied with one another to become China's next great unifying dynasty. The period of the Five Dynasties lasted from 907 to 960, when a warlord regime called Song finally managed to impose some measure of enduring unity to the majority, but not all, of historically Chinese territory. The Song lasted from 960 to 1279, when all of China was conquered by the Mongol descendants of Chinggis Khan (Genghis Khan).

Tang government was efficient and effectively organized. The first beginnings of the well-known Chinese civil service examination system date back to Han times, but during the Tang the system was further institutionalized as one way for the government to recruit bureaucratic personnel. Tang testing evaluated a candidate's cultural knowledge, literacy, handwriting, and even physical appearance, and background investigations of promising candidates helped the government learn more about their general characters and reputations. Candidates who passed these multiple levels of assessment were then put on a waiting list for government jobs. Perhaps only one in every five hundred candidates who began the entire process ever attained a government job. The majority of people who got such jobs came from old aristocratic families. Occasionally a hometown boy with no prominent family background succeeded at the examinations, but this was the exception. The Tang was a predominantly aristocratic society.

New officials started with lowly positions in areas distant from the Tang capital, but as their careers progressed they gradually climbed the ladder of government promotions. The Tang government had a highly organized system of ranks and salaries for its officials, who were not allowed to remain in any one locality for very long. The government feared, probably with justification, that an official who remained in an area too long might become too comfortable there, put down roots, and eventually become corrupt. Every three years or so, the Tang government rotated its officials throughout the Chinese population of the Tang empire.

The "equal fields system" was the Tang's way of dealing with the age-old landlord problem. In this system, most large private land holdings were simply confiscated and remanded to government ownership. (This idea was not the Tang's but came from previous dynasties during the Period of Division; however, the Tang was the first dynasty to give it widespread implementation.) The government then distributed plots of its land to peasants to farm, but not to own. That is, although the peasants were given sole right to farm land for their own living, nobody could buy it from them and they could not sell it to anyone. This was land, not real estate. Able-bodied males from age 16 to 60 were given exclusive rights to plots of land approximately 14 acres in size, and in exchange for these rights, the peasants were required to pay three types of taxes to the government: grain, corvée (a fixed number of days of laboring on government-sponsored construction projects), and cloth. In essence, peasants rented the land long term, with tax payments as rent. Of course, the Tang government instituted the equal fields system so that it would not have to compete with landlords and mortgage sharks for revenue from the land. Extensive government surveys underpinned this system, and with a powerful and highly organized government it all worked for a while. When the government weakened after the An Lushan rebellion in 755, the landlord problem gradually began emerging once again, and eventually the system fell apart.

Many Chinese view the Tang as China's single greatest age for poetry. During China's last dynasty, the Qing (1644–1912), a compilation of Tang poetry called *Three Hundred Tang Poems* became very popular, and even today some cultured Chinese families still encourage their children to memorize large parts of it. Famous Tang poets include Li Bo, Du Fu, Bo Juyi, and Li Shangyin.

EMPEROR AND KHAN: TANG RELATIONS WITH THE TURKS

Li Yuan's son, the second Tang emperor, is known to Chinese history as Tang Taizong. An energetic and assertive personality, Taizong was much more aggressive and ambitious than his father. Taizong secured what his father could not even imagine: the submission of the Turks to Tang overlordship. He understood the Turks well and knew their psychology. During the 620s, when the Turks were making threatening moves toward the Tang, Taizong twice dashed out of the gates of Chang'an on horseback and rode into the Turk encampments, where he actually challenged the Turk khans to personal combat. Overawed by his bravado and confidence, the Turks on both occasions backed off. Taizong predicted that the Turks would eventually weaken themselves through civil war, and in the late 620s his predictions came true. In 630 the Turks decided to avoid self-destruction by submitting to the Tang, and they agreed to recognize Taizong as their "Heavenly Khan." With this, Taizong became without question the most powerful man in the world. He reigned as emperor over the Chinese and Heavenly Khan over the hordes of warlike Turkic mounted warriors on China's northern frontier. Tang domination over the Turks endured for half a century. The Tang then deployed Turks along its northern frontiers as guards. Other Turks went into China and were eventually assimilated into Chinese civilization.

This peculiar relation between the Chinese and the Turks symbolizes Tang China's approach to the outside world in general. Chang'an, the Tang capital, became the cultural and economic center of Asia. The Japanese and Koreans greatly admired Tang civilization and sent many envoys to learn its culture and methods of government. The Japanese even modeled their first capital cities after the Tang capital. Nara and Heian were virtual scaled-down copies of Chang'an, and the "Japanese" tea ceremony and the formal kimono dress were based on Tang precedents. Silla dynasty Korea (A.D. 668–935) copied Tang governmental organization in extensive detail, and the earliest literature in both Korea and Japan was in large part written in pure Chinese. Taizong himself was part Turk and so could not entertain arrogant or condescending attitudes toward foreign peoples and cultures. He had a very open-minded attitude toward all peoples, and his style was reflected and perpetuated throughout the rest of the dynasty. He fostered and protected foreign religions, and in Chang'an were found Buddhist temples, Jewish synagogues, Islamic mosques, and Nestorian Christian chapels. (Nestorian Christianity was condemned as heresy at the Council of Ephesus in A.D. 431 because of its seemingly heterodox views of Jesus Christ. It eventually declined in the West but spread through much of Asia, where it achieved its greatest extent from the seventh through tenth centuries.) China in Tang times was wide open to the outside world, more so than in any other period until the twentieth century. China imported much from the rest of the outside world and gained its widespread taste for tea, an important Southeast Asian crop, during this time. It also gained a taste for foreign wines.

For the Chinese, Tang domination of the Turks was evidence that China and its emperors truly possessed the Mandate of Heaven; how could they *not*, when all of China and the majority of its erstwhile enemies recognized Tang leadership? From the Turks' point of view, however, this period of submission was an unfortunate step they had to take to prevent their own dissolution. With Taizong's death in 649, things began to change when the young Turks began to question their fathers' loyalty to Tang China. By 680 the Turks had formally broken away from Tang control and asserted their independence. Patriotic Turk hotheads began to bemoan the fact that their people had ever submitted to Chinese overlordship at all. The Turks pursued their own national destiny until 744, when they were conquered not by the Chinese but by the Uighurs, a related Turkic-speaking people. In 745 the Uighurs presented the Tang Chinese with the head of the last Turkish khan to prove that they were now the masters of the steppe lands on China's northern borders. The Uighurs never did accept an inferior position vis-à-vis China. In fact, in many ways, the Uighurs lorded it over China because the Tang had, in the 750s, asked for and received their help in quelling the An Lushan rebellion. Tang China after An Lushan owed its empire to the Uighurs and knew it, so Tang authorities never dared cross the Uighurs. Uighur horsemen haughtily pranced about the streets of Chang'an, seemingly aware of popular Chinese resentment against them but caring little about it.

PARTIAL RECOVERY: SONG, 960–1279

The Tang dynasty came to an end in 907, when the last Tang emperor gave up his throne. With this abdication, China entered a brief period of disunity called the Five Dynasties period, which lasted from 907 to 960. Each of the Five Dynasties lasted only a brief time before being overthrown by another, and all of them ruled only in northern China. (During this period, the south was ruled by a series of motley regimes that were later called the Ten Kingdoms.) During the Five Dynasties, a powerful barbarian people on China's north, the Kitans, conquered a portion of northern China and proclaimed a new dynasty of their own: the Liao (907–1125). The portion of northern Chinese territory occupied by the Kitan Liao was not recovered by a native Chinese dynasty until 1368.

Lasting unity over most of China's historical territory was finally achieved in 960 by Zhao Kuangyin, who became the founding emperor of the Song dynasty (960–1279) and is known in Chinese history as Song Taizu, or "Grand Progenitor of the Song." Taizu was originally a general for the last of the Five Dynasties, but he turned against it when he deemed its fortunes were finished. The story of his rise to power is known to every educated Chinese. According to some Song historical materials, Zhao (the future Taizu) awoke one morning in his military camp and was startled to find a yellow robe draped about his shoulders. He immediately understood the momentous meaning of the robe: yellow was the imperial color, and only the emperor could wear a yellow robe. He thrice protested his inability and unworthiness to be emperor, but his lieutenants were so insistent, and the voice of the people was so enthusiastic, that he finally agreed reluctantly to bow to the popular will and proclaim his own dynasty, the Song, with its capital at Kaifeng (which was then known as Bian or Bianliang). His dynasty lasted for over 300 years when it was overthrown by the Mongol descendants of Chinggis Khan in 1279.

Zhao was probably more ambitious and less reluctant to assume power than this idealized version of the events indicates. He was unhappy that the emperor of the dynasty against which he rebelled was a mere child and probably concluded that he himself was more qualified to unify China, and the unification of China was very much on his mind after he proclaimed his dynasty. He had two great tasks before him: first, the conquest of the south and the internal unification of China and second, recovery of the parts of northern China conquered by the Kitans. He had his work cut out for him.

One of Taizu's steps in securing his power over China internally was to reign in the military. He was, of course, quite self-conscious about his own rise to power through a military mutiny, and he wanted to ensure that nobody else would be able to challenge his power in this way. He carefully and deliberately deprived his lieutenants of their own military authority and transferred it into his own hands. Another well-known story gives an idealized and dramatic account of how all this happened. One night at a sumptuous wine-and-dine affair with his comrades in arms, Taizu (who was apparently quite drunk) began to weep bitterly. Surprised and taken aback by this, his lieutenants asked him why he was crying. He responded that he could not bear the thought that his own military comrades, here so convivially gathered with him on this evening, might one day launch a military rebellion against him. Each of them protested that this would never happen and sought to console him. Eventually they agreed that in order to get

Taizu's spirits back up, they would remand all of their military authority over to him in symbolic exchange for one more round of wine. Taizu took them up on this (maybe he was not so drunk after all), and with one momentous toast he deprived them of their military autonomy. His success at this is known, if not universally celebrated, as the "exchange of military authority for a cup of wine."

However it actually happened, Taizu's consolidation of military authority in his own hands, as well as his insistence that the civilian arm of the government should have unquestionable control over the military, had important and long-range consequences. First of all, these developments significantly weakened the military. In his efforts to achieve control over the military and prevent any challenge to his power from that quarter, Taizu also reduced the size of the military, which eventually had a disastrous effect on the Song's national security. Second, they led to an overall climate during the Song that was disdainful and untrusting of the military. Taizu canceled military conscription and relied on an all-volunteer army. As a result, the army had trouble attracting quality men. Its ranks were eventually filled with large numbers of sentenced criminals, ne'er-do-wells, and the dregs of society. A popular saying of the time went that "good iron should not be made into nails, and good boys should not serve as soldiers."

All in all, the Song was a weak dynasty militarily. The traditional Chinese assessment of the dynasty is succinct and to the point: "heavy on civilian government, light on the military" (*zhongwen qingwu*). Patriotic Chinese today do not generally look upon the Song with much favor, and some disparagingly refer to it as "the little dynasty" (*xiao chaoting*) and even blame it for the humiliating military defeats China suffered at the hands of the British and other aggressive European powers nine centuries later. The Song's military weakness is probably traceable to Taizu's concerns about military threats to his government, and in retrospect it is evident that he probably overreacted to this possibility. His dynasty never grew to the size or power of the mighty Han or Tang empires. It did not rule over a far-flung empire or have a long arm of territory extending far out into Central Asia, and it failed to attract as much international admiration or envy as the Tang had.

Taizu was not content simply to have increased control over a weakened military. He also had concerns about the social sphere—namely the political or economic pressure that prominent families and lineage groups might bring to bear on his government. Taizu did not like the aristocratic style of the former Tang dynasty, and he took steps to prevent a new Tang-style aristocratic class from emerging during his dynasty. He wanted the vast majority of civilian officials in his government to get their positions because of what they knew, not who they knew or what their family backgrounds were. Accordingly, he reestablished and greatly expanded the examination system, and eventually the majority of his government officials were people who had no aristocratic family backgrounds but had secured their government employment by passing civil service examinations. This ensured that he had a fresh flow of new, nonaristocratic blood in his government bureaucracy. Of course, each new recruit into the Song government knew that he owed his position and allegiance to Taizu's dynasty and government, and not to the wealth, prestige, or influence of his own family. In short, Taizu's government was a meritocracy, not an aristocracy. As the sole assessor and rewarder of merit, the Song government was secure and not in a position to be manipulated by the interests or pressures of prominent families.

After eliminating any possible military and social challenges to his position, Taizu turned his attention to challenges from the government bureaucracy itself. Accordingly, he reorganized government ministries, weakened their ties with one another, and placed them beneath him hierarchically to foster ambiguous and adversarial ties among them. At the same time, he took care to strengthen and clearly define each ministry's direct power relationship with himself. By weakening the horizontal ties between ministries and strengthening the vertical ties between them and himself, Taizu consolidated his own power over the government bureaucracy. If there was a disagreement over government policy, it was between the ministries, and he was left as the sole, unchallengeable arbiter of these differences. The man was a political animal, and he played the game well.

All of this was somewhat ironic, given the Song's very humble territorial position. Externally, China had not been as weak since the Period of Division, when one barbarian regime after another occupied huge tracts of Chinese territory. Song China did not command the respect or admiration of its international neighbors, and the Kitan Liao (and two other barbarian states on the Song's western and southern frontiers) frequently humiliated China with attacks on its borders and insults to its national honor. Internally, however, the first Song emperor gathered unprecedented amounts of civilian and military power into his own hands. Thus, the Song was externally weaker and internally stronger than any previous major dynasty. It is almost tempting to conclude that the one was the cause of the other, or that Zhao and his successors increased their own power internally precisely because they and their state were so weak on the international scene. As far as power relationships were concerned, a certain amount of anxiety or self-consciousness may have shaped the form and style of Song government.

Taizu died in 976 without completely eliminating the last of the holdout Chinese dynasties in the south. This was accomplished by his brother and successor, known in Chinese history as Song Taizong (Grand Ancestor of the Song). Afterward Taizong moved to recover the northern Chinese territories lost earlier in the century to the Kitans, but his two attacks against the Kitan both ended in humiliating defeat. (During the second attack, Taizong was hit by two Kitan arrows and had to be transported back to Song territory in a donkey cart.) He died in 997 without having recovered the lost territory, and a timid and vacillating emperor known as Zhenzong ("Naive Ancestor") succeeded him.

The Kitans attacked China in 1004, perhaps in revenge for the Song's two earlier attacks against them. To their probable surprise, however, the Kitans found that Song China stoutly resisted their invasion, and the next year the two states concluded a formal peace agreement called the Shanyuan Treaty. The treaty stopped all fighting between the Song and the Liao dynasty of the Kitans, and peace between the two states prevailed for over a century. The major results of the treaty were that the Liao called off the attack and an agreement was made that the Song would annually pay the Kitan Liao 100,000 ounces of silver and 200,000 rolls of silk. The fight ended in a draw between the two sides, but each regarded itself as victorious. The Song proclaimed victory because the Kitans stopped the attack and retreated, while the Kitans told their people that the Song was so terrified that it agreed to pay them every year if they would just go away. Regardless of which side "won," the treaty stopped the fighting and helped usher in one of China's greatest centuries: the eleventh. In spite of its external weakness, eleventh-century China was, overall, a very peaceful and prosperous place. Some of China's most significant intellectual, economic, and technological innovations were made during this century.

The peace and prosperity came to an end in the early 1100s with the emergence in the north of another barbarian power: the Jurchens and their Jin dynasty (1115–1234). The Jurchens, a seminomadic people, challenged the Kitans for power north of China and eventually defeated them in battle. Song China made tentative peaceful gestures to the Jurchens but eventually went back on them, and in reprisal the Jurchens attacked the Song and took over huge amounts of its territory, including its capital city. One member of the Song royal family managed to flee to southern China, where he and his supporters set up a new capital city in Hangzhou (then called Lin'an) in 1127. From here the remnants of the Song dynasty endured until 1279 and the Mongols' complete conquest of China. This period of Chinese history is usually called Southern Song, reflecting the dynasty's move to the south. (The period of Song history before this was eventually called Northern Song.)

The Southern Song initially was not prepared to give up all of the territory it lost to the Jurchens without another fight. The majority opinion in Southern Song seems to have favored an attempt at reconquest of the lost territories, but there was some opposition to this. In the late 1130s and early 1140s, the two main principals of this disagreement were a general named Yue Fei, who favored reconquest, and the emperor's chief councilor, named Qin Gui, who opposed it. (These two men have been called, respectively, the greatest patriot and the vilest villain in all of Chinese history.) Yue Fei launched his attack but was recalled by Qin Gui and thrown into prison, where he died. The Jurchens were so angry at being attacked that they demanded formal recognition of their claim to the Chinese territory they had already conquered, an increase in the annual silver and silk payments over and above what used to be paid to the Kitans, and, most humiliating of all, China's acceptance of "vassal" status vis-à-vis the Jurchens' Jin dynasty. Acting very much against prevailing public opinion, the Southern Song government accepted these demands in 1142. Subsequently, Yue Fei was celebrated as a hero who had died fighting in the noble cause to recover lost territory for the motherland, and Qin Gui was almost universally vilified. Even today there are temples to Yue Fei's memory in Taiwan, and on the mainland, crowds of Chinese patriots have been known to show their contempt for Qin Gui's "capitulationist" policies by spitting on a statue of him and making demeaning gestures to the statue of his wife.

The national humiliation of being a vassal to the Jin did not last long. In the 1160s fighting broke out again between Jin and Southern Song, but this time the Song acquitted itself well on the battlefield and agreed to end the hostilities only after the Jin assented to eliminating China's vassal status.

After this, life dragged on in the Southern Song. Being so far south, the Song government and its people became more oriented to trade along China's coastline, and soon Hangzhou emerged as a thriving metropolis that engaged in maritime trade with many nations. Even so, however, Hangzhou did not have the same open-minded attitudes toward foreigners that Chang'an did during the Tang. China, by late Southern Song times, had learned to fear foreigners and was not as fascinated with their cultures as Tang China had been.

The great Mongol conqueror Chinggis Khan emerged in 1206 as the undisputed leader of all pastoral nomadic peoples north of China. He and his successors in the Mongol world empire intermittently attacked the Jin dynasty of the Jurchens until it fell in 1234, and after this the Mongols and the Southern Song shared a border. The Southern Song government in Hangzhou was probably not very sad to see the Jurchens defeated, but they occasionally wondered if they would be the next target of the conquering Mongols. Their worst fears were realized in the 1250s, when the Mongols began attacking southern China. The fight with the Mongols was long and hard, but by 1279 the Mongol leader Khubilai (Kublai Khan) had succeeded in conquering all of China and proclaiming a new dynasty: the Yuan. This was the first time in history that *all* of China, and not just part of it, had fallen to foreign conquerors.

SONG FOREIGN RELATIONS WITH THE KITAN LIAO, 1005–CA. 1120

In 1988 Jingshen Tao, a prominent historian of Song diplomacy and foreign relations, published a book entitled *Two Sons of Heaven: Studies in Sung-Liao Relations.* The purpose of his startling title was to point out that Song foreign relations were unique in Chinese history. The Song was one of only a very few periods in Chinese history when the Chinese emperor explicitly and publicly recognized a foreign ruler as the equal of himself.

Actually, the Song had no choice. The Kitans and their Liao dynasty to China's north had proven to be more than a match for Song China. Because the Liao was a militarily powerful state that ruled over a significant Chinese population, it demanded to be treated diplomatically as an equal. The Liao would hear of no pejorative or condescending references to its regime or people, and its rulers would be called emperors (*huangdi*), and not something lesser such as sovereigns (*jun*), kings (*wang*), or lords (*zhu*). The Liao was also greatly concerned about its border security and insisted on strictly demarcating exactly where its territory began and the Song territory ended.

After the Shanyuan Treaty, the Song and the Liao recognized each other as "brotherly states" and their emperors as familial relations. These fictitious kinship ties were taken quite seriously, and both states carefully monitored the changing relationships between their emperors. (For example, an older brother/younger brother relationship would be altered to an uncle/nephew relationship when the older brother passed away and a new emperor took his place.) A fairly complex pattern of diplomatic relations between the Song and the Liao eventually emerged during the eleventh century. This diplomacy involved the frequent dispatch of ad hoc envoys and their retinues who traveled to the neighboring emperor's court for a time and then left; the European norm of fixed embassies and permanent residential diplomacy was almost completely unknown in premodern China, as the British and other Western nations were to discover during the late eighteenth and early nineteenth centuries.

Two types of traveling embassies were exchanged annually between the Song and the Liao: birthday felicitation envoys and new year felicitation envoys. Several other types of embassies were dispatched on an irregular, as-needed basis when reigning emperors, empresses, or dowager empresses passed away and new ones were enthroned. All of these embassies were of course purely ceremonial, but at a minimum they did maintain yearly diplomatic contact between the two states and served as reminders of the inviolability of the Shanyuan Treaty. Other types of embassies conducted substantive, negotiatory contact between the two states.

Song relations with the Jurchens basically followed the precedents established after the Shanyuan Treaty. With the exception of the period from 1142 to the 1160s, when the Song was nominally a vassal to the Jin, Song and Jin emperors continued to regard and address each other as equals in their diplomatic communications and ritual.

NEO-CONFUCIANISM

During the late Tang period, a reaction against Buddhism was developing among China's intellectual elite. An essay written by the late Tang scholar Han Yu (768–824), encouraging a Tang emperor not to receive a reputed finger bone of the Buddha as a sacred relic, is widely regarded as the opening salvo against Buddhism and the beginning of a Confucian revival that flourished during the subsequent Song period and beyond.

Neo-Confucianism was a rediscovery or reassertion of China's Confucian past, often seemingly at the expense of the Buddhist heritage from India. The Song dynasty framers of Neo-Confucianism attempted to show that authentic Confucian thought could address many of the profound cosmological and metaphysical concerns dealt with by Buddhism. Neo-Confucianists argued that a Confucian cosmology could be abstracted from some of the most ancient Chinese texts, and they eventually identified a corpus of these texts to serve as an authoritative statement of Confucius's ideology and the very ancient thought to which they argued he subscribed. Their purpose seems to have been to show that the secular and this-worldly concerns of Confucian thought could be expanded or conflated into a more comprehensive consideration of the universe. Buddhism was not the only cosmological game in town; Confucianism too could be shown to be profound and cosmological.

Neo-Confucianism eventually developed into two distinct strands. One school, given definitive expression by the great Southern Song philosopher and synthesizer Zhu Xi, was very rationalistic and centered on the study of principles (*li*), which it taught inhered in all things. *Li* were nonmaterial realities that were manifest in the material world, or *qi*. The greatest or ultimate expression of all *li* was the Supreme Ultimate (*taiji*), and the universe itself was the result of the various interworkings of these two great cosmological realities. Zhu Xi's cosmology was perhaps a dualism, or a philosophy holding that the universe is composed of two basic and irreducible entities. Another school, definitively developed by the Ming scholar Wang Shouren (Wang Yangming, 1472–1529), was more or less a monism, or a conception of the universe as composed of only one ultimate reality. Wang Shouren and like-minded Song philosophers before him argued that the universe was not ultimately two but one; *li* and *qi* were ultimately reducible to a single complete unity, and this perfect oneness inhered in people's minds or hearts (*xin*). Thus, contemplation of external phenomena and meditating on their *li* or principles was not as important as recovering the unity of the cosmos that was reflected within each individual.

By Song times, Buddhism was no longer the intellectual darling of the elite. Elites during the Song and subsequent dynasties were more explicitly Confucian in their public and ideological lives than their Tang predecessors had been, but many of them retained, like Han Yu himself, some measure of attachment to Buddhism and Buddhist principles in their private lives. It would be a mistake to conclude that China's intellectuals had by Song times completely turned their backs on Buddhism; and, of course, Buddhism continued to flourish throughout other segments of Chinese society well into modern times.

THE TANG-SONG TRANSITION: MAJOR CHANGES IN CHINESE CIVILIZATION

Historians of China have noticed some fundamental changes in China between the mid-Tang and late Song periods. One fundamental change was China's relationship with the outside world. In mid-Tang times, prior to the An Lushan rebellion, China was preeminent in the world and knew it. The Chinese had little reason to fear the outside world and seemed to find it endlessly fascinating. By the middle of the thirteenth century, this viewpoint had changed drastically. China had been recognizing the Liao and Jin states and rulers as equals, and the Mongol conquest of all China was rumbling on the horizon. Thirteenth-century China had every reason to be fearful and distrusting of the outside world, especially the barbarian warrior tribes on its northern borders.

Relations between the emperor and the bureaucracy changed as well. In mid-Tang times the emperor was *primus inter pares*, or first among equals, and he debated policy matters with his government ministers. By late Song times the emperor of a considerable weaker dynasty was, ironically, quite a bit more powerful internally vis-à-vis his bureaucracy than his Tang predecessors had been. He no longer debated policy but listened to rival factions of officials at court debate policy while remaining aloof from the fray. The emperor in late Song times was the final arbiter, and no longer one of the principals, of policy debates. Ministers who came into the presence of the Song emperors were much less relaxed than their Tang counterparts had been.

Most of the elite of Tang society were aristocrats, or people who came from families who had served Chinese governments for centuries. Being a member of the cultural and policy-making elite in Tang China was, on balance, just as much a matter of who you were as what you knew or how competent you were. Tang officialdom was largely an aristocracy. By late Song times, on the other hand, a slight majority of the elite came from families that had little or no heritage of government service. The Song dynasty had expanded its civil service examination system and had made official careers more available to men of talent, regardless of their bloodlines. The Song government did not want to be dominated by prominent aristocratic families and their interests. This style was started by the founding Song emperor, who wanted a class of officials more dependent on him for their positions than on any other segment of society. Song officialdom was, on balance, more of a meritocracy than an aristocracy.

Taxation changed. In Tang China, prior to the An Lushan rebellion, taxes were largely levied on people, not on land. Peasants farmed land owned by the state, and the taxes they paid to the state were more or less the rent for their land. By late Song times, on the other hand, private ownership of land was recognized, and taxes were levied on the land itself, according to how productive or fertile it was. Sources of tax revenue also changed over the Tang-Song transition. Mid-Tang revenues were largely drawn from agricultural taxes, but by late Song times commerce had expanded so much that commercial taxes accounted for fully half of the government's tax revenue.

The monetary system also changed. Tang China used copper coins as money, but by late Song times paper money was in widespread circulation. Marco Polo described to an astonished Europe the use of paper currency he encountered in Chinese cities just after the Mongol conquest of China.

There were also important population and demographic shifts. Chang'an, the Tang capital, had been more or less China's only major city, but by late Song times there were more than 10 cities with populations of one million or more. Hangzhou, the capital of the Southern Song, had a population of four million, which is quite large even by modern North American standards. Marco Polo described the teeming population, abundant luxuries, and unimaginable wealth and ingenuity he had encountered in Hangzhou, or "Quinsai" as he called the city, during the late thirteenth century. The population of Song China was already 100 million by 1100, far surpassing the Tang population high mark of 60 million. Urbanization, of course, was a major trend as a greater proportion of the Chinese population lived in cities by the end of the Song. Demographic shifts accompanied the population growth and urbanization as southern China was opened up to wet rice cultivation, which feeds more people per square unit of surface area than the dry cropping practiced in the north. In mid-Tang times the majority of China's population lived in the north, but by the late Song slightly over half of China's population lived in the south.

The quality of life of elite women worsened over the Tang-Song transition. In Tang times it was not unusual for an elite gentleman to view an educated and articulate woman as a very desirable companion, and she would often accompany him at drinking or social occasions. By Song times, however, several developments made life grimmer for women. The cult of female chastity, seldom prevalent in Tang times, was in full swing by the late Song, as was the idea that a chaste and virtuous woman should never remarry, even if her first husband died while in his youth. Concubinage was also much more common during Song times. Perhaps most bizarre of all, the practice of foot binding emerged during Five Dynasties and Song times. Foot binding catered to the foot fetish of elite Song men, who found unnaturally tiny feet attractive and normal-sized feet repulsive. To achieve the standard of feminine beauty in foot size, or "three-inch golden lotuses" as tiny feet were often called, many of the daughters in elite families had their feet deformed from an early age. Tightly wrapped bandages gradually broke the arch of the foot and caused the toes and heel to grow inward toward one another. This excruciatingly painful process was complete by the girl's late teens, at which time she was deformed for life. Chinese literature abounds with stories of mothers who wept bitterly as they wrapped their daughters' feet; they knew that the process hurt, but if their daughters did not have small feet, they would never be able to marry a prominent man and achieve social standing. Foot binding continued well into the first decades of the twentieth century but was finally abandoned when China bowed to modern ways and international norms.

THE MONGOL CONQUEST

In 1279 Khubilai Khan, grandson of the Mongol conqueror Chinggis Khan (Genghis Khan), prevailed over the last vestigial Song loyalist resistance and brought all of China under Mongol rule. This was the first time in history that all of China had been conquered by a foreign people. The Yuan dynasty (1279–1368) established by Khubilai was only part of a larger Mongol world empire that included other "khanates" or regions conquered and ruled by the Mongols: the Golden Horde in Russia, the Il Khanate in Persia and other areas of the Middle East, and the Chagadai Khanate in Central Asia. Together, these khanates formed the largest land empire the world has ever known. Khubilai Khan was *Khaghan*, or Grand Khan, over all of these khanates. He was, in the words of Marco Polo, "the most powerful man since Adam." His only significant failures were the abortive invasions of Japan he made during the later years of his reign.

The Mongol conquest of China was a long time in the making. Its roots go back to the twelfth century when a young man named Temujin, abandoned by his clan when his father was poisoned by political enemies, began building up a personal following in the steppe regions north of China, an area we know today as Mongolia. By dint of determination, luck, and the guidance of his mother, Temujin expanded his power over several rival tribes and finally became ruler of them all. In 1206, at a great assembly of pastoral nomadic warriors, he was proclaimed Chinggis Khan, which means "Universal Ruler" or "Khan from Ocean to Ocean." Chinggis Khan attacked the Jurchen Jin dynasty in northern China, and for a time the Jin seemed willing to submit to his rule. Ultimately, however, the Jin rebelled against Mongol overlordship and was never fully subjugated by Chinggis Khan, who devoted much of his life after 1206 to conquering Central Asia, including many

Chinggis Khan (Genghis Khan). (Instructional Resources Corporation)

Islamic regions. When Chinggis Khan died in 1227 he had not subjugated the Jurchens, and the task was left to his son and successor, Ögödei Khan, who completed it in 1234.

With this, all of northern China came under Mongol control. For a time Ögödei considered exterminating all the Chinese in northern China and converting it into grasslands for pastoral nomads, but his ethnic Kitan advisor, Yelü Chucai, talked him out of it, convincing him that Chinese peasants made agriculture possible, which in turn was responsible for the enormous wealth he was extracting from China.

In 1251 Möngke Khan, Ögödei's cousin, became Grand Khan of the Mongol world empire and decided to undertake two great conquest campaigns: one against Persia and one against China. Möngke personally mounted the campaign against Southern Song China and sent his younger brother Hülegü to attend to the conquest of Persia, which was accomplished by 1256. The Southern Song campaign was more difficult, however, and Möngke died in 1259 without having accomplished it. That honor was left to his brother Khubilai, who became Grand Khan in 1260 but did not conquer the Southern Song until 1279.

The outright conquest of China may not have been Chinggis Khan's original intention; he seems to have wanted to intimidate China from a distance the way the Xiongnu and Turks had done before him.

Painted portrait of Khubilai Khan (Kubla Khan). (Courtesy Artdaily.org)

Möngke and Khubilai, however, had grown up near China and were somewhat familiar with Chinese culture and history. They may have wanted to replicate Tang Taizong's fate of becoming both emperor to the Chinese and Grand Khan to the nomadic peoples. At any rate, Khubilai took up the conquest of China with relish; however, China was not conquered for almost another 20 years. China was the most difficult, and also the last, of the great Mongol conquests. Khubilai had named his regime in China the Yuan a few years before 1279, but from the traditional Chinese point of view the Yuan dynasty did not become legitimate until the last Song emperor died in 1279, after drowning at sea near modern Hong Kong.

The Yuan dynasty lasted for less than a hundred years, and its decline set in after Khubilai's death in 1294. Yuan China was administratively unstable because some Khans after Khubilai favored a more "native" or Chinese style of governance in China; others were more "traditional" or Mongolian in their approach and sought to exploit China for the good of the larger Mongol empire. This produced an inconsistency and unpredictability in Yuan government that did not bode well for its long-term longevity.

The Mongol conquerors of China seldom fully trusted Chinese officials and appointed Mongolian or Central Asian commissars to supervise them and keep close tabs on their activities. Very few governmental decisions or orders made by Chinese officials were valid without the cosignatures of the commissars. The Mongols also canceled the Chinese civil service examinations for most of the Yuan dynasty, preferring other methods of recruiting government officials. In some surprising ways, Mongol rule in China was not as harsh as might be imagined. Capital crimes and executions in Yuan China were actually *fewer* in number than they had been during the Song. Mongols imposed laws to reduce animal suffering in China and specified quick and humane means of slaughter. The Mongols did discriminate against the Chinese, and in particular against the southern Chinese. This probably was not racism, as some scholars have labeled it, but more of a hierarchy of assessed loyalties. That is, Mongols tended to trust people who had been loyal to them the longest. Central Asians had mostly submitted to the Mongols during Chinggis Khan's lifetime; the northern Chinese were conquered in 1234; and the Southern Song Chinese were not subjugated until 1279.

The Yuan period was not a cultural void in China. Painting flourished, as did drama and vernacular literature. A robust debate within the Confucian tradition occurred as Chinese scholars wrestled with the question of whether to serve their new Mongol masters. Some refused to work for the Mongol barbarian invaders, while others concluded that now more than ever, China needed the cultural and moral influence that Confucianism could exert. Traditional Chinese education was maintained in many private academies run by Neo-Confucian scholars. In fact, it was during the Yuan that the Four Books, known and largely memorized by every scholar in Ming and Qing times, were made the authoritative canon of Neo-Confucian ideology.

The Mongols ultimately failed to maintain order in China and contributed to many of the late Yuan's problems, including inflation, unemployment, neglect of water conservation projects, and botched famine relief efforts. By 1368 the Chinese had had enough, and a rebel leader among them named Zhu Yuanzhang overthrew their dynasty, sent most of the Mongols packing back to Mongolia, and founded the Ming dynasty, which was to endure until 1644.

MING RECOVERY: 1368–1644

Zhu Yuanzhang was the first commoner since Liu Bang, the founding emperor of the Han dynasty, to rise from the status of commoner to emperor. He was born to very poor peasant parents and was orphaned at an early age. As a teenager he became a Buddhist monk and then turned to the wandering life of a beggar when times got bad. He joined a quasi-religious movement against the Mongols and quickly rose to leadership. He had established a regime in Nanjing by 1367, and the next year he moved northward to Beijing, where he defeated the Mongol rulers and expelled them to Mongolia. He named his dynasty Ming.

Zhu gathered an unprecedented amount of political and military power into his own hands, more than the Tang or even Song emperors had. He was an extraordinarily competent and energetic ruler who attended to a myriad of administrative details himself. He was the apex of the Ming governmental pyramid, and he made all important governmental decisions himself. This was the famous "Ming despotism," which refers not to his harsh treatment of his subjects (Zhu was in fact a populist who advocated social leveling policies and instituted soak-the-rich taxation) but to his consolidation and concentration of power into his own hands, at the expense of the bureaucracy. In fact, he may have been reacting against the late Yuan dynasty's *lack* of effective, centralized power.

Zhu Yuanzhang was a gifted leader, but his shortcomings were startling. Toward the end of his life, he grew paranoid and suspicious of all those around him, even his lifelong associates and supporters, and he had many of them dismissed or worse. He was hypersensitive to criticisms and slights, real or perceived, and touchy about his personal ugliness.

The Ming government functioned well when a competent emperor such as Zhu Yuanzhang ruled over it, but when subsequent mediocre emperors came to power, the results were often disastrous. In such cases, governmental power often devolved to the eunuchs, the emasculated personal attendants of the emperor, and they were not always the most scrupulous of men. The late Ming period, in particular, was a time of administrative gridlock and decay as emperors neglected their governmental responsibilities while eunuchs ran the country as they saw fit, for their own aggrandizement.

The third Ming emperor, Yongle (r. 1403–1425), moved the capital from Nanjing to Beijing, where it remained for the rest of the dynasty, because his power base was mostly in Beijing and because the city was a convenient base from which to launch periodic raids into Mongolia and keep an eye on any possible attempts to reestablish Mongol domination over China. Perhaps because he was nervous about the perceived legitimacy of his succession to the throne, Yongle dispatched the Muslim navigator Zheng He (Cheng Ho) on seven maritime expeditions to areas as far away as India and even the Swahili Coast of Africa. His purpose might have been to cultivate more diplomatic contacts and thus new legitimizing recognition for the new emperor.

As the Ming dynasty wore on there was a distinct inward turn in China, and some xenophobia and isolationism emerged, although international trade and contacts were never completely curtailed. The overall Ming mood was certainly less cosmopolitan, less international, and less open than the Tang. The Ming, of course, did have its share of trouble from foreign peoples, particularly the Mongols.

MING-MONGOL RELATIONS

By far the greatest foreign policy concern for the Ming was the Mongols, who after all had conquered and ruled China for nearly a century before being overthrown and expelled. The Mongols made frequent noises about restoring the Yuan dynasty and recovering China, and for several decades after their return to Mongolia they maintained the fiction of a Northern Yuan regime. The Chinese built the Great Wall of China during the Ming dynasty to counter Mongol revanchist threats and refused, for almost the entire dynasty, to come to any sort of a trade accommodation with the Mongols. As a result, the Ming was subjected to raids and harassment along its northern borders to an extent unparalleled in Chinese history.

Yongle's strategy for dealing with the Mongol threat was to invade Mongolia periodically and play off rival Mongolian groups against one another, usually Western Mongols against Eastern Mongols. After his death, however, Ming China reverted to a more passive and defensive strategy. In 1449 a Western Mongol leader launched a massive invasion of Chinese territory and fought his way to Beijing. The Ming emperor himself went out to meet the Mongols on the battlefield, but this action ended in defeat and his capture. The Western Mongols thought they now had a hugely valuable bargaining chip with the Chinese, but the Ming simply enthroned another emperor. Thus deprived of their leverage with Ming China but still fearful of Chinese reprisals if the captive emperor were harmed, the Western Mongols returned the hapless emperor the next year. The entire incident embarrassed the Ming but also spelled the end of the Western Mongols' prestige and power in the steppe lands.

The next threat to Ming China came from the Eastern Mongols, who could lay claim to the lineage of Chinggis Khan. By the 1500s the Eastern Mongols were regularly launching cavalry raids on the Ming's northern defenses, and this continued for most of the century. In 1570, however, a formal peace treaty and trade agreement between most of the Eastern Mongols and Ming China ended most of the fighting. After 1570 the Mongols converted en masse to Tibetan-style Buddhism, which reduced their martial ardor. By 1600, the threat to China was no longer the Mongols but the Manchus, the descendants of the Jurchens.

THE EXAMINATION SYSTEM

The Ming reinstituted the examination system from Song times and developed it to its full extent. Like many other Qing institutions, the Qing examination system was based almost completely on the Ming precedent. To pass the examinations, candidates were expected to study Neo-Confucian teachings, which typically entailed a lifetime from childhood of rote memorization of the Four Books and the Five Classics of Chinese antiquity.

There were four main levels of the Ming examinations. The first was a qualifying examination at the county (*xian*) level. Candidates who qualified took the prefectural (*fu*) examinations, which were held twice every three years. The tiny minority of candidates who passed earned the title or degree of *Shengyuan*, sometimes known more collo-quially as *Xiucai*, literally "flowering talent," and were designated members of the gentry class, a distinction that exempted them from corporeal punishment and corvée requirements. The next rungs of the system were harder to achieve. Provincial examinations were held once every three years at provincial capitals, where candidates were locked up in individual examination cells for several days while they wrote essays. Only about 1 percent of the candidates passed these examinations and earned the coveted degree of *Juren*, literally "recom-mended man." *Juren* degree holders were eligible to participate in the final level of the examination system, the capital or metropolitan examinations held once every three years in Beijing. These examina-tions involved written essays and also a personal audience with the emperor himself, at which the candidate was evaluated on the basis of his speaking ability and personal deportment. Candidates who passed this final level were granted the coveted title *Jinshi*, literally "advanced scholar," and were virtually guaranteed a lifetime of presti-gious government employment.

In theory, the examination system was open to talented individuals of every socioeconomic class. In practice, however, the system was stacked in favor of the wealthy, who could afford the leisure necessary for scholarship and had a family atmosphere that encouraged learning. Still, however, a significant minority of boys from unprivileged backgrounds did succeed at the examinations, and their entry into the bureaucracy guaranteed the Ming and Qing governments a steady stream of fresh, new administrative talent.

The examination system made and destroyed lives. Most bright young boys who started out their childhoods with dreams of success at the examinations and the honor it would bring to their families and ancestors eventually had their hopes dashed, and they faded away into discouraged and disappointed obscurity, perhaps as local gentry who would have some measure of influence and prestige in their local communities but would never achieve national prominence in the government. People who passed the examinations were frequently listless and colorless yes-men who had long since learned to give the government what it wanted and to stop thinking for themselves. This submissive flatness may indeed have been exactly what the government wanted. The examination system did succeed in guaranteeing that government bureaucrats at least knew Confucian teachings, even if they did not always abide by them or believe them. Three things could be said of men who made it all the way through examinations up to the *Jinshi* level: they were smart, they were tough, and they were disciplined. Slow, delicate, and individualistic men did not have what it took to earn the *Jinshi* degree. It was smart, tough, and disciplined officials the government wanted to man its bureaucratic posts.

MANCHU CONQUEST: 1644–1912

Administrative negligence eventually produced a crisis during the last century of Ming rule. Bad government, as well as a simple lack of government, contributed to social unrest and desperation in the countryside. Peasant rebellions in northern and southern China became widespread by the 1630s, and in 1644, when a peasant rebel named Li Zicheng entered Beijing, the last Ming emperor committed suicide. This paved the way for the Manchu conquest of China.

In 1644 the Manchus poured into China and captured Beijing, where they restored order and defeated the rebel Li Zicheng who had captured the city. Li, and not the Manchus, had toppled the Ming dynasty, and the Manchus claimed that they had come to restore order in Beijing and in all of China. They named their dynasty Qing and remained in power until 1911.

The Manchus did not come out of nowhere. In their ancestral home-land in Manchuria they had been building a conquest dynasty for several decades. The Qing state started with a leader named Nurhachi (1559–1626), who broke down the old Manchu tribal affiliations and unified the Manchus as a people. Nurhachi nursed an enormous grudge against the Ming for its complicity in the death of his father, and like his Jurchen ancestors, he dreamed of conquering China. But he died in 1626, much too early to see his dream realized. His successors carried on his "great enterprise" of constructing a conquest dynasty, and as things worsened in Ming China a steady stream of Chinese peasants defected to Manchuria and served the Manchus, who were ruling over a more orderly society. In 1636 the Manchus declared a new dynasty, Qing, which signaled their intentions to the Ming. In 1644 a Ming Chinese general allowed massive numbers of Manchu troops to enter China through a pass in the Great Wall, and with this action the Ming dynasty was finished.

The Ming-Qing transition was one of the less traumatic dynasty transitions in Chinese history. The Manchu Qing regime was attractive to many Chinese because it presented an alternative to the chaos and misrule of late Ming China and because it perpetuated Chinese institutions virtually unchanged. Indeed, the Qing was undoubtedly the most Chinese of all the conquest dynasties. Resistance to Manchu rule continued in southern China for a few more decades, but it was completely eliminated in 1683, the year the first great Manchu emperor, the Kangxi emperor (r. 1662–1722), invaded the island of Taiwan, crushed a Ming loyalist regime there, and formally incorporated the island into Chinese territory as a prefecture (fu) of Fujian province.

One token of submission the Manchus required of all Chinese males beyond the age of puberty was, on pain of death, the Manchu coiffure, sometimes called the Manchu "queue" or "pigtail." The Manchu hairstyle for men specified that the front half of the head be shaved bald and the back portion of the hair be grown long and gathered into a single, tight braid. Many have seen pictures of men in "old China" with these hairstyles, but they should remember that this is a Manchu imposition, not a native Chinese coiffure. Starting in the nineteenth century, Chinese opposed to continued Manchu rule in China announced individual and collective rebellion by cutting off their queues and letting their hair grow out in front.

The Qing was one of China's greatest dynasties. Eighteenth-century China was the wealthiest, most powerful, and most populous nation in the world, and Europeans often idolized China and outdid themselves for the privilege of trading with the Chinese. The first great

Manchu ruler, the Kangxi emperor (r. 1661–1722), became well known in both China and Europe for his Sixteen Moral Maxims in elegant literary Chinese, which were displayed prominently throughout the Qing empire and later expounded upon through colloquial moral fables.

1. Encourage filial piety and brotherly submissiveness, that human relations may be deepened.
2. Strengthen kinship clans, that harmony may be manifest.
3. Harmonize local communities, that lawsuits may cease.
4. Attend diligently to agriculture and sericulture, that there may be sufficient food and clothing.
5. Give place to frugality, that there may be sparing use of resources.
6. Dignify the schools, that scholarly habits may improve.
7. Condemn heresies, that orthodoxy may be exalted.
8. Expound on the law, that the foolish and wayward may be admonished.
9. Elucidate civility and humility, that manners and customs may be improved.
10. Attend to your proper calling, that the determination of the people may be resolute.
11. Instruct the children, that wrongdoing may be prevented.
12. Desist with frivolous lawsuits, that the good and conscientious may be protected.
13. Forbid the harboring of fugitives, that sharing in their fate may be avoided.
14. Fully remit taxes, that pressure for payment may be avoided.
15. Unite community tithings, that brigands and bandits may be apprehended.
16. Resolve strife and quarrels, that the body and life may be esteemed.

The second great Manchu ruler, the Qianlong (r. 1736–1796) emperor, was a household word in elite European families, and Enlightenment philosophers in Europe wrote quite approvingly of the Qing's overall secular approach to government.

During the nineteenth century, when the Qing slipped into serious decline, Chinese patriots began blaming the Manchus for most of China's woes. China would not have suffered as much from external imperialism and internal upheaval, they imagined, if the Chinese themselves were running the dynasty. This, however, was smug conceit, and events after the overthrow of the Manchus in 1911 showed that the Chinese themselves were probably not any more up to facing the challenges of modernity than the Manchus had been. A thoroughgoing political revolution, and not ethnic cleansing of the topmost levels of government, was what finally made the difference for China.

THE QING TRIBUTARY SYSTEM

The Qing was not simply a Chinese dynasty, but a multiethnic empire. The overwhelming majority of the Qing's subjects were of course Chinese, but the ethnically Chinese core of Qing China (sometimes called China Proper) accounted for only around half of Qing territory. While the Qing's governance of China Proper was based largely on Ming precedent, non-Chinese administrative practices and institutions were used for other areas. Until well into the nineteenth century, the Qing separately administered Manchuria more or less as an exclusive ethnic park and ancestral homeland for the Manchus. Other non-Chinese areas of the Qing empire, such as Xinjiang, Tibet, Qinghai, and Mongolia, were administered by the Court of Colonial Affairs (*Lifanyuan*), a high-level central government agency that exercised Qing sovereignty over these areas and directly governed them on behalf of the Qing emperors. Of all these non-Chinese areas, only Outer Mongolia (Mongolia north of the Gobi Desert) managed to escape Chinese control in the twentieth century and became an independent nation. Today Xinjiang, Tibet, and Manchuria (which the Chinese now prefer to call *Dongbei*, or the northeast) are very much under the direct control of the People's Republic of China.

Over surrounding areas not directly under its administrative control, the Qing exercised not sovereignty but a more vaguely defined suzerainty, which was essentially a variety of feudal overlordship. A Qing institution called the Bureau of Receptions (*Zhukesi*) managed relations with quasi-independent vassal states or kingdoms that included Korea, Vietnam, Burma, Siam, Cambodia, the Malay Peninsula, and even the Sulu Archipelago (today part of the Philippines, between Mindanao and Borneo). In accordance with established schedules, these nations sent envoys who offered tribute (local products) to the Qing emperor and performed before him the *kowtow*, a ritual of extreme obeisance that involved prostration and audibly knocking the forehead on the floor. This was a symbolic recognition that their countries were humble vassal states of the mighty Qing empire.

These nations subjected themselves to this humiliating procedure because the benefits they received for mere gestures of submission to the Qing outweighed any fleeting chagrin they might suffer. In return for offering tribute and performing the *kowtow*, the Qing conferred a title of recognition on the nation's king and showered him and his envoys with lavish gifts out of all proportion to the worth of the tributary items presented. Tribute missions were allowed to remain in

Beijing and trade for several days after their audiences with the Qing emperor, and this trade was fabulously lucrative. Enfeoffment by the Qing emperor often conferred legitimacy and prestige on royal families in these nations and made challenging their power quite difficult; it was no trifling matter to contemplate toppling a royal house that had received a Qing patent. Implicit in these tributary arrangements was also a guarantee of Qing military assistance in case of aggression by a third power.

Contrary to popular opinion, not all nations of the world were regarded as participants in the tribute system, which Harvard's John K. Fairbank once labeled the "Chinese world order." For instance, the Qing never regarded Japan or India as tributary states. Some European nations that wanted favorable trade relations with China seemed to accept elements of the system, and the resulting misunderstanding and friction led, in the nineteenth century, to war between China and some Western European powers.

QING INTELLECTUAL TRENDS

The fall of the Ming was deeply troubling to many Chinese intellectuals, and for the rest of the seventeenth century and beyond many Chinese contemplated the reasons for the Manchu conquest. What had gone wrong? Several scholars seem to have concluded that one major problem was Neo-Confucianism itself. Perhaps, they speculated, the Song and Ming Neo-Confucianists had not properly understood Confucian thought after all; perhaps Neo-Confucianism was too heavily tainted with Buddhist ideas, terminology, and analytical categories.

An intellectual movement arose among many scholars who had reservations about Neo-Confucianism. For them, the best way to recover the authentic Confucian vision was a back-to-the-basics, back-to-the-original-texts approach. They sought to look back into Chinese antiquity before the Song Neo-Confucian thinkers to see what the texts really said. Many scholars concluded that the compelling inner logic of Neo-Confucianism had distracted scholars into neglecting basic textual scholarship. What did the texts themselves say apart from Neo-Confucian commentaries and glosses?

Could the texts speak for themselves? Many concluded that they could and devoted themselves to developing long-neglected textual skills. Scholars poured their lives into careful philology, or the study of origins, meanings, and authenticity of ancient texts. Some scholars devoted their lives to reconstructing ancient pronunciations or pin-pointing ancient place-names. All of this work was done with the faith that, in the end, the texts now carefully understood would reveal the authentic Confucian moral vision. Implicit in all this careful textual scholarship, which the Chinese called *kaozheng*, was the assumption that Confucius was indeed correct about Chinese antiquity. It was the understanding of Confucianism, and not authentic Confucianism itself, that was the problem. Large numbers of Chinese intellectuals did not begin questioning the appropriateness and applicability of Confucianism itself in the modern world until the early decades of the twentieth century.

Qing scholarship was not all a matter of hairsplitting textual research. Many Qing scholars continued to think in cosmological terms, and some of them mounted sustained criticisms of *kaozheng* scholarship, which seemed at times to miss the philosophical forest for the philological trees.

TECHNOLOGICAL INNOVATIONS

Chinese technological prowess and inventive genius seem to have tapered off after the Mongol conquest. The Tang and Song periods, however, saw some extraordinarily important technological innovations that changed the course of world history.

Everyone knows that the Chinese invented gunpowder, but many people are surprised to learn that Chinese alchemists were seeking an elixir of immortality when they discovered the formula for gunpowder. (The Chinese term for gunpowder is *huoyao*, literally "fire medicine.") Chinese alchemists as far back as Han times had experimented with sulfur and were appalled by its toxic and volatile nature when heated. To "subdue" or tame the sulfur before heating they added other substances (often saltpeter) to it. Later, during Tang times, alchemists discovered that adding charcoal to unheated mixtures of sulfur and saltpeter yielded a compound that was instantaneously combustible, even explosive, when heated. The formula for gunpowder was perfected during subsequent centuries, and during the eleventh century the Song scholar Zeng Gongliang published this formula for the first time in world history. In the West today, conventional wisdom holds that, although the Chinese invented gunpowder, they never applied it effectively in military technology. This, however, is untrue. During Song and Yuan times, the Chinese invented and used grenades, land mines, flamethrowers, and bombs in warfare. Rockets were invented in Song China during the eleventh century, and the world's first true guns appeared in China during the Song-Yuan transition. Gun technology then quickly spread from China and reached Europe by 1320.

China was the first civilization to print books, although printing itself was not invented in China. (The use of carved seals to stamp names on various surfaces goes back to the ancient Mesopotamian civilization of Sumeria, which far outdates Chinese civilization.) The Chinese did invent and perfect woodblock printing, or the art of carving obverse images and hundreds of words onto fruitwood blocks, which were then inked and applied to paper. The first complete printed book in world history was probably a Buddhist work, the *Diamond Sutra*, in Tang China in 868. By early Song times entire collections of writings were printed and circulated among friends. A 130-volume set of the Confucian classics was published in Song China in 953 and sold to the public. Korea was the first country to which Chinese woodblock printing spread, and from Korea it probably was transmitted to Japan.

It is almost universally believed in the West that Johann Gutenberg was the first in the world to invent movable type printing in 1458. (Some Koreans have also argued that movable print type was first invented in Korea.) Recent studies in Chinese technological history have shown that movable type was actually another Chinese first. Song scholar Shen Gua records the first use of a complete set of movable printing type in China during the 1040s. Even so, movable type technology did not find immediate and extensive use in China because of its impracticability. Thousands of individual characters were used in ordinary Chinese writing, and the meticulous process of arranging individual character types was often more difficult than simply carving up entire page blocks from scratch. Movable type was more practically applicable to alphabetic languages, and its first revolutionary effects were undeniably felt in the West.

Other lesser-known inventions of the Chinese are somewhat surprising. The world's first mechanical clock was invented in Tang China during the eighth century. By the eleventh century, the ingenious Chinese inventor Su Song had perfected a mechanical clock that ran in good time from 1092 until Kaifeng, the Northern Song capital, was overrun by the Jurchens in 1126. Descriptions of his and other Chinese mechanical clocks eventually made their way to Europe, where a working mechanical clock was first constructed in the early fourteenth century.

The Chinese also understood the principles of what Europeans call Mercator map projections, or the flat maps of the world that typically show Greenland to be much larger than it really is in relation to North

America. European historians usually credit the first Mercator projections to the Flemish cartographer Gerardus Mercator, who lived and flourished during the sixteenth century. But manuscript Mercator projection star maps go back to the tenth century in China, and in the late eleventh century Su Song published Mercator-style maps in one of his many technical books.

The world's first inoculation against smallpox probably occurred in China during Northern Song times; by sixteenth-century Ming times, it was widely practiced. The Chinese even made the world's first phosphorescent paintings in Northern Song times, centuries before phosphorescent substances were first introduced in the West during the eighteenth century.

5

The Tumultuous Nineteenth Century: External Aggression and Internal Chaos

JOHN BULL IN THE CHINA CLOSET

During the late eighteenth and early nineteenth centuries the British, having failed to persuade China to alter its business and diplomatic practices to their own liking, and aghast that the Chinese would dare attempt to interdict British narcotics trafficking, simply bullied their way into China and imposed their will on the hapless nation through brute force. The Opium War, fought between the two nations from 1840 to 1841, ended with British victory and the Treaty of Nanking, which compelled Qing China to cede the island of Hong Kong to the British crown in perpetuity, pay Britain an enormous war indemnity, and open several coastal cities to British residence and trade. The Opium War and its aftermath inaugurated China's "Century of Humiliation," which endured until 1949 and the final victory of the Chinese Communist revolution. During this long and challenging century, the British, and also other foreign powers following at their heels,

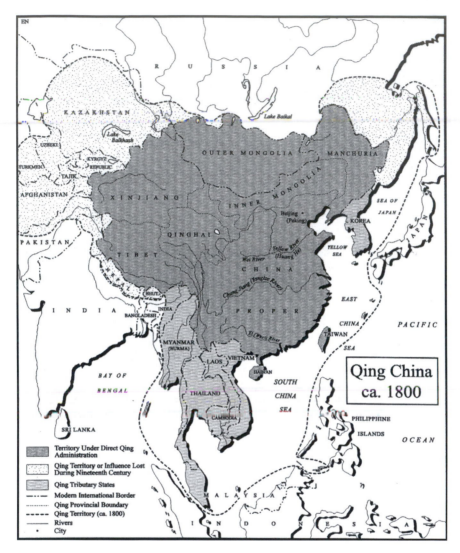

Qing China.

dominated but never quite subjugated the Chinese. China did manage to escape the utter ignominy of India, which was completely conquered and incorporated into the British empire.

The main grievances the British had with the Chinese concerned commerce and diplomacy. Much to the dismay of anxious British merchants and investors, the Chinese trade restrictions were myriad. Since the mid-eighteenth century, trade had been restricted to the single port city of Canton (Guangzhou) in southern China, where trade could be conducted only from October through January. British ships sailing to Canton were required to submit to numerous inspections, measurements, fees, and irregular tariffs. Venal Chinese functionaries hinted broadly that generous "presents" or bribes would grease the gears of commerce. Other expenses incurred involved the hiring of Chinese go-betweens, ship pilots, and linguists who communicated with the Westerners in a puerile language known as "pidgin" English, which applied English vocabulary to Chinese word order (which fortunately was largely the same as English). Items to be traded had to have been cleared and contracted for a year in advance, and prices for the goods were fixed by Chinese merchant guilds without open competition or bidding, to the great frustration of British and other Western traders who coveted maximum profit for their transactions. Western merchants had "factories" (actually warehouses) where they could stay while they traded, but they were not permitted to tarry in Canton for long and were expected to leave the city soon after they had concluded their business. They were not allowed to bring their wives to Canton, and their mobility in the city was restricted to a few hundred yards around their factories. They were also forbidden to communicate with Chinese government officials, draw undue attention to themselves, or learn the Chinese language. Qing law was another source of apprehension for the British, who found it incomprehensible and were terrified of the penalty (usually death by garroting) meted out for any number of legal infractions.

The British found it difficult and frustrating to communicate with the Chinese government about their grievances with the trading procedure. On the two notable occasions when the British did present their grievances and requests directly to the Chinese government, diplomatic tensions arose when the two peoples discovered that their models and notions of diplomacy were vastly dissimilar. For the British, as well as all other Western nations, diplomacy was conducted between equally sovereign and independent nation-states, each of which stationed full-time residential diplomats in other nations' capital cities to facilitate official government-to-government contacts. This was not at all the way Qing China conducted foreign relations with its neighbors. The Chinese considered their country the center of world civilization, and all people were naturally drawn to China because of its wealth, prestige, and power. Accordingly, foreign countries would dispatch envoys to China as humble tribute bearers who meekly petitioned for an audience with the emperor. While in China, the envoys would naturally perform the *kowtow* to the emperor. And when their diplomatic functions were concluded, the foreign envoys might graciously be allowed to remain in China for a few days of trading and sightseeing before being required to return to their native lands. Any notion of other nations being China's equals or of foreign diplomats remaining in China indefinitely would have been unthinkable. Furthermore, the Qing government viewed involvement with commerce as beneath the dignity of the Chinese government; commerce involved private contact between petty men concerned with profit, a somewhat ignoble motive in traditional Confucian moral estimations, and did not require government-to-government contact.

In short, neither nation had a full appreciation of the diplomatic sensibilities and norms to which the other subscribed. This became quite apparent in June 1793, when the British government sent Lord Macartney to the Qianlong emperor (r. 1736–1796) with a wish list for, among other things, residential diplomatic representation in Beijing, trade throughout China, and exemption for British subjects from Chinese legal jurisdiction. The Qing government received Macartney and his retinue as tribute bearers coming to congratulate the Qianlong emperor on the occasion of his 83rd birthday. Macartney, however, steadfastly refused to perform the *kowtow,* which would have led to a considerable diplomatic contretemps for both sides had the emperor not ultimately dispensed with the requirement.

The substance of Macartney's requests were summarily denied in a highly condescending missive from Qianlong to King George III. One might well imagine how badly the smug ethnocentricity of this letter would have clashed with what the French have called *la morgue britannique,* or British haughtiness.

AN IMPERIAL EDICT TO THE KING OF ENGLAND:

You, O King, are so inclined toward our civilization that you have sent a special envoy across the seas to bring our Court your memorial of congratulations on the occasion of my birthday and to present your native products as an expression of your thoughtfulness. On perusing your memorial, so simply worded and sincerely conceived, I am impressed by your genuine respectfulness and friendliness and greatly pleased.

As to the request made in your memorial, O King, to send one of your nationals to stay at the Celestial Court to take care of your country's trade with China, this is not in harmony with the state system of our dynasty and will definitely not be permitted.... There has never been a precedent for letting them do whatever they like.

The Celestial Court has pacified and possessed the territory within the four seas. Its sole aim is to do its utmost to achieve good government and to manage political affairs, attaching no value to strange jewels and precious objects. The various articles presented by you, O King, this

time are accepted by my special order to the office in charge of such
functions in consideration of the offerings having come from a long distance with sincere good wishes. As a matter of fact, the virtue and prestige of the Celestial Dynasty having spread far and wide, the kings of
the myriad nations come by land and sea with all sorts of precious
things. Consequently there is nothing we lack, as your principal envoy
and others have themselves observed. We have never set much store
on strange or ingenious objects, nor do we need any more of your country's manufactures. (Teng and Fairbank 1963, 19)

In 1816 Britain made one last attempt to alter China's business and
diplomatic practices peacefully. Lord Amherst, a former governor of
India, traveled to China with a wish list more or less identical with
Macartney's. Like Macartney, he refused to perform the *kowtow* and
was ultimately unsuccessful in his mission.

THE OPIUM WAR

The balance of Sino-British trade was very much in China's favor
throughout the eighteenth century. The Chinese commodity the British
most desired was tea, but they also purchased large quantities of silk
and porcelain. The Chinese purchased a few odd woolens and knick-
knacks from the British, but it was mostly silver that flowed out of
Britain and into China. Finally the British hit upon one commodity
for which the Chinese would pay most handsomely: opium, a highly
addictive narcotic that was usually smoked. British opium was produced in Bengal and then sold to smugglers who ran the drug into
Chinese harbors in small, fast boats under cover of night. Opium
flowed into China in insignificant amounts during the eighteenth century, but by the early decades of the nineteenth century the opium
habit began taking hold in southern China, and addiction rates soared
exponentially, first equalizing the balance of trade between the two
countries and then tipping it massively in Britain's favor by the early
1830s. By the middle 1830s southern China's opium problem was
reaching crisis proportions. The British East India Company claimed
all the while not to have anything officially to do with the opium trade,
but it was an open secret that the British were now essentially dope
pushers who were growing enormously wealthy at the expense of an
addicted Chinese populace that would do and pay just about anything
to sustain its drug habit. (Not to be outdone by their erstwhile colonial
masters, some Americans in wealthy New England families increased
their fortunes by selling opium made in Turkey to the Chinese.)

In 1834 the British East India Company was disbanded, and private traders made their moves to get in on the lucrative opium trade. Knowing that a multiplication of private British traders would require greater governmental facilitation, the British government sent Lord William John Napier to China as superintendent of trade, an official government position. Napier, a pompous and overbearing man from a family line that served British imperialist interests, was overly anxious to extend the dignity of the British crown and his own office to the Chinese. In presenting himself to the Chinese authorities in Canton he violated just about every Chinese sensibility and regulation imaginable, and when they were taken aback by his brusque demeanor he blustered that Britain was quite ready for war with China. He called in British warships and announced that he would "hand his name down to posterity as the man who had thrown open the wide field of the Chinese Empire to the British Spirit and Industry" (Hsü 1990, 175). The spirited captains of British industry and commerce were considerably less enthusiastic about his saber rattling and the disruption of trade it produced, and they refused to support him. Napier eventually backed off and returned in September to Macao, where he died the next month. After the Napier incident, the British government appointed Captain Charles Elliot superintendent of trade in 1836 and instructed him to be less confrontational in dealing with the Chinese. Elliot eventually engaged in open military conflict with China over opium.

By the late 1830s the Qing government decided, after a brief flirtation with the idea of legalizing the opium trade, to interdict opium. A fiery and energetic Chinese official named Lin Zexu was appointed imperial commissioner and sent to Canton as the emperor's personal representative to rid China of the opium problem once and for all. Commissioner Lin arrived in Canton in March 1839 and gave the foreigners (mainly the British) a deadline for surrendering all their stockpiles of opium. When his deadline passed with no action, Lin blockaded the foreign factory area in Canton, trapping several foreigners inside, including Charles Elliot himself. After several weeks passed, a crisis atmosphere emerged as foreigners in the surrounded factories began running out of food and supplies. Then a remarkable idea dawned on Elliot: he would simply give Commissioner Lin exactly what he wanted. In his official capacity, Elliot issued a proclamation making all of the opium in Canton the property of the British crown, and no longer the property of the private traders. His motive was simple: if Commissioner Lin trifled with Crown property, it would be sheer effrontery to Her Majesty. This in turn would constitute a Chinese provocation and serve as a perfect pretext and justification for war with the Chinese.

> Now I, the said Chief Superintendent . . . do hereby, in the name and on the behalf of Her Britannic Majesty's Government, enjoin and require all Her Majesty's subjects now present in Canton, forthwith to make a surrender to me, for the service of Her Said Majesty's Government, to be delivered over to the Government of China, of all the opium belonging to them or British opium under my control . . . and I . . . do now, in the most full and unreserved manner, hold myself responsible, for and on the behalf of Her Britannic Majesty's Government, to all and each of Her Majesty's subjects surrendering the said British-owned opium into my hands to be delivered over to the Chinese government. (H. Chang 1964, 264–65)

On June 6 (the Opium Prohibition Day formerly celebrated annually in Nationalist China), Commissioner Lin accepted the surrendered opium and destroyed it. Elliot then reported this "outrage" to the British government, and in the late 1839 he learned that a British expeditionary force would be sent to China. In early 1840, Britain declared war on China.

The expeditionary force did not arrive until June 1840, when British warships took the fight right to the emperor's doorstep, anchoring off the shore of Tianjin, Beijing's outlet to the sea. When Qishan, the Manchu governor-general of the region, persuaded the British to return south to Canton for talks without firing a shot, he was handsomely rewarded by the Qing government and appointed to deal with the British. When the talks began, Qishan was aghast at British demands for payment of an indemnity for the lost opium and permanent cession of the island of Hong Kong, demands he knew Beijing would never accept. Ultimately unable to placate the British any further and unsuccessful at preventing a resumption of Sino-British hostilities, Qishan was recalled in disgrace and exiled to northern Manchuria.

Eventually a British naval force sailed up the Yangtze River to the city of Nanjing and poised itself to bombard the city if a formal peace agreement were not forthcoming. The thought of this was more than the Qing government could bear, and in August 1841 the Treaty of Nanking was concluded aboard a British ship anchored outside Nanjing. The treaty provided for the formal cession of Hong Kong in perpetuity to the British Crown, the opening of five other port cities along China's southern and eastern coasts to British trade, payment to a large indemnity, abolition of the trade restrictions disliked by the British, and a uniform tariff. A subsequent agreement gave the British some measure of extraterritoriality, or exemption from Chinese legal jurisdiction.

For the Chinese, the Opium War was about just that: opium. They had not asked the British to come to China, after all, and yet they were willing to accommodate Britain's insatiable appetite for commerce as long as the British respected Chinese ways and ceased selling dangerous and addictive narcotics. The British, on the other hand, insisted that the Opium War was fought because of China's obstreperous impedance of commerce, indignities offered the Crown, and refusal to bend to Britain's diplomatic norms. The British pretended that opium itself was a mere epiphenomenon compared to these larger issues, and they won their point through simple force of arms.

As the first of the humiliating "unequal treaties" imposed on China by imperialist powers, the Treaty of Nanking endures in infamy in the modern Chinese nationalistic consciousness. This was the treaty that began it all, that led to China's descent from the rarified heights of the Celestial Court to a terrestrial nadir as the "Sick Man of Asia." The British had drawn first blood in China, and soon other Western nations smelled the blood in the water. In July 1844 the Treaty of Wanghsia was concluded with the Americans, and in October 1844, the Treaty of Whampoa with the French. The rest of the nineteenth century was a time of sustained nibbling away at the edges of the Qing empire by imperialist powers (mainly Britain, Russia, and Japan) in specific instances too numerous to discuss in detail in this brief narrative. With the Treaty of Nanking, China's Century of Humiliation had begun, one that would be compounded synergistically in future decades by internal upheavals.

The Opium War did not solve all of the friction between Britain and China, and the Treaty of Nanking did not provide for Britain's ultimate goal of diplomatic representation in Beijing itself. Even though other coastal cities or "treaty ports" were opened to British commerce and residence as per the Treaty of Nanking, the city of Canton refused to admit the British. Attempts to open Canton and extend trade to other Chinese cities were unsuccessful, and by the mid-1850s the British had concluded once again that only war would convince China to bend to their demands. All the British needed was a *causus belli*, a provocation to justify military action. This came on October 8, 1856, not this time as an indignity to the Crown, but to the flag. The *Arrow*, a Chinese-owned but British-registered ship flying the British flag, was boarded near Canton by Chinese forces searching for a wanted pirate. When the British protested the boarding, the Chinese coolly informed them that this was none of their affair: the ship was owned by Chinese and was boarded by Chinese in Chinese waters. The ship's flag was all that mattered to the British, and in response they shelled Canton for five days in late October. After this the British sent Lord Elgin (who had been Governor-General of Canada from 1847 to 1854) at the head of another expeditionary force, this time joined by the French, to chastise the Chinese. In December 1857, marines under Elgin's command stormed Canton, captured the defiant and xenophobic governor-general who resided there, and carried him away in captivity to British India. Elgin's force then sailed northward to Tianjin in early 1858 and menaced the city. The terrified Qing government sent negotiators to deal with the British, and Elgin bullied them into signing the Treaty of Tientsin on June 26, 1858. The treaty provided for residential British diplomacy in Beijing, the opening of several new ports, indemnities for Britain and France, and unrestricted travel through all parts of China for all foreigners, including Protestant and Catholic missionaries. (Before the treaty, missionaries and other foreigners had been allowed only in the treaty ports.)

But the fighting was not over yet. In March 1859 the Qing government offered minimal resistance when the British ambassador attempted to travel to Beijing to take up his post there. This provoked Britain into dispatching *another* expeditionary force against China, once again led by Lord Elgin. This time British and French ground troops made it all the way into Beijing, and eventually they burned the Manchu emperor's Summer Palace (*Yuanming Yuan*) to the ground. This was the first time a modern imperialist power had ever stormed into a Chinese capital, and tales of it still elicit Chinese indignation. (The site of the ruins of the Summer Palace is preserved today as a hallowed, nationalistic ground for the Chinese, much as the hulk of the U.S.S. *Arizona*, lying at the bottom of Pearl Harbor and marked with a monument, is for Americans.) On October 24, 1860, Lord Elgin dictated to the Chinese the Convention of Peking, which allowed the British once and for all to station residential diplomats in Beijing. Other provisions included more indemnities, the cession to Britain of the Kowloon Peninsula opposite the island of Hong Kong, and the right of French Catholic missionaries to own property in the Chinese hinterland.

THE TAIPING REBELLION

If the intrusion of the British and other Westerners was China's great external calamity of the nineteenth century, by far its most disastrous internal upheaval was the Taiping Rebellion, a pseudo-Christian uprising that very nearly toppled the Qing dynasty. It was suppressed in 1864 only with the greatest of difficulty, and not before 40 million people had died in what was, and still is, the most cataclysmic civil war in world history. Overpopulation led to the disastrous calamity. By the nineteenth century, China's population had grown to unmanageable proportions, and millions of people in the Chinese countryside were facing malnutrition and even starvation. By the 1840s millions of peasants unable to eke out an existence on their tiny plots of land abandoned farming altogether and began to roam the countryside as bandits.

The leading figure in the Taiping Rebellion was Hong Xiuquan, a mentally unstable and intensely imaginative man who was convinced that he was the younger brother of Jesus Christ. He was born to a poor peasant family in southern China's Guangdong province, but it was quickly apparent to Hong's family that he was a bright, precocious boy. Accordingly, his extended family clan exempted him from all manual labor and allowed him to study for the imperial service examinations. Hong, however, failed the examinations repeatedly and eventually suffered a nervous breakdown. During his feverish delirium he saw images of a venerable old man with a long white beard who gave him a sword and told him to exterminate demons. A middle-aged man also figured into the hallucinations.

Soon, after the fever broke and Hong returned to the rhythms of everyday life, he picked up a Christian tract he had accepted a few years earlier and was astonished to find in it the interpretive key to his earlier dreams. He concluded that the Biblical "Kingdom of Heaven" mentioned in the tract was none other than China, that the demons were the Manchus, and that the elderly and middle-aged men he saw were none other than God the Father and Jesus Christ, respectively. All of this he interpreted as personal instructions to rise up against the Qing regime and reclaim the Heavenly Kingdom of China in the name of his vision of the Christian faith. In 1847 he sought religious instruction from Issachar Roberts, an American Southern Baptist preacher from Tennessee. Roberts, who found Hong venal and unstable and in general unsuitable for Christian conversion, eventually refused him baptism and distanced himself from him.

This did not seem to matter to Hong, however. He began gathering followers and converts to himself. He read in Acts 2 about the early Christian community of believers and attempted to replicate this communal sharing among his followers. Subsequent reading in the Old Testament about the armies of Israel further enthralled him, and by the early 1850s he had transformed his following from a few desperate peasant fighters into a militant pseudo-Christian movement the members of which cut their queues and proclaimed allegiance to the *Taiping Tianguo*, or the Heavenly Kingdom of Great Peace. His armies eventually proceeded northward through Hunan province, captured the city of Changsha, and made their way to the Yangtze River with tens of thousands of dedicated fighters. The "Taipings," as they came to be known, were victorious wherever they went. They built a large navy and floated all the way down the Yangtze to Nanjing, which they captured in 1853, and named the capital of their new theocratic government after mercilessly slaughtering every Manchu they found in the city.

Hong's seditious intentions were abundantly clear the moment he named his movement a "kingdom" and had his followers cut off their queues. He made good on these intentions by attacking Peking, but for once he was defeated and beaten back. After 1855 he decided to remain in Nanjing and consolidate his power there. Nanjing in the late 1850s and early 1860s contrasted quite favorably with the rest of China; its streets were cleaner, its people happier, and its women much freer. (Taiping women did not bind their feet and were given the unprecedented freedom to walk around in public on city streets.)

Foreigners, initially fascinated with the Taipings, eventually backed away from them and remained neutral as the Qing government moved to crush the rebellion. Christian missionaries had concluded by the early 1860s that Hong's garbled version of Christianity was quite heterodox, and Western merchants and diplomats began to fear that the favorable agreements they had reached with the Qing might be subject to cancellation should the Taipings actually create a new dynasty in China.

Western Christians were not the only ones who viewed the Taipings as heterodox. To Chinese traditionalists, the ideology and religion of the Taipings seemed the very antithesis of Confucian ethical teachings. The Qing government, by this time quite Chinese in its world outlook, resolved to crush the Taipings at all costs. In the 1850s the Qing government entrusted the fight against the Taipings to one man: a high government official named Zeng Guofan, a native of Hunan (a province the Taipings had largely devastated). Regular Qing armies had tried but failed to defeat the Taipings. Zeng was given free reign to raise and train new armies and fight the Taipings as he saw fit. The Qing dynasty more or less turned its destiny over to Zeng and trusted him implicitly.

Zeng named his new army the Hunan Braves and in 1854 captured the central Chinese city of Wuhan from the Taipings, but the Taipings soon recaptured it. A stalemate between Zeng and the Taipings then developed and endured until 1860. In 1862 Zeng finally launched a massive attack on the Taiping stronghold at Nanjing. Li Hongzhang and his Anhui Army (Huai Army) also helped out with the final attack, as did forces under General Zuo Zongtang. In 1864, after the Taipings had fought valiantly to the very last man, Nanjing was finally recaptured.

The Qing dynasty was never the same after the Taiping Rebellion. Even though Zeng Guofan surrendered power over his army shortly after the defeat of the Taipings, the power of the Qing central government had drastically declined during the rebellion and never recovered. Regionalism in China began to develop as provinces far from Beijing more or less began to pursue their separate destinies and were less and less influenced by Qing directives. During the next decade, the weakened Qing government was unable to resist foreign attacks on its territory: a brief Japanese occupation of Taiwan in 1874, a Russian invasion and occupation of part of Xinjiang from 1871 to 1881, and a French invasion of Vietnam, a Qing tributary state, in 1885. Weakness and regionalism endured beyond the fall of the dynasty in 1912 and reached its tragic culmination in the warlord period, which lasted from around 1917 to 1927.

The Taiping Rebellion inspired future revolutionaries in China. Sun Yat-sen, the founder of the Republic of China, admired the Taipings and grew up hearing heroic tales about Hong Xiuquan's exploits. The Chinese Communists today regard the Taipings as protorevolutionaries who did the best they could against the Qing government and foreign imperialism without the guiding ideology of Marxism-Leninism-Mao Zedong thought.

SELF-STRENGTHENING: HALFHEARTED REFORMS

The Qing dynasty, having narrowly escaped ruin during the Taiping Rebellion, attempted to recover some prestige for itself and restore order and confidence in China. It launched a fairly superficial program of institutional and technological modernization, often known as the Self-Strengthening Movement, which lasted from 1861 to 1895. During this time the Qing government instituted something roughly equivalent to a foreign diplomacy office, established schools for foreign language instruction, reformed and expanded its customs service (which was, much to the humiliation and consternation of later generations of Chinese patriots, run directly by the British), and learned the rudiments of international law.

Zeng Guofan and especially Li Hongzhang, the two main heroes of the civil war with the Taipings, emerged as enthusiastic advocates of Self-Strengthening and emphasized selective adaptation of Western technology, particularly military technology. Many Chinese during the Self-Strengthening period were convinced that China could retain all of its traditional heritage and needed only to learn how to make and use the superior weaponry of the West to overcome foreign domination. The Chinese provinces utilized foreign assistance and consultation to modernize the Chinese military and to establish arsenals, shipyards, mines, textile mills, and telegraph lines. A modern Chinese navy began to take shape. These modernization efforts appeared impressive but ultimately proved to be limited in scope and vision because they had very little leadership or coordination from the Qing central government, which had been greatly weakened in the wake of the Taiping Rebellion. Provincial rather than national in scope, self-strengthening efforts failed because they were not accompanied by all of the sweeping changes necessary for effective modernization. The advocates of self-strengthening were too selective in what they sought to learn from the West; they did not understand that the key to the West's great military power was not based on technological superiority alone but also on its social, political, and economic systems. Experience ultimately showed that equaling the West in military power would entail many more changes in China than the Self-Strengtheners were willing to contemplate. As a result, China, toward the end of the nineteenth century, was woefully unprepared for its first modern military clash with a much more effectively modernized state: Japan.

THE FIRST SINO-JAPANESE WAR 1894–1895

War between China and Japan, over Korea, which had been a tributary state to China since early Ming dynasty times, broke out in 1894. A newly modernizing Japan insisted in the 1870s that Korea was an independent state. In essence, Japan wanted to transfer Korea from the Chinese to the Japanese orbit. Japan's desire to dominate Korea intensified in the 1890s, and in July 1894 a Japanese warship sank a Qing ship in Korean waters. On August 1 China and Japan declared war on each other. Thousands of Japanese troops landed in Korea, and much to the surprise of the international community, the smaller but faster, and better-trained Japanese navy defeated the Qing fleet. The provisions of the Treaty of Shimonoseki, signed in April 1895, included cession of the Liaodong Peninsula and Taiwan (which had been made a province in the 1880s) to Japan, formal Qing recognition of the independence of Korea, and payment of an enormous war indemnity to Japan.

Subsequent Qing investigation into the defeat of the Chinese fleet uncovered extensive corruption and incompetence in the navy. Funds earmarked for naval development had gone elsewhere, and it was even discovered that some of the Qing ships' magazines contained not gunpowder but sand. Prewar preparations and combat readiness were also inadequate. Before the war, when the noted writer on Asia Sir Henry Norman inspected a Chinese battleship, he found after the canvas had been removed from a quick-firing gun that its barrel had been filled with chopsticks and was generally littered with rice and pickles (Paine 2003, 155–56).

China's defeat in the First Sino-Japanese War marked the emergence of Japan, not China, as the preeminent military and economic power in East Asia. It also revealed the full extent of China's weakness as the "Sick Man of Asia." Soon other vultures were circling overhead, demanding their fair share of the "Chinese melon" that was being divided among "the Powers," or the imperialist nations. In 1895 the Russians joined the French and the Germans and intimidated Japan into surrendering its hold over the Liaodong Peninsula. Not long after this, the Russians secured railway rights in Manchuria and seized the port cities of Dairen and Port Arthur on the southern tip of the Liaodong Peninsula for themselves. In 1897 the Germans pressured the Qing into leasing part of Shandong province to them for 99 years. The next year, China was once more John Bullied into surrendering more territorial sovereignty to the British; this time the New Territories opposite the island of Hong Kong on the mainland were leased to Britain for 99 years. (The lease finally expired in 1997, when the British gave the New Territories, as well as Kowloon and the island of Hong Kong, back to China.) The Americans, busy in 1898 with their war with Spain and their subsequent beginnings of empire in the Philippines, Guam, Cuba, and Puerto Rico, were too slow to get in on the divvying up of the Chinese spoils.

Many Chinese patriots were humiliated by the aftermaths of the First Sino-Japanese War and concluded that the halfhearted self-strengthening efforts were insufficient to modernize China and enable it to stand up to the international community. Some advocated more radical reform programs; others such as Sun Yat-sen espoused outright revolution against the Manchu Qing regime.

The Taiwan Republic

In May 1895 a short-lived republic was declared on Taiwan in an attempt to stave off the impending Japanese colonial takeover of the island. This "Republic of Taiwan" or "Republic of Formosa" was headed by Tang Jingsong (Tang Ching-sung, 1841–1903), the former Qing governor of the island. James Wheeler Davidson, an American (and later Canadian) adventurer and journalist in Taiwan at the time, was an eyewitness to the rise and fall of this republic. Many of his accounts of it are priceless because much Chinese documentation of the republic is no longer available. Davidson recorded, for example, the English version of the republic's official declaration of independence, which no longer exists in its Chinese original:

Official Declaration of Independence of the Republic of Formosa

The Japanese have affronted China by annexing our territory of Formosa, and the supplications of us, the People of Formosa, at the portals of the Throne have been made in vain. We now learn that the Japanese slaves are about to arrive.

If we suffer this, the land of our hearths and homes will become the land of savages and barbarians, but if we do not suffer it, our condition of comparative weakness will certainly not endure long. Frequent conferences have been held with the Foreign Powers, who all aver that the People of Formosa must establish their independence before the Powers will assist them.

Now therefore we, the People of Formosa, are irrevocably resolved to die before we will serve the enemy. And we have in Council determined to convert the whole island of Formosa into a Republican State, and that the administration of all our State affairs shall be organized and carried on by the deliberations and decisions of Officers publicly elected by us the People. But as in this enterprise there is needed, as well for the resistance of Japanese aggression as for the organization of the new administration, a man to have chief control, in whom authority shall centre, and by whom the peace of our homesteads shall be assured, — therefore, in view of the respect and admiration in which we have long held the Governor and Commander-in-Chief Tang Ching Sung, we have in Council determined to raise him to the position of President of the Republic.

An official seal has been cut, and on the second day of the fifth month, at the *ssu* hour [9 a.m. May 25], it will be publicly presented with all respect by the notables and people of the whole of Formosa. At early dawn on that day, all of us, notables and people, farmers and merchants, artizans [sic] and tradesmen, must assemble at the Tuan Fang Meeting

House, that we may in grave and solemn manner inaugurate this under-
taking.

Let there be neither delay nor mistake.

A Declaration of the whole of Formosa.

[Seal in red as follows] An announcement by the whole of Formosa
(Davidson 1896; Davidson 1903, 279–80)

Davidson, an American republican, whose beliefs led him to see this declaration as important, was disappointed in its reception. His account of the public reaction to the declaration the next day in Taiwan is a classic for its acuity and substance:

The first day of the new republic was greeted with a drizzling rain. The mass of the Chinese were unable to appreciate the seriousness of their position; in fact the Declaration of Independence appeared to them to be of but little more importance than any other piece of official business. I expected that the memorable day would find the streets filled with holiday makers arrayed in their best clothes, the houses gay with flags, and the day noisy with fire crackers. It was not so; for all jogged along as usual. The pretty tea-girls (and Formosa has some pretty girls) were picking tea with no addition to their old time coquettishness, the tea-box makers and painters were working away in their usual busy style. Not a new flag or a fire cracker in the settlement. At the president's yamen, however, the court was crowded with enthusiasts, the whole square was brilliant with new flags, including two large banners which bore the characters, "The President of the Republic of Formosa"; while above them all, floated the new flag of the nation; a blue background with the centre decorated by a hungry looking yellow tiger possessing a tail of greater length than is customarily allotted to a real tiger. The people, principally officials and their friends, fired off crackers and chattered and buzzed away with the idea, no doubt, of mutual encouragement; for the lack of enthusiasm with which the townspeople regarded the affair must have been rather disheartening to the leaders. It was somewhat amusing to note how many of the Chinese merchants condemned the movement wholly, because the ex-governor had introduced it during the busy season. As one local tea merchant informed me: "My talkee that new fashion blong velly good, but just now my too muchee pidgin, no have got time." [I think this new thing is very good, but I have too much business, and I have no time."] (Davidson 1903, 281–82)

Davidson's description of the republic's flag is valuable because only half of the flag has survived to the present. Modern re-creations of the flag take Davidson's account into primary consideration, particularly his depiction of the tiger's long tail.

Advocates of Taiwan independence occasionally tout this short-lived regime as the first republic in East Asia and as a historical precedent for the independence of their island, but they sometimes neglect to mention that the republic recognized the suzerainty of the Qing dynasty and the Emperor of China over it and that Tang Jingsong designated himself as "President of the Republic of Formosa and Ex-Acting Governor of Formosa." (Indeed, Tang even called his republic a tributary state to China.) Tang Jingsong and his successors in the fledgling republic fled to the mainland when the Japanese army was drawing near, and the entire republic collapsed after only a few months. Japanese colonial rule over the island lasted until the end of World War II in 1945, when the United States defeated and occupied Japan.

THE HUNDRED DAYS REFORM

The most prominent of the radical reformers was Kang Youwei, who eventually emerged as an enthusiastic advocate of thoroughgoing reform and a constitutional monarchy for China on the Japanese and British models. Kang was a highly intelligent and idealistic man who had passed his *Jinshi* examinations with the distinction as Optimus (*Zhuangyuan*), the top-ranked examination graduate in all of China. In 1898 Kang began to barrage the throne with passionately written memorials arguing for the necessity of drastic reform if China as a nation and civilization were to survive in the modern world. The Guangxu emperor (r. 1875–1908) was impressed with Kang's forthrightness and summoned him for a personal audience in June 1898. The audience lasted for an unprecedented five hours, during which Kang Youwei convinced the emperor of the validity of his reform program.

From June through September 1898, there issued from the throne a series of imperial edicts for reform. Because the reforms were announced over a period of approximately 100 days, they subsequently became known to Westerners as the Hundred Days Reforms. The wide-ranging edicts called for drastic changes in China's laws and the examination system. They also advocated overhauling the Qing government into a federalized constitutional monarchy, complete with a parliament, various administrative branches, and the treatment of the Qing emperor as head of state. This was more than the emperor's aunt, the Empress Dowager Cixi (a cunning and ruthless woman who had been the real power behind the Qing throne since 1862), could stand. On September 21 she had her nephew arrested and assumed control of the Qing government herself. She quickly reversed all reform edicts and issued arrest warrants for Kang and his supporters. Kang managed to flee to Japan, where he was given a hero's welcome. He remained there for many years, where he advocated his vision of a modernized constitutional monarchy for China and established his Emperor Protection Society (*Baohuangdang*), a body that favored the retention and protection of the Manchu emperor.

Kang's reforms failed because they offended the empress dowager's sensibilities and because he did not secure the backing of the military. Chinese Communist historians today regard him as a bourgeois reformist whose class and educational background deceived him into thinking that mere institutional reform would save China. The failure of his reforms convinced revolutionaries such as Sun Yat-sen that the Manchu dynasty would have to be overthrown by means of violent revolution.

6

Revolution and Republic

THE BOXER UPRISING

At the dawn of the twentieth century a xenophobic and superstitious popular movement was sweeping through northern and central China. Known in English as the Boxer Rebellion or the Boxer Uprising and initially in Chinese as *yihequan* (more or less Righteous and Harmonious Fists), by the summer of 1900 its followers had surrounded foreign legations in Peking and were poised for the wholesale slaughter of foreign diplomats, businessmen, and missionaries. The Boxers, as they were called by Westerners, were practitioners of traditional Chinese martial arts who sought to eliminate foreigners and foreign influence in China. The movement was quelled in August 1900 when an allied force of almost 20,000 troops from several Western nations and Japan arrived in Peking and put the Boxers to flight, but not before 231 foreigners in several areas of northern China had been killed by the insurgents, including two medical missionaries educated at Princeton. The subsequent Boxer Indemnity, which became an enormous burden for the Qing dynasty, proved to be one of the factors that led to its overthrow in 1911.

A good portion of the Boxers' anger was originally directed at the Manchus and their Qing government, which they perceived as incompetent to resist the inroads the foreigners had made into China. A native Chinese government, they believed, would have been better able and better equipped to cope with the Western challenge. The Boxers' xenophobia focused particularly on Protestant and Catholic missionaries, who were, especially in the countryside, the most visible reminder of China's semicolonial subjugation. Chinese everywhere were acutely aware that the missionaries had entered China in the wakes of their nations' gunboats, and popular resentment against them festered because of their occasionally haughty attitudes and the presumptuousness of some of their converts. There was also considerable animosity toward Christianity as a religion. Economic difficulties and urban unemployment caused by the influx of cheap European textiles contributed to popular restlessness, as did frequent floods and other natural disasters in China in the late nineteenth century, all of which seemed to suggest a pending loss of the Mandate of Heaven for the Qing government.

One major center of Boxer activity was Shandong province, an area devastated by floodwaters in 1898 when the dikes of the Yellow River burst. By 1899 Boxing was a craze in Shandong, and thousands of people began believing Boxer claims that mental and physical discipline through martial arts training would make them impervious to foreign bullets and bayonets. Even the governor of Shandong was impressed with the Boxers, and in 1899 he changed their name to the more flattering and official-sounding Righteous and Harmonious Militia (*Yihetuan*).

Foreigners in Shandong were horrified by the increasingly bold and public displays of Boxer xenophobia, and their governments pressured the Qing into dismissing the governor for his unseemly support of the movement. In April 1900, however, Empress Dowager Cixi became more or less converted to the Boxer cause, and she approved of Boxer militia organization efforts in several northern Chinese provinces. By May, Boxing had become a craze, and the foreign legations in Peking were becoming increasingly alarmed by news of foreigners being murdered in the provinces and by the obviously hostile intentions of the Boxers in Peking who constantly paraded and protested outside legation compounds. Several legations got word to their governments that the situation might well become critical and require military assistance.

The empress dowager, far from doing anything to allay these concerns, goaded the Boxers into further boldness. On June 3 Boxers cut the railway link between Tianjin (then called Tientsin) and Peking, effectively cutting the foreign legations off from contact with the outside world. By June 13 mobs of Boxers were rampaging freely throughout Peking, burning foreign homes and churches, murdering Chinese Christians on sight, and desecrating foreign graves. Most ominously of all, on June 19, the empress dowager announced to the legations that she was breaking off diplomatic ties with all foreign nations and gave diplomats 24 hours to leave China under military protection. Some left, but some were so worried about their personal safety that they elected to remain behind in Peking. These concerns were not entirely unwarranted; the next day, the German minister, Clemens von Ketteler, was murdered by a mob.

The foreign legations, convinced that the Boxers and the empress dowager meant to destroy their compounds and murder all foreigners, had managed to get word out about their impending peril before things got out of hand. Assembling an international relief force took time, however, and until it arrived the diplomats and other foreigners who had taken refuge in the legations had to endure a low-level, muted siege. There was a lull in hostile demonstrations in July, and at times the surrounding of the compounds was obviously halfhearted and done more for show than anything else. By late July, real hostilities against the legations were launched again, and the legations were not relieved until August 14, when a combined force of 18,000 troops from Japan, Russia, Britain, the United States, France, Austria, and Italy arrived, lifted the siege against the legations, and then proceeded to loot the city. Humiliated supporters of the Boxers committed suicide, and the next day the empress dowager fled the city along with the puppet emperor she dominated.

Li Hongzhang was left in Peking to negotiate with the foreigners. Negotiations for a peace settlement and indemnities dragged on until September 1901, when the Boxer Protocol was finally concluded. Its provisions included huge indemnities for more than 10 nations. Punishments were also specified for the hard-liners in the government who had supported the Boxers and for the cities where Boxer activity had been the most intense.

The Boxer Uprising and the allied relief expedition that quelled it were both exceedingly humiliating to China. The predations of what the Chinese dubbed the Allied Armies of Eight Nations robbed China of much of its national esteem, and some Chinese turned from condescension toward foreigners to outright fear of and toadying to them. The onerous Boxer Indemnity payments impeded economic growth in China, accelerated imperialistic designs to "carve up the Chinese melon" among the foreign powers, and convinced many Chinese patriots that the Qing government, which had done more than its share to produce the entire crisis in the first place, had to go—now only outright revolution, no longer simple reform, could save China. The Boxer Rebellion also damaged the image and reputation of China in foreign countries, and in the West talk of the "yellow peril," or the implacable hostility of the "yellow race" for the "white race," became widespread.

It should be remembered, however, that the Boxer Rebellion was largely a northern Chinese disturbance; many provinces in the south more or less concluded separate peaces with the foreigners and were not attacked by allied forces. The Qing central government had been severely weakened in the wake of the Taiping Rebellion, and at no time was this more apparent than during the Boxer Rebellion, when it was clear that Peking's real authority extended only to the provinces in the north. The rest of China was more or less free to deal with foreign governments in whichever ways they saw fit, and many provinces did just that.

SUN YAT-SEN AND THE REVOLUTION OF 1911

The moribund Qing dynasty limped along for a few more years and launched a few halfhearted reforms, but its days were numbered. The empress dowager died in 1908, just after having her nephew, the Guangxu emperor (r. 1875–1908), murdered. A child emperor was installed, and one last imperial regency was established, but the Chinese had had enough. On October 10, 1911, a mutiny that broke out in the central Chinese city of Wuchang quickly spread. In early 1912, the last Manchu emperor of China abdicated peacefully and amicably, without a cataclysmic final showdown between dynastic and revolutionary forces. China's last dynasty passed into history not with a bang, but a whimper.

Many Chinese worked long and hard to promote and achieve this revolution, but the most well-known of them all is undoubtedly Sun Yat-sen, a Chinese patriot and medical doctor born in Guangdong province in 1866. In his youth, Sun was quite impressed with the order and cleanliness of the British and other foreign settlements in Canton. Early in his life he began envying the wealth, power, and good order of the West, and he nursed a nationalistic sense of regret that China was not the equal of the West. He followed his brother to Hawaii in 1879 and, once again favorably impressed with the West, enrolled in a Christian school. In the 1880s he went to Hong Kong and Canton and earned a medical degree, and in the early 1890s he began his medical practice.

His heart, however, was not in medicine but in treating the disease of his native land. In 1894 he traveled to Peking and sought an interview

with Li Hongzhang himself to discuss possible cures for China's
national ills. Li, however, did not have time to discuss national affairs
with a nobody who had a Western medical degree but no *Jinshi* creden-
tials. Sun resented the snub for the rest of his life, and the incident
helped him resolve to overthrow the Qing dynasty. The Manchus, he
concluded, were holding China back; China would be better off led by
a native Chinese regime. By 1895 he had abandoned his medical practice, and he went to Canton and Hong Kong to foment revolutionary
sentiment. There he broadened his contacts with secret Chinese frater-
nal orders and launched an abortive revolutionary uprising in Canton.
This was foiled, however, and he fled to Hong Kong and thence to
Japan, where he was given a hero's welcome. In Japan Sun decided that
he would need more money for his revolutionary program, and the best
source for that was the relatively wealthy community of overseas
Chinese in Japan, Hawaii, North America, and Britain. In all of these
places he appealed to the Chinese communities for money for his cause
and tried to inspire them with a vision of his anti-Manchu revolution.

Sun continued his globe-trotting, fund-raising, and anti-Manchu
rhetoric in London the next year, in 1896. There he was lured into the

Sun Yat-Sen. (Library of Congress)

Qing embassy and arrested by Qing officials, who intended to take him back to China for trial and certain execution. Sun managed to get word of his "kidnapping" out to the British public, and when the story was splashed all over the London newspapers, the British Foreign Office pressured the embassy into releasing him. With this incident, Sun had become a celebrity in Britain and the rest of the world. He remained in Britain until late 1897 where he formulated the ideology for his revolution: the Three Principles of the People, or nationalism, socialism, and democracy.

Sun then went to Japan and preached revolution there, but the response was tepid. He was startled to find that the Japanese were more enthusiastic about his revolutionary program than the Chinese there were. He was bitterly disappointed that his own Chinese people were apparently fatalistic, apathetic, and living in fear of Manchu reprisals, but he had an ideological rival in Japan: Kang Youwei, who was arguing for a constitutional monarchy in China. Sun, a thoroughgoing republican by this time, would not hear of this and debated with Kang vigorously. Kang, for his part, shared Li Hongzhang's contempt for Sun as a nobody without so much as a *Shengyuan* degree.

Sun's revolutionary cause was given a shot in the arm in 1903 with the publication of the virulently anti-Manchu tract *The Revolutionary Army*, written by an 18-year-old racist and Chinese patriot named Zou Rong. This pamphlet, which was an instant success among the Chinese community in Japan, berated the Chinese for their slavish and shameless acceptance of Manchu rule and tyranny over them. *The Revolutionary Army* did for the Chinese what Sun had largely failed to do: it energized them and helped tip the balance of public opinion in favor of revolution for China and away from Kang Youwei's Emperor Protection Society. Two passages from it will perhaps convey some of the flavor, an almost hysterical patriotism and anti-Manchu racism, of Zou Rong's tract:

Revolution! Revolution! Why should my 400 million fellowcountrymen embark on revolution today? I first cry out (and I put all I know into it):

Unjust! Unjust! What is most bitter and unjust in China today is to have to bear with the wolvish ambitions of this inferior race of nomads, the brigand Manchus, our rulers. And when we seek to be wealthy and noble, we wag our tails and beg for pity, we kneel thrice and make ninefold kowtows, delighted and intoxicated to find ourselves under them, shameless and unable to come to our senses. Alas, fellowcountrymen, you have no feelings of patriotism! Alas, you have no racial feelings, no feelings of independence!

As for the Manchu scoundrels, our common foes and antagonists, 260 years of their slavery can still be thrown off, let alone a few score years of it. . . . Let us steel ourselves in deadly struggles to drive out the Manchu scoundrels who humiliate us, tyrannize over us, slaughter us and debauch our women, in the end to restore the great China of our heritage, to recover our natural rights, to win back the freedom which should be ours from birth.

Let there be revolution in China! Let there be revolution in China! The French carried out three revolutions, the Americans the Seven Years War (of Independence). Therefore there should be revolution in China. . . . I should like to hold the whip daily, to take part in the revolution of my fellowcountrymen, to implore my fellowcountrymen to carry out their revolution.

How can I bear to see robes and regalia of the Upper Land fall to the barbarian? Let us lead the heroes of the Middle Plain to win back our rivers and hills.

Is this the resolve of my fellowcountrymen, too? (Tsou/Lust 1968, 65, 82)

In 1904 Sun traveled once again to Hawaii and the United States where he politicized the secret Chinese fraternities there and converted them to his anti-Manchu program. The next year, he organized a union of these fraternities called the Tongmenghui, or United Chinese League. Initiates into it were told that they were no longer subjects of the Qing or the Manchus. The league's membership grew quickly, and by 1906 branches of it had been established in many places throughout the world and were contributing money for the revolution in China. Meanwhile, Sun's supporters and other like-minded Chinese patriots were attempting to make several more uprisings in China. The last of the unsuccessful uprisings against the Manchus was attempted in the Canton suburb of Huanghuagang in April 1911, in which several dozen insurgents lost their lives.

The uprising that touched off the revolution instead of being crushed as just another rebellion occurred on October 10, 1911, in the city of Wuhan, Hubei province. Wuhan was chosen because of its central location in China. Republican revolutionaries were in control of the city by noon, and two weeks later a neighboring province, Hunan, announced its break with the Qing. Other provinces quickly followed suit, and by December 1911, more than half of China had declared its independence from the Qing government.

Sun Yat-sen read about the October 10 uprising while he was in Denver, Colorado, on one of his many globe-trotting fund-raising trips. Sun did not immediately return to China upon learning of the subsequent success of the uprising but instead made efforts to secure

American and European support for the new republican regime. Although Sun was an effective agitator for revolution, he did not command as much military power as he would need to sustain a new republican regime once it was established. Someone else, however, did. He was an unscrupulous and conniving general named Yuan Shikai, who had long served the Manchus. After the success of the October 1911 revolution, Sun did not insist on becoming the president of the new Republic of China himself, but turned the presidency over to Yuan Shikai on February 2, 1912, one day after the final and official abdication of the last Manchu emperor.

Sun had wanted the capital of the republic to be in Nanjing. Because Beijing had been the capital of two conquest dynasties (Mongol Yuan and Manchu Qing), he and other Chinese patriots antagonistic toward the Manchus wanted to relocate the nation's capital to a city more identified with native Chinese rule. (Nanjing was the capital of the early Ming and had been the capital of several native Chinese dynasties during the Period of Division.) Yuan Shikai, however, wanted the capital to be located in his base of power in Beijing, and Sun reluctantly assented to this.

In one sense, Sun's republican revolution was quite decisive—it ended over 250 years of Manchu imperial rule—but his revolution was not thorough. China needed more than an end to the *ancien régime* to become a functional republic: it needed a stable and functional government, which unfortunately neither Sun nor Yuan could provide. The results for China were tragic. Yuan made a mockery out of republican rule and soon scrapped it altogether in favor of a constitutional monarchy, with himself as head of state and head of government. His death in 1916 did little to prevent China from sliding into a decade of regional warlordism. Sun Yat-sen meanwhile retreated to Canton in southern China and tried in vain to rally China and the world to his cause. He died a disappointed and frustrated man in 1925, before his dream of seeing China unified under a strong and modern republican government could be realized.

YUAN'S MISRULE

Yuan Shikai turned out to be no friend of the revolution. To the disgust of Sun Yat-sen and many others who had high hopes for China after the 1911 revolution, it soon became apparent that Yuan meant to do little more than replace the Qing dynasty with one of his own. Yuan soon convinced himself and a coterie of Western advisors, including an American who had been president of Johns Hopkins University, that China was not ready for republican rule and was much more suited for a monarchy. Accordingly, he had a constitution drawn up in 1914 that gave him unlimited power and the lifelong right to rule over China. The Japanese helped him, flattered that he admired the imperial style of governance in post–Meiji Japan. To curry favor with them, he gave in to Japan's infamous Twenty-one Demands, which included such humiliating provisions as Japanese control of key Chinese industries, including steel production. This became intolerable to many provinces, and in late 1915 a southern province declared its independence of his rule. Several provinces followed suit, and once again a regime collapsed. By May 1916, Yuan found himself abandoned by several provinces and his erstwhile Japanese supporters, and he died the next month.

THE WARLORD PERIOD

The collapse of Yuan's regime led to a decade of chaos and division in China. It produced a power vacuum that no regime could hope to fill, and China disintegrated into several geopolitical regions, all more or less dominated by military commanders dubbed "warlords" by Western writers. The warlord period was so confusing that most foreign governments simply chose to recognize whichever regime occupied Beijing as the legitimate government of China. Warlords fought and allied with one another in an execrable and Byzantine pattern of intrigue, cooperation, and betrayal. Several civil wars between warlord armies raged, and almost invariably the warlords claimed to be fighting not for their own selfish purposes but for the good of China. While it is easy to be cynical about these claims, it is important to remember that few if any of the warlords claimed to be legitimate governments; in their view, political legitimacy would come after they had established order in China. They did not usually pretend to be governments in their own right, although they certainly dominated many local and regional governments and often intimidated them into doing their bidding. And they craved the legitimacy and recognition that could be conferred on them by official governmental documents and properly signed and sealed appointments. Many even sought to have their photographs and biographies published (in Chinese and English) in the "who's who in China" books popular in the early twentieth century.

THE MAY FOURTH MOVEMENT AND PERIOD

The warlord-dominated regimes were often interested in little more than the raw exercise of power and seldom took much thought for matters of public ideology. What mattered to them was not what people thought or believed about the state, but that they would obey rather than defy the state. The lack of an official ideology in China after the fall of the Qing certainly had its drawbacks, but in one way it helped the intellectual revolution. The very absence of an ideology fostered much debate and speculation about just what China's guiding ideology should be. Because the warlord armies cared little for safeguarding any particular state orthodoxy or dogma, Chinese students and intellectuals during the warlord period were freer than ever before or since to speak their minds and earnestly discuss what philosophy or guiding system of thought China ought to espouse in building its future. Marxism-Leninism-Mao Zedong Thought, which became China's official state ideology in 1949, had its birth in the discussions among students and intellectuals during the May Fourth period.

The May Fourth period is so named because of a large, nationalistic protest movement against Japanese aggression that was held on May 4, 1919. Because the protest typified much of the nationalistic energy and intellectual openness of its time, the entire period between the late 1910s and early 1920s is now generally referred to as the May Fourth period. The Chinese of this time knew intuitively that their nation was at an intellectual and political crossroads, and what they discussed and wrote still has ramifications for China today.

The epicenter of the May Fourth period in China was Peking University, or Beida, as it is usually abbreviated in Chinese. Beida was (and still is) the Harvard of China, and it often set trends that other Chinese universities followed. During World War I, many Chinese intellectuals who had been studying abroad in Japan, Europe, and the United States came home to China, and many of the best and brightest of them were recruited to Beida to become professors or administrators. Foremost among the promising and talented young Chinese returning home were Chen Duxiu and Cai Yuanpei from Europe, Lu Xun from Japan, and Hu Shi from the United States. All were to emerge as bright stars in Beida's intellectual constellation.

Cai Yuanpei was particularly important. He had earned his *Jinshi* degree in the 1880s, but in 1907 he went to Germany to study. He was appointed China's minister of education after the 1911 revolution, but Yuan Shikai's subsequent antics so disgusted him that he returned to Europe for further study in Germany and France. With Yuan's death in 1916, however, he returned once again to China and was soon appointed chancellor of Beida. Cai's chancellorship transformed Beida into a modern, first-class institution of higher learning. Beida had formerly been more or less a training college for government hacks, and its standards of commitment and scholarship for both students and faculty members were abysmal. Cai changed all of this and insisted that Beida become a committed and energetic place where study and absolute academic freedom would be taken seriously. Beida would no longer be a place where students simply partied their educational careers away and made interpersonal contacts that would last them through a lifetime of service to the government. Furthermore, there would be no party line to toe; Beida would be an intellectually alive place where the expression of all varieties of thought would be allowed and even encouraged. The new intellectual atmosphere, openness, and commitment fostered by Cai Yuanpei were enormously attractive to China's rising generation of young and energetic intellectuals, and many of them flocked to Beida. In 1916 Cai had set the stage for the intellectual renaissance that would follow.

Chen Duxiu, who had earned a *Shengyuan* degree in 1896, studied in Japan and France. He returned to China in 1915 to protest Japan's infamous Twenty-one Demands, and in Shanghai he published a monthly magazine called *New Youth*, in which he relentlessly slammed what he considered the intellectual sources of China's backwardness. He regularly skewered Confucianism and the traditional Chinese family in the pages of *New Youth* and urged China's young people to reject much of their traditional heritage, including traditional attitudes toward women. (Chen was recognizably feminist in some of his thought.) He was antitraditional but not anti-Chinese. Like all intellectuals of his era, he deeply loved his country and was passionately committed to creating a better future for an imperiled China. In 1917 Chen was made a professor of literature at Beida, and there he continued to influence young Chinese intellectuals. Chen himself also underwent a transformation at Beida. He began studying Marxism-Leninism along with Li Dazhao, the newly appointed head librarian at Beida. (In Li Dazhao's employ at Beida was a young library assistant named Mao Zedong.) Chen and Li Dazhao would, a few years later, emerge as the cofounders of the Chinese Communist party.

Hu Shi was America's man in China. Hu, like the other key members of the May Fourth period, had a dual intellectual heritage: he had pursued traditional Chinese learning in his youth and then

Western studies. Hu went to the United States in 1909 at the age of 18 and entered Cornell University, where he learned English well and became convinced that written Chinese ought to reflect the spoken vernacular Chinese instead of being highly literary, allusive, and formulaic. He later took his Ph.D. in philosophy at Columbia University, where he was influenced by the study of evolution and the pragmatic philosophy of John Dewey. Hu eventually went to Beida, where he attracted quite a following of energetic young Chinese students. Like Chen Duxiu, Hu Shi detested Confucianism and wanted an end to it. Hu argued that Confucianism, shown by pragmatism to be inapplicable to modern Chinese realities, should be discarded. "Down with the Confucian establishment" or "Put Ye Olde Confucian Curiosity Shoppe out of business" became favorite slogans at Beida and elsewhere. As replacements for Confucianism he tirelessly promoted "Mr. Science" and "Mr. Democracy" as the new guiding ideology and institution for China. He also widely promoted the use of plain vernacular language in published writing. Plain language was, he argued, much easier to learn and would increase literacy in China. The plain language movement turned out to be Hu's most enduring contribution to China; it eventually won out over the old literary language, and today the newspapers and books of China are published in the vernacular or semivernacular style. The old literary language now appears almost exclusively in historical records. Indeed, modern writing in the old classical language is now often regarded as pretentious, anachronistic, or just plain silly.

Inspired by Hu Shi, Chen Duxiu, and others, Beida students founded a vernacular magazine called *New Tide* that promoted critical thinking and language reform. Other student magazines eventually joined in the fray, and soon many aspects of traditional China were under attack and ridiculed in these publications. Warlordism, constitutional monarchy, traditional customs, filial piety, and patriarchy were singled out for special scorn in the pages of these student periodicals, and new issues were eagerly awaited and snatched up as soon as they became available.

Beida was an exciting and intellectually alive place. Many foreign intellectuals, including John Dewey and Bertrand Russell, traveled to China and spoke with interested and engaged students about the best alternatives for China's future. During the May Fourth period, Chinese students sampled many ideologies and "-isms," including socialism, liberalism, anarchism, and even social Darwinism. Some foreign intellectuals commented that there was much more interest in their ideas in China than there was in their own home countries.

THE MAY FOURTH PROTEST

Into this lively academic atmosphere came a protest against Japanese aggression on May 4, 1919. At the center of the upheaval was the fate of Shandong, a Chinese province. Shandong had more or less been a German colony since 1898, when Germany leased Jiaozhou as a naval base for 99 years and set up beer breweries in nearby Qingdao. When World War I broke out, China at first remained neutral. This changed in September 1919, when the warlord-dominated government in Beijing entered into secret discussions with Japan about Shandong.

The Japanese, who sensed Germany's impending defeat in the war, had begun to covet the German holdings in Shandong and were soon scheming for a way for them to be transferred to Japan at war's end. The Japanese made a substantial loan to the Beijing government in exchange for Beijing's recognition of Japan's claims to Shandong and for granting rights to Japan for constructing railroads and stationing troops throughout the province. All of this was unknown to the Chinese public.

Meanwhile, Chinese students and intellectuals at Beida and other universities had high hopes for the Versailles Peace Conference at the end of World War I. They hoped that the idealistic principles voiced by U.S. President Woodrow Wilson and other international leaders would result in the righting of wrongs China had suffered at the hands of foreign powers ever since the Opium War. The Chinese delegation to Versailles was bitterly disappointed to learn that the conference would address only matters immediately pertaining to World War I, and it was outraged to learn of its own government's secret negotiations with Japan that would even deprive China of the Shandong territory it had lost to the Germans in 1898. The final adjudication of Shandong's fate came at Versailles on April 28, 1919, in Japan's favor.

When word of this adjudication reached China, the Chinese public was enraged. Student hotheads began calling for the defense of Shandong and cabled the Chinese delegation in Versailles with impassioned pleas not to sign the final peace agreement. On May 4 a major demonstration was organized. Angry crowds marched past the house of the foreign minister who had approved the secret agreement, and police responded by arresting several student demonstrators. This arrest, in turn, led to a larger general strike in Beijing, and a boycott of Japanese goods followed. Unprepared for the magnitude of public indignation at its actions, the Beijing government released the students a few days later and informed the delegation in Versailles that it could decide for itself whether or not to sign the final peace treaty. When

Chinese students in Paris were told about this, they immediately surrounded the quarters of the Chinese delegation in an around-the-clock vigil. As a result, the Chinese delegation did not sign the final peace agreement ending World War I.

TO GO WEST OR GO EAST, YOUNG MAN: THAT IS THE QUESTION

The Versailles settlement was deeply disappointing to many Chinese intellectuals and led many of them to become disillusioned with the West. Perhaps the West, after all, did not have the answers to China's problems. Western Europe, which many Chinese intellectuals had looked to as the pinnacle of modern civilization, had very nearly destroyed itself in World War I. What had caused the tragic war—excessive materialism, rampant nationalism, unfeeling capitalism? Western Europe and North America then stood by and did little to blunt Japanese ambitions toward Shandong. Were they really China's friends after all? Many disillusioned students began listening to voices critical of the West, including Chinese nativists and, more important, the Bolsheviks. Perhaps the answers were in Eastern Europe and Russia. One of the most extensive and penetrating critiques of Western civilization was Marxism-Leninism, an ideology that both excoriated the West's domination of the world and predicted its eventual collapse. Such ideas were comforting and powerfully appealing to a generation of young Chinese hotheads angry with how the West sold out China at Versailles. Out of this anger and disillusionment came renewed interest in Marxism-Leninism and the Bolshevik Revolution in Russia. Perhaps in a very real way, the West's failure to emerge as China's friend at a crucial historical moment turned a good portion of modern China's key transitional generation away from the West and toward the East.

THE FOUNDING OF THE CHINESE COMMUNIST PARTY

In order to make sense of the history of communism in China, it is necessary to have a rudimentary understanding of Marxist-Leninist dogma, which holds that history is driven by class conflict and unfolds in five main stages. The most primitive historical stage is "slave society," in which slaves are ruled over by masters. Eventually the slaves rise up and overthrow their masters, and this leads to a "feudal society." In the feudal society, serfs eventually overthrow their lords and advance on to a "capitalist society," in which the "bourgeoisie," or city-dwelling capitalists, exploit the "proletariat," or laboring industrial class. When the proletariat overthrow the bourgeoisie, the advancement is to a "socialist society." Eventually socialist society advances to a "communist society" in which there is no more exploitation or class conflict. This historical model seems to resemble the linear conception of historical development in Judaeo-Christian thought, but with social perfection replacing God's judgment as the final culmination of all history.

Almost all Communists agreed that China was stuck in a "feudal" society and would need to have a "bourgeois revolution" to capitalism. After the bourgeois revolutionaries had outlived their usefulness, their capitalist society would be overthrown and China would advance to socialism. Marxist-Leninist study groups came to this conclusion during the heady days of the May Fourth period. The May 1, 1919, issue of Chen Duxiu's *New Youth* was dedicated to Marxism, although most of the articles appearing in this issue were critical of the ideology. Earlier study groups had been considering Marxism-Leninism in some detail, but this May Day edition of *New Youth* introduced it into the broader intellectual communities at Beida and elsewhere. Li Dazhao, Beida's head librarian, had been holding such study groups earlier, and his office became affectionately known as the "Red Chamber" by his adoring students and groupies, including the future leader Mao Zedong. Li had, in fact, written the lone article in favor of Marxism in the May 1 issue; Chen at this time was still undecided. Chen's adherence to Marxism came in mid-1920, after he had left Beida. Chen concluded that multiparty democracy on the Anglo-American model was nothing but a sham, a tool for the bourgeoisie to maintain political control over capitalist society.

In 1920, then, there were two centers of Marxist study in China: one at Beida under Li Dazhao, and one in Shanghai under Chen Duxiu. In the Soviet Union, the Comintern learned about this and dispatched an agent, Grigory Voitinsky, to organize a Communist party in China. Voitinsky met with Li and Chen and helped young Marxists in China organize the Chinese Communist party. The party's First Congress was held in a girls' school in Shanghai's French concession area in July 1921. The First Congress decided that the Communists would cooperate with Sun Yat-sen and accommodate his ideology for the time being because Sun was, in their estimation, China's best hope for a bourgeois revolution. Ironically, neither Chen Duxiu nor Li Dazhao attended this First Congress, but they are still honored as the two cofounders of the party in China. (Mao later revised his favorable impression of Chen and maintained that Li, who saw a greater revolutionary role for China's peasants than Chen did, was the more ideologically correct of the two).

The Chinese Communist party (or CCP, as it is sometimes abbreviated in English) organized youth leagues and held foreign language classes to prepare China's brightest minds for further training and indoctrination in Moscow. It also helped organize several labor unions and strikes in Shanghai. Labor unions then spread to other Chinese cities, where suspicious Chinese warlords sometimes violently opposed them. In Peking, for instance, the warlord Wu Peifu opened fire with machine guns in February 1923 on striking railroad workers, killing or wounding several hundred of them.

By July 1922 the CCP had over 100 members in several Chinese cities, and the Second Congress had decided to place the CCP under the Comintern's control and direction. This meant that Moscow would, in theory at least, be in charge of ideological and doctrinal matters pertaining to communism in China. This would eventually lead to some friction in China between more orthodox Communists who followed Moscow's guidance for "bourgeois" and "proletariat" revolution on the one hand and the peasantist group (including Mao Zedong) on the other, which advocated a greater revolutionary role for China's millions of peasants.

THE FIRST UNITED FRONT

The warlord period did not drag on forever. The geopolitical division and intellectual openness it fostered had both come to an end by 1927, when Chiang Kai-shek, one of Sun Yat-sen's key generals, finally defeated most of the warlord regimes and more or less allied or entered into a state of detente with the rest of them. In achieving a nominal unification of China, Chiang Kai-shek also broke off all ties with the Chinese Communists. This led to periodic civil war in China until 1949 and the final Chinese Communist triumph.

After Yuan Shikai betrayed Sun's republican revolution, Sun once again went abroad for a time, seeking more funds from his followers and eventually regrouping them into a more tightly organized body, which he named the Nationalist Party, or Guomindang (sometimes also known as the KMT, after the initials of its old-style spelling, Kuomintang). He eventually returned to China and established a government of his own in southern China to serve as an alternative to the various warlord-dominated regimes in Beijing.

The Soviets wanted to export their Bolshevik Revolution, and Russian interest in China increased after the May Fourth protests. Their purpose was to advance China from feudalism to capitalism and, ultimately, to socialism. Accordingly, Soviet agents from the Comintern, an international organization that sought to export the Bolshevik Revolution to other countries and guide them along the Marxist-Leninist paradigm for revolution and social salvation, searched for suitable candidates for a bourgeois revolution in China. At first they thought warlords could fill this role, but after several warlords rebuffed Soviet overtures, the Soviets finally "discovered" Sun Yat-sen in southern China and identified him as their man. They planned to use Sun Yat-sen to accomplish the bourgeois revolution and then dispose of him after he outlived his usefulness and a new socialist revolution had taken hold in China.

Sun Yat-sen himself was by no means a Communist and clearly rejected communism as unsuitable for China. He was, however, interested in working with the Communists temporarily in order to achieve his immediate objective of toppling the warlord-dominated governments in China and achieving real and lasting national unification. Sun turned to the Communists and the Soviet Union because no other Western nation showed much interest in cooperating with his political program for China. By the early 1920s he was thoroughly disillusioned with the West and regarded the Soviet Union as the only European power even remotely interested in seeing a republic established in China. Accordingly, in 1922, he allowed Chinese Communists to join his own Nationalist Party, but he made it clear that they were joining as individuals, not as a political bloc. Sun did not envision or approve of a union between the two parties. Both parties, then, hoped to outlive the other after national unification and the defeat of the warlords. Only one party could win at this precarious game, and in 1949 the Communists emerged as the victorious party.

Sun's decision to admit the Chinese Communists into the Nationalist Party is still controversial. Some rabidly anti-Communist officials in his own party objected adamantly to this, but he overruled them and argued that all Chinese had the right to join in his revolution and that Soviet aid might go elsewhere in China if he refused to accommodate the Chinese Communists. Besides, he argued, there was some conceptual overlap between his Three Principles of the People and Marxist-Leninist ideas.

Accordingly, in the early 1920s, the Soviets sent an agent to help Sun achieve this alliance between the two parties and also to help him reorganize the Nationalist party along more Leninist, Bolshevik lines.

Chiang Kai-shek, one of Sun's main generals, was sent to Moscow for political indoctrination and training. While in Moscow, Chiang Kai-shek developed an enmity toward the Soviets and communism that endured for the rest of his life. He repeatedly wrote to Sun warning him about the real Soviet intentions for him and for China, but Sun brushed off these warnings as the loyal but overheated anxieties of a hot-blooded young Chinese patriot. Chiang Kai-shek bit his lip and did not dare cross Sun, but after Sun died in 1925 he assumed the leadership of the Nationalists and decided to break with the Chinese Communists. That break came in 1927 with blood and terror. This first period of cooperation between the Nationalists and the Chinese Communists became known as the First United Front.

THE NORTHERN EXPEDITION

After he established working political and military ties with the Soviets, Sun Yat-sen was eager to launch his Northern Expedition, a military campaign against the warlords, and destroy their power. (He had

Nationalist Chinese leader Chiang Kai-shek. (Library of Congress)

long since given up on any purely political solution to the problem of warlordism in China.) He died, however, in March 1925 from cancer before his long-envisioned march could take place. Sun was a giant of a man with enormous prestige and following in China, and no single leader could take his place. His mantle of leadership fell on two main figures. Political leadership went to Wang Jingwei, a left-wing Nationalist politician who was somewhat sympathetic with the Chinese Communists. The all-important command of the military, however, went to Chiang Kai-shek, who by this time had pronounced right-wing tendencies and a deep and abiding hatred of the Chinese Communists.

On July 27, 1926, Chiang began the Northern Expedition, and it went more smoothly than almost anyone had anticipated. By September the Nationalists and their Communist allies had captured Wuhan, the centrally located and strategically important city where the Revolution of 1911 had first broken out, and left-wing elements of the Nationalist government soon moved their capital to the city from Canton. Chiang Kai-shek then marched on Shanghai and Nanjing, and in March 1927 his troops entered Shanghai unopposed and also captured Nanjing, where Chiang Kai-shek set up his own right-wing government. Chiang then turned with a vengeance on the generally pro-Communist labor unions in Shanghai. On April 12, 1927, he launched a brutal and bloody anti-Communist campaign in the city. His agents and police ruthlessly tracked down Communist cells and shot suspected Communists on sight. The Nationalist government in Wuhan was appalled at his actions and sought to distance itself from his Nanjing regime, but by February 1928 the Wuhan government, having concluded that it would be unwise and futile to confront Chiang Kai-shek militarily, dissolved itself and recognized Chiang's Nanjing-based regime as the new capital of the restored republic. (Nanjing was, after all, where Sun Yat-sen had wanted China's new capital to be located.) By 1929 Chiang had marched on Beijing, expelled the warlord Zhang Zuolin, and renamed the city Beiping, which means "Northern Peace" or "Pacified North."

By 1929, then, Chiang Kai-shek had emerged as China's new strongman. His forces had broken the warlords' power, nominally unified China under the control of a Nanjing-based government, and expelled the Chinese Communists from Shanghai, Beijing, and other major cities. The Communists had not been defeated, however, but simply driven underground. They quickly reemerged in the countryside where they organized peasant resistance movements. For the next two decades, Chiang tried in vain to rid China of communism. By 1931 a new and ominous threat would emerge: Japanese militarism and aggression.

THE CHINESE COMMUNISTS IN THE COUNTRYSIDE

After Chiang's coup against them, the Chinese Communists were down but not out. Many of them went into hiding in the cities where they continued, at the Comintern's insistence, to foment classic proletariat uprisings in the major cities. All the urban uprisings failed. Typically, they lasted for three days and were then suppressed by massive numbers of KMT forces who were sent to the cities. By 1930 enthusiasm among Chinese Communists for urban uprisings was waning.

A minority of Chinese Communists, led by Mao Zedong, had meanwhile retreated to the countryside, beyond the immediate reach of Chiang's city-based forces. Mao returned to his native province of Hunan, and in 1927 he led an unsuccessful peasant uprising, but he was not discouraged. In August of that year several thousand KMT troops defected to the Chinese Communists, among them Zhu De, who eventually became the commander of the Red Army, and Zhou Enlai, who later served as China's premier and was, after Mao, the second most powerful leader in China.

Mao Zedong, leader of the Chinese communists. (The Illustrated London News Picture Library)

Mao and Zhu eventually relocated to Jiangxi province, where they organized a rural soviet, a Communist-led regime that confiscated land from greedy landlords, punished or executed them, and redistributed their land to poor peasants. This simple program of land reform was tremendously appealing to Jiangxi's peasantry, and by early 1930 Mao's Communist movement in the province was gaining enormous popular support. This was ominous for Chiang Kai-shek, but he found even more unsettling Zhu De's command over a Red Army emerging to protect the new soviet from attack. In November 1930 Chiang Kai-shek launched the first of five "encirclement and extermination" campaigns against the Jiangxi soviet. The first four were unsuccessful, but the fifth in October 1933 succeeded in dislodging the Chinese Communists and sending them on the epic Long March. They finally relocated in Yan'an in the faraway northern province of Shaanxi.

JAPANESE AGGRESSION

Japan was undeniably the first nation in East Asia to modernize itself effectively, and by the early twentieth century some Japanese chauvinists and militarists envisioned that Japan would emerge as the next conquest dynasty in China and rule over the Chinese as the Mongols and Manchus had done in previous centuries. Japanese militarists regarded themselves and their country as the force that would save the rest of East Asia and the Pacific islands from the twin perils of communism and white man's imperialism. This would also allow Japan to establish its own empire in the same area, but the Japanese imagined that East Asia would prefer Japanese imperialism to Western imperialism. Eventually Japan originated a charming euphemism for its East Asian empire: the Greater East Asia Co-Prosperity Sphere.

Japan's aggression against China began on September 18, 1931, when Japanese forces manufactured a pretext to conquer Manchuria, or China's northeast. The Japanese claimed that on this day a bomb exploded on a train in Mukden, Manchuria, and that Japanese troops investigating the explosion were fired upon. Japan therefore had no choice but to take over all of Manchuria in self-defense. This action, known as the Manchurian Incident or the Mukden Incident, was the beginning of World War II for China. The next year, Japan transformed Manchuria into an "independent" state and named it Manchukuo, or the "Nation of Manchuria." Japan then installed a puppet government in Manchukuo that was headed up by Henry Pu Yi, the last Qing emperor who was only a child of about three when his dynasty abdicated in early 1912. The rest of the world was not fooled by Japan's claims that the people of Manchuria had begged Japan to make theirs an independent state, and the League of Nations criticized Japan for its aggression. Japan responded by withdrawing from the League and more or less thumbing its nose at the rest of the world. Japan's lack of concern for its international image became further apparent in January 1932, when it attacked and occupied the Chinese areas of Shanghai and did not withdraw until the middle of the year, after several foreign powers intervened to help negotiate a truce. But Japanese occupying troops remained in Manchuria, and during the early and mid-1930s the tentacles of Japanese military occupation spread to other areas of northern China. The Japanese knew that Chiang Kai-shek's government in Nanjing was too busy with the Chinese Communists to resist their invasions effectively.

DISEASES OF SKIN AND HEART

The great and pressing question for Chiang Kai-shek's government during the Japanese aggression of the 1930s was who to fight first: the Japanese invaders or the Chinese Communist insurgents. This question, in turn, boiled down to an assessment of which was the greater threat, the invasion from without or the subversion from within. For Chiang Kai-shek there was little question that the Communists posed the greater peril to China. Comparing the Japanese to a disease of the skin and the Chinese Communists to a disease of the heart, he reasoned that only a strong and internally unified China freed of subversion could successfully resist the Japanese invasion. Accordingly, he continued his relentless search for Chinese Communists in the cities and continued the fight against the rural soviet regime in Jiangxi.

THE EXTERMINATION AND ENCIRCLEMENT CAMPAIGNS

Chiang Kai-shek had launched the first of his ominously named extermination and encirclement campaigns against Jiangxi in November 1930. This was a disastrous failure: 40,000 Red Army troops defeated 100,000 Nationalist troops. Undeterred and undiscouraged, Chiang attacked a second time from February through June 1931, but with similar results: 30,000 Red Army troops defeated an army of 200,000 Nationalist men. Chiang personally led 300,000 troops on the third campaign in the summer of 1931 and penetrated deep into Jiangxi, but Mao and Zhu successfully divided the army into small, isolated units and then ambushed them individually, inflicting enormous casualties. A fourth campaign launched in mid-1932 against other soviets in other provinces also ended in defeat for Chiang Kai-shek's government. The fifth and final campaign, launched against Jiangxi in October 1933, was a massive, well-coordinated assault, with 750,000 Nationalist troops, air support, and German military advice. The Chinese Communists were defeated in this attack and were forced to evacuate the province.

The reasons for the Communists' defeat in this last campaign are controversial. Mao, a classic guerrilla warrior, disliked traditional positional warfare and preferred to lure enemy units into isolation and then wear them down through hit-and-run guerrilla tactics. Other Communist strategists and Otto Braun, a German military advisor to the Chinese Communists, opposed Mao's tactics and pointed out that soviets in other provinces had defeated campaigns against them through European-style positional warfare. They ultimately had their way, and the results for the Chinese Communists were disastrous. Chiang's massive fifth campaign was intelligently conceived and competently coordinated, and his troops advanced slowly and steadily instead of rushing forth and being "lured in deep." They built block-houses and left reinforcements in conquered areas before advancing farther, and a slowly constricting ring of troops was eventually established around the Communists, cutting them off from the outside world and depriving them of salt, a commodity in desperately short supply. By late 1934, facing impending defeat, the Chinese Communists decided to concentrate all of their firepower and break out of the encirclement at one point. Mao disagreed with these tactics and argued for classic guerrilla tactics: Communist troops should slip through the encirclements at night in small fire teams and regroup later elsewhere. Once again overruled, Mao angrily watched the breakthrough successfully achieved in late 1934, but at a very high cost to the Red Army. The Long March had begun.

THE LONG MARCH OF THE CHINESE COMMUNISTS

The Long March is one of the pivotal events in the history of the Chinese Communist movement. Around 400,000 people started out, but only 40,000 made it all the way to Yan'an. The rest deserted or were killed or captured. It was a make-or-break struggle for the Chinese Communists who participated in it, and the few who survived became a core generation for Chinese leadership well into the 1980s and even the 1990s. For the Chinese Communists, the Long March became the stuff of legends. It was a crucial, nation-making event, and to have participated in it was like having fought at Vimy Ridge in World War I for Canadians or having wintered at Valley Forge for Americans. The Long March today is immortalized in China in movies, television dramas, novels, plays, and ear-splitting arias sung by rosy-cheeked peasant girls. Chinese space rockets today are called Long March rockets, and the CCP still occasionally touts "the Yan'an spirit" as a pristine and selfless ideological puritanism to counter what it sees as the corrosive cultural and economic influences of the modern Western, capitalistic world.

In reality, the Long March was the long retreat of a defeated army and regime. The Nationalists called it the "Great Rat Scamper" (*da liu-cuan*), and many old Nationalists in Taiwan today still chuckle at its glorification and exaggeration in mainland China. KMT aircraft followed the course of the Long March and regularly bombed and strafed it, so that the marchers eventually had to march at night and rest during the daytime. Hostile foot soldiers often ambushed them and decimated their numbers. The Long Marchers suffered terribly and often went without shoes, warm clothing, and adequate nutrition. (Photographs of Mao taken right after the Long March show him to be gaunt and emaciated, and the few months after he arrived in Yan'an were the only time in his adult life when he was not overweight.)

On January 5, 1935, the Long Marchers stopped in the town of Zunyi in Guizhou province where they conferred on their damage and progress. One Communist leader after another stood up to denounce those who had insisted on positional warfare in fighting against the last Nationalist extermination campaign. This pleased Mao, who, of course, had also criticized the nonguerrilla style of warfare and argued that the decision to break out of the encirclement in one block had produced needless casualties. Mao was given strategic leadership over the Red Army and also admitted to the Standing Committee of the Politburo, the highest policy-making body of the CCP. Ever after this, Mao was the dominant personality of the Chinese Communist movement. The conference at Zunyi made his career, and throughout the rest of his life he retained supreme command over the Red Army.

The adventures and narrow escapes encountered and overcome by the Long Marchers are too numerous to recount in detail. One challenge, however, the crossing of the Luding Bridge in a steep and mountainous region in Sichuan province, stands out as the most notable. The bridge was a suspension bridge from which KMT troops had removed the wooden planking. Large numbers of KMT troops waited on the other side of the bridge, ready to resist any Communist troops who attempted to cross it. At great odds and with enormous casualties, the Long Marchers captured and crossed the bridge and moved on.

The Long March finally ended in Shaanxi province in October 1935, and by 1936 the Communists had holed up in the town of Yan'an, a strategically important area that was nearly impossible to bomb from the air because the dwellings were dug into the faces of nearly vertical cliffs. There the Chinese Communists remained headquartered until the end of World War II in August 1945, beyond the reach of Japanese and KMT foes alike. The time in Yan'an was a breather for Mao, and there he received foreign sympathizers, gave interviews to adventurous American journalists, wrote theoretical essays, fine-tuned his ideology, and regained his lost weight.

THE XI'AN INCIDENT AND THE SECOND UNITED FRONT

The KMT government of Chiang Kai-shek was, of course, not content to allow Mao and the Communists to remain unchallenged in Yan'an. Because the approaches to Yan'an were heavily defended, Chiang blockaded the entire area around the town to starve the Communists out by choking off their supplies. He also continued his campaign of hunting down other pockets of Communist activity in China and violently eliminating them.

This did not always play well in Chinese public opinion. Many Chinese who otherwise had reservations about the Chinese Communist movement wondered why, during Japan's ongoing invasion of China, Chiang was intent on ignoring the Japanese and killing large numbers of his own Chinese people who happened to be Communists. Was not an invasion by foreigners a greater threat and shame than insurrection by a few thousand misguided rebels? By late December 1935, students in Beiping and Shanghai were protesting against the anti-Communist campaigns. Their simple insistence that "Chinese must not kill Chinese" had a direct and powerful appeal to large segments of the Chinese public, including the very military units in Shaanxi that were manning the blockades and fighting the Chinese Communists.

These units were under the control of a young general named Zhang Xueliang, son of a former warlord and himself only nominally allied with Chiang Kai-shek's KMT government. Zhang and his men were not at all enthusiastic about fighting the Communists while the Japanese invasion was unfolding, and by the summer of 1936 Zhang had significantly downscaled his anti-Communist campaigns and was, by some reports, even conferring with Chinese Communist leaders. Continuing reports to this effect were distressing to Chiang Kai-shek, and in early December 1936 he boarded a plane and flew to Xi'an, the provincial capital of Shaanxi, intending to persuade Zhang Xueliang to continue with the anti-Communist struggle. He arrived in Xi'an on December 10 and soon realized that he was getting nowhere with Zhang.

What happened next is a matter of some controversy. In the early hours of December 12, Zhang and his men apparently surrounded Chiang Kai-shek's quarters to kidnap him. Chiang attempted to escape but was soon captured by Zhang's men, who treated him well but insisted that he call off the anti-Communist campaign and instead fight the Japanese. On December 25, 1936, Chiang Kai-shek was released and allowed to fly back to Nanjing, but with Zhang Xueliang in his company as a prisoner. Once back in Nanjing, Chiang Kai-shek did call off the anti-Communist offensive but placed Zhang under house arrest. (Zhang endured this punishment after the removal of the Nationalist government to Taiwan in 1949. He was finally released in the late 1980s by Chiang Kai-shek's son and allowed to move to Hawaii. Astonishingly, Zhang was still alive in the year 2000, aged 101.) In early 1937 Chiang's government declared all-out war on the Japanese invaders, much to the relief and satisfaction of the Chinese Communists and much of the rest of China's educated population as well. This was the beginning of the Second United Front, a period of renewed cooperation between the Nationalists and Communists. In the First United Front the common enemy had been the warlords, and now the common enemy was Japan. The Second United Front lasted until 1941, when it largely fell apart as both parties renewed armed attacks on one another.

Was Zhang a sacrificial lamb of sorts? Was an agreement reached during the Xi'an Incident that enabled Chiang Kai-shek to call off the anti-Communist offensive while saving face? Did Zhang agree to become Chiang's prisoner in exchange for the cancellation of his war against the Communists? Only Zhang Xueliang knew the real answers to these questions, and hopefully he had them recorded somewhere for the benefit of history prior to his death in the early twenty-first century. In the People's Republic of China today, Zhang is highly revered, and if while he was alive he had ever chosen to return to the mainland, he would have received a tumultuous hero's welcome.

WORLD WAR II IN CHINA

Europeans usually date the beginning of World War II to 1939 and Adolf Hitler's invasion of Poland. Americans often date it to December 7, 1941, and the infamous Japanese sneak attack on Pearl Harbor. For the Chinese, it began with the Japanese invasion of Manchuria in September 1931 and did not end until Japan's defeat by the United States in August 1945.

World War II in China was at times a complicated three-way war, with the Chinese Communists and Nationalists sometimes fighting each other as well as the Japanese. Each side accused the other of secretly collaborating with the Japanese and waging half-hearted war against them. The truth is that, after the American entry into the war in late December 1941, *both* sides became convinced that the United States would eventually prevail against Japan, and they decided to retain their best forces in reserve for the civil war and final showdown they knew would follow Japan's surrender. Some U.S. forces were committed to the war effort in China. General Joseph Stilwell commanded American army units in southern China and found Chiang Kai-shek's refusal to wage an all-out war against the Japanese supremely frustrating, and rogue fighter pilots under Claire Chennault of American Flying Tigers fame shot down many Japanese aircraft for Chiang Kai-shek in the early months of America's involvement in World War II. (Chiang reportedly paid $500 for each Japanese plane shot down.) In the end, however, American forces in China did not play a decisive role in defeating the Japanese. The major actions of the United States against the Japanese empire occurred in the Pacific War.

World War II in China proved to be the Chinese Communists' salvation. The power vacuum created in China by the Japanese invasion and the Second United Front gave them the opportunity to recover and consolidate their hold over vast areas of Chinese territory. Without the Japanese invasion the Chinese Communists would never have come to power; Mao directly admitted as much to Tanaka Kakuei, the prime minister of Japan during the early 1970s (Li 1994, 567–68). During the war Mao apportioned his efforts as follows: 70 percent to Communist expansion, 20 percent to cooperation with the KMT, and 10 percent to fighting the Japanese invaders (Hsü 1990, 589).

Unnerved by the Second United Front and the prospect of fighting a China united against them, in July 1937 Japanese militarists unleashed a full-scale invasion of China. They soon occupied several major Chinese cities, and by December they had captured Nanjing, then internationally recognized as China's capital and the seat of Chiang Kai-shek's government. Chiang abandoned the city to the Japanese but did not surrender to them; he and his government relocated far up the Yangtze to the city of Chongqing (Chungking) in mountainous Sichuan province, where they remained for the duration of World War II. Frustrated that their capture of Nanjing did not result in China's official surrender, the Japanese invaders brutally murdered more than 300,000 innocent and unarmed civilians in the city. The Rape of Nanking, as it became known in the West, shocked the world and led to deep shame in Japan at the end of the war when the Japanese public learned about it. The Rape of Nanking, a historical reality still denied by right-wing extremists in Japan, remains today a source of considerable anti-Japanese feeling in China, in part because of the Japanese government's continual refusal to apologize for it officially. A recent book written by Iris Chang, *The Rape of Nanking: The Forgotten Holocaust of World War II* (1997), contains graphic descriptions of Japanese atrocities in Nanjing, including murder, torture, and widespread rape. Many booksellers in Japan today are afraid to display or sell the book for fear of violent and destructive reprisals by ultraconservative Japanese groups.

By 1944 the Japanese controlled roughly the eastern half of China, but they never succeeded in conquering the entire country. Chongqing and Yan'an, the wartime capitals of the Chinese Nationalists and Communists, respectively, remained beyond their reach throughout the war, although Japanese aircraft bombed the cities whenever they could. Japanese power in China had begun evaporating by late 1944 and early 1945 as troops were pulled out of China for the anticipated defense of the Japanese home islands against advancing American forces.

7

The People's Republic: From First Breath to Mao's Death

Mao Zedong was both the Lenin and the Stalin of the Chinese Revolution, both the revolutionary founder and the post-revolutionary tyrant.

Maurice Meisner (Meisner 2007, 192)

CIVIL WAR IN CHINA

The use of two atomic bombs by the Americans against Japan in August 1945 ended the war sooner than anyone in China expected. Chiang Kai-shek returned in triumph to Nanjing in the fall of 1945, but soon the ebullient mood in China was muted by what everyone knew was on the horizon: the final showdown between the Nationalists and the Communists.

For a time the Americans tried to mediate in China and prevent civil war. This, however, turned out to be an impossibility because each side was determined to defeat the other and was not sincerely interested in any sort of reconciliation. At the same time, however, both sides attempted to curry favor with the United States and tried to humor the idealistic American diplomats who sought to reconcile the Nationalists and the Communists. The U.S. government was sympathetic with the Nationalists for the simple reason that Chiang Kai-shek's regime was almost universally recognized as China's government at the time.

Immediately after Japan's surrender, American diplomat Patrick Hurley, a cantankerous and apparently prematurely senile man, tried to get the two sides together to conduct discussions. Yielding to U.S. pressure, Chiang Kai-shek invited Mao to Chongqing, but Mao balked because he feared a KMT trap. After Hurley gave the assurances of the U.S. government that there would be no trap, Mao boarded an airplane for the first time in his life and flew from Yan'an to Chongqing in mid-August 1945. Six weeks of talks yielded no practical results, however, and Mao went back to Yan'an determined to prepare for all-out war with Chiang Kai-shek. Hurley returned to the United States a discouraged and disillusioned man, but the Americans were not yet ready to give up on China. In December 1945 the United States sent another envoy to China, General George C. Marshall, the originator of the Marshall Plan for the postwar recovery of Europe. Because of Marshall's enormous prestige, the Nationalists and Communists came to the negotiating table once more in early 1946 and feigned a tentative settlement of their differences. By March, however, both sides were fighting once again. "Talk, talk, fight, fight" was the guiding principle for the Communists at this time, and it might as well have been for the Nationalists as well. Marshall finally left China in January 1947, thoroughly disgusted with the refusal of both sides in the Chinese civil war to engage in peace talks in good faith.

After Marshall's departure from China, civil war flared up in Manchuria. American military advisors had encouraged Chiang to maintain his hold over southern China rather than spread his forces too thin in the Communist-dominated north. Chiang, however, stubbornly refused to heed their advice and had the American military airlift thousands of Nationalist troops to areas throughout northern China. Chiang's insistence on attempting to recapture the north was simple from the Nationalists' point of view: Manchuria and other parts of northern China had been occupied by Japanese invading forces since 1931, and one major reason for China's war with Japan was over these very areas. Strategically, however, Chiang's moves against the north were quite foolish, and his campaigns turned out just as American military advisors had feared: his widely spread forces were eventually outmaneuvered and overwhelmed. By late 1947 his armies in Manchuria had been largely wiped out, and in December 1948 Beijing (then still called Beiping) fell to the Communists.

Nanjing itself fell to the Communists in April 1949, and on October 1, 1949, Mao was confident enough in the Communists' ultimate victory that he proclaimed in Beiping (now renamed Beijing) the liberation of China and the founding of the new People's Republic of China to jubilant throngs of celebrants in Tiananmen Square. He announced to China and the world that China had stood up. Meanwhile, the remnants of Chiang Kai-shek's corrupt government and discouraged military fled to the island of Taiwan, where it has remained ever since.

THE KOREAN WAR

The Korean War came as a surprise to the new Chinese Communist regime. The People's Republic of China on the mainland was initially enthusiastic about extending its land reform program throughout the rest of the country and "liberating" Taiwan by armed attack. The Korean War, however, interrupted these plans and indirectly saved Chiang Kai-shek's regime on Taiwan. Mao was initially content to let Korea fight its own civil war, but when it became apparent that General Douglas MacArthur, the American commanding general of the United Nations forces defending southern Korea against northern Korean aggression, quite possibly intended to invade China, Mao decided to commit Chinese ground troops to the war.

At the end of World War II, Korea was divided at roughly the 38th parallel, with a Soviet-backed Communist dictatorship north of it and an undemocratic dictatorship backed by the United States to the south. On June 25, 1950, North Korean forces launched a massive blitzkrieg-style attack on the south and quickly overwhelmed it. Two days later, a Security Council resolution passed at the United Nations condemned North Korean aggression and decided to commit UN ground troops to Korea. (The Soviet Union did not participate in this resolution because it had boycotted the Security Council to protest the UN's refusal to seat the new Communist Chinese regime's representatives on the Security Council.) This same day, U.S. President Harry Truman ordered elements of the U.S. Seventh Fleet into the Taiwan Strait to save Taiwan from Communist attack. The United States has more or less been committed to the defense of Taiwan ever since.

In September 1950 UN forces under MacArthur successfully launched a daring surprise amphibious landing at Inchon on Korea's west coast and quickly put the North Korean invaders to flight, pushing them back to north of the 38th parallel. In historical hindsight, this retreat of North Korean forces probably should have been the end of UN involvement in the war. But it did not end there, and by late October the UN forces had advanced far into North Korean territory and occupied Pyongyang, the North Korean capital. MacArthur continued to drive northward and to make reckless statements about pushing on to the Yalu River (the boundary between China and Korea) and even beyond it into China. The war in Korea was now suffering from "mission creep" and was turning into an entirely new war.

Washington and the United Nations ignored repeated warnings from China that it would not stand idly by if MacArthur continued in this reckless plan. Finally, on November 26, 1950, millions of Chinese Communist "volunteers" (many armed only with clubs or spears) who had been massed at the Yalu River invaded Korea and swarmed southward in overwhelming numbers, driving the UN forces southward to the 38th parallel and beyond. The withdrawal in the face of Chinese human-wave tactics was the longest retreat in the history of the U.S. Army. On January 4, 1951, Chinese Communist troops captured Seoul, the capital of South Korea. By April 1951, however, UN forces had once again driven the Chinese and their North Korean allies back north of the 38th parallel. After this, MacArthur began talking again about advancing to the Yalu River. This was too much for President Truman, who fired and recalled MacArthur on April 11. After this the war degenerated into a protracted conflict of attrition and stalemate. The Chinese abandoned their earlier human-wave tactics and practiced classical guerrilla warfare, resulting in thousands of UN casualties. The war dragged on inconclusively until July 1953, when a cease-fire was reached that essentially reestablished the prewar boundaries in Korea.

The Korean War was technically a UN action, but the United States assumed a disproportionate amount of the war burden: 54,000 of the 57,000 non-Korean UN troops who died in combat were Americans. China today regards the Korean War as an American operation and seems to forget that the war was sanctioned by a vote at the United Nations. Today, many patriotic mainland Chinese are fond of imagining that China "taught the United States a lesson" in the Korean War by fighting the most powerful military machine in the world to a standstill. Thus, in this view, China was announcing to the world that the People's Republic was here to stay and that the Chinese military was no longer the ragtag collection of listless and ineptly led ragamuffins against whom Japanese forces had prevailed so easily during the 1930s in Manchuria. China's "victory" over U.S.–dominated forces in Korea is, indeed, part of the national patriotic mythology in China. In fact, however, UN forces were gradually succeeding in pushing Chinese and North Korean forces back north of the 38th parallel when the war ended. The Chinese "victory" was achieved at an enormous and disproportionate burden to China: over one million died in combat. Not all of the Chinese troops were volunteers, and some 14,000 of them who were captured elected to go to Chiang Kai-shek's Taiwan rather than live under communism in mainland China.

Chinese intervention in the Korean War did not fundamentally alter the situation in Korea. The war started and ended with the Communist North Koreans largely confined north of the 38th parallel and the non-Communist South Koreans south of it. This situation remains to this day, with a truce rather than a formal treaty keeping the peace between the two sides of the divided Korean peninsula. Today North Korea is still internationally isolated and economically backward, but China has in recent years reined in some of North Korea's excesses and encouraged it to open to the outside world.

Brainwashing

The Chinese Communist use of brainwashing or coercive indoctrination became known to the outside world in the 1950s, especially after the outbreak of the Korean War, when Chinese Communist forces began capturing UN troops and the practice came to the attention of Western governments and media. The Chinese Communists called the practice "thought reform" or "reform through labor"; the term "brainwashing" was coined by the American journalist Edward Hunter in 1950 to describe the way the Chinese Communists used "struggle groups," physical and mental abuse, and social deprivation to coerce reluctant or defiant individuals into supporting their cause. The effects of brainwashing were not always long lasting, although the practice did succeed in permanently altering the thinking of some people.

Two examples of more lasting effects of brainwashing are the cases of Allyn and Adele Rickett, married students of Chinese language at the University of Pennsylvania who received Fulbright grants in 1948 to study in China. In Beijing they engaged in intelligence work for the U.S. Naval Intelligence Service, and after the outbreak of the Korean War they were arrested and imprisoned for espionage. During their captivity the Ricketts were subjected to psychological and physical torment, including verbal abuse and being forced to wear handcuffs for long periods or to stand for several hours at a time. Adele Rickett recalled her treatment in a Chinese Communist prison camp in the following terms:

As we heard the doors being locked in preparation for turning in, Jeng Ai-ling suddenly asked, "What have you been thinking about the last couple of hours?"

Tears of self-pity welled in my eyes as I answered, "I've been thinking about all the terrible things the imperialists have done in China."

Jen Ai-ling exploded, "Filthy spy! You really have all the tricks!" She turned to Mei Chi-yün, "Just look at her, trying to gain our sympathy. She's running true to form." Then back to me, "You don't have a human heart at all. You've got a dog's heart, haven't you?"

Afraid that denial would bring on further accusation of obstinacy, I remained silent, head drooping.

"Answer me! You've got a dog's heart, haven't you?"

I nodded and replied in a tiny voice, "Yes, I guess I have."

"Ha! Shouted Mei Chi-yün. "That's a fine thing. Defiling your parents like that. If you're a dog, what does that make them? Really you have the character of a filthy spy."

Just then the whistle blew. The two women looked at each other hesitantly for a moment and then Jeng Ai-ling said, disgustedly, "Get to bed. And you'd better think about your attitude."

The next two or three days were spent in a struggle to make me face up to those elements in my character which made me one moment cringing and fawning, the next obstinate and defiant. Over and over they resorted to the method of having me stand on the floor two or three hours at a time, hoping that this would stir me to take a serious look at myself. It was obvious, however, that my continued standing weighted on Jeng Ai-ling's mind, for she used the flimsiest of pretexts to excuse me and let me sit down. (Rickett 1981, 246)

After their release from Chinese Communist captivity in 1955 and their subsequent return to the United States, the Ricketts continued to have generally positive opinions of the Chinese Communists and of their experience in China. "In our own personal lives we have found that the experience in China has been of tremendous value," they wrote in 1981. " . . . [W]e are both convinced that what we learned during our prison experience has made us far happier and more active people" (Rickett 1981, 343).

Life in the thought reform camps was sometimes unspeakably brutal. Bao Ruo-wang (Jean Pasqualini) recalls a summary execution inmates at his prison farm were required to witness:

The first one to come before us was Wang, our one-armed warder, and he was quickly joined by the brigade leader in charge of production, a man named Yen, [and] perhaps a dozen guards. . . . In the middle of them all was the barber, tied up in chains and fetters. A rope around his neck and cinched at the waist kept his head bowed. His hands were tied behind his back. The guards shoved him directly in front of us. He stood there silently, like a trussed penitent, as the steam wisped up around his feet. Yen had a speech.

"I have something awful to speak about. I'm not happy to do it and it's nothing to be proud of. But it is my duty and it should be a lesson for you. This rotten egg here was jailed on a morals charge—homosexual relations with a boy. He only received seven years for this offence. Later, when working in the paper mill, his behaviour was constantly bad and he stole repeatedly. His sentence was doubled. Now we have established that while here, he seduced a young prisoner nineteen years old—a mentally retarded prisoner. If this happened in society, he would be severely punished. But by doing what he did here, he not only sinned morally but he also dirtied the reputation of the prison and the great policy of Reform Through Labour. Therefore, in consideration of his repeated offences, the representative of the Supreme People's Court will now read you his sentence."

The man in the blue uniform strode forward and read out the somber document, a recapitulation of the offences that ended with the decision of the People's Court: death with immediate execution of sentence.

Everything happened so suddenly then that I didn't even have the time to be shocked or frightened. Before the man in the blue uniform had even finished pronouncing the last word the barber was dead. The guard standing behind him pulled out a huge pistol and blew his head open. (Bao 1973, 189–90)

Harry Wu (Wu Hongda) was an intellectual arrested in 1960 for speaking up for himself, which was considered a crime during the Hundred Flowers campaign. He was subjected to similar intimidation:

Around midnight a duty prisoner called my name from the doorway. I tried to still my growing panic as I followed him outside into a small, bare room. A police captain sat behind a single table. "Squat down," he barked without looking up. He shone the desk lamp onto my face. "State your name, age, occupation, and the nature of your crime."

"I am a counterrevolutionary rightist," I answered quickly. "In the Hundred Flowers campaign I attacked the Communist Party. I still have a lot of poisonous ideas."

"We know all that. What else? What else?" shouted my interrogator. "Don't you understand the Party's policy? Lenience to those who confess, harshness to those who resist reform." He stood up, walked around me, then kicked open a second door. I saw a body hanging from the rafters, then another sprawled on the wet floor. I couldn't see their faces or tell if they were unconscious or dead. "This is what happens to those who resist the Party's authority," he snapped. "You're a young student. I'll give you another chance. Tomorrow night come back and confess fully." Terribly shaken by the glimpse of those who had apparently resisted reform, I returned to my slot on the kang [bed]. I had no idea what I would say at the next session. I knew only that if my answers sounded false or incomplete I too would be hanging from the interrogation room ceiling. I didn't sleep at all that night. (Wu 1994, 49–50)

NATIONAL RECONSTRUCTION EFFORTS, 1949–1956

The end of the Korean War brought some stability and normalcy to China for the next few years. Ultimately, however, Mao became concerned because China was getting down to the practical tasks of peacetime reconstruction and rational economic planning and seemed no longer to possess the ideological focus and revolutionary ardor of pre-liberation days. Longing to see China realize his revolutionary objectives before his own death, Mao attempted to propel China quickly along the revolutionary path to socialism. In this he was excessively theoretical and idealistic and ignored the real-world on-the-ground consequences of his adventurism. As a result, China was plunged into two decades of chaos and turmoil. From 1956 until his death in 1976, Mao more or less had his way with China and set the cause of modernizing his country back 20 years. In retrospect it is clear that Mao was a fine fighter and theoretician but largely a failure as a practical peacetime leader. Mao's contributions to China essentially ended with liberation in 1949.

The first decade of the People's Republic started out well enough. The Korean War was a brief but significant interruption to China's plans for domestic reconstruction and political consolidation. Even during the Korean War, however, some reforms proceeded. Positive reforms included the land reform program of confiscating all farmland and redistributing it to landless peasants and reform of marriage law, which outlawed concubinage and polygamy and made it easier for women to obtain divorces. Negative development included a nationwide roundup and execution of more than 500,000 "counterrevolutionaries" (basically anyone deemed hostile to the new Communist regime, including former Nationalist officials and people who had voiced disapproval of what the Communists were doing) and new "reform through labor" techniques that employed backbreaking physical labor and subtle psychological torture. The object of reform-through-labor efforts was to change the thought patterns of people deemed hostile to the new state but not deserving of the death penalty.

The People's Republic used Soviet models and five-year plans to achieve its socialist transformation. For its first four years, the People's Republic of China, or PRC, focused on education, industrialization, and health care. The first formal Soviet-style-five-year plan, which extended from 1953 to 1957, continued efforts to improve education and health care, but it was concerned primarily with improving heavy industrial and agricultural production. Industrial output steadily increased during this period, thanks largely to the assistance of Soviet industrial experts. Agriculture was, however, a different story. Mao and the more idealistic of the Chinese Communists envisioned an agricultural collectivization scheme under which China's peasants would combine themselves into agricultural producers' cooperatives (often abbreviated APCs) of between 40 and 300 households. These cooperatives would, they anticipated, pool labor and create much more efficient agriculture. In practice, however, the results of collectivization were disappointing, and more practically minded national leaders sought the dissolution of the APCs. The practical camp eventually prevailed over the idealistic camp, and by 1955 several thousand APCs had been disbanded.

THE HUNDRED FLOWERS CAMPAIGN

Mao and his ideological colleagues viewed these disbandments with alarm but for a time could do nothing about them. Mao was careful and deliberate in conducting warfare, but when it came to peacetime national reconstruction he proved to be an impatient and impetuous man. He saw the relative peace and prosperity of the 1950s as a step away from the old revolutionary commitment he had known in the Long March and Yan'an days. He sat and stewed at the dissolution of the APCs but could do little about it because he was outvoted in the Politburo. But votes were not everything, and Mao knew quite well that he was still the dominant personality of the Communist party and had an enormous reservoir of esteem and good will among the common people. In early 1957 he published an important essay entitled "On the Correct Handling of Contradictions Among the People" in which he urged those who disagreed with his policies to come forward and offer constructive criticisms and suggestions. "Let a hundred flowers bloom and a hundred schools contend" was his message, and it eventually backfired on him.

The magnitude of the response might have surprised Mao. Thousands of intellectuals took Mao at his word and criticized the Soviet Union, Mao's impetuosity in the agricultural collectivization movement, and even socialism and the CCP itself. Some posters put up by students in Beijing were almost frenetic in their denunciations. By May 1957 Mao announced that criticisms of socialism and the party would no longer be tolerated, and a distinction was drawn between "fragrant flowers" and "poisonous weeds." Those who had already uttered "poisonous weeds" were tracked down by the hundreds of thousands and "sent down" to the countryside for backbreaking agricultural "reform through labor."

Did Mao plan all of this from the start and use the Hundred Flowers movement as a ruse to smoke out his critics and then crack down on them, or did he start the movement with the best intentions, only to be taken aback by the magnitude of the negative response? Many scholars, as well as many Chinese people who lived through this period, disagree on the answer to this question.

THE GREAT LEAP FORWARD

For reasons that are not altogether clear, Mao and his critics in the highest levels of the CCP worked out a reconciliation among themselves in the summer of 1957. Perhaps they were fearful of the groundswell of public opinion voiced against them and their party during the abortive Hundred Flowers movement. At any rate, by the summer of 1957, a largely united effort was made by the CCP leadership to push forward the agricultural collectivization movement once more. Mao had argued all along that the APC movement had failed in the mid-1950s because it was not pushed *fast* enough. He was impatient to see the agricultural transformation of China through to its completion, and his former critics apparently decided to go along with him and give it one more try.

The CCP launched the Great Leap Forward in September 1957. Its purposes were twofold: to collectivize agriculture and thereby dramatically increase agricultural production, and to surpass Great Britain in industrial production within the impossibly lofty goal of 15 years. The collectivization of agriculture was accomplished by October 1958. In industry it was decided that China would follow a decentralized approach, with thousands of small-scale industrial enterprises located throughout the countryside. Huge numbers of peasants were transferred to these local, rural industrial efforts, which led to a shortage of agricultural labor. The results for Chinese agriculture were catastrophic.

Enthusiasm for the Great Leap Forward and its goals was tremendous throughout China. In the countryside a movement against the "four pests" (flies, rats, sparrows, and mosquitoes) was launched, and so many sparrows were killed that the numbers of insects actually *increased* because the sparrows, their natural predators, were disappearing. With the boundless enthusiasm prevailing in the countryside and the completion of agricultural collectivization, elevated agricultural production goals were announced in the summer of 1958, and bumper crops were expected. Peasants and agricultural leaders naively believed that these impossibly high goals were actually achievable. Government propaganda was at its shrillest pitch in the fall of 1958, and one famous report claimed that peasants at one APC had successfully planted grain so closely and densely together that children could stand on top of the planted stocks and not sink down to the ground.

In industry, the most well-known efforts were the so-called backyard furnaces or small-scale steelmaking efforts that had sprung up all over the countryside by the fall of 1958. Almost 100 million people were diverted for labor in these efforts, and in their enthusiasm to achieve elevated production quotas, millions of ordinary Chinese even donated their pots and other metal tools to be melted down. The results were catastrophic; the steel produced was of inferior, unusable quality, and millions of peasants had been distracted from their agricultural work, naively believing that agricultural collectivization would somehow make up for the absence of their labor.

The autumn harvest of 1958 was disastrously small, but government propaganda reported that agricultural production had doubled. (The vast majority of the APCs did not want to disappoint the government with accurate production reports, so they grossly exaggerated them.) The government took these inflated production figures at face value and collected grain tax according to them. As a result, millions of people in China starved to death during the winter of 1958–1959 before the government could get food to them. By early 1959 there was grain rationing in the cities, and meat all but disappeared from the markets because farm animals could not be fed what little grain and other crops had been produced.

Written eyewitness recollections of starvation during the Great Leap Forward are relatively rare, and living memory of the famine will have all but disappeared by approximately 2030. A few telling descriptions of it do survive, however, including a harrowing account by an old woman who lived in Anhui province near Fengyang along the Huai River at the time:

> The communal canteen did not serve any proper food, just wild grasses, peanut shells and sweet potato skins. Because of this diet we had terrible problems. Some were constipated but others had constant diarrhoea and could not get beyond the front door. Yet if they found that a house or the area around it was dirty, they would place a black flag outside. If it was clean, they put up a white flag. I had to try and clean up the mess but at the time I had difficulty walking.
>
> My legs and hands were swollen and I felt that at any moment I would die. Instead of walking to the fields to look for wild grass, I crawled and rolled to save energy. Several old women tried to get grass from ponds or rivers but because they had to stand in the water their legs became infected.
>
> All the trees in the village had been cut down. Any nearby were all stripped of bark. I peeled off the bark of a locust tree and cooked it as if it were rice soup. It tasted like wood and was sticky.
>
> At the time the villagers looked quite fat and even healthy because they were swollen but when they were queuing up at the canteen to eat, they would suddenly collapse and could not get up. Some could only walk using a stick . . .
>
> More than half of the villagers died, mostly between New Year [1960] and April or May. In one of our neighbours' houses, three boys and a girl starved. In one brother's family two children died. Another family of sixteen died. Many families disappeared completely with no survivors at all. The production team chief's daughter-in-law and his grandson starved to death. He then boiled and ate the corpse of the child but he also died. When the village teacher was on the verge of death, he said to his wife, "Why should we keep our child? If we eat him then I can survive and later we can produce another child." His wife refused to do this and her husband died. (Becker 1996, 135–36)

Bao Ruo-wang (Jean Pasqualini), a Chinese and French citizen, was imprisoned in late 1957 on charges in the course of the anti-rightist campaign, and his prison memoirs recall the widespread eating of "food substitutes" in China at the time in vain attempts to stave off hunger pangs and give a sense of satisfied fullness in the stomachs of starving people:

> The signal that truly desperate times were upon us came in early December, when a horse-drawn cart entered the compound and a

prisoner detail began unloading the cargo: dark brown sheets of an unknown material, rigid and light, each one measuring about three by five feet. No one had any idea of what they were. Two weeks later we were called into the auditorium to hear the answer. The stuff was paper pulp, and we were going to eat it. Food Substitute, the prison officials called it—*dai shipin*. I'll never forget the words. Since there wasn't enough food to go around in China, the search was on for something to replace it and we prisoners had the honor of being the guinea pigs for the various ersatzes the scientific community came up with. (Bao 1973, 216–19)

Harry Wu (Wu Hongda) describes his own ordeal by hunger in a brainwashing camp during this time:

Day by day, our hunger became more intense. Without food, the body uses calories stored in muscle tissues and even in bones to provide energy and sustain life. I began to understand the process of starvation. When death strikes in the camps, malnutrition is rarely the direct cause. The heart does not stop beating from lack of nourishment. Depending on your overall health, you can survive for a week, even two, with no food or water at all. In such a depleted state, it is other things that kill you.

Sometimes you catch cold, your lungs fill with fluid, and finally you stop breathing. Sometimes bacteria in the food cause continuous diarrhea that leads to death. Sometimes infection from a wound becomes fatal. The cause of death is always noted in your file as pleurisy or food poisoning or injury, never as starvation. (Wu 1994, 95–96)

Wu Ningkun, another intellectual who spoke his mind during the feigned openness of Mao's Hundred Flowers campaign, wound up in a brainwashing camp in 1960. He was fortunate enough to have family members who could bring him some food during the worst months of the famine, but other inmates were not as lucky.

One of the have-nots was a young scholar of classical Chinese who slept on my right on the kang [bed]. One day he handed me a note written in his elegant calligraphy in the style of the great classical calligrapher Liu Gongquan. "I beg you to lend one of your pancakes, professor. I solemnly promise to pay you back with double interest when my wife comes from Hunan province to bring me food from home." I hesitated, because I felt I had no right to be generous with the food, which represented the sacrifices of my relatives were making to save my life. A second note contained the same message with a proverb added: "He who saves a man's life does a deed greater than building the Buddha a seven-story pagoda." My heart melted at his elegant Liu-style calligraphy. I had always admired and envied people who were expert at the Liu style, which I had imitated in vain in my school days. Such elegant calligraphy reduced to such abject circumstances! What had the nation come to, the nation that tirelessly flaunted its ancient culture! When the others were not looking, I handed Lao Liu a pancake. He gobbled it up in no time.

"You don't know how good it tasted, Lao Wu," he told me in his Hunan accent the next day when he was being removed to the cell set aside for the sick, whose continued presence in the regular cells the offers thought was demoralizing to the other inmates. (Wu 1993, 134–35)

During the heady euphoria of the "backyard furnace" fiasco in late 1958, Mao himself never seriously doubted the inflated production figures. The enthusiasm and creative energies of the masses unleashed during the Great Leap Forward were more important to him than strictly accurate production reports. The serious nationwide shortage of food in December 1958 was unknown to Mao because "no one was willing to tell him the truth" (Li 1994, 283). When he did finally learn the terrible truth about the Great Leap Forward, he refused to assume responsibility for it. Mao subscribed to the popular traditional Chinese idea that the emperor could do no wrong himself; he could only be deceived and misguided by his advisers and court officials. "As the emperor, he believed in his own infallibility. If wrong decisions were made, wrong policies introduced, the fault lay not with him but with the information provided him. The emperor could not be wrong, but he could be deceived" (Li 1994, 296).

By the summer of 1959, everyone in China realized that something had gone disastrously wrong with the Great Leap Forward, but very few people dared say so openly for fear of offending Mao and his supporters. One person who did dare say that the emperor had no clothes was Peng Dehuai, a general with a reputation for bluntness who had been with the Chinese Communists since the Long March days and was a hero of the Korean War. At a meeting of the Politburo (a small and powerful core group of high-level leaders within the Chinese Communist party) held in the summer of 1959 in Lushan, Peng Dehuai circulated a letter that was scathingly critical of Mao's policies and the disastrous results of the Great Leap Forward. Mao was offended at the tone and content of the letter and was aghast to learn that Peng had probably circulated it at the suggestion of Soviet leader Nikita Khrushchev. Peng's blunt criticisms forced Mao to own up to the errors of the Great Leap Forward, but Mao excused himself for them with the banal observation that everyone makes mistakes. He then moved with a vengeance against Peng Dehuai and denounced him as a traitor to China who had done a foreigner's bidding. Seeing which way the wind was blowing, Peng's supporters (including Deng Xiaoping) abandoned him, and he alone took the fall for his impolitic criticisms of Mao. Peng, who was dismissed as Minister of Defense and replaced by Lin Biao, was hounded during the Cultural Revolution over his confrontation with Mao and eventually died in a prison of cruel neglect in 1974. Today, however, Peng's reputation has been posthumously rehabilitated, and he is admired even in Taiwan for his courageous and forthright criticisms of Mao's policies.

Mao decided to learn the truth about the Great Leap by traveling to his home village of Shaoshan in Hunan. There he would encounter no carefully staged performances or artificially inflated agricultural production figures. He could trust his fellow provincials and home villagers to speak forthrightly and honestly with him. His trip there awakened him to the horrible reality of the Great Leap Forward, but even then he still did not want to do anything to dampen the enthusiasm of the masses. His basic confidence in the movement remained unshaken. His confidence was not fully undermined until 1960:

> Mao of course was immune to the tribulations of famine, and everyone tried to shield him from its effects, but he knew the severity of the crisis. The documents he received every day now allowed him no escape from the truth. Reports were coming in from all over the country, and by the summer of 1960, he had become so depressed that he took again to his bed. He seemed psychologically incapable of confronting the effects of the famine. (Li 1994, 339)

Mao did, however, finally did make one concession to the famine: He stopped eating meat. "Everyone is starving. I can't eat meat," he said (Li 1994, 340).

Mao never did admit that his Great Leap Forward was a complete failure. He was finally forced to admit that at least some of the responsibility for the disaster was his, but it came across as insincere and even staged. He was distressed that party and state began operating independently of him. He became depressed and took to his bed during his disgrace within the party during the early 1960s, all the while craving popular approval and adulation and plotting his next political moves. He rarely attended meetings but did read the daily transcripts of the proceedings in the Great Hall of the People. He became increasingly suspicious of the loyalty of Liu Shaoqi and saw Lin Biao as one of his few true supporters. Mao also admired Chen Boda for defending the Great Leap Forward:

> Confronted two years later with the massive starvation during the Great Leap Forward, Chen dismissed the millions of deaths. "This is an unavoidable phenomenon in our forward march," he declared. No wonder Mao liked this mean, petty, and ambitious man. In one simple sentence, he absolved Mao of responsibility for one of the greatest catastrophes the country had ever faced—a catastrophe for which Mao's policies were directly responsible. (Li 1994, 390)

The Great Leap Forward was, in reality, a great leap backward. An estimated 20 to 40 million people died of starvation between 1959 and 1962 because of the food shortages created by the movement. (This number, already appallingly tragic enough, would have been much higher had not Canada and Australia sold, over Washington's objections, thousands of tons of wheat to China.) Agricultural production in China did not recover its 1957 levels until the early 1970s. The Great Leap scandalized the Soviets and solidified their determination to distance themselves from Mao's madcap adventurism. For the Nationalists on Taiwan, it was just one more instance of Chinese Communist tyranny. This time, however, instead of fearing and loathing the Communists, the Nationalists simply laughed at them. Ever since Great Leap days, the idiom "primitive methods for making steel" (*tufa liangang*) has been a part of popular speech in Taiwan as an idiom for doing things in a comically outmoded and inefficient manner.

During the famine associated with the Great Leap Forward, "Mao knew that people were dying by the millions. He did not care" (Li 1994, 125). He often shocked foreign visitors with his callous attitude toward human life. India's Prime Minister Jawaharlal Nehru was appalled when Mao told him not to fear the atom bomb; it is nothing but a "paper tiger" because "China has many people. They cannot be bombed out of existence. . . . The deaths of ten or twenty million people is nothing to be afraid of" (Li 1994, 125). Later he expounded on his "paper tiger" theory again to Soviet leader Anastas Mikoyan. Mikoyan was so taken aback by Mao's nonchalance about China's potential loss of tens of millions of lives in a nuclear war that he sought out Dr. Li and had a heart-to-heart conversation and a stiff drink with him. In the wake of Khrushchev's visit to Beijing in 1958, he shocked Dr. Li with the following tirade:

> Khrushchev doesn't know what he's talking about. . . . He wants to improve relations with the United States. . . . Let's get the United States involved. . . . Maybe we can get the United States to drop an atom bomb on Fujian. Maybe ten or twenty million people will be killed. Chiang Kai-shek wants the United States to use the bomb against us. Let them use it. Let's see what Khrushchev says then. (Li 1994, 262)

This was not mere blusterous rhetoric on Mao's part. The shelling of the Nationalist-held island of Quemoy off the shore of Fujian in 1958 was carried out with this in mind and was an attempt to undermine Khrushchev's quest for peace. "Mao was convinced that Chiang Kai-shek wanted the United States to drop an atom bomb on Fujian province," Dr. Li informs us, "and Mao would not have minded if it had. His shelling of Quemoy was a dare to see how far the United States would go" (Li 1994, 125).

In late 1960 future Canadian Prime Minister Pierre Elliott Trudeau traveled with one of his ideological confreres to China at the official invitation of the Chinese government. For almost six weeks their Communist minders took the two Canadians to carefully selected and prepared industrial and agricultural sites to showcase the putative accomplishments of Mao's Great Leap. They knew they were being handed propaganda, but they endured it with grace and good humor. The next year Trudeau and his friend published their travel diaries in French as *Deux innocents en Chine rouge*. An English translation as *Two Innocents in Red China* appeared in 1968 after Trudeau was elected Prime Minister of Canada.

While the two innocents never really denied persistent contemporary reports of famine in China, they did downplay them to some extent and sidestepped the issue of the famine's severity:

> Hold on a minute, please! Isn't famine raging in China at this very moment?
>
> Do you mean the famine in which the conservative press of the West takes such delight? The famine of which the Formosan [Nationalist Chinese] government speaks with such cheerful compassion? It is true that dispatches from Hong Kong report a "shortage of provisions that in some districts verges on famine." It is true that during our journey people mentioned to us droughts in the south and floods in the north. . . . All the same, it has to be acknowledged: it would take more than that to overturn the government of Mao Tse-tung [Mao Zedong] . . .

In fact a famine ... today will do less harm than in the past, for there will be no financial sharks to speculate in misery. And the instruments of distribution and apportionment (roads, trucks, staff) are better organized today than they used to be.

Conclusion: the Chinese will continue to listen to the teachers of Marxism at the weekly meeting. (Trudeau and Hébert 2007, 178–79)

But now we know much more about Great Leap China than we did in the early 1960s. A Chinese translation of *Deux innocents* was published in book form in China in 2006, and in the introductory Chinese-language material there was not one word about what is now known about the famine and starvation.

The next year, in his long introduction to the 2007 republication in Canada of the English translation of *Deux innocents*, Alexandre Trudeau (son of Pierre Trudeau, who died in 2000) acknowledged that "The Great Leap Forward caused a great famine" and that it was the Chinese Communist Party's "first great catastrophe," but he did not discuss the magnitude of the resultant starvation (Trudeau and Hébert 2007, 26–27). "This charming period piece gives us a memorable picture of a China that has largely vanished," writes Canadian historian and popular commentator Margaret MacMillan on the jacket of this republication. But if Great-Leap China has indeed largely disappeared, the Chinese people can only celebrate in jubilation and relief and hope that no man-made famine ever stalks and starves them again.

THE LULL BEFORE THE STORM

Mao was an unpopular man in China in the early 1960s, and he knew it. In 1961 a play called *Hai Rui Dismissed from Office* became quite popular and was performed in Beijing before sellout audiences. The plot of the play was an oblique historical condemnation of Mao's role in the Great Leap Forward and a celebration of Peng Dehuai's courage in criticizing him over it. The historical Hai Rui was a loyal and upright official during the Ming dynasty who bluntly criticized a Ming emperor's policies and was, as a result, dismissed from office in disgrace. Anyone who saw the play and had a finger on the pulse of political developments in China knew that the character Hai Rui was the historical and literary counterpart to Peng Dehuai, while the stubborn and obtuse Ming emperor who failed to heed the loyal minister's remonstrations was none other than Mao himself. Jiang Qing, a woman with literary and cultural interests who had been Mao's wife since Yan'an days, quickly caught on to this and urged Mao for years to do something about it.

Mao made only one public appearance in 1962. During this year he was angry and hurt about the way practical officials had more or less shunted him aside and regarded him as a "dead ancestor." He feared that bureaucrats and governmental cogs were now in control of China and that the country was slowly watering down Marxist-Leninist dogma. In his youth he had accepted Marxism-Leninism and saw class struggle as the driving force of history. Now, in the wake of attempts to recover from the Great Leap, there was little evidence of continuing class struggle, and this troubled him.

One segment of Chinese society that was not critical of Mao was the People's Liberation Army (or PLA), led by Lin Biao. Lin knew that the basis of his power and authority was his loyalty to Mao, and during the early 1960s he flattered Mao and was obsequious in his behavior to him. When others criticized Mao for the Great Leap catastrophe, Lin praised it and glorified Mao for attempting it. Lin fostered a personality cult centered on Mao in the PLA, and he printed and circulated among PLA troops the famous "Little Red Book," or *Quotations from Chairman Mao Zedong*, which he encouraged officers and men to read and memorize reverentially. Mao was pleased with all this attentiveness and by 1965 was encouraging China to learn from the PLA's ideological zeal and personal dedication to him. Mao encouraged the formation of a personality cult centered on himself, partly for his own glorification but mainly for the mass dedication to his ideology that it might produce.

By late 1965 Mao was once again confident enough in his own leadership to fire a salvo at his critics and detractors. He finally unleashed the fury of his wife Jiang Qing and her ultra-leftist cronies against those they regarded as impeding class struggle in China, and in November they had newspapers in Beijing and Shanghai publish a tirade against the Hai Rui play. By the end of the year Mao had convened a meeting with top Chinese officials about the play and lashed out at his critics, questioning their devotion to the revolutionary cause. In February 1966 he told Lin Biao and the PLA about his vision of a "great socialist cultural revolution" that would fundamentally change China's culture by rooting out the vestiges of old or feudal ways. With this done, Mao believed, his critics would finally be silenced and China could proceed farther and faster along the revolutionary path toward the ultimate goal of pure communism.

CHINA GOES MAD: THE CULTURAL
REVOLUTION, 1966–1976

Mao was intensely dedicated to the task of seeing the revolution through in China during his lifetime. Rather than see his revolution derailed, he threw China into a decade of chaos and turmoil that would, he hoped, maintain China's revolutionary ardor and keep the nation on track to achieve socialism in his lifetime. Mao plunged China into one of its darkest decades of the twentieth century because the revolutionary ideals and goals of his youth remained unrealized. He was, as his physician wrote in the 1990s, dedicated to socialism for socialism's sake and cared little about the practical consequences or real-world human suffering that his attempts to realize his theoretical ideals entailed (Li 1994, 377).

Frustrated that the majority of the Chinese government was apparently abandoning China's revolutionary charter and following a more revisionist path similar to the Soviet Union, Mao essentially threw a temper tantrum; he went over the heads of the government and appealed directly to the people for support. Mao tapped into a vast reservoir of youthful discontent in China and told a generation of Chinese youth that it was acceptable for them to rebel against authority figures in families, schools, workplaces, and local and provincial governments; many personnel in these organizations were, after all, revisionist or counterrevolutionary and deserved contempt and censure. That was all that a generation of angry and disenchanted urban youth needed to hear, and by the summer of 1966 China was in the throes of a nationwide upheaval that would last, to a greater or lesser extent, until Mao's death in September 1976.

May 1966 was a big month in the developing momentum for the Cultural Revolution. Mao's most prominent critics were dismissed in May, and this same month Lin Biao asserted that these critics were part of a "black line" in the party that was out to restore bourgeois interests in Chinese society. Only a thorough housecleaning within the party and an intensified revolution in Chinese society and culture could reverse these ominous developments. Sensing which way the wind was blowing, Mao's longtime associate Zhou Enlai named the developing movement the Great Proletarian Cultural Revolution. Also in May, an ultra-leftist philosophy professor at Peking University (Beida) placed "big-character posters" throughout the campus condemning the university president's policies forbidding student protest movements. Mao's discovery and approval of the posters had two results: the dismissal or assailing of many professors and administrators at

Peking University and the popularization of big-character posters (large posters written with bold Chinese characters) as a means of airing opinions and attacking ideological opponents.

In June 1966 the anarchy in China began. Many young students left their studies and joined the exciting new movement to protect Chairman Mao and his Thought from revisionists, the standard bogeyman label for anyone who dared voice disagreement with Mao. Revisionists were members of the over-thirty generation; how could young people ever dare resist the smiling Chairman Mao who was telling them that it was acceptable to rebel against the older generations? In August Mao publicly and approvingly designated his new young supporters the "Red Guards" and heartily approved of their slogan "to rebel is justified." And rebel they did, in the name of a personality cult centered on the thought, and the person, of Chairman Mao. Mao took his famous swim in the Yangtze River in July 1966 to announce to China and the world that he had the renewed political and physical prowess necessary to direct the turmoil he was about to unleash in China. (In reality, the swim as a feat of physical fitness was quite unremarkable; Mao simply let the current carry him along as he floated on his back, supported by the buoyancy of his considerable stomach.)

Mao's sycophants and flatterers in the PLA were proud of the role they had played in starting the movement. Happy to be included in Mao's vision of cultural revolution and ideological purification in China, the PLA's *Liberation Army Daily* published the following piece in its August 1, 1966 edition:

> Chairman Mao wants us to run our army as a great school. Working mainly as a fighting force, it concurrently studies, engages in agriculture, runs factories, and does mass work; it carries on and further develops the fine traditions of our Party and our army, and trains and tempers millions of successors to the proletarian revolutionary cause, so that our people's army of several million can play a still greater role in the cause of socialist revolution and socialist construction. It is a great school for the study, implementation, dissemination, and safeguarding of Mao Zedong's Thought. (Schurmann and Schell 1967, 623)

In this same piece the *Liberation Army Daily* ingratiated itself with Mao by lashing out at his critics at Lushan:

> The . . . big struggle took place at the same time as our Party's struggle against the Right opportunist anti-Party clique in 1959. Taking advantage of the important posts they had usurped in the army, the principal members of the anti-Party clique—who were exposed at the Party's Lushan

Conference—made a great effort to do away with the Party's absolute leadership over the army, to abrogate political work, to reject the army's tasks of participating in socialist construction and doing mass work, and to abolish the local armed forces and the militia; in this way, they tried to completely negate Chairman Mao's thinking on the people's army and the people's war. They vainly hoped to refashion our army according to the bourgeois, revisionist military line so that it would become an instrument for their usurping leadership of the Party and the government, and for realizing their personal ambitions. The Enlarged Session of the Military Commission held after the Party's Lushan Conference thoroughly settled accounts with them in regard to their crimes and dismissed them from office. This was a great victory for Mao Zedong's Thought! (625)

On August 5, Mao egged the Red Guards on by posting his own big-character poster saying "Bomb the headquarters!" at the door of the Communist Party Central Committee Headquarters. Unnerved, the Central Committee gave in to Mao's tactics by dismissing moderates and recruiting radical Maoists into its ranks.

On the dawn of August 18, 1966, Mao propelled his new personality cult to a frenzy among the Red Guards when he spoke to one million of them at a rally in Beijing's Tiananmen Square. He mingled and chatted with the crowds for several hours, and the next day news of the rally was splashed all over China's newspapers. This produced a craze for Red Guard rallies at Tiananmen Square for much of the rest of the year. The last rally, held in November 1966, was the largest, with more than 2.5 million people attending.

These huge Red Guard rallies were possible because students all over China simply quit school and adventurously traveled all over China to "make revolution" and do quixotic battle against the phantom counterrevolutionaries and reactionaries. They were given free passage on China's train and bus system to just about anywhere, which enabled the Red Guard generation to see more of China than any other generation in Chinese history. The ultimate destination for millions of Red Guards was, of course, Beijing, especially after the news media reported that Mao himself was known to review the rallies at Tiananmen Square. The fondest dream of any Red Guard was to lay eyes on the Chairman, even if only for a few fleeting and frenzied seconds. Liang Heng, a young student who traveled all the way from Hunan in southern China to attend a Red Guard rally at Tiananmen Square, conveys in his memoirs the intensity and flavor of the rallies:

If there was any single thing that meant ecstasy to everyone in those days, it was seeing Chairman Mao. Ever since I had been in Peking [Beijing], the possibility had been in the back of my mind, and, like every other Red Guard, I would have laid down my life for the chance.

Chairman Mao's car was first, a Peking-brand army jeep. As in a dream, I saw him. He seemed very tall to me, magnificent, truly larger than life. He waved his hat as the jeep drove slowly through the throng. The soldiers forming the passageway stood at attention, but the tears poured down their faces in rivulets. Nevertheless they managed to sniffle their refrain, "Please keep Revolutionary order! Please keep Revolutionary order!"

I was bawling like a baby, crying out incoherently again and again, "You are our hearts' reddest, reddest sun!" My tears blocked my vision, but I could do nothing to control myself. Then Chairman Mao's car was past, and Premier Zhou's followed.

The people in front hadn't realized what had happened, and were still chanting. "We want to see Chairman Mao!" with their backs turned to all the action. As they discovered him in their midst, however, they nearly mobbed the car, obstructing its passage completely. . . . It was only when the crowd was told that the Chairman wanted to climb the gate-tower to see the fireworks that they separated and let the car go through.

When it was all over everyone ran to the post office to telegraph the good news to their families all over China. I waited more than two hours to trace out the trembling words, "This evening at 9:15 I became the happiest person in the world." I knew my father would need no further explanation. (Liang and Shapiro 1983, 121, 124–25)

The throngs of Red Guards collected Mao memorabilia, wore red armbands emblazoned with three characters meaning Red Guard, sang songs in praise of Chairman Mao's wisdom and benevolence, and above all read his works, especially the Little Red Book or *Quotations from Chairman Mao Zedong*. Mao's *Quotations* were carried by every good Red Guard wherever he or she went. The original edition of the *Quotations*, issued by the PLA in a cheap, red plastic cover, had 270 pages of text and measured about $5 \times 3\frac{1}{2} \times \frac{3}{4}$ inches. A generation of Red Guards reverentially pored over the *Quotations* and knew them largely by heart; many even committed the entire book to memory. (The *Quotations* achieved popularity with the 1960s hippie generation in the United States and Canada.) Stridently anti-American, the *Quotations* contained frequent and shrill denunciation of the United States:

People of the world, unite and defeat the U.S. aggressors and all their running dogs! People of the world, be courageous, dare to fight, defy difficulties and advance wave upon wave. Then the whole world will belong to the people. Monsters of all kinds shall be destroyed. (Mao 1976, 82)

Mao was supremely confident in the ultimate victory of the socialist revolution all over the world:

The socialist system will eventually replace the capitalist system; this is an objective law independent of man's will. However much the reactionaries try to hold back the wheel of history, sooner or later revolution will take place and will inevitably triumph. (24)

It is my opinion that the international situation has now reached a new turning point. There are two winds in the world today, the East Wind and the West Wind. There is a Chinese saying, "Either the East Wind prevails over the West Wind or the West Wind prevails over the East Wind." I believe it is characteristic of the situation today that the East Wind is prevailing over the West Wind. That is to say, the forces of socialism have become overwhelmingly superior to the forces of imperialism. (80–81)

The ultimate victory of the socialist and communist revolutions would be accomplished through brute force of arms:

Every Communist must grasp the truth, "Political power grows out of the barrel of a gun." (61)

... only with guns can the whole world be transformed. (63)

We are advocates of the abolition of war, we do not want war; but war can only be abolished through war, and in order to get rid of the gun it is necessary to take up the gun. (63)

Revolution was, in fact, a brutal and messy business, and in what was probably the most famous statement of his life, Mao told his followers that they should not expect it to be otherwise:

A revolution is not a dinner party, or writing an essay, or painting a picture, or doing embroidery; it cannot be so refined, so leisurely and gentle, so temperate, kind, courteous, restrained and magnanimous. A revolution is an insurrection, an act of violence by which one class overthrows another. (11–12)

The Cultural Revolution was an exciting time for the Red Guards and other perpetrators, but for its victims (variously called counterrevolutionaries, reactionaries, revisionists, capitalist roaders, and the like) it was a time of enormous suffering and hardship. Mao detested intellectuals because they thought for themselves and did not always reverentially lap up the dogma he poured out to them. It had been the intellectuals, after all, who had spoken out most vociferously against Mao's policies during the Hundred Flowers campaign. Always conscious of his own lack of formal advanced education, Mao was especially suspicious of any intellectual who had studied abroad. During the Cultural Revolution, thousands of patriotic, foreign-educated Chinese who had returned to China after the 1949 revolution were hunted down and sent to the countryside for back-breaking reform through labor on farms. Hundreds of physicists and other scientists were reduced to demeaning tasks such as shoveling pig manure and cleaning latrines. Intellectuals in general were referred to as the "stinking ninth category," ninth being the last of a list of undesirables in Chinese society that included criminals and "bad elements." Red Guards took special delight in bursting into their teachers' homes in search of anything that could possibly prove them antagonistic to Mao or pro-Western in their tastes: books, music, paintings, and even Western-style clothing. People who aroused the slightest suspicion of the Red Guards were taken out and "struggled," or verbally and physically abused before large crowds of accusers and detractors. Chinese writer Jung Chang recalls how her father, an intellectual, was tormented but remained defiant during the Cultural Revolution:

> A standard opening was to chant: "Ten thousand years, another ten thousand years, and yet another ten thousand years to our Great Teacher, Great Leader, Great Commander, and Great Helmsman Chairman Mao!" Each time the three "ten thousand"s and four "great"s were shouted out, everyone raised their Little Red Books in unison. My father would not do this. He said that the "ten thousand years" was how emperors used to be addressed, and it was unfitting for Chairman Mao, a Communist.
>
> This brought down a torrent of hysterical yells and slaps. At one meeting, all of the targets were ordered to kneel and kowtow to a huge portrait of Mao at the back of the platform. While the others did as they were told, my father refused. He said that kneeling and kowtowing were undignified feudal practices which the Communists were committed to eliminating. The Rebels screamed, kicked his knees, and struck him on the head, but he still struggled to stand upright. "I will not kneel! I will not kowtow!" he said furiously. The enraged crowd demanded,

"Bow your head and admit your crimes!" He replied, "I have committed
no crime. I will not bow my head!"

Several large young men jumped on him to try to force him down,
but as soon as they let go he stood up straight, raised his head, and
stared defiantly at the audience. His assailants yanked his hair and
pulled his neck. My father struggled fiercely. As the hysterical crowd
screamed that he was "anti-Cultural Revolution," he shouted angrily,
"What kind of Cultural Revolution is this? There is nothing 'cultural'
about it! There is only brutality!" (Chang 1991, 331)

Zhai Zhenhua, who now lives and works in Canada, recalls in lurch-
ing, harrowing detail her Red Guard days and her raid on the home of
a supposed class enemy named Xiuying:

We searched high and low, everywhere except under the bricks on the
floor, but we didn't find money or anything worthwhile, let alone a
gun or counter-revolutionary leaflet. And the woman was arrogant!
She wouldn't even talk to us or answer our questions. I was annoyed.
Everything about her—her loose, large body, her flaccid face, and her
fishy eyes—was hateful. "You don't want to talk with us? All the better,
save me some saliva. Beat her!" I ordered my soldiers.

As soon as they started to strap her with their belts, she slid down
onto the floor with her back against the wall and from then on hardly
moved. Her eyes never looked up. Before we left, we grabbed some of
her belongings at random to turn over to our headquarters.

The next morning, as I walked towards the headquarters' office,
Xiaoli, a Red Guard from the third grade of junior school, was leaving.
We exchanged hellos as we passed each other. After a few steps, she
suddenly stopped, turned, and asked me, "Did you raid Xiuying's home
yesterday?"

"Yes, I was in charge."

"She's dead," Xiaoli said casually.

"Dead?" I repeated.

She nodded several times and went on her way.

My heart jumped. Dead? She was alive yesterday when we left. Or
wasn't she? It wasn't our habit to check whether our victims were dead
or alive when we left them. But I didn't mean to kill her! I didn't!
Although I had no problem beating people hard to make them suffer,
I never wanted to kill anybody and I never beat people on their heads.
Perhaps Xiuying committed suicide after we left or had a heart attack
during our beating. No! It was impossible. Why should she die on the
only home raid I was in charge of? Xiaoli must have made a mistake.
Or maybe she was kidding with me. I wanted to go after her to find
out, but I didn't have the courage. It was too frightening. I wasn't about

to ask the headquarters either—let them come to me. If Xiuying was dead and I had to pay the price, I would do so.

I never discovered whether she died or not, but I suspected that there were many victims of home raids who had died during or after the attacks. Xiuying's death would hardly have been news, but the thought that I might have killed her weighed heavily upon me for days. Still, eventually I managed to persuade myself it was all right. We were in a war and there are always casualties on the battlefields. I shouldn't be intimidated by the death of one class enemy. The revolution had to succeed, and I had to continue to do my part. When I was assigned new tasks, I tried to be as brave as before. (Zhai 1994, 97–98)

By November 1966 Mao was taken aback by the viciousness of the attacks against teachers and other authorities and tried to remind the Red Guards that not all people in authority were revisionists or capitalist roaders. He did not, however, rein in the movement at this time, and things steadily worsened. Several high officials in China's government were hauled out of their homes, struggled, and more or less forced to admit to trumped-up accusations against them. During the summer of 1967, mobs broke into Peng Dehuai's house and dragged him out to a struggle session. A mob broke into the British embassy in Beijing, terrorized British diplomats, and burned a part of the British embassy compound. Anarchy prevailed in several major Chinese cities as rival groups claiming to be the most loyal of Chairman Mao's Red Guards fought and murdered each other. One Chinese intellectual remembers how university and urban life was violently disrupted as the city of Hefei in Anhui province descended into lawlessness:

At the university, the sixteen-year-old daughter of Colonel Li, still in junior high, made herself famous by being one of those daredevil Red Guards who prided themselves on their blood lineage. She sported a dagger with éclat, because both of her parents had served in the early Red Army. One day, while roaming the streets with a band of teenagers of her faction, she saw a teenage boy coming toward them.

"Who is that? Friend or enemy?"she asked her companions. "I have not seen him before. Enemy, I believe," one of the boys said. "Then what are we waiting for? Let's get him," she urged, walking up to the solitary youth. "Stop! Who are you, kid? Which faction?" "You have no right to stop me or ask me questions. Let me go by."

"Here's for your impudence, you dog!" Her dagger went straight into the youngster's heart. Her companions were dumbfounded. "Come on!" she said cheerfully. "I'll treat you to ice-suckers to celebrate our heroic deed." Leaving the youngster dying on the street in a pool of blood, she walked up to a man peddling ice-suckers and clenched the bloody dagger between her teeth while she fumbled in her pockets for change. "Ten ice-suckers for Chairman Mao's true Red Guards!" she said proudly. The peddler was so frightened that he dared not take money for the ice-suckers. The dead boy turned out to have belonged to the same faction as the killer. (Wu 1993, 206–7)

Hundreds of thousands of people met with violent deaths in China during the Cultural Revolution. Nien Cheng's daughter Meiping was murdered in Shanghai during the Cultural Revolution, and after the 10-year nightmare finally ended, Nien Cheng began to seek justice and resolution of Meiping's case. She wrote many petitions seeking redress until a government official finally asked her to stop writing them and to be patient.

"I have come here today to tell you to stop writing petitions. In due course your case will be reviewed, since it is the policy of the Party and government to review all cases of the Cultural Revolution."

"How much longer will I have to wait?" I asked him.

"Do you know how many cases we have to deal with in Shanghai? Ten thousand people died unnaturally in this city. Their deaths were all related directly or indirectly to the Gang of Four and their followers. Many times that number were imprisoned. Many are still detained. Our first priority must be to examine these cases immediately and to release the innocent people. Then we will examine the cases of those who are out of prison and are still living, like yourself. After that we will come to the cases of those who are dead, like your daughter . . . "

What he said seemed reasonable. I had not realized the magnitude of the problem facing the officials charged with reviewing the cases.

"It's good of you to take time off to visit me today. I want to thank you and the government you represent. I must say your visit has somewhat restored my confidence. You are very different from the officials I have had to deal with during the past ten years."

"Of course I'm different. I've only recently been rehabilitated myself," the man said with a twist of his mouth that might have been a bitter smile. (Cheng 1986, 488)

Things became ominous in the summer of 1967 when entire shipments of weapons disappeared and mob rule prevailed in the southern Chinese city of Guangzhou. When it appeared that the PLA itself might also be sliding into chaos, Mao finally concluded that his Cultural Revolution had gone too far and tried to restrain it. When he toured the provinces in September, he was appalled at the extent of the social disruption he saw. Mao also reined in Jiang Qing and her group of writers, but he kept them in reserve to use as attack dogs against his political opponents when it suited him. Order in China was not quickly restored, and in July 1968 Mao had to instruct the PLA to restore order to China's cities through all the necessary means, including military force. That same month he summoned student and Red Guard leaders to a discussion and more or less told them that the party was over now. One way to get the Red Guards out of the cities was to send them out to the countryside to learn from the peasants. This he did in 1969, and millions of students went to work on farms. Some went willingly and enthusiastically, but most had to be compelled. In the countryside they learned nothing but bitterness for Mao, who seemed to have no concern for them now that they had outlived their usefulness.

In addition to its mindless brutality, the Cultural Revolution was a time of destruction to China's artistic heritage. (Tibet was hit particularly hard, with almost all of its monasteries destroyed. Only the Potala Palace in Lhasa was spared the destruction, on the personal orders of Zhou Enlai.) Red Guards destroyed innumerable relics and *objets d'art*. A wealthy Chinese woman whose house was raided and ransacked by Red Guards recalls the wanton destruction she witnessed in heartrending detail:

> The Red Guards had taken from the storeroom the crates containing my father's books and papers and were trying to open them with pliers. Through the open drawing room door, I saw a girl on the ladder removing the curtains. Two bridge tables were in the middle of the room. On them was a collection of cameras, watches, clocks, binoculars, and silverware that the Red Guards had gathered from all over the house. These were the "valuables" they intended to present to the state.
>
> Mounting the stairs, I was astonished to see several Red Guards taking pieces of my porcelain collection out of their padded boxes. One young man had arranged a set of four Kangxi winecups in a row on the floor and was stepping on them. I was just in time to hear the crunch of delicate porcelain under the sole of his shoe. The sound pierced my heart. Impulsively I leapt forward and caught his leg just as he raised his foot to crush the next cup. He toppled. We fell in a heap together. My eyes searched for the other winecups to make sure we had not broken them in our fall, and, momentarily distracted, I was not able to move aside when the boy regained his feet and kicked me right in my chest. I cried out in pain . . .

The young man whose revolutionary work of destruction I had interrupted said angrily, "You shut up! These things belong to the old culture. They are the useless toys of the feudal emperors and the modern capitalist class and have no significance to us, the proletarian class. They cannot be compared to cameras and binoculars, which are useful for our struggle in time of war. Our Great Leader Chairman Mao taught us, 'If we do not destroy, we cannot establish.' The old culture must be destroyed to make way for the new socialist culture." (Cheng 1986, 73–74)

The fall of 1968 was the end of the Cultural Revolution proper, and it was officially declared over in the spring of 1969. Its lingering effects, however, continued to reverberate until Mao's death in 1976. After 1969 movements reminiscent of the Cultural Revolution flared up occasionally but were not given the full rein they had in 1966 and 1967. Mao knew that his Cultural Revolution was, like his Great Leap Forward of the late 1950s, a monumental failure, but this time he made sure that nobody like Peng Dehuai would dare come forth and criticize him. This time the odds were stacked in his favor; the highest levels of the CCP were packed with his allies, and he always had Jiang Qing and her group of literary hatchet men ready to slice up any potential critics.

Mao continued to be concerned about the state of the revolution in China, but by the late 1960s and early 1970s he was becoming preoccupied with another matter, the growing Sino-Soviet split. Mao became convinced during this time that the greatest threat to Chinese and international security was not the United States but the Soviet Union, which had distanced itself from China in horror after the lunacy of the Great Leap Forward and the Cultural Revolution and had begun menacing China along the Sino-Soviet borders.

The Cultural Revolution was a complex phenomenon, and making sense of it is not an easy task. Indeed, several scholars who have devoted their careers to plumbing its depths have not been able to come to full grips with its causes and the course of its development. The Cultural Revolution was more or less officially launched in mid-1966, but after that it seems to have assumed a momentum and meaning all its own, quite apart from what Mao originally foresaw or intended. It ended with the deaths of more than one million Chinese and massive disruptions in the lives of almost all of China's urban population. (Disruptions were less extensive in the countryside.) Perhaps we never will fully understand the Cultural Revolution, but at present it appears that it was more or less a failed attempt by Mao and his ideological supporters to see the revolution through to completion. Mao's appeal to China's angry young people was an attempt to harness their energy and restlessness for the revolutionary cause, but instead of furthering the revolution they plunged China into social and economic chaos.

MAO'S LATER YEARS AND DEATH

By 1970 Mao was so concerned about the perceived threats posed to China by the Soviet Union that he began to make his first tentative openings to the outside world. He tried to oust the Chinese Nationalists from the United Nations and to seat representatives of his own government on the world deliberative body. In 1970 Chiang Kai-shek's Nationalists were still representing China at the United Nations and stubbornly maintaining the fiction that they, and not the Chinese Communists, were the legitimate government of all China. On October 1, 1970, Mao appeared publicly in Tiananmen Square with Edgar Snow, an American journalist who during the 1930s had written about the Chinese Communist movement. Newspaper coverage of this appearance stated pointedly that the people of the world, including Americans, were China's friends. The government of Canadian Prime Minister Pierre Elliott Trudeau diplomatically recognized the People's Republic of China in 1970, and in 1971 U.S. President Richard Nixon surprised the world by personally visiting China and chatting with Mao. Later that year, the Chinese Communists were admitted to the United Nations and Chiang Kai-shek's Nationalists were ousted. Nixon's decision to "play the China card" against the Soviet Union began the process of normalizing relations between China and the United States, but official U.S. recognition of Mao's China did not come until early 1979. In 1972 Japan, reeling from the "Nixon shock" caused by the president's trip to China, established diplomatic relations with the People's Republic of China and cut off ties with the Nationalists on Taiwan.

Lin Biao, Mao's designated successor and supposedly loyal comrade in arms, did not like Mao's anti-Soviet stance and his outreach to foreign countries. In August 1971 Lin Biao apparently launched a failed attempt to assassinate Mao and then attempted to flee to the Soviet Union, where he probably had supporters. Historians disagree on the ultimate cause of Lin Biao's death, but one fairly widely accepted account holds that a plane he boarded to flee China ran out of fuel and crashed in Mongolia, killing all aboard. News of

Lin Biao's perfidy shocked the Chinese public, and soon there were massive anti–Lin Biao rallies. Lin's introduction to Mao's *Quotations* was dutifully cut out of millions of copies, and today a first-printing copy of the *Quotations* with Lin Biao's introduction still intact is something of a rarity and a collector's item.

The fall of Lin Biao led to a power struggle between the Maoist radicals and the more moderate voices in the Chinese government, chief of whom was Zhou Enlai. Zhou was designated as Mao's heir-apparent, and this did not sit well with the radicals. The center of the radicals' power was the Politburo, which included Jiang Qing and her radical literary and cultural supporters. Two of these radicals were, in fact, members of the Standing Committee, a five-or six-member core group within the Politburo. Zhou led the moderates and attempted to reduce the power of the radicals. Zhou brought Deng Xiaoping, a fellow moderate, back to power in 1974, and the next year Zhou announced China's "Four Modernizations," or goals to improve and modernize agriculture, industry, defense, and science. The radicals were incensed by this and accused Zhou and Deng of plotting to restore capitalism in China.

Zhou Enlai died in early January 1976 of cancer, and all of China mourned. He might have lived a little longer had Mao not refused to allow him treatment for his cancer. Zhou's death led to a power struggle over whether a moderate or a radical would be named as Mao's successor. Deng Xiaoping, who had no other source of support than Zhou, found himself in an awkward and precarious position. Mao designated a compromise candidate as his successor, a relatively unknown figure named Hua Guofeng, and reportedly told him that "with you in charge, my mind is at ease." Meanwhile, the battles between radicals and moderates continued. By March the radicals were attacking Zhou's memory and vilifying him as a capitalist roader, an opprobrious bogeyman tag somewhat equivalent to being labeled a "commie" during the 1950s in the United States. This infuriated millions of people who knew that Zhou had been a moderating force behind the darkest days of the Cultural Revolution and had blunted its sharpest edges; without him, the Cultural Revolution might well have been much worse. Zhou, in fact, and not Mao, was by 1975 the most beloved man in China. In April millions of people marched to Tiananmen Square and celebrated his memory by placing huge mounds of wreaths and poems at the foot of the Monument to the Heroes of the People in the middle of the square. Mao's ordering of the removal of these tributes on April 5 led to the Tiananmen Incident, a huge demonstration in response. After angry crowds burned the police station near the square, the army moved in with truncheons to clear the square. The radicals on the Politburo then blamed one of their number, Deng Xiaoping, for the disturbances. Deng was expelled from the Politburo and sent into internal exile. He retained only his party membership, but he was too major a figure to be forgotten. He eventually came back to power after Mao's death and was China's leading figure until his death in 1997.

The radicals then gained the upper hand, but they did not enjoy their day in the sun for long. Mao fell gravely ill in the summer of 1976 and finally died on September 9. China mourned his passing, but not with the same grief that attended Zhou's passing earlier in the year. The main question for China after Mao's death was, once again, who his successor would be. Then, as now, the Chinese public would have nothing to do with the selection of his successor. Because China was not a democracy, the death of a national leader was typically followed not by an orderly transition, but a raw power struggle between unelected, high-ranking political figures. Hua Guofeng was the nominally designated successor, but he knew that his base of support was limited and that he would probably not prevail in a protracted power struggle. So he decided to strike first. The PLA, by now sick and tired of all the upheavals and instability in China, responded positively to his appeal for military support, and on October 6, 1976, Jiang Qing and three of her fellow radicals were arrested. These four people, dubbed the Gang of Four, were made scapegoats for most of China's suffering over the past decade. Everyone knew that Mao did find the Gang of Four useful at times and occasionally gave his support to them as he saw fit, but Mao was still too much a revered figure to share in the blame. Mao was the unnamed fifth man in what was really a gang of five.

Mao was a political revolutionary and an important national symbol, but he made most of his contributions to China prior to 1949. After that he proved to be largely an impediment to peacetime growth and development in China. He understood neither economics nor military operations. Contrary to conventional wisdom, Mao was not a military genius; the military writings and victories commonly credited to him are actually attributable to other figures in the Red Army (Wei 2002, 229–48). After his death in 1976 his mistakes were openly recognized, and the Chinese people in their innately good sense decided that China would never again allow the disruptive national movements and class struggle he so treasured.

One of Mao's most insightful biographers comments on the ironies of Mao's transition from liberator to tyrant:

> Mao Zedong thus stands in a long line of revolutionary tyrants—revolutionary in that they contributed to great socio-economic progress, tyrannical in their political methods. Mao began his political career as a servant of China's impoverished peasants and made himself their master in the process. He liberated the Chinese nation from the shackles of a century-long foreign impingement, only to bind the people of the nation to the alien shackles of his own deified image . . . The ill-fated Great Leap Forward campaign marked the transition from Mao as the dominant leader of an authoritarian Leninist party to a personal tyrant ruling above the Party. (Meisner 2007, 194)

Ever since he had become a Marxist during his student days at Beida, Mao Zedong was an idealogue in a hurry who valued socialism for its own elegant, purely theoretical sake. He wanted to see the completion of the Marxian stages of socioeconomic development and the final emergence of a truly classless, communistic society in China. He longed for the culmination of this grand historical process during his own lifetime and was annoyed by the possibility that he might not live to see it. Thus, during the 1950s as he began contemplating his own mortality, he grew impatient with the slow, grinding gait of historical process and sought to impel or accelerate it, to make History bend to human (i.e., his) will. For China, the results of Mao's impatience with the unfolding of Marxian fantasy were utterly disastrous:

> . . . Mao's subjective desire for socialism proved far more powerful than the influence of Marxist teachings on the objective material prerequisites of the new society. Thus, by the late 1950s, Mao's Marxian insistence on proceeding through the necessary stages of socio-economic development gave way to the notion of a "permanent" or "continuous" revolution, one that bypassed the "bourgeois-democratic" phrase altogether; he claimed to have completed "the transition to socialism" in a few short years, and then proclaimed the imminence of communism. . . . By late 1957 Mao Zedong had thrown off all conventional Marxian restraints on the revolutionary will, permitting him to embark on the tragic adventure of the Great Leap Forward. Standing above all institutions, he now became a tyrant as well as a utopian prophet, nearly oblivious to the human and social costs of his "great leap" to communism—and to the costs of the Cultural Revolution, an upheaval which in large measure grew out of the political tensions generated by the failure of the Great Leap. (Meisner 2007, 197)

The Chinese Communist Party knows full well that Mao and Maoism have little if anything to do with what is going on in China today, and he and his ideology are now largely repudiated. (In fact, China today pointedly distances itself from Maoist guerilla insurgencies in Nepal and Peru.) But this repudiation must be kept under wraps and cannot go too far without undermining the legitimacy of continuing Communist rule over the country. (Lu Decheng fond this out in 1989 when he threw dye-filled eggshells at Mao Zedong's gigantic portrait facing Tiananmen Square in Beijing and was sentenced to over a decade and a half in prison for the act. Lu, who now lives in Calgary, is the subject of a recent book by Denise Chong.) So Mao is now revered at a distance but disavowed close up. In today's China, Mao is indeed a "dead ancestor," both literally and figuratively. China has outgrown him.

8

Deng's China

The arrest of the Gang of Four led to widespread celebration in China, not so much because the Chinese people knew a great deal about each member, but because it seemed to portend a final stop to the endless and exhausting mass movements that Mao and the radicals so loved to promote. In the summer of 1977 all four members were expelled from the party. Meanwhile, Deng Xiaoping was making a comeback. In early 1977 he was allowed to go back to Beijing, and he quickly emerged as the party's dominant personality, effectively shunting Hua Guofeng aside. It simply did not matter any more that Mao had apparently designated Hua as his successor; people were fed up with Mao and his antics. Deng was soon leading the charge against the radicals and moved, along with the fellow moderate Hu Yaobang, to purge the party of its extremists. The pendulum had swung the other way, and now the radicals who had joined the party during the heady days of the Cultural Revolution were subject to summary expulsion. Deng and his supporters then launched an enormously popular program of reform in China.

Deng detested the personality cult that Mao and his devotees had fostered, and he quickly dismantled it. Huge statues of Mao were

Deng Xiaoping in 1978. (AP Photo)

pulled down all over China, and Deng rejected all attempts to create a similar personality cult around himself. Deng wanted to change China, but he would do it from behind the scenes, without the heroically high profile of Chairman Mao, the Great Helmsman. In August 1977 Deng stated in a major party speech that Mao had actually made mistakes. On this occasion, he also propounded his famous principle "seek truth from facts." By this he meant that the Chinese Communists should henceforth be less concerned about ideological purity and doctrinal rigidity and be more flexible and pragmatic in their thinking: whatever worked was good, and whatever did not was bad. Deng's star was rising, and by the end of the year he and his fellow moderates Hu Yaobang and Zhao Ziyang had been admitted to the Politburo. Deng, labeled a capitalist roader during the Cultural Revolution, was now emerging as China's preeminent leader. Political developments turned on a dime in China.

To the relief of China's population, Deng announced that there would be no more mass movements and that the nation would henceforth concentrate on building its economy and improving the lives of its citizens. Deng allowed, even encouraged, individual enterprise and found nothing wrong with material incentives. Diehard conservative Communists stewed about his restoration of "capitalism" in China, but their day was now gone and they could do nothing about it but rant among themselves. Deng was doing for China what Mao would never do—providing a peaceful, orderly environment in which stable economic development could take place. To the relief of millions of peasants, the last vestiges of the communes and agricultural cooperatives were disbanded in the countryside in the early 1980s.

Economic development proceeded most quickly along China's eastern and southern coastal cities. In 1980 Deng announced the formation of four Special Economic Zones on China's southern and eastern coastline where exports, joint ventures, and foreign investment would be encouraged and facilitated. The largest of these was Shenzhen (north of Hong Kong), today a thriving metropolis of crass commercialism and unbridled capitalism. Other areas in the Chinese hinterland, away from the prosperous coastal regions, lagged behind in economic development and began to nurse a sense of resentment and alienation from the rest of the nation.

University life was restored to sanity, and thousands of students and faculty members returned to their studies and research. By the late 1970s and early 1980s, thousands of Chinese students were beginning to go abroad for graduate study in North America and Europe, and foreign students and teachers were invited to China and treated like royalty when they did come. An entire generation of young people who had suffered through the Cultural Revolution embraced China's new openness with enthusiasm and abandon.

Probably the single most unpopular of Deng's reforms was the announcement in 1979 of his one-child policy, which would, he hoped, level off the rate of China's population growth sometime in the twenty-first century. Mao possessed only a rudimentary grasp of demographics and adhered to a crude Marxist faith in the productive capacity of the proletariat, which he expressed as the ability of two hands to feed one mouth. The more people in China the better, he believed throughout his life, and nobody could convince him that China would ever face a crisis of overpopulation. Mao, after all, based his career on his faith in, and affection for, China's peasant masses. Deng and other more rational political minds, on the other hand, could clearly foresee a demographic catastrophe for China if population growth were not controlled. The outstripping of China's premodern agricultural productivity by its burgeoning population was, after all, one of the major contributing factors to China's decline in the nineteenth century. The one-child policy was more rigorously enforced in the cities than in the countryside, however, and it contributed to female infanticide, always a problem in a nation where baby boys are valued above baby girls. The children in Chinese orphanages today are overwhelmingly female, and an unnaturally high proportion of males to females has developed in some areas of China. Many couples in Chinese cities used amniocentesis to discover the sex of unborn children and abort female fetuses, hoping to try again for a boy. Today there are even disturbing reports of abortions being forced on women who have already given birth to one or more children. Overpopulation is one of China's most pressing problems today, and the implications of both ignoring it and remedying it present vexing ethical questions.

Deng was in many ways an enthusiastic reformer, but the one thing he was determined not to allow in China was democracy. China would develop and modernize its economy and other aspects of its society, but it absolutely would not tolerate challenges to the final authority and power of the Chinese Communist Party. Communist doctrine, like some varieties of ultraconservative political thought in the United States, holds that the democracy practiced in the capitalistic West is in reality a "bourgeois" democracy, in which the bourgeoisie or monied classes control the political system from behind the scenes and manipulate it for the advancement of their interests, all the while fooling the public into thinking that they actually have some say in the selection of their leaders and policies. Of course, a more obvious reason for Deng's refusal to allow democratization in China was that if China's government were made directly accountable to the Chinese people, Deng and other members of the Communist party might well find themselves voted out of their jobs and power. Deng was determined that economic and social liberalization would not lead to political liberalization. China would, in his words, "open the window but not let in the flies and mosquitoes."

This became quite apparent in 1978 with the appearance of the "Democracy Wall" in Beijing, a place where the police allowed big-character posters criticizing some aspects of the government's policies to remain up for a time. Placing big-character posters on the Democracy Wall became something of a craze for a while, but when the posters began demanding democratization and authentic freedom of expression, Deng shut the wall down. In early 1979 he announced his Four Cardinal Principles, parallel guidelines that people would need to keep in mind as they participated in Zhou Enlai's Four Modernizations, of which Deng Xiaoping heartily approved. These four principles dictated that the Chinese people were not permitted to question socialism, the dictatorship of the proletariat, the Communist party's leadership, or Marxism-Leninism. In other words, China would modernize in just about every way but politically and ideologically. These were the limits of China's newfound freedoms and prosperity. The Chinese people could pursue private wealth, but not democracy.

FOREIGN POLICY

During the late 1970s Deng fundamentally reoriented China's foreign policies and began to throw his weight around on the international stage. In January 1979 he became the first Chinese leader ever to visit the United States. Deng was a hit with the American public and media, and in China he was seen on television warmly shaking hands with President Jimmy Carter and wearing a Texas-style ten-gallon hat. This was quite a change from Mao's deliberate isolation of China from the rest of the world. Soon thousands of Chinese students were applying for visas to study at American universities. In Moscow, Soviet leaders fumed and stewed at the new coziness between China and the United States.

Deng's most dramatic move in the international arena was his invasion of Vietnam in early 1979. In the 1970s China supported the murderous Khmer Rouge regime in Kampuchea (Cambodia), headed by Pol Pot of "Killing Fields" infamy. Pol Pot's murders of hundreds of thousands of city residents in the mid-1970s led to a domestic crisis in Kampuchea as huge numbers of refugees flooded into neighboring Vietnam. Vietnam was concerned about Khmer Rouge atrocities and was further angered and alienated when Pol Pot began mistreating Kampuchea's large Vietnamese population. By December 1978 Vietnam had had enough of Pol Pot and invaded Kampuchea, capturing its capital city Phnom Penh in January 1979. China, incensed that Vietnam dared invade a regime that it supported, decided to reassert the historical tradition of Chinese influence in East Asia. In February Deng ordered the PLA to invade Vietnam and force it to withdraw from Kampuchea. His purpose was not to occupy Vietnamese territory but to "punish" or "chastise" Vietnam for daring to trifle with Beijing's ally. The invasion, however, failed to dislodge Vietnam from Kampuchea and resulted in very high casualty rates. The Chinese campaign in Vietnam ended in failure and defeat, but the Chinese government-controlled media still insisted that China had taught Vietnam a lesson. As with the Chinese invasion of Korea in 1951, however, the only real "lesson" China taught anyone was that it was willing to expend huge numbers of Chinese lives when it did not like developments in its neighboring countries.

If his invasion of Vietnam was his greatest foreign policy failure, Deng's most significant foreign policy success was the U.S. government's diplomatic recognition of the People's Republic of China. The U.S. government continued to recognize the Nationalists on Taiwan and the fiction of their claim to be China's sole legitimate government until late 1978, when it finally faced reality and switched recognition to the People's Republic of China. Nevertheless, the American public and Congress were in no mood to abandon the Nationalists on Taiwan, and in 1979 the Taiwan Relations Act (TRA) was passed and signed into law. The TRA, as it is known in American diplomatic and foreign policy circles, states that the United States will remain committed to the peaceful resolution of the fate of Taiwan and that any armed aggression on the island by Beijing will be a matter of "grave concern" to Washington. Over Beijing's objections, the U.S. government continued allowing arms sales to Taiwan even after diplomatically recognizing Beijing.

Deng's regime negotiated successfully with Britain for the return of the British Crown Colony of Hong Kong to China in 1997. Although the Treaty of Nanking stated that the island of Hong Kong was to be ceded in perpetuity to the British crown, the New Territories, an extension of the Hong Kong colony leased to Britain in 1898 for 99 years, were the most important part of the colony. Without them, the island would be cut off from water, electricity, and other contacts with China. London could not, therefore, realistically expect to return the New Territories and retain the island. Nonetheless, the British government was concerned about the residents of Hong Kong coming under Communist rule after 1997. Deng, however, reassured Britain and the rest of the world that China would largely leave Hong Kong alone for 50 years after its return to Chinese control. This would be possible under Deng's new "one country, two systems" principle, which held that socialism would be practiced on the mainland but that Hong Kong could retain its own social and economic system and largely govern itself. Deng, no doctrinaire Communist, could see that it was plainly in China's economic self-interest to maintain Hong Kong's capitalistic business contacts after 1997. What ultimately mattered was not the economic system in Hong Kong, but the former colony's recognition of itself as a part of China and its freedom from any foreign government or colonial administration. Britain ultimately accepted Deng's formula and in 1984 successfully negotiated arrangements for the orderly return of the colony to China in 1997.

Deng's "one country, two systems" principle was not formulated only with Hong Kong in mind. Deng and his supporters also insisted that the principle would apply to Taiwan when it eventually reunified with the mainland. Taiwan could retain its own military, its own form of government, and its own economic system. What was required of Taiwan was that it lower its Nationalist flag and recognize itself as being a part of China. Taiwan, however, understandably remained skeptical of Beijing's trustworthiness on this matter and sought reassurance from Washington that the United States would not stand idly by in the event of an attack on the island from the mainland.

EVALUATING AND SUCCEEDING MAO

In the early 1980s Deng moved to clarify his attitude toward Chairman Mao. Deng and his moderates could not completely condemn Mao without undermining their own legitimacy as ruling members of the Communist party, so they issued an official judgment of Mao as 70 percent good and 30 percent bad (about a C+ on a standard academic marking scale). This is now more or less the official evaluation of Mao in China today. Hua Guofeng could see by this time that his time was up; the 70 percent verdict was not a strong enough foundation on which to base his claims of being Mao's successor and the leader of China. That position and honor would clearly go to Deng Xiaoping, and Hua stepped down from power. Unlike Mao, Deng never became party chairman, but that no longer mattered in China; what mattered was influence, and Deng had plenty of that.

With the new liberalization and openness came some challenges for Deng's government. Many conservatives growled about "spiritual pollution" (Western popular music, discos, sunglasses, pornography, immodest dress, human rights concerns, demands for multiparty democracy, and so on), and a campaign against it was launched in 1983. Worse yet, the problem of governmental corruption, never much of a problem during Mao's days, raised its ugly head in the 1980s. As the decade progressed many Chinese people came to resent the culture of corruption in government and the perks and privileges enjoyed by high-ranking party and government officials.

Inflation and uneven economic development were creating tensions in China by the mid-1980s, and this in turn led some people to conclude that the political system in China needed reform in order to govern over a more market-oriented economy. Astrophysicist Fang Lizhi became a leading dissident figure. He argued tirelessly for sweeping political reform, and he developed a strong following among Chinese students. In 1986 large student demonstrations demanded political liberalization at campuses in Shanghai and several other major Chinese cities. Hu Yaobang, general secretary of the Communist Party, expressed some sympathy for the views of Fang and the students, and for this he became a hero among them. For Deng, however, this was "bourgeois liberalism" that had gone too far, and he pressured Hu into resigning his position in January 1987. Hereafter, Hu Yaobang was both a hero and a political martyr in the eyes of the students.

By the late 1980s, the fast-moving pace of Chinese political developments had cast Deng and his supporters as conservatives, or people who had reservations about the demands for democratization in China. Reformers, on the other hand, were now people who favored more extensive liberalization. Hu Yaobang and Zhao Ziyang, once thought of as moderates in Deng's camp, had by now emerged as more progressive and pro-reform than Deng. (Conservatives as now defined were, of course, still far less committed to class struggle and mass movements than the radical Maoists had been in the 1960s and 1970s.) In 1987 and 1988 conservatives launched an anti–bourgeois liberalization campaign, but it soon ran out of steam. Something of a standoff between reformers and conservatives had developed by 1988, and it did not resolve itself in favor of the Dengist conservatives until the tragic Tiananmen Square Massacre of June 1989.

THE RAPE OF PEKING: THE BEIJING SPRING AND THE TIANANMEN SQUARE MASSACRE

In the early hours of June 4, 1989, dozens of tanks and thousands of Chinese troops from the 27th Army of the PLA entered Tiananmen Square in Beijing and brutally slaughtered hundreds, if not thousands, of unarmed students and civilian protestors. The bloody crackdown was ordered by Deng Xiaoping himself, who feared that the protests, which had been occurring almost constantly since April 15, would threaten his power and that of the Chinese Communist Party. The slaughter was broadcast in living, gory color to a horrified world via satellite feed. The massacre at Tiananmen Square put the Chinese people and the whole world on notice that the Chinese Communists would brook no serious challenge to their rule over China. In so doing they undermined their legitimacy and moral standing domestically and abroad. Beijing still suppresses the truth about the Tiananmen Square massacre, but sooner or later it will come out. Those responsible for the massacre and those who still voice approval of it, including former current Chinese leader Jiang Zemin, will one day stand condemned in history for their complicity in the gratuitous and brutal

A lone and unknown man (sometimes called "Tank Man" in the West) holds up a column of tanks on the streets of Beijing in the aftermath of the Tiananmen Massacre. His fate remains unknown today, even though this photograph is world famous. (Reuters/Corbis)

murders of their own countrymen. The perpetrators of the Tiananmen Square Massacre will, as the Chinese saying goes, "leave behind a historical stench for ten thousand years" (*yichou wannian*).

The popular student-led protest movement of 1989 was often called a pro-democracy movement in Western journalism, but this was probably a mistake, or at least an overstatement. True enough, many of the students touted "democracy" as a corrective for China's problems, but few if any of them possessed a sophisticated knowledge of democracy or democratic societies. Most of them emphasized their patriotism and their desire to create a legal opposition within China's socialist system. Only a small fraction of them actually advocated the overthrow of the Chinese Communist Party, the dissolution of the socialist system, and the full-fledged introduction of multiparty, Western-style democracy in China. Instead, they were reacting to the disruptions, corruption, inflation, and mismanagement in an economically liberalizing country ruled over by an ossified, authoritarian Leninist gerontocracy, or rule by old men. These problems were largely of the Chinese Communists' own making because they did not fully understand how to govern a nation that had fairly quickly transitioned from a clunky, socialist command economy to a more open and market-oriented economy which sanctioned the accumulation and investment of private capital and largely accommodated the profit motive. Put simply, the Chinese Communists did not understand political economics, and the people they ruled over suffered as a result.

Some students seemed to have a naive faith in a vaguely defined "democracy" as the panacea or cure-all for corruption, low education budgets, and abysmal civil rights, and in this they were reflecting the convictions of their May Fourth–era predecessors of the late 1910s and early 1920s. Official corruption was probably the single greatest grievance the students had with the government, and in voicing an objection to it they had the concurrence and support of millions of workers, intellectuals, and other ordinary citizens. What millions of people thought, the young and brash students shouted from the tops of their lungs in Tiananmen Square, to the thrill and delight of residents in Beijing and many other major Chinese cities. These were intoxicating and heady times, and eventually millions of people joined the student protests. The students were, in fact, more likely to get away with these protests than the ordinary run of people would have been because of China's traditionally paternalistic and tolerant attitude toward youthful student enthusiasm. While the students were being tolerated in their protests, large segments of the rest of society joined with them, cheered them on, and coddled them with free food, beverages, and frozen confections in the late spring heat.

The "Beijing Spring," or the popular protests against the Chinese Communists' tyranny and corruption, began on April 15 and came to a decisive end with the June 4 bloodbath (see Yu and Harrison 1990, 15–34). The movement was led by university students in Beijing, with students at Beida (of May Fourth–era fame) the most influential among them. Former General Secretary of the Chinese Communist Party Hu Yaobang, who had expressed sympathy with previous student movements in China during the 1980s and was a hero to most Chinese students, died of a heart attack on April 15, 1989. The next day students at campuses all over Beijing put up big-character posters commemorating him and attacking the governmental corruption he so heartily abhorred. When wreaths placed in Tiananmen Square in his memory were removed on April 17 (a Monday), some 3,000 Beida students marched to Tiananmen Square in protest and demanded that the government reevaluate Hu Yaobang's achievements, grant freedom of the press, increase funding for education, allow freedom of protest and demonstration, and publish the financial holdings of several high government officials they suspected of massive corruption. The students had no way to know it at the time, but their march would inaugurate 47 days of student protests in Beijing and other major

Chinese cities. Often these protests were joined and supported by large nonstudent segments of urban populations.

On April 18, 5,000 students, largely from Beida, marched to Tiananmen Square shouting slogans such as "Down with tyranny,""Down with corruption," and "Long live democracy." On April 22, Hu Yaobang's funeral was held, and the eulogy was delivered by Zhao Ziyang, another top official known to be very sympathetic with the students and their high estimation of Hu. Students from all over China poured into Beijing the next day to commemorate Hu and join in the protests, and the government responded by imposing censorship. To counter this, 35 Beijing universities staged a student strike. The burgeoning movement and increasing boldness among the students irked Deng Xiaoping, who probably felt personally insulted by some of the things that were said about him, including a comparison of him with the Dowager Empress Cixi. On April 26, the *People's Daily*, the government's main newspaper, published an editorial, probably written by Deng himself, entitled "The Banner Against Turmoil Must Be Raised." The editorial claimed that the student movement was a riot planned by a handful of depraved troublemakers and conspirators. Beijing's police force forbade any unapproved demonstrations or marches.

This unwise and intemperate editorial was a red rag to a bull as far as the students were concerned, and deadlock, not dialogue, resulted from it. The editorial polarized the confrontation between the students and the government in stark black-and-white terms and seemingly left no room for compromise or understanding. It was grievously insulting to thousands of students, and ultimately it was counterproductive. Thousands more students joined in the protests, as much to dispute the government's mischaracterization of their movement as to voice their discontent with official corruption and the lack of freedom of expression. On the next day, April 27, 200,000 students marched in protest in Beijing and were cheered on by more than a million onlookers. On April 28, Wuer Kaixi, a hot-blooded young Uighur from China's northwestern Xinjiang autonomous region, presented demands for liberalization and dialogue with the government. The next day a high official did meet for some discussion with several student leaders, but Wuer Kaixi was pointedly not invited. On April 30, several students were allowed to meet with high government officials, including the mayor of Beijing. In an attempt to defuse a potentially volatile situation with the student protestors, Zhao Ziyang stated on May 3 that the Chinese Communist Party supported student demands for an end to corruption and more development for education. Notably absent from his statement of student demands the government endorsed were democracy and freedom of expression.

May 4, 1989, was the 70th anniversary of the May Fourth Movement, and Beida students were well aware of their university's heritage of protest movements. (The students also noted that 1989 was the 200th anniversary of the French Revolution and its principles of liberty, equality, and fraternity.) Determined to make something of the anniversary, 200,000 students marched to Tiananmen Square and demanded that the government recognize the student movement as patriotic and not antigovernmental. At their protest rally they presented a "New May Fourth Declaration" demanding democracy in the universities and in the Chinese political system. Some placards at this and other rallies said simply "Hello, Mr. Democracy" (*De Xiansheng, ni hao*). People with even a minimal knowledge of Chinese history recognized immediately the comparison the students were making between themselves and their May Fourth–era predecessors.

The student protestors were so distressed with the government's refusal to open any kind of dialogue with them that, on May 13, 3,000 of them started a hunger strike in Tiananmen Square. They reiterated their demands that a government dialogue with them be broadcast live on national television. On May 15, 800,000 people visited Tiananmen Square to show support for the hunger-striking students and their demands. By May 16, it was becoming quite apparent to the government that there was massive popular support for the students' demands, and the old Communists became gravely frightened for their own positions and safety. On May 17, Deng and a selected few senior party members held a meeting to decide what to do about the burgeoning popular movement against them. Zhao Ziyang recalls the substance of this meeting in his political memoirs, published without the Chinese communists' approval in 2009:

> On the 17th, I phoned to request to see Deng. Later, a member of Deng's staff asked me to go to Deng Xiaoping's home in the afternoon for a meeting. All the members of the Politburo Standing Committee plus [Yang] Shangkun were already there. At the time, Wan Li, who would have attended, was still abroad. Since I had asked for a personal meeting with Deng, only to have Deng call for a full Standing Committee meeting at his home, I realized that things had already taken a bad turn.
>
> First, I expressed my views, roughly as follows:
>
> > The situation with the student demonstrations has worsened and has grown extremely grave. Students, teachers, journalists, scholars, and even some government staff have taken to the streets in protest. Today,

Chinese Communist Party General Secretary Zhao Ziyang at Tiananmen Square calling on student hunger strikers, May 19, 1989. (AP Photo/Xinhua)

there were approximately 300,000 to 400,000 people. Quite a large number of workers and peasants are also sympathetic. . . . The key issue blocking dialogue with the students is the judgment passed by the April 26 editorial. . . . If the hunger strike continues and some people die, it will be like gasoline poured over a flame. If we take a confrontational stance with the masses, a dangerous situation could ensue in which we lose complete control.

While I was expressing my views, Deng appeared very impatient and displeased. As soon as I had finished speaking, Li Peng and Yao Yilin immediately stood up to criticize me. (Zhao 2009, 27–28)

The Tiananmen Papers, a book published in 2001 that purports to contain transcripts of discussions and deliberations by top Chinese Communist officials on how to respond to the Tiananmen student protests, conveys Zhao's comments at this key meeting as follows:

Martial law could give us total control of the situation, yes; but think of the terror it will strike in the minds of Beijing's citizens and students. Where will that lead? . . . In the forty years of the People's Republic, our Party has learned many lessons from its political and economic mistakes. Given the crisis we now face at home and abroad, I think that one

more big political mistake might well cost us all our remaining legitimacy. So I see martial law as extremely dangerous. The Chinese people
cannot take any more huge policy blunders. (Zhang 2001, 192)

At this meeting Deng and his hard-line supporters decided two
things: the students' demands for democracy and freedom in China
would mean the dissolution of the Communist Party's power, which
they absolutely would not tolerate, and the protest movements could
be quelled only by force.

On May 18, the government finally agreed to meet with student protest leaders, but the students were not satisfied with the conditions.
Premier Li Peng and two other high officials met with student leaders
Wuer Kaixi, Wang Dan, and others, but Li Peng insisted that the only
subject for the dialogue would be how to help the students on hunger
strike. The fiery Wuer Kaixi was incensed at this and repeatedly interrupted Li Peng, demanding that other matters be addressed. Wang
Dan demanded that the government retract the April 26 editorial, recognize the peaceful and patriotic nature of the protests, and broadcast
the dialogue. Li Peng, stunned at Wuer Kaixi's temerity and the stark-
ness of Wang Dan's demands, ended the meeting.

The next day, an infuriated Deng Xiaoping stated in a Politburo
meeting that he would never allow a reversal of the April 26 editorial.
Only 2 of the 18 members at the meeting declined to label the movement a riot. One of them was Zhao Ziyang, and Deng ever after
viewed him as a traitor and stripped him of all power. Nevertheless,
that day Zhao went out to the square and spoke tearily with the students, knowing what they did not: the movement would be crushed
by force if it did not disperse of its own accord. He convinced them
to end their hunger strike.

The next day, May 20, Premier Li Peng announced the imposition of
martial law in Beijing. No more protests or marches would be permitted, and news coverage would henceforth be censored. Satellite broadcasts of the movement by foreign television crews was cut. Ominously,
large numbers of troops and armored personnel carriers began rumbling about Beijing streets.

By May 24 Beijing was full of soldiers. Perhaps the students should
have realized that something foreboding was in the offing, but several
thousand of them vowed to continue their occupation of Tiananmen
Square no matter what. The government, for its part, was determined
to bring the movement to a decisive end. The Communist gerontocrats
were tired of being challenged, interrupted, and instructed by young
hothead students who apparently cared very little for the historical

struggles endured by the Communists to come to power. In the earthy words of the crusty old veteran and high-ranking Communist official Chen Yun, "We must not let the next generation pour a bucket of shit on our heads" (Dietrich 1996, 295). "We seized power and established the People's Republic," Chen Yun told an emergency meeting of senior military officials on May 24, "after decades of struggle and fighting, in which hundreds of thousands of our revolutionary heroes lost their lives. Are we to give it all up just to satisfy the students?" (Hsu 1990, 930).

Sensing the perilous situation the students in Tiananmen Square were facing, demonstrations in support of them were held in several major Chinese cities over the next few days. A rock concert held in Hong Kong on May 27 raised $12 million for the benefit of the protesting students in Beijing. The Beijing students' spirits and defiance were elevated on May 30 when a huge statue called the Goddess of Democracy, obviously patterned after the Statue of Liberty in New York City, was brought into the square before dawn. This attracted journalistic coverage all over the world and seemed to be the last straw for the government; the movement had gone too far in publicly utilizing a well-known American symbol of democracy and freedom, and it would now be crushed.

At 6.00 P.M. on June 3, 1989, the Chinese government issued three warnings over state-run media that the movement was about to be violently suppressed. According to Canadian journalist Jan Wong, who was an eyewitness to these warnings and the subsequent massacres, this was counterproductive and probably increased rather than decreased the number of lives lost (Wong 1996, 248).

By several accounts, the soldiers who murdered unarmed civilians and students had been heavily doped with amphetamines and did not seem to know where they were or what they were doing (Yu and Harrison 1990, xxiii). Wong witnessed the butchery as Chinese soldiers rampaged through the streets of Beijing and Tiananmen Square. She described the horrific scenes just after midnight on June 4, 1989. She stayed up all night during the massacre, trying to contain her horror because she knew she was witnessing a horrific historical event:

> In the darkness I could make out a double row of soldiers, approximately one hundred and twenty men across. At 2:35, they began firing into the crowds as they marched across the square. With each volley, tens of thousands of people fled toward the hotel. Someone commandeered a bus, drove it toward the soldiers and was killed in a hail of

gunfire. The crowd began to scream, "Go back! Go back!" The soldiers responded with another hail of bullets.

By 2:48, the soldiers had cleared a wide swath at the north end of the square. The crowd had thinned a bit. At 3:12, there was a tremendous round of gunfire, lasting several minutes. People stampeded down the Avenue of Eternal Peace.

The soldiers strafed ambulances and shot medical workers trying to rescue the wounded. Some cyclists flung bodies across the back of their bicycles. Others just carried the wounded on their backs. Beijing's doughty pedicab drivers pitched in. Between 3:15 and 3:23, I counted eighteen pedicabs pass by me carrying the dead and wounded to the nearby Beijing Hospital. (Wong 1996, 253)

Toward dawn, the soldiers moved on Tiananmen Square and slaughtered students there:

At 5:17, the soldiers allowed the frightened students to file out through the south side of the square, making them run a gauntlet of truncheons and fists. The students straggled past the Kentucky Fried Chicken outlet and then north. As they turned west onto the Avenue of Eternal Peace, they saw a row of tanks lined up between them and the square. A retreating student hurled a curse. Suddenly, one of the tanks roared to life and mowed down eleven marchers from behind, killing seven instantly. (Wong 1996, 256–57)

The slaughter that is named after Tiananmen actually took place in the streets of Beijing in the vicinity of Tiananmen Square. Shen Tong was an eyewitness to the bloody events of the night of June 3–June 4 at the intersection of Xidan and Chang'an Avenue, near his house:

I fought my way through the crowd, trying to get into the avenue, but I stopped when one of the soldiers fired rapidly at my feet. I wasn't hurt, so I tried to look for the shells, to see whether the bullets were real. Hundreds of people rushed into the avenue to put up barricades, but as soon as they reached the middle of the street, a spray of machine-gun fire scattered them. People who had been hit fell to the ground and lay still. *Those people are dead*, I thought to myself. *The bullets are real*. I couldn't believe it. It was as if this were all happening in a dream ...

... three soldiers jumped from an armored car and shot into the crowd. A flash of bright orange light went up a few meters away; two buses had been set on fire by the people. I walked toward the wreckage and stood behind a tree, watching the flames, which actually looked beautiful against the night sky. More shots were fired at my feet. When I looked in the direction of the gunfire, I found myself staring at a soldier's face. His eyes were popping, bloodshot, and dazed, as if he were on drugs. (Shen 1990, 322–23)

Not all of the people who died in the streets of Beijing in the vicinity of Tiananmen Square were civilians. Enraged crowds also killed soldiers, and in subsequent news of the Tiananmen Massacre by China's state-controlled media, the government played up the deaths of soldiers and mostly ignored the larger numbers of civilian dead.

> ...Smoldering army vehicles were everywhere, and I could smell the fumes of the burning rubber and paint.
> When we entered one alley, we saw a man in an official-looking green uniform being chased by an angry mob of Beijing residents, who caught up with him at a construction site and picked up pieces of brick to hit him with. The man didn't make a sound. I jumped off the bicycle, almost knocking over my uncle, and ran toward them. Pushing the people aside, I saw him lying face down, with blood pouring out of his nostrils as he exhaled rapidly. He looked about eighteen years old.
> "Stop hitting him!" I pleaded with the crowd.
> "It's none of your business," a man said, shoving me away.
> "Please stop it," I begged. "We have to take him to the hospital, we have to find him an ambulance."
> My uncle pulled me away from the mob. "Forget it, Yuan Yuan. He's almost dead—there's no use."
> He put me back on his bicycle and rode off quickly.
> "The solders are killing the people, the people are killing the soldiers, right in the middle of the capital," I mumbled. (Shen 1990, 326–27)

At daybreak the butchery was over, and the 27th Army was busy piling up bodies in Tiananmen Square and covering them with canvas. For the next few days they burned the bodies and had helicopters fly the ashes away. The bodies of most of the people murdered in Tiananmen Square and the streets of Beijing were never recovered.

On June 7 a government spokesman declared that the demonstrations had been counterrevolutionary riots and set up a hotline for informants to turn in people who had participated in them. Two days later Deng Xiaoping himself appeared on television and *congratulated* the soldiers who had crushed the movement. "They are truly the people's army, China's Great Wall of steel. They have stood and passed this test." He did not mention the hundreds of unarmed civilians murdered by the soldiers. Of them he said only, "Their aim was to topple the Communist Party, socialism, and the entire People's Republic of China, and set up a capitalist republic." He ended with a flat statement that his Four

Cardinal Principles forbidding any opposition to the Communist Party were correct (Yu and Harrison 1990, 34). The government then made mass arrests of several thousand people. Some of them were given mock trials and shot in the back of the head. By mid-July the government had issued nationwide arrest warrants for the student ringleaders, but many managed to escape to the West with the help of Chinese sympathizers. Among them were Chai Ling, who entered Princeton, and Wuer Kaixi, who went to Harvard.

9

China in the 1990s

Deng Xiaoping was a popular leader in China until June 1989. His decision to murder his way out of the challenges posed by the student-led protest movements will eventually stain his historical legacy, but a decade into the twenty-first century, the official government line is still that the suppression was warranted. Deng continued to rule over China's modernization efforts until his death in February 1997.

After Tiananmen, Deng's first order of business was to appoint people who would support him to the highest levels of the party and government. He dismissed Zhao Ziyang from his position as head of the Chinese Communist party and replaced him with the relatively unknown Jiang Zemin, who had been mayor of Shanghai. Jiang, a polyglot but otherwise a relatively bloodless figure and unoriginal intellect, parroted the line for Deng and emerged as his replacement and the paramount leader of China in the late 1990s and beyond.

Deng then rounded up thousands of students and their supporters who had participated in the Tiananmen demonstrations. Several student leaders managed to escape from China and flee to freedom abroad, but others did not, including Wang Dan, who was sentenced to 4 years in prison and then resentenced after his release to another 11 years in

1996. Trials of the arrested student leaders and other dissidents were held in 1991, when the world's attention was focused not on China but on the first Gulf War in Kuwait and Iraq. The United States did not draw much attention to these trials, and there was probably some sort of tacit agreement with China during this time: the United States would tone down its denunciation of the Tiananmen Square Massacre if China, with its permanent seat on the Security Council, would not veto the United Nations resolution authorizing the Gulf War.

By 1991 Jiang Zemin was poised to succeed Deng Xiaoping, having consolidated political and military power into his own hands. He now concurrently held positions as party head, president of the People's Republic of China, and the all-important chairmanship of the Military Affairs Commission. He then attempted to achieve a measure of popular support and legitimacy from the Chinese public by appealing to their innate patriotism and by continuing to foster economic development. The pursuit of wealth and continuing resentment of foreign (i.e., mainly American and Japanese) criticism and badgering of China would, he hoped, distract the Chinese people from seeking liberal democracy and freedom. He and Deng Xiaoping both concluded that the Communist regime in China would have fallen in 1989 had China not begun growing wealthy during the 1980s, so they continued to foster and encourage economic development. Jiang and Deng rejected notions that free market economic development always leads to democratization and were determined to make China a wealthy authoritarian state. For them, in other words, economic development in China was not the path *toward* democratization, but away from it.

Western journalists in the 1980s and 1990s often concluded that China had "gone capitalist," but the Chinese government rejected this. "Socialism with Chinese characteristics" was the government's preferred description for what was happening in China. That is, while some private sector enterprises were developing, most businesses continued to be publicly owned and managed, but with a relatively free market rather than central planning determining production and prices. The government continued to apply five-year plans for China, but these were much less artificial and intrusive into the private market than they had been during the 1950s.

By 1995, after Deng had slipped into ill health and senescence, Jiang was more or less running the country. A new leadership group, with Jiang Zemin at the core, had taken over in China. After months of insisting that he was in fine health, the Chinese media announced on February 19, 1997, that Deng Xiaoping had finally died, and Jiang's transition to formal leadership of China was relatively uneventful.

Deng Xiaoping, the architect of China's post-Mao stability and the man who ordered the massacre at Tiananmen Square, died just short of his stated goal of seeing the return of Hong Kong to China on July 1, 1997. Jiang led China in celebrating Hong Kong's return to Chinese control. For Jiang, 1999 was also a banner year because in December of that year the former Portuguese colony of Macao was also returned to China.

The honeymoon period between China and the Western world came to an abrupt end in 1989 after the Tiananmen Square Massacre. The disintegration of the Soviet Union in 1991 deprived the United States and China of the common foe that had in the 1970s driven them into each other's arms in the first place, and the two countries were soon eyeing each other resentfully and suspiciously. Relations between China and the United States grew increasingly rocky during the 1990s as the United States and China began thinking of each other more as rivals than allies or strategic partners. From China's perspective, the American-dominated Western world seemed to be harassing and criticizing China constantly about anything and everything, including its human rights abuses, its oppression of Tibet, its mistreatment of girl orphans, its burgeoning trade deficits, and its piracy of foreign intellectual property (including CDs, videotapes, movies, books, and computer program software). Beijing flew into a towering rage in 1995 and fulminated against Britain in its newspapers for weeks when Chris Patten, the last British governor of Hong Kong, held free elections for the colony's Legislative Council and introduced other democratic institutions. (Beijing dissolved the Legislative Council immediately after it took control of Hong Kong in July 1997 and replaced it with its own Provisional Legislature packed with unelected, pro-Beijing appointees.) Also in 1995, Beijing was infuriated that the United States granted a travel visa to Lee Teng-hui, President of the Republic of China on Taiwan. Lee's purpose in going to the United States was to give an address at his Ph.D. alma mater, Cornell University. But Beijing perceived ulterior motives behind Lee's trip and excoriated him and the American government for weeks over his brief visit to the United States. During the flap over Lee's visit, the campus of Nanjing University was plastered with government posters denouncing Lee and the United States. Ordinary university students, however, seemed to care very little about their government's anti-American tirades and were consistently friendly and polite to American students.

Paranoia in the Chinese leadership and populace grew in the 1990s as more and more people became convinced that the United States and its allies in the West were out to "contain" or "restrain" China and deny it its rightful place among the major nations of the world. Concern over human rights was, in the estimation of the Chinese government and many ordinary Chinese citizens, simply a fig leaf to mask American animosity toward China. How could the United States, with its astronomically high murder rates, race riots, homelessness, urban blight, drug abuse, spectacular mass murders, gang warfare, racism, and gun proliferation seriously expect its preachy pronouncements on human rights to be taken seriously? Something more sinister lurked behind America's insistence on respecting human rights, they concluded.

In the West, on the other hand, there was increasing concern about China's growing swagger and its increasingly defiant attitude toward the outside world. China, after all, supplied harsh dictatorships with nuclear technology and utilized slave labor in prisons to manufacture cheap toys for sale in the West. Would the rest of the democratic and industrialized world be able to convince China to comply with internationally accepted human rights standards and behavioral norms? Right-wing elements in the U.S. Congress and in private American think tanks began in the mid-1990s to characterize China as a potential threat to American security and global dominance, and the publication in 1997 of the influential book *The Coming Conflict with China* by Richard Bernstein and Ross H. Munro fed these fears to a wider American reading public. Concern that Chinese spies had stolen American technology for miniaturizing nuclear warheads, which would greatly boost any nuclear missile program, emerged during the late 1990s and further muddied the already troubled waters of Sino-American relations. Even though he was an immigrant from Taiwan, Chinese-American nuclear physicist Wen-ho Lee was arrested and charged with divulging nuclear secrets from the Los Alamos National Laboratory in New Mexico to the Chinese Communists. (He was later cleared of the most serious of these charges in September 2000.)

The United States was not the only Western nation whose relations with China were strained in the 1990s. The Chinese government expressed continual irritation with Western censure of China's human rights abuses, and its response was always the same old tired, predictable song: China as a sovereign nation was free to abuse its citizens in any way it saw fit, and any criticism from the West of how China governed itself constituted gross interference in China's internal affairs. The Chinese government turned a deaf ear to the explanation that human rights belonged to human beings regardless of their citizenship and thus transcended considerations of national sovereignty. The lens through which China continued to view the rest of the world was, first and foremost, colored by national sovereignty.

The single greatest strain on Sino-Western relations since the Tiananmen Square Massacre came in May 1999, when NATO aircraft bombing the Serbian capital city of Belgrade destroyed the Chinese embassy there. NATO claimed that the bombing was accidental and immediately apologized profusely to the Chinese government for it, but this did not mollify public opinion in China. Some Western strategic analysts speculated that the bombing was a deliberate response to the Chinese embassy's communications assistance to Serbian forces, whose own communications infrastructure had been largely disrupted during NATO's bombing campaign against Serb atrocities in Kosovo. Enraged mobs in Beijing and other major Chinese cities surrounded American and British diplomatic compounds, foreign student dormitories, and any other place they identified with the Western presence, including even American fast-food outlets, and pelted them with projectiles. Security forces worked hard to maintain order and minimize the destruction, but rioters were permitted to throw almost any object light enough to pick up at the American and British embassies in Beijing. Mobs denounced President Bill Clinton as Adolf Hitler and equated NATO with the Nazis, and on American television Li Zhaoxing, the Chinese ambassador to the United States at the time and a diplomat with only a mediocre command of English, lectured American journalists on the evils of NATO rather than listening and responding to their questions. In Beijing, the American ambassador and several members of his staff remained sequestered in diplomatic offices and away from their residences for several days. Electronic mail and other forms of international communication and news coverage remained intact throughout the crisis. Although a few Westerners in various parts of China were roughed up and spat on, none were killed or seriously injured.

Several Western journalists insisted that the riots were planned and orchestrated by the Chinese government, but this is untrue. With a few notable exceptions, Western print and media journalists do not understand China and greatly underestimate the depth of patriotic and nationalistic feeling there today. They come close to libeling the Chinese people as mindless automatons who do not express outrage at Western atrocities unless their government tells them to do so. The anti-NATO riots were in fact almost completely spontaneous, and the Chinese government did not organize or orchestrate them; *facilitate* might be a better word. That is, the government decided to go along with the gathering protest movements rather than risk resisting them and thereby inflaming antigovernment as well as antiforeign sentiment. Popular uprisings in China are very frequently two-edged swords that can cut against the government as well as foreign indignities. The Boxer Uprising of 1899 and 1900 was originally antidynastic until the Qing government coopted it, redirecting popular indignation away from itself and toward Western powers and their embassies. The anti-NATO riots of May 1999 did not start out as antigovernment protests, but they easily could have turned against the Chinese government if it had been seen as being too soft on NATO or condemning of the outburst of antiforeign sentiment. So Chinese government officials went along with the protestors to some extent, appearing on television to express understanding of their indignation but warning them to maintain order. In Beijing the government provided buses for protestors to ride to the American and British embassies, where Chinese security forces permitted vandalism of embassy property but thwarted attempts to storm the embassy compounds. The Chinese government had wisely released a safety valve, and within a few days the entire crisis had dissipated and life went back to normal. Jiang Zemin and his core leadership group parried a potential crisis for their government and walked, with calm and finesse, a delicate tightrope between alienating Western business interests in China on the one hand and alienating the enraged and nationalistic Chinese masses on the other.

In Beijing, many of the very same students who had hurled brick shards at the U.S. embassy a few days earlier soon lined up there to obtain their student visas to study at American universities. The majority of them harbored secret plans to remain permanently in the United States. (Fewer than one-third of the Chinese students who go to America ever return to China.) Their brickbat-and-visa relationship with the American embassy reflected the larger comic complexity of young Chinese intellectuals' love-hate attitude toward the United States: the America that had enraged them a few days before was now doing them a favor. The same might be said of the Chinese government, for which the anti-NATO protests could not have come at a more opportune time. In May 1999, the 10th anniversary of the Tiananmen Square Massacre was looming on the horizon, and nervous Chinese government officials were contemplating various ways of maintaining June 4, 1999, as just another ordinary day. The anti-NATO riots were exactly the distraction the Chinese government needed, and the critical date passed in Beijing and elsewhere in China without commemoration, gathering, or comment.

Sino-American friction continued throughout the rest of the year. American officials responded to the anti-American riots in China by leveling new charges of espionage against Chinese scientists living in the United States. A loosely knit group of American researchers concerned about China's ultimate strategic intentions gained considerable influence with conservative representatives and senators in the U.S. Congress. Known informally as the Blue Team, this group villified the Beijing leadership and encouraged the U.S. government to pursue a harder line with China. Some Blue Teamers even went so far as to speculate that the running of the Panama Canal by the Hong Kong-based harbor management firm Hutchison Whampoa Limited was actually a Chinese Communist plot to gain control of Central America and deploy nuclear missiles there aimed at the United States!

China had legitimate historical grievances against the Western world and Japan; it would be impossible for reasonable people who review China's modern history to conclude otherwise. The fear in some quarters in the 1990s, however, was that China might eventually translate its accelerating development and nascent historical resentments into a confrontation, or perhaps even open warfare, with the West. Perhaps China would even attempt to ally itself with other nations and civilizations hostile to the West in this cause. In his influential book *The Clash of Civilizations and the Remaking of World Order*, Harvard scholar Samuel Huntington argued that in the post-Cold War world, China's relations with Islamic countries and Russia might well be "less conflictual," while its relations with the West will probably be "more conflictual" (Huntington 1996, 245). Would a Sino-Islamic entente eventually emerge to threaten or challenge the West?

During the 1990s an angry and xenophobic book entitled *China Can Say No* (a book that drew the inspiration for its title and content from *The Japan That Can Say No* by Japanese nativists) created something of a firestorm of discussion and public debate in China. Other such shrill, ultranationalistic books soon became available in China, even in respectable, mainstream bookstores. One of the most prominent of these was *China's Road Under the Shadow of Globalization* (*Quanqiuhua Yinyingxia di Zhongguo zhi Lu*; Beijing: *Zhongguo shehui kexue chubanshe*, 1999) by Fang Ning, Wang Xiaodong, and Song Qiang. More than a mere rant piece about the bombing of the Chinese embassy in Belgrade, their book was a sustained polemic, a protracted diatribe, against the government and people of the United States of America. Loving China necessarily entails hating America, they argued. No accusation against Americans was too fanciful or far-fetched for them. The book claimed that the United States did not care about its relations with China: America wanted rather to trample China beneath its feet, America obtained considerable strategic benefit from its bombing of the Chinese embassy in Belgrade, patriotism for Americans amounts to world domination, and America is the most unfriendly nation in the world.

As with paranoid conspiracy theorists and ultranationalists everywhere, they filled their writing with bold-faced type and half-digested works of real scholars they sought both to denigrate and to emulate. Also like conspiracy theorists the world over, they speculated on the hostile intentions of foreign nations, bemoaned their fellow countrymen's lack of nationalistic consciousness, exhorted them to recover their former greatness, and railed against liberalism, intellectuals, globalization, and free trade. They themselves were middle-aged men born in the 1950s, but they were trying their best to convert China's younger generations to their xenophobic point of view.

Their book contained a discussion of race and a crude treatment of the "biological differences between races." White Americans and other Westerners, they claimed, were looking into the possibility of conducting race-discriminating biological warfare (195), and it was undeniable that most of the people able to utilize the technology of the information age are currently white people (196). African Americans avoided racial extinction at the hands of white Americans because they were "physically stronger and more suited to slavery in plantations" (192), and regional separatism is not the problem in the United States that it is in Canada or Northern Ireland because white Americans came very close to "completely and utterly wiping out all Indians" (193–94).

They seemed unable to grasp the essential points and arguments of distinguished Harvard scholar of international relations Samuel Huntington in other than racist terms. The "clash of civilizations" that Huntington and other Western scholars foresee was, they argued, actually a conflict between races (222). There is a Chinese saying that perfectly describes their approach to Huntington: "With the hearts of petty men, they attempt to measure the innards of a gentleman." If the paranoia and ultranationalism of the book could somehow be divorced from its cultural particulars, the book's overall paranoid approach and xenophobic tone might well have been indistinguishable from the far right-wing neo-fascist trash available at a typical American gun show.

It would be comforting and reassuring to assume that the people who adhered to such extremist ideas were amateur autodidacts and other frustrated cranks who washed out of Ph.D. programs because of their lack of focus and discipline. In fact some such ultranationalists were affiliated with respectable institutions in mainland China and even in Taiwan. For example, a professor of foreign languages at National Taiwan University in Taipei, Taiwan, argued with shrill, emotive intensity that freedom would make China lax and democracy will make China collapse. What was so great about freedom, and what was so good about democracy? Power was much more important to China than democracy. Because Westerners were frightened by China's enormous population of 1.1 billion, they used freedom and democracy to divide and weaken the Chinese. The professor warned Chinese compatriots that "when Westerners give you the thumbs-up and call you 'good,' you are nothing but an unmitigated traitor to China!" These rants were contained in a multiauthored book that slavishly parroted the Chinese Communist party line and overflowed with spite and venom toward Chinese dissidents and overseas exiles ("Xiang jianshe Zhongguo di iwan tongbao zhi jing" [My respects to the hundreds of millions of compatriots building China], in Lin and Wei 1999, 206–8).

Of course there were many rational voices in China in the 1990s that discussed China's international relations in more sober and reasoned terms. Many Chinese intellectuals were embarrassed by the shrill tone of such ultranationalistic works and preferred to direct foreigners to more solid and reasoned works by China's large community of responsible intellectuals. The debate in China about democracy, liberalism, and human rights was maturing during the 1990s and was not controlled by extremists who ranted about "Asian values" and rejected respect for human rights as unworkable in China. Contemplations of China's future by such renowned scholars as Yan Xuetong and Li Shenzhi were much more rational and evenhanded.

China changed fundamentally in the 1990s. During this decade the youth of China turned away from agitating for increased liberalization, democracy, and freedom in China and turned toward making money and indulging their ultranationalist impulses, usually at the expense of the United States and Japan. The long and time-honored tradition of student protests and marches was killed at the Tiananmen massacre of June 1989. In 1995 at a Kentucky Fried Chicken store on the Bund in Shanghai, a young Chinese man who was a university student during the 1980s said it all to me: "Since Tiananmen, nobody cares about democracy and freedom any more. Now we're only interested in making money." The students and youth of China today have traded their political birthright for a mess of economic pottage.

10

The Twenty-First Century: Dealing with a Pushy China

"China does not do small," mused CBC Radio One's Jian Ghomeshi on his cultural affairs talk and variety show "Q" shortly after the end of the 2008 Beijing Olympics and the grandiose spectacles of its opening and closing ceremonies. But for China, the ceremonial and athletics of the 2008 Beijing Olympics were what they had been for South Korea 20 years earlier, in 1988: an international debut, a sassy and stylish showcasing of the country's accomplishments, a way of saying to the outside world, "We've come a long way, we're here, and we matter." In China, the fact that Beijing was hosting the games at all was widely regarded as a significant symbolic victory over the United States, which had led a campaign in the 1990s to deny Beijing the 2000 Olympics because of China's human rights abuses.

Indeed, China neither does nor is small. It is a truly massive country by just about any measure imaginable. It is now rapidly emerging as a major world power, and historically, for approximately 2,000 of the past 2,500 years, China has in fact been the world leader economically, militarily, demographically, and culturally. China longs very deeply to resume its historical position as the world's most powerful state, and it has already taken many of the concrete steps required to do so. This will only continue—a prospect that has some people terrified.

As China becomes more powerful and influential, it has been growing more restive and acting with increasing swagger and confidence on the world stage. Some critics of China now maintain that the country has even become abrasive, vindictive, and pushy. Concerns that China might turn out this way date back a number of years. In 1996 Singapore's colorful and controversial former prime minister (and now Senior Minister) Lee Kuan Yew gave an important speech in Washington, D.C., at a dinner hosted by The Nixon Center in which he argued that the United States should take the lead in effectively engaging China and absorbing its energies over the next 50 to 100 years in order to prevent China's emergence once again as a hegemonic behemoth, one attempting to dominate the rest of Asia and perhaps even the world:

> In the triangular relationship between the US, Japan and China, the US-China leg is the most important factor for stability in East Asia. US-China bilateral relations will set the tone, structure, and context for all other relationships in East Asia. A stable US-China relationship will mean stability and growth. An ad hoc and spasmodic relationship will cause uncertainty and instability, and inhibit growth throughout East Asia . . .
>
> As China's development nears the point when it will have enough weight to elbow its way into the region, it will make a fateful decision—whether to be a hegemon, using its economic and military weight to create a sphere of influence in the region for its economic and security needs, or to continue as a good international citizen abiding by international rules to achieve even better growth . . .
>
> . . . China should be given every incentive to choose international cooperation which will absorb its energies constructively for another 50 to 100 years. This means China must have the economic opportunities to do this peacefully, without having to push its way to get resources like oil, and have access to markets for its goods and services . . .
>
> If such a route is not open to China, the world must live with a pushy China. In this event the United States will not be alone in being concerned about what China will do when it is able to contest the present world dispensation. All countries in Asia, medium and small, have this concern: will China seek to re-establish its traditional pattern on international relations of vassal states in a tributary relationship with the Middle Kingdom? Any signs of this will alarm all the countries in the region, and cause most countries to realign themselves closer to the US and Japan.

> The United States should use the time available to encourage and help China to integrate itself into the world community, and to play a part in shaping the international order. Then China will find it worthwhile to accept its obligations as a global citizen. (Lee 1996)

So does the United States' failure to engage effectively with China and mentor it in becoming a good international citizen account for China's newfound pushiness? The answer to this question is open to debate, but up to the present, at least, this much is clear: Beijing is not prickly or pushy about everything. Incidents and developments that elicit Beijing's diplomatic ire and incite China into throwing its weight around in the international arena pertain almost exclusively in some way to China's perceptions of its territorial integrity or internal stability. Thus, activities and personalities seen as favoring or agitating for the independence and secession of Tibet, Xinjiang, Inner Mongolia, or Taiwan from China are on Beijing's diplomatic hit list, as also are the Falun Gong and its leadership.

The number of victims on that diplomatic hit list is growing, and individual companies and even universities are now feeling Beijing's wrath. After the Obama administration approved of a massive arms sale to Taiwan in 2010, Beijing engaged in its same diplomatic invective about U.S. interference in China's "internal" affairs, but this time there was concrete economic action. Beijing targeted Boeing (one of the firms involved in the Taiwan arms deal) by deciding to purchase several dozen commercial aircraft from Airbus, Boeing's European rival.

Beijing can be quite prickly at times about its sovereignty over Tibet and the activities of the Dalai Lama, a man Beijing sees primarily as someone who wants to harm China's territorial unity and integrity by tearing Tibet away from China. While the West may see the Dalai Lama primarily as an inspiring teacher, speaker, and Nobel laureate, in China he is usually depicted as a conniving "splittist" who has figured out how to manipulate public opinion and the media in Western countries. The West sees the Dalai Lama primarily as a religious leader, while China sees him primarily as a political leader. The truth of the matter is, of course, that he is both. China is sensitive about Western universities awarding the Dalai Lama honorary academic degrees and deplores visits and meetings in any capacity between the Dalai Lama and the political leaders of any country. The Dalai Lama has recently claimed that he no longer seeks the independence of Tibet from China, but it is still difficult for Beijing to see him as a non-political leader because he maintains a government in exile in

Dharamsala, India and still upholds a constitution for an independent Tibet.

CAPITALISM AND/OR SOCIALISM AND/OR COMMUNISM: MODERN CHINESE ECONOMIC DEVELOPMENT

In one of the first major popular books about modern China to come out after Deng Xiaoping's decision to institute economic reforms and open up to the outside world, *Time* magazine journalist Richard Bernstein recorded in his 1982 book *From the Center of the Earth: The Search for the Truth About China* his discussions with Chinese friends and students about the relative merits of socialism versus capitalism:

> In Chungking [Chongqing] . . . I talked in an officially arranged meeting with a couple of one-time capitalist entrepreneurs, men who had owned factories in the past, possessed chauffeur-driven cars, liveried servants, had frequently traveled abroad, and who now, after long periods of suffering and persecution, were allowed to give advice to the local government on industry and commerce and foreign trade. I asked them if they weren't discouraged by China's poor record of the recent past, if they, as former capitalists, weren't convinced that the market system with its rewards and incentives, its flexibility and speed, would provide a better solution for China than a centrally planned system. The answer, inevitably, was: "In a few years, you will see the superiority of socialism." (Bernstein 1982, 70)

In the fall of 1980 Bernstein met with a group of university students in Chengdu and attempted to have a frank discussion with them:

> . . . These days, when you want to learn about technology or management or even music, where do you look? To the capitalist countries! When you want to send students overseas, you send them to the United States, France, West Germany, Japan, not Yugoslavia. Can you name a socialist country that has done better than an otherwise comparable capitalist country—South Korea versus North Korea, East Germany versus West Germany, Czechoslovakia versus Austria? No, in every case the capitalist country has done better. Therefore it is fair to ask, what makes you so confident of the superiority of socialism?
>
> The students crowded around a table in their classroom clearly excited to have this contact with a foreigner. They were nice kids, bright, friendly, unaffected. But their answers were clichés of the mandatory kind: "Under socialism there is no exploitation. Under socialism you are guaranteed a job for life. In China you are not at the

mercy of a boss who can fire you if he doesn't like your nose." Then, echoing the optimism of the former capitalists, the students declared: "Come back in a few years and you will see the superiority of socialism." (Bernstein 1982, 71)

Now, nearly 30 years after these discussions, one may well ask if the optimism of Bernstein's friends in the early 1980s was warranted. To be sure, China is now much more economically developed than it was in 1981, but the gap between rich and poor is increasingly larger now. (In fact, this gap is greater in China today under the Communists than it was during the Nationalist period under Chiang Kai-shek.) Unemployment and job security are now economic issues that Mao's command economy never faced. Some Chinese workers, particularly miners and textile workers, are driven like slaves in very dangerous workplaces. Rich people have access to the best health care, and poorer people with serious illnesses are often simply left to die. Chinese cities are vastly wealthier than the Chinese countryside. The coastal provinces of eastern and southern China are much more economically developed than the hinterland provinces. All in all, the spectacular inequality of wealth distribution in China today would have shocked Sun Yat-sen.

Is China still a communist or even a socialist country today? Outsiders have been asking this question since the early 1980s. Many commentators and observers have their doubts, and the views expressed by British journalist and writer Jonathan Fenby are typical:

Is China still socialist, as Hu Jintao proclaims? The predominance of market economics, lack of social care, pollution, recurrent food scandals, growing wealth disparities and illiteracy that is estimated to have risen by 30 million people in five years argue otherwise. At the end of 2008, new high school history textbooks in Shanghai cut the text on socialism to one short chapter out of 52 while giving a single sentence to pre-1978 Chinese Communism and making one reference to Mao. The workers in whose name the CCP claims to rule have lost out. Encouraging output through market mechanisms has proved a lot easier for this authoritarian system than defending its citizens from the adverse effects of growth. The Maoist "iron rice bowl" welfare safety net is gone. The World Bank estimates that the share of wages in the PRC's gross domestic product dropped from 53 per cent in 1998 to 41 per cent in 2005 (compared to 56 per cent in the USA.)

China's leaders still call themselves Communists, but what does this mean for them? . . . How can followers of Communism privatize on an enormous scale, throw millions out of work at state enterprises,

pass laws to defend private property and introduce bankruptcy regulations that recognize shareholders and relegate the rights of workers?
(Fenby 2009, 675–76)

These are pressing and telling questions. But as tedious and evasive
as the basic answer to the question "Is China still a communist or socialist country?" may sound, it really does depend on to whom the question
is addressed and what is meant by "communism." During the 1960s,
virtually anyone queried on the streets of Beijing or Shanghai
about his or her personal belief in Marxism-Leninism-Mao Zedong
Thought would have enthusiastically and unhesitatingly affirmed it.
During the heady days of the 1950s and 1960s, the Chinese public was
brimming with confidence in the leadership of the Chinese Communist
Party, and they bought it all—Mao's personality cult, the necessity of
class struggle, the Marxist idea about the five progressive historical
stages of socioeconomic development (slave, feudal, capitalist, socialist,
and ultimately communist societies), and even Mao's insistence that
some of these historical stages (for example, the transition from feudal
society to socialist society) could be leapfrogged in only a few months
through mass movements and the transformative power of political
education.

Today, however, the same query in the same places would likely
produce blank stares. No, of course the overwhelming majority of
Chinese people do not believe in that *laotao* (old stuff) any more—they
believe in getting rich and, in the process, making China great again. If
the Party can provide the social stability and infrastructural development necessary for continued economic growth, then fine, the public
will support the Party and not challenge its rule over China. Thus, in
one sense, in terms of the public acceptance and legitimacy of basic
Marxism-Leninism-Mao Zedong Thought, the answer to the question
is an emphatic "No," China is no longer a communist country. Communist ideology died with Mao in 1976 and was buried in 1978 when
Deng Xiaoping's reforms were announced.

For the Party itself, however, the answer is another matter entirely.
The Party today continues to be communist in purely ideological
terms. That is, it and its members continue to believe in the basics of
Marxism-Leninism. For them, the question is not whether Marx's
theory of the five stages of socioeconomic development are correct—
they are. The question is *where* along the continuum of these five stages
China is at present. Mao believed that China leapfrogged from feudal
society right over capitalist society during the mid-1950s and was well
advanced into the socialist stage by the late 1950s, perhaps even on the

runway to authentically classless society and communism. (It was this confidence that led him to launch the Great Leap Forward in an attempt to see communism realized in China during his lifetime.) But today, the Party holds that Mao was wrong about this and that China's progression through the five stages must proceed and unfold in an orderly and natural manner, with no more artificial shortcuts or mad-cap mass movements launched in vain attempts to accelerate or do end-runs around orderly historical progression.

So where in the five-stage progression is China today? It is transitioning from capitalist society into the *preliminary* stages of socialism and socialist society. Thus, with China at this stage of socioeconomic development, capitalist economic activity is not simply permissible or tolerable: It is *necessary*—it is quite essential. (There are, accordingly, no real ideological qualms about allowing successful entrepreneurs to join the Party today.) When socialism will have matured is anybody's guess—perhaps by the middle of this century? And the advent of a classless communist society, if it is envisioned at all, is relegated to the very distant and unforeseeable future—perhaps many centuries from now.

Thus, internally and doctrinally, the Party is still communist, or more precisely Marxist-Leninist, in its basic ideology. It has simply corrected a few of Mao's ideological errors or deviances. The Party does not crave much public legitimacy because that is not very important at this historical stage of socioeconomic development. But the Party does occasionally fret about its public "crisis of faith" and envisions a time when its ideological legitimacy with the Chinese public will once again become very important and necessary. But not for now.

So, is China still a communist or socialist country today? The answer really does depend on who is asked.

How did China develop economically to the point that its very existence as a communist or even socialist country is now a point of discussion and contention? The trajectory of China's economic growth over the past three decades, even in piecemeal, incremental format, is indeed breathtaking. But while contemplating China's economic growth with some awe, it is essential to remember this: China recently surpassed Japan to become the world's second largest economy. In terms of per capita GDP, China has a very long way to go before it can equal the advanced industrialized democracies of the world. In per capita GDP China lags behind even Belize, Botswana, and Brazil.

Chinese economic development, along with earlier economic development in Japan and South Korea, has helped alter the center and focus of the world's economy from a trans-Atlantic one to a trans-Pacific one.

Since 1978 the Chinese economy has expanded 14 times in real terms. By the early 1990s China had, after some false starts and obstreperous objections from left-wing diehards and obtuse Marxist ideologues in the 1980s, completed the transition from a clunky socialist command economy to a modern, efficient, primarily market economy.

By the beginning of this century, there were already more cell phones and television sets in China than anywhere else in the world. Today it seems that the cell phones work everywhere in China; spotty coverage is not the problem it is in North America. No area seems too remote or rural for cell phone coverage in China.

Traditional heavy industries have also experienced phenomenal growth in China over the past decade, and because of the voracious Chinese demand for scrap iron, the world price for scrap iron went from $77 U.S. a ton in 2001 to $300 U.S. a ton by the end of 2004. To meet the demand, manhole covers began turning up missing in cities all over the world, including Beijing itself, as thieves made off with them and sought to cash in. (After losing 24,000 manhole covers, Beijing began experimenting with composite manhole covers that would have little recycling value.) In the United States, stainless steel beer kegs were next because they were worth more than the deposits paid on them. Resourceful criminals in Ukraine even stole a vintage steam locomotive from an open-air museum and sold it to a scrap dealer. In 2006, thieves in Vancouver tried to steal an entire Telus phone booth. That same year, thieves in Quebec brazenly stole copper from the roofs of the St-Charles-de-Limoilou and St-Francois-d' Assise churches in Montréal.

China has weathered some fairly serious economic storms, such as the stock market's loss of more than 60 percent of its value in 2007, when property prices began faltering. Inflation has become a problem, primarily because of skyrocketing prices. But China takes these economic fluctuations in stride, and there is no serious talk in the country of ever turning away from capitalism and returning to the inefficiencies and inadequacies of planned command economies.

Economic growth in China has been fueled by extensive direct foreign investment and also by domestic capital; thrifty Chinese families typically save or invest a staggering 50 percent of their income. By 2008 China was holding an estimated two trillion dollars U.S. in foreign exchange reserves. Late that year China passed Japan as the single largest holder of U.S. government bonds and other debt. Indeed, by 2009 it had become abundantly clear that China's economic health was crucial to the world's economic well-being. That year a posting laconically and sardonically summarizing modern China's economic history made its way like lighting around the globe among Chinese Internet users:

> 1949: Only socialism can save China.
> 1979: Only capitalism can change China.
> 1989: Only China can save socialism after the fall of the Soviet Union.
> 2009: Only China can save capitalism. (Fenby 2009, 679)

And the trends continue. Today China has the most Internet connections of any country in the world. By late 2009 China became the world's largest market for automobiles, surpassing even the United States. The most popular automobile brand in China is, perhaps somewhat surprisingly, the United States' General Motors. Wealthier Chinese prefer European cars, but China's growing middle class sees American automobiles as solid and dependable and seems, by and large, to prefer them over Japanese cars.

China's sustained double-digit rates of annual economic growth have broad implications both internationally and domestically. China today is emerging all over the world as a major market for export growth. A few years ago China surpassed the United States as Japan's largest trading partner, and by 2009 China beat out the United States as Brazil's top trading partner. As China becomes wealthier its own domestic markets for manufactured products, foreign and domestic travel, and leisure activities will also grow and become increasingly important parts of the national economy.

Leisure and tourism are up-and-coming growth sectors in China, and wise investors may want to take note of this. Zhao Ziyang, the heroic General Secretary of the Chinese Communist Party who in 1989 opposed the bloody crackdown on Tiananmen protestors and was subsequently placed under house arrest for the rest of his life, loved to golf. In the mid 1980s there were no golf courses in China, but by 2007 China had the fifth-highest number of golf courses in the world, and the game continues to grow in popularity.

Three generations of post-Mao leaders have ruled over this economic transformation of China: Deng Xiaoping, Jiang Zemin, and now Hu Jintao. During the late 1990s Hu Jintao, a native of Anhui (one of China's poorer provinces) born in 1942, was obviously being groomed to succeed Jiang Zemin as China's strongman. Hu, a technocrat by background and temperament, was originally appointed to engineering posts before his star began rising in the Chinese Communist hierarchy.

In 1987 he was appointed to the Party's Central Committee, and in 1988, as party head over Tibet, he made his bones by suppressing pro-independence marches in Tibet and imposing martial law. By 1992 he had risen to the Standing Committee of the Politburo, and by 1999 he was a member of the Central Military Commission. In 2002 he became General Secretary of the Chinese Communist Party. The next year, Hu became the President of the People's Republic of China when Jiang Zemin stepped down from the position. Hu's accession to supreme power was complete in 2004, when he succeeded Jiang Zemin as Chairman of the Central Military Commission. As president, Hu is nominally China's head of government, but his leadership over the Party and the Chinese military assure that he is China's key strongman.

The accession of Hu Jintao and his cohorts to supreme power marks the consolidation of the "fourth generation" governing China. Wen Jiabao (born 1942), a native of Tianjin who by profession is an engineer and geologist, is currently China's Premier, or nominally its head of government. (Even so, Hu is without question the more powerful of the two men.) Together, their rule over China is sometimes called the "Hu-Wen administration."

Over the past decade, then, leadership over China has passed from Jiang to Hu. Remarkably, the term *jianghu* in Chinese, in all but one of the constituent components for Hu's surname, means something like "tough guy from the 'hood" or "slick and worldly-wise." But perhaps not surprisingly, there does not seem to have been any comment on this singular coincidence in the Chinese press.

CHINA'S FUTURE CHALLENGES

Will the synergistic effects of intense, convergent crises produce a "perfect storm" that leads to the overall collapse of China? We cannot know for certain, but several crises or challenges, each unprecedented in all of human experience in its magnitude, loom ominously on the horizon of China's future.

The Natural Environment

First-time international visitors to urban China today are almost uniformly impressed with the country's economic accomplishments and development, but virtually all of them are also aghast at the spectacular environmental pollution they see all around them. China today is one of the most grossly polluted countries in the world, and in 2007 an official report by the World Bank stated that 750,000 people die prematurely in China each year due to causes traceable to extremely high air and water pollution. Also according to the World Bank, 16 of the 20 most polluted cities on earth in 2007 were in China. Major Chinese cities are, by and large, fairly miserable places in which to live, being polluted, crowded, noisy, hot, and too sparsely appointed with public parks and green spaces.

The breakneck pace of China's economic and industrial development is unsustainable environmentally, and so are the rising standards of living in Chinese cities. If all urban Chinese want to live and consume like North Americans, with air conditioners, flat-screen TVs, and privately owned and operated automobiles, China will collapse under the environmental strain. Many environmentalists in China are quite aware of this, but they often strain to make their voices heard by government officials, businesspeople, and economic planners who value development far above all else. Many thoughtful Chinese intellectuals also know that pollution is a very serious issue in China, although a large majority of them seem cynically resigned to the proposition or observation that every developing country fouls its nest environmentally for a period before it learns how to clean up after itself. But how long will this take? Can China afford to wait much longer? China's economic juggernaut has spawned a crassly materialistic worldview that often seems to have little time or space for environmental concerns.

A. Air

In a 2007 *Reader's Digest* survey of the environmental livability ("living green") of six dozen major world cities, Beijing came in dead last. (For comparison, Calgary came in at 59, Los Angeles at 57, Toronto at 50, Ottawa at 33, Berlin at 32, London at 27, San Francisco at 26, Vancouver at 24, Chicago at 23, New York at 15, Paris at 4, and Stockholm at 1.) Open-air visibility in Beijing is often only two or three blocks, and it is typically difficult even to see from one end of Tiananmen Square to the other. Beijing's Forbidden City, once hidden from public view by secrecy and security policy, is now often largely obscured from public view by smog. Visitors to Beijing who get back to their hotel rooms and blow their noses after a long day of seeing the sights will notice on their tissues the startlingly brown-black residual evidence of the air pollutants they have been breathing in all day. It is now something of a commonplace observation that people often cannot see their shadows outside in broad daylight in Beijing, not for cloud cover but for pollution cover. Clear blue days are very few and far between in Beijing. During the lead-up to the Olympics in 2008, industrial operations and the driving of private automobiles were severely restricted long enough to give Beijing a brief respite of reasonably clean air for the games. Some Olympic athletes were so concerned about Beijing's air quality that they flew in just before their events and flew out again as soon as they were over. Right after the Olympic torch had been extinguished in Beijing, the city was back to its old polluting ways, and air quality is now once again as bad as it ever was, if not worsening.

In 2007 China surpassed the United States as the world's top emitter of greenhouse gasses, and acid rain created by the emissions from China's iron foundries and coking plants now spreads all over the rest of East Asia. Most of the air pollution in China is due to bounding increases in coal burning and motorization. China currently accounts for about one-third of the earth's coal combustion, and this is increasing by 10 percent per year. The demand for coal in China is so great that some business interests and government officials look the other way as unregulated and unsafe coal mines operate in China, and every year hundreds of Chinese workers perish in mining accidents. The situation in Shanxi province, the heart of China's coal mining and coal industry operations, is especially serious. An early 2009 report in the *New York Times* relates the essentials and contours of the persistent mining safety problem in China:

> In January, Zhao Tiechui, a senior official in charge of coal mine supervision, told Xinhua about problems regulating the industry. The government has said that 80 percent of the 16,000 mines operating in China are illegal.
>
> "Coal mines often experience the most serious accidents because so many of them are operating illegally," he said. "The industry also sees the most frequent covering-up of accidents."
>
> But mining is lucrative for those at the top. The owners of large mining companies are among China's wealthiest people. (Wong 2009)

The most polluted city in the world is Shanxi province's Linfen, a city of over four million people. There, the air quality is so bad that residents quite literally choke on coal dust, and as a result there are rising rates of lung cancer, pneumonia, and bronchitis. "Don't bother hanging your laundry" in Linfen, advised *Time* magazine in 2007. "It'll turn black before it dries." Canadian journalist Geoffrey York limned the environmental tragedy of Linfen in black, smudgy hues in a 2009 article on the city for Toronto's *Globe and Mail*:

This is the toxic centre of China's coal-producing heartland. It's an apocalyptic vision of clanking factories, spewing smokestacks, burning flames, suffocating fumes, slag heaps, constant haze and relentless dust...

On a winter morning, the smog is so thick that a visitor can barely see 100 metres ahead. Buildings disappear into the haze. The Buddhas in the ancient temples are black with coal dust. Even the sun is barely visible in the darkened sky. Linfen is a ghost city, inhabited by people who loom out of the smog like spectral presences. (York 2009)

Few foreigners venture to live in Linfen, and of course not all Chinese cities are quite this bad in terms of environmental quality. Still, visitors to China must remember that China is an environmentally degraded and dangerous country and should take appropriate precautions before and during travel there.

B. Water

China has approximately the same amount of freshwater resources as Canada, but well over 40 times Canada's population. Put another way, China has about 7 percent of the world's freshwater resources but over 20 percent of its population. Water is thus a very scarce resource in China, with annual per capital availability at only one-fourth of the global average. The once-mighty Yellow River, which historically was feared because of its periodic catastrophic floods on the North China Plain, often does not even flow to the Yellow Sea anymore because its waters are all utilized by agriculture and industry. (In 1997, for example, the river did not flow into the sea for 7 out of 12 months.) The Wei River, once a major geographical feature in Shaanxi province, is now little more than a muddy creek. Two-thirds of China's demand for water is met by groundwater, but overutilization of groundwater has led to saltwater intrusion and land subsidence. Aquifers and water tables beneath Chinese cities, especially in the north, are being drained at catastrophically unsustainable rates. In a memorable 2007 story in the *New York Times* about China's looming water crisis, Jim Yardley vividly describes the problem in the following terms:

Hundreds of feet below ground, the primary water source for this provincial capital of more than two million people [Shijiazhuang, Hebei province] is steadily running dry. The underground water table is sinking about four feet a year. Municipal wells have already drained two-thirds of the local groundwater.

Above ground, this city in the North China Plain is having a party.
Economic growth topped 11 percent last year. Population is rising. A
new upscale housing development is advertising waterfront property
on lakes filled with pumped groundwater. Another half-built complex,
the Arc de Royal, is rising above one of the lowest points in the city's
water table.

"People who are buying apartments aren't thinking about whether
there will be water in the future," said Zhang Zhongmin, who has tried
for 20 years to raise public awareness about the city's dire water situation.
(Yardley 2007)

What is more, available water in China is often very badly polluted
with infectious and parasitic diseases, industrial chemicals, and heavy
metals. Around 700 million Chinese, or more than half of the country's
entire population, consume water containing excessively high levels of
human and animal waste. (Most urban sewage is dumped untreated
directly into lakes and rivers.) Sixty percent of China's rivers and
90 percent of its underground urban water is polluted with sewage
and industrial chemicals, and around 25 percent of China's people
have no access at all to safe drinking water. In 2007 there was so much
toxic algal bloom from nearly 3,000 chemical factories choking Lake
Tai in Jiangsu province, China's third largest freshwater lake, that
two million people in Wuxi city were left without drinking water.
The Huai River in central China is now one of the most polluted rivers
in the world, and an environmentally degraded Huai River basin now
gravely threatens the health and well-being of 150 million people.
Cancer mortality rates in the region are skyrocketing. In Shanxi province, arsenic pollution in the water has led to a province-wide outbreak of arsenicosis.

C. Soil and Land

China has over 20 percent of the world's population but only 7 percent of the farmland. What arable land there is has been spectacularly
altered by the hand of man. According to National Geographic's 2008
Atlas of China, "The large population in eastern China has resulted in
one of the most human-altered landscapes in the world, mostly in the
form of agriculture." (34)

China has one of the most serious soil erosion problems in the world
today. A recent nationwide survey in China found that more than
100 million people in southwest China will lose the land they live on if
soil erosion continues at present rates. Likewise, harvests in northeast

China may eventually drop by almost half if current erosion trends are not halted. Every year illegal logging and slash-and-burn agriculture consume up to 5,000 square kilometers of virgin forest. Over the past two decades, forest cover in central and northern China has been reduced by almost half. The problem has become so serious that the Chinese government has instituted a credible program of reforestation and has begun teaching the Chinese public about its importance. A massive reforestation project is currently underway in the Yangzi watershed.

China is already at least 20 percent desert, and it loses thousands more square miles of land each year to desertification, a major environmental crisis in China with root causes traceable mainly to deforestation and overgrazing perpetrated during Mao's rule. Desertification is now double what it was in China during the 1950s, when Mao's rule began. Old deserts are expanding and new deserts are forming. Ironically, Mao's most enduring influence on China may not turn out to be his revolutionary ideology, relentless promotion of class struggle, or rash attempts at leapfrogging of Marxian stages of historical development, but rather the environmental degradation inflicted on China by his headlong rush to control and exploit nature.

D. The Three Gorges Dam

The Three Gorges Dam, located on the Yangzi River in Hubei province, is a massive hydroelectric dam at the town of Sandouping, about halfway between the major Yangzi River cities of Chongqing and Wuhan. It is the world's largest dam, hydroelectric or otherwise. It was first proposed around 1920 by Sun Yat-sen and later endorsed by Chiang Kai-shek, and Mao Zedong, ever the romantic warrior fighting against the Japanese, the Chinese Nationalists, and nature itself, rhapsodized poetically about the project. Its construction was authorized in 1992, and since that time it has proven extremely controversial.

The dam was completed in 2006 and began producing hydroelectric power soon thereafter, although its full electrical generating potential will probably not be achieved until sometime in 2011. Over the course of its construction, one million residents had to be removed because of the large man-made lake created by the dam, and several important archaeological and cultural sites were flooded out. Environmentalists began sounding the alarm about silting and other ill effects of damming up the Yangzi, but in China, where political will trumps environmental concerns along with everything else, concerns about the dam's environmental impact fell largely on deaf ears. Fear that too much environmentalism might lead to social unrest, always a major dread of the Communist Party, often led not so much to government censorship of public discourse on the topic per se, but to voluntary self-censorship born of long-ingrained instincts for survival and self-preservation.

Since the dam's completion, however, even Communist Party hardliners have had to admit that the dam's critics and detractors have been right. Toxic algal blooms have appeared on the Three Gorges Lake. The dam has triggered landslides, which have in turn produced massive, ocean-sized waves 60 feet in height. It is now widely recognized in China that there will be some difficult environmental consequences created by the dam, including heavy siltation within only a few years, the alteration of entire ecosystems, the extinction of entire species of fish, an increase in waterborne diseases, water shortages created by decreased water flow, and salination as sea water creeps farther upriver. The dam and its lake may be changing weather patterns, leading in particular to decreased rainfall.

The physical vulnerability of the dam is itself a major issue. Geological fault lines cross the dam, and if it ever broke the results would be catastrophic; the lower Yangzi delta area has some of the highest and densest population clusters on earth. Some geologists have speculated that the sheer weight of the water backed up behind the dam might trigger earthquakes. In addition, irresponsible people in Taiwan have threatened to bomb the dam if the mainland ever attacks the island. Terrorists, both foreign and domestic, might target the dam.

Proponents of the Three Gorges Dam tout its very real benefits: its production of electricity without hydrocarbon combustion and also its flood storage capacity, which will ameliorate the perennial problem of seasonal floods along the great river's course. A very long time ago in ancient China, however, Yu the Great figured out that the best flood control measure is ultimately not to contain floodwaters, but to give them somewhere to go—to channel them away. If unexpectedly large floods in the future swell the Three Gorges Lake beyond its containment capacity, the result could be an unthinkable human catastrophe unprecedented in all of human experience.

The relative benefits and detriments of damming rivers have recently come under increased scrutiny and are now important topics of discussion and debate in environmental studies. This, however, has been ignored or downplayed in China. Dams impede or contain the flow of both water and silt, and in this the Three Gorges Dam is no exception. There are concerns that excess accumulation of silt upstream from the dam may eventually clog upstream port cities, while a reduction of sediment flow downstream from the dam may lead to the erosion and sinking of coastal cities on the Yangzi Delta, including the great metropolis of Shanghai itself. China's Grand Canal, a once-ballyhooed major water conservancy project completed during the Sui dynasty (589–618), was eventually rendered useless because of unmanageable siltation. The Aswan High Dam on the upper reaches of the Nile in Egypt, completed with Soviet assistance in 1970, is (or should have been) a cautionary tale for China. The dam's lake, Lake Nasser, flooded out important cultural and archaeological sites and deprives the rest of the Nile of the very silt that made the Nile Delta so fertile agriculturally. On the Nile Delta the interruption of silt flow has led to erosion, salination resulting from the inundation of the Mediterranean Sea, and decreased agricultural yield. The same problems await China because of its Three Gorges Dam, and perhaps on a much larger scale.

Health and Health Care

If American public health is threatened by the obesity epidemic, the greatest threats to Chinese public health today are cancers caused by environmental pollution and cigarette smoking. Nearly two-thirds of all Chinese men smoke, and increasing numbers of Chinese women are also taking up the filthy habit. The manifold ill effects of smoking are clearly known to the medical care profession in China, but nearly half of all male doctors in China still smoke. Meanwhile the Chinese government, which operates and profits from the tobacco industry, is doing little or nothing to encourage its citizens to kick the habit. In the foreseeable future the number of lives prematurely snuffed out in China due to lung cancer and emphysema will only increase, and probably quite dramatically. It is already projected that over the next decade in China's cities, more than half a million people each year will die prematurely from air pollution. The situation is even worse in the countryside, where one in four deaths are associated with respiratory diseases caused by air pollution, cigarette smoking, or both. In some cities in China, cancer mortality rates are so high that they are referred to simply as "cancer cities."

Health care in Chinese cities is vastly superior to that in the countryside, and patients who have the most money to spend get the best health care. The rural and urban poor are largely left to die of their illnesses.

What Canadian surgeon Norman Bethune once said of health care in Depression-era North America is true of China today: "There is a rich man's tuberculosis and a poor man's tuberculosis. The rich man recovers and the poor man dies. This succinctly expresses the close embrace of economics and pathology." (Spence 1969, 217)

Sex Ratio Imbalance

China's growing sex ratio disparity could endanger internal social stability in the country and even damage its relations with neighboring countries. An important recent study of excess male populations in Asian countries has speculated that in some regions of China and India, "bare branches" (single men with no prospects for marriage) are causing rising crime rates and social instability (Hudson and den Boer 2005, 230–41). Perhaps the Qing dynasty's legislative preoccupation with specifying harsh punishments for rootless, vagrant, sexually aggressive males (Sommer 2000, 96–101) had something to do with sex ratio disparity. Much more recently, there have been indications that human smuggling along the China–North Korea border involves almost exclusively North Korean women who have been bought by Chinese men desperate to find wives (Kim 2008, 81–101). According to the Coalition Against Trafficking in Women, tens of thousands of women are bought and sold in China each year, especially in the provinces of Yunnan, Sichuan, and Guizhou, and China is also a popular destination for trafficked women from Russia and Ukraine. Organized crime gangs in China have recently begun discovering how lucrative human trafficking can be when individuals and families are willing to pay the equivalent of thousands of U.S. dollars to traffickers for baby boys or for girls at or near marriageable age. Wife-selling, kidnappings of girls, and prostitution, along with all of the attendant social ills associated with these crimes, will be the natural consequences of China's grossly unnatural gender imbalance problem.

Energy Dependency

China does not have enough natural resources, in particular energy resources, to sustain its burgeoning economic development. Thus China, like most industrialized countries, must look to outside sources to meet its energy needs. China understands its utter dependency on oil from the Middle East and is presently beefing up its military capabilities, particularly its navy, to guarantee the unimpeded flow of Middle Eastern oil into Chinese ports. China's military does anticipate, or at least plan for, possible future competition or even war with advanced industrialized countries over uninterrupted access to energy resources.

China is seeking to secure energy supplies and other natural resources from other regions and countries as well, such as Canada. Unlike most countries, which are content to have an embassy in Ottawa and perhaps two or three consulates in Toronto, Montreal, and Vancouver, the world's three largest national economies (the United States, China, and Japan) are all smart enough to have diplomatic offices in Calgary, the economic capital of Alberta's extensive oil and natural gas resources, widely estimated to be the world's second largest after Saudi Arabia.

China is also looking to Africa in a big way to satisfy its endless energy demands. It offers many African states one variation or another of a very tempting proposal: extensive economic development assistance, with few if any strings or preconditions attached, in exchange for guaranteed access to petroleum, mineral, and timber resources. "Give us unfettered access to that oil well, that forest, and that mine," China more or less says, "and we'll build you railways, highways, and irrigation networks, and perhaps update and reequip your military," all with the understanding, tacit or otherwise, that China will not get involved with matters such as human rights, democracy, or freedom of expression and religious belief.

In concerning itself more with the natural resource wealth of African states than with the quality of their governments and their human rights records, China has propped up some very unsavory regimes and individual leaders in Africa. For example, Robert Mugabe, Zimbabwe's contumacious and reviled dictator and erstwhile revolutionary, is still in power today in part due to Chinese economic support. How to compete economically and diplomatically with radical Muslims and the Chinese energy juggernaut in Africa while at the same time holding true to cherished principles and respect for human rights is a major challenge that the free and democratic world will face with increasing urgency in the future.

Political and Social Stability

The Chinese Communists have staked their all on continued economic development and prosperity in China. In their view, economic development is the way to keep the Communist Party in China from suffering the fates of the parties in other countries such as the Soviet Union, Romania, Poland, and Hungary, among others. But for development and prosperity to continue, there must be political and social stability in China. Several potential challenges to this stability exist, including corruption, turmoil in the countryside, religious movements, human rights abuses, and the free flow of information.

A. Corruption

In his now-classic *The Coming Collapse of China*, an apocalyptic vision of China's political and economic future published in 2001, Gordon Chang argued that China will someday go the way of the Soviet Union, collapsing and disintegrating into several smaller countries. This will be, Chang argues, because of the ineptitude and corruption of the Chinese Communist Party; the weakness of China's banking system, which will one day endanger the savings of ordinary, thrifty Chinese; and China's raucous and traumatic adjustment to the global trading system. One overheated chapter in his book is entitled "Lake of Gasoline: The Discontent of the People is Explosive," and in it Change even declares that into this lake one individual "in some small town, or large city, will have only to throw a match" (Chang 2001, 44).

As of this writing (2011), Chang's dire predictions about China's future have not materialized. But this certainly does not mean that corruption in China has gone away or is now less of a problem. On the contrary. Public perception in China still holds corruption as China's most pressing problem. The Berlin-based nongovernmental organization Transparency International compiles an international Corruption Perceptions Index, and from 2001 through 2006 this ranked China among the most corrupt one-third of the nations of the Earth. A recent audit in China found that from 1996 through 2005, fully 8 percent of public funds in China were improperly appropriated or spent. According to Minxin Pei, Director of the China Program at the Carnegie Endowment for International Peace, "We can suppose that 10 percent of government spending, contracts, and transactions is used as kickbacks and bribes or is simply stolen" (Pei 2007, 2).

Corruption is an especially big problem in land transactions and infrastructural projects:

> Half of provincial transport chiefs in China have been sentenced to jail terms (some have even been executed) for corruption. Corruption is also widespread in the acquisition and transfer of land. Typically, local officials use illegal (and sometimes violent) means to acquire farmland at low prices and later sell the user rights of the land to developers in exchange for bribes.... According to the head of the Regulatory Enforcement Bureau at the Ministry of Land Resources, the government

uncovered more than one million cases of illegal acquisition of land between 1299 and 2005. (Pei 2007, 3)

The tentacles of corruption invade most sectors of the Chinese economy, but in the financial sector it is especially serious:

> Kickbacks for loan approval, massive theft by insiders, misuse of funds, and large-scale fraud are routine in Chinese banks, brokerage houses, insurance companies, and rural credit cooperatives. In 2004, China's banking regulations uncovered 584 billion yuan in misused funds; in 2005, they found 767 billion yuan in misused funds. A large number of top executives in China's largest banks have been jailed for corruption. (Pei 2007, 5)

Corruption does in fact harm China in very real terms and could become politically dangerous for the Chinese Communists if it leads to popular discontent and turmoil:

> The total costs of corruption in China are huge. The direct economic loss owing to corruption represents a large transfer of wealth—at least 3 percent of GDP per year—to a tiny group of elites. This annual transfer, from the poorer to the richer, is fueling China's rapid increase in socio-economic inequality and the public's perception of social injustice. . . . Corruption at the local level sparks tens of thousands of riots and violent collective protests each year, undermining social stability and necessitating extra spending on internal security. Corruption has also contributed to China's massive environmental degradation, deterioration in social services, and the rising costs of housing, health care, and education. (Pei 2007, 5)

Corrupt Chinese government officials are nothing new. Bribery was so common during late imperial times that the Qing government paid its officials "integrity nourishing allowances" to supplement their regular salaries and, hopefully, keep them from taking bribes. But even so, paying off government officials was so extensive that the Qing government usually looked the other way at what John K. Fairbank of Harvard called "the squeeze"; that is, unless it became so outrageous that it led to popular unrest and came to Beijing's attention. If it came to Beijing's attention, the corrupt official in question would be in real trouble. The trick was, accordingly, to maintain bribe-taking and other corrupt activities at just below the boiling point.

Corruption in late imperial times was not limited to officialdom. On the local village and small town scene, members of the gentry class, or those who had passed at least one of the three rungs of the imperial civil

service examination system, were also often bribed by unscrupulous
businessmen and shady underworld figures involved in prostitution
and gambling. Party members in the People's Republic of China today,
who play and fill many of the roles and functions that the gentry did
in late imperial times, also have more or less the same opportunities
for accruing ill-gotten gain. And they, like Qing gentry, need to know
how to keep things from boiling over and coming to Beijing's attention.

B. Turmoil in the Countryside

The benefits of China's breakneck economic growth are by no means
shared by everyone in China. Eastern and southern coastal areas reap
a highly disproportionate share of China's newfound wealth, while
many hinterland provinces lag behind. Standards of living in China's
major cities are far ahead of almost all rural areas in the country. The
CIA estimates that there is a fluid and mobile population of about
200 million rural laborers and their dependents wandering around
China seeking employment and opportunity in large cities. In spite of
the contributions these laborers make to China's economy, they are
widely exploited and mistreated. During the Olympics, Beijing shooed
them out of the central parts of the city in order to present a more
pleasant urban face to the outside world and its cameras. Peasants in
the countryside and rural laborers in the cities are increasingly angry,
and they are speaking up and protesting.

A lengthy report on the lives of peasants in Anhui province entitled
"Investigations into the Chinese Peasantry" (*Zhongguo nongmin diao-
cha*) was published in a magazine in China in 2003, and the issue
quickly sold out. The report spread like wildfire and made its way
onto websites throughout China before it was finally published in
book form in December of that year by the prestigious People's Literature Publishing House. The first printing of 100,000 copies sold out
within a month, and the book proved so infuriating to so many people
in China that Beijing simply banned it as of March 2004, yanking the
book from the shelves of bookstores.

This book, which has been translated into English as *Will the Boat
Sink the Water?*, paints a bleak picture of the lives of peasants in Anhui
and how they suffer at the hands of cruel, vindictive local officials and
cadres who care nothing for their well-being and exploit them. The
book's first chapter, entitled "The Martyr," is about how one peasant,
Ding Zuoming, was murdered for daring to expose corruption and
oppression in his village. After he complained about the corruption

to a deputy of township security named Peng Zhizhong, Peng had three hired thugs beat him severely:

> Against Ding Zuoming's protests, Peng said to the three men, "The lout has no manners. Too spirited. Soften him up a bit." Then he retired.
>
> The three men knew what was meant by "softening up." One of the men present, Zhu, had been Ding's classmate in high school and now sneaked out to avoid a personal confrontation. But he knew that Boss Peng would never be satisfied unless they could break Ding, so before leaving, he suggested that the other two try the "horse's walk," one of their cruellest forms of torture.
>
> Ji and Zhao dragged Ding Zuoming from the cell into an unused reception room to do the "horse's walk." Of course Ding resisted. Despite having spent twelve years in school, Ding was no pale scholar. Having been toughened by years of farm work, he was more than a handful for Ji and Zhao, who could hardly subdue him, not to mention doing the horse's walk. Just then another security man, Wang Jinjun, came in with a club. Ji and Zhao clamoured that Ding Zuoming was attacking them, so Wang raised his club and struck Ding right and left. Ding tried to defend himself, but was hit repeatedly on the arms and the back. Although he was groaning in pain, he would not give in. Ding resisted the "horse's walk," and Wang beat him mercilessly with the club. When the club split, he kicked Ding and used an electric prodder to get him to a kneeling position. When Wang, exhausted, stopped the beating, Ji picked up the stump of a broken shoulder pole and continued where Wang had left off.
>
> By now Ding Zuoming had stopped moaning. He was filled with shock and fear when he realized that as long as he did not "soften up," these thugs would kill him. But he still would not give in. Glaring at Ji, Zhao, and Wang, he shouted at the top of his voice, "True, I accused the village cadres. They are bleeding the peasants. It's against Party policy. Kill me, but I won't give in. If you kill me, my ghost will haunt you all!" Ji looked up and met Ding Zuoming's bloodshot eyes and the piece of wood slipped from his hand. This enraged Wang, who screamed hysterically, "You spineless bastard! Afraid of him! How dare he talk big in this place!" Goaded, Ji picked up the stump and went after Ding again. Meanwhile Zhao took a dirty rag and stuffed Ding's mouth. The three men continued hitting Ding for another twenty minutes. (Chen 2006, 15–16)

Ding Zuoming died of his injuries the next day. Seven men involved in his death were captured and severely punished. Wang Jinjun, who wielded the club, was sentenced to death. Ding Zuoming did not die in vain because his case led to the significant reduction of peasants' tax burdens.

Will the Boat Sink the Water? also details in other chapters how angry peasants appointed representatives to travel to Beijing to petition the highest authorities of the land for relief and how they were sometimes intercepted, mistreated, and returned to their homes without results. Tens of thousands of oppressed and angered people from the countryside still travel to Beijing with petitions for redress of their grievances, and they are routinely rounded up, imprisoned in secret prisons called "black houses," mistreated, and sent back home. According to Andrew Jacobs of the *New York Times*, China's petition system has been overwhelmed recently:

> According to the state media, 10 million petitions have been filed in the last five years on complaints as diverse as illegal land seizures and unpaid wages. The numbers would be far higher but for the black houses, also called black jails, the newest weapon local officials use to prevent these aggrieved citizens from embarrassing them in front of central government superiors. Officially, these jails do not exist. In China's authoritarian state, senior officials tally petitions to get a rough sense of social order around the country. A successfully filed petition—however illusory the prospect of justice—is considered a black mark on the bureaucratic record of the local officials accused of wrongdoing.
>
> So the game, sometimes deadly, is to prevent a filing. The cat-and-mouse contest has created a sizable underground economy that enriches the interceptors, the police and those who run the city's ad hoc detention centers.
>
> Human rights activists and petitioners say plainclothes security officers and hired thugs grab the aggrieved off the streets and hide them in a growing constellation of unmarked detention centers. There, the activists say, the aggrieved will be insulted, roughed up and then escorted back to their home provinces. Some are held for weeks and months without charge, activists say, and in a few cases, the beatings are fatal. (Jacobs 2009)

Thousands of incidents of public unrest have occurred in China every year for the past several years. Most but not all of them occur in the countryside. Kristin Jones of The Committee to Protect Journalists states succinctly the major reasons behind the turmoil:

> "Mass incidents" is the term the Chinese government uses to describe demonstrations, riots, and group petitioning. In January 2006, the Ministry of Public Security announced that there were 87,000 such incidents in 2005, a 6.6 percent increase over the previous year. Protests over corruption, taxes, and environmental degradation caused by China's breakneck economic development contributed to the rise. But some of

the most highly charged disputes have occurred over government seizure of farmland for construction of the factories, power plants, shopping malls, roads, and apartment complexes that are fueling China's boom (Jones 2006)

The *New York Times* website occasionally posted video footage of protests and disturbances, but in 2006 China issued new restrictions on foreign media that required all news reports to be cleared and vetted with Xinhua News Agency, China's state-controlled propaganda arm. Websites for the *New York Times* and many other foreign news media outlets are frequently blocked by "The Great Firewall of China," or the Chinese Communists' Internet filters.

C. Religious Movements

The Chinese Communists dislike organized religion primarily because they look at it in political terms and see in it a possible source of social turmoil and national upheaval. (One has only to recall the Taiping Rebellion of the nineteenth century to see that concerns about the political and even military implications of organized religion are, or at least have been, somewhat warranted.) If they could, the Chinese Communists would simply eliminate organized religion altogether, but they know they cannot. Even Mao once speculated that in the future, in a truly classless and communist society, religion might still exist.

China claims that its citizens enjoy freedom of religion, and indeed they are much freer religiously than they were during Mao's rule. But China is careful to cut off Chinese religious groups from any foreign connections and watches over them closely. This is because the Chinese Communists fear any organization of whatever type that can rival the Communist Party in numbers and influence. Chinese Protestants, for example, are required to belong to the "Three-Self Patriotic" state church, the "three self" referring to the church being self-administering, self-financing, and self-propagating, all without foreign interference or participation. The Chinese government micromanages the state church and carefully monitors the doctrines it teaches and the numbers of Bibles it uses. (The state church is required, for example, to teach that Mao Zedong has gone to heaven, and not to hell.) Many Chinese Protestants resent the officiousness of the official state church and attend unofficial "House Church" congregations in private homes. Surveillance and persecution of the House Churches varies with time and region. Mainland China is a much less religious place than Hong Kong or Taiwan, where Buddhist and Taoist temples and Catholic and Protestant chapels, and also an occasional Islamic mosque, are ordinary parts of any large city or small town. Years of anti-religious propaganda and Marxist-Leninist materialism in the mainland have taken their toll, but there is evidence that religious life is gradually making a comeback.

Of all Chinese religious groups, it is probably Falun Gong that has received the most media attention, both domestically and abroad. Falun Gong, also called Falun Dafa, is a spiritual discipline first made public in China by Li Hongzhi in 1992, toward the end of China's "*qigong* boom." The practice includes a regimen of *qigong* meditation but distinguished itself from other *qigong* disciplines with a moral philosophy rooted in Buddhist tradition, centered on the tenets of Truth, Compassion, and Tolerance. Although the practice does not maintain formal rituals, temples, or the worship of any specific deity, it fits within commonly accepted definitions of a religion in that it seeks to enable the practitioner to attain higher states of being or enlightenment.

Li traveled throughout China between 1992 and 1994 giving lectures to the public. By late 1998, government estimates put the number of Falun Gong adherents in China at over 70 million. In 1996 a rift formed between Falun Gong and the government-run *qigong* association. Li Hongzhi withdrew from the association in March of 1996, and some scholars have speculated that Falun Gong was bullied out of it because Falun Gong failed to accept the authority of the association over its religious operations.

Although some individuals and departments in the government continued to encourage Falun Gong's growth, the group felt under increased scrutiny following its split from the state *qigong* association. Its books were banned from further publication in 1996, and government monitoring of Falun Gong exercise groups gradually increased, culminating in the April 1999 beating and arrest of several Falun Gong practitioners in the city of Tianjin. In response, some 10,000 Falun Gong adherents gathered peacefully outside the central appeal office, adjacent the government compound at Zhongnanhai, to request official recognition and an end to the escalating harassment against them. Premier Zhu Rongzhi met with several representatives and agreed to address their concerns, and the crowd dispersed as quietly and suddenly as it had formed. President Jiang Zemin, however, was deeply unsettled by Falun Gong's ability to summon such a large gathering without the government's knowledge and reportedly felt threatened by Falun Gong's popularity and independent moral philosophy. That evening, Jiang sent a letter through the party ranks declaring that the atheist ideology of the Communist Party must "defeat" Falun Gong.

In the months that followed, Jiang formed a new department called the Falun Gong Control Office. The office was charged with overseeing the eradication of Falun Gong and was given extrajudicial power to execute its mandate. Lawyers were prohibited from representing Falun Gong cases, and on July 22, 1999, the government issued an official ban on the practice of Falun Gong. It also prohibited citizens from protesting the ban.

Reports of the crackdown that followed alleged the arrests and detentions of hundreds of thousands of Falun Gong followers in prisons, labor camps, and mental hospitals. There have also been consistent reports of beatings and torture of Falun Gong practitioners, and two-thirds of all Chinese torture cases reported through the United Nation's special rapporteur on torture have involved Falun Gong practitioners. The U.S. Department of State estimates that Falun Gong adherents comprise as much as half of China's reeducation-through-labor camp population.

In 2006, persistent reports emerged alleging that China's organ transplant industry has been supplied in part with the organs of non-consenting Falun Gong prisoners. Assessing the veracity of these reports is difficult, but later in 2006 Canadian human rights lawyer David Matas and former Canadian Secretary of State David Kilgour concluded that large-scale organ seizures from unwilling Falun Gong practitioners were fairly common in China.

Falun Gong's response to persecution has been nonviolent, focusing primarily on grassroots education campaigns. Perhaps their most common form of resistance has been through the establishment of a network of largely autonomous, underground printing houses that produce and distribute literature about the persecution throughout China. Falun Gong practitioners outside China have established dissident media outlets, including a Chinese-language satellite television station, to broadcast information to mainland China. In 2001, Chinese-American Falun Gong practitioners developed now-widely used software to circumvent China's Internet blockade. In late 2004, some Falun Gong dissidents began circulating a series of critical commentaries on the Chinese Communist Party. Falun Gong practitioners claim that many millions of Chinese have severed all affiliations with the Party as a result of these critical commentaries.

Falun Gong maintains a robust presence in North America and frequently sponsors media campaigns, cultural events, and protests against the Chinese Communists' restrictive policies against their religious practices. The *Epoch News* is an English-language newspaper with ties to Falun Gong, and its Chinese version (*Dajiyuan*) is often among the most popular newspapers in North American Chinese communities. It seems certain that Falun Gong will remain a thorn in the side of the Chinese Communists for some time to come. Religious persecution in China is focused for now on Falun Gong, and perhaps on militant Islam in Xinjiang as well, but waves of it have coursed through the history of the People's Republic of China, and it may well return to some extent in the future. Religious tolerance and freedom are important indicators of the maturity and freedom of a country, and where they are lacking, freedom in general is also lacking.

D. Human Rights Abuses

China is prickly about criticisms of its human rights abuses. The Chinese Communists do not see in human rights concerns the same potential for political and social turmoil that they do in organized religion, but they still remain surprisingly touchy about the subject, perhaps because they are more concerned about their international image than about the human rights of their subjects at home. China is a signatory nation to the Universal Declaration of Human Rights (UDHR), adopted by the United Nations General Assembly in late 1948. The text of the UDHR clearly and unambiguously outlines specific inalienable rights possessed by every individual throughout the world, regardless of the country in which they were born or in which they reside. People enjoy human rights simply by virtue of being human beings, and human rights transcend and trump considerations of national sovereignty and national territorial borders.

China frequently claims to abide by the UDHR, but its actions belie its words. China today often seeks desperately to argue that human rights are culturally and nationally relative concepts and not the absolute, unambiguous rights as outlined in the UDHR. Chinese Communists and the Chinese intellectuals who serve them sometimes also attempt to cast aspersions over the entire concept of human rights by caricaturing it as an instance of anachronistic Western pushiness or cultural imperialism.

Every year the U.S. Department of State issues a report on human rights in other countries, including China, and every year China responds with its own report detailing American human rights issues, thus focusing on the accuser rather than on the substance of the accusation.

But it is not just the U.S. government that accuses China of having a very poor human rights record. Amnesty International regularly reports on China's human rights abuses, as does Freedom House, a nonpartisan group founded in 1941 that monitors the states of democracy, human rights, and political freedoms throughout the world. (According to its own website, Freedom House "has been a vigorous proponent of democratic values and a steadfast opponent of dictatorships of the far left and the far right.") Freedom House has consistently ranked mainland China as "not free" and noted in 2009 that, "Despite expectations that it would enact at least symbolic human rights improvements during its year as host of the Olympic Games, the Chinese government in 2008 increased restrictions on online writers, human rights lawyers, democracy activists, migrant workers, and individuals seeking to petition the central government on abuses by local officials." In 2009 Freedom House also awarded China its lowest rating for political rights and its second lowest rating for civil liberties. Interestingly enough, that same year Taiwan achieved Freedom House's highest score for its political rights and the second highest score for its civil liberties.

E. The Free Flow of Information

Gone forever are the days when strict government control over telephones, radios, radio transceivers, newspapers, books, and magazines could accomplish the obscurantist purposes of the state. Information technology has now exploded beyond the ability of any government or state on earth to control it. The Chinese Communists fear the unimpeded free flow of information because it will lead, among other things, to public discovery of their own party's past and present misdeeds and misgovernment.

The "Great Firewall of China," which the Chinese Communists attempt to use in restricting their subjects' access to information, is something of a problem for Chinese Internet users today. But resourceful and computer-savvy people in China always find a way around it. Proxy servers outside China do help, as does software that can circumvent Great Firewall restrictions. The Chinese Communists periodically block major world news sites such as BBC, CNN, and the *New York Times*.

In 2010 the Internet search engine giant Google announced that it was growing weary of the Chinese Communists' insistence on censoring all search results within China. Google also went public with complaints about the constant barrage of cyber-attacks originating within China against its computer facilities. Google even floated the possibility of withdrawing from the China market entirely rather than

continue accepting and condoning censorship in China while enduring cyber-attacks.

A famous example of how the Chinese Communists require Google
to censor search results involves entering the term "Tiananmen" into
the uncensored, international Google images search engine (images
.google.com) and comparing the results with those obtained by entering the same term into the censored Chinese version of Google image
search (images.google.cn). Typically the uncensored international
version of Google will include photographs of tanks and gore from
the 1989 Tiananmen massacre among its first images, whereas the first
images retrieved by Chinese version will be mostly of smiling tourists,
colorful Tiananmen historical sites, and the like. But things can get
interesting when graphic photographs of the Tiananmen massacre
make it among the images called up by the Chinese version and
remain up for a few hours or even days before China's army of tens
of thousands of hyper-vigilant cyber-cops finally takes them down.

As might be expected, Baidu, the indigenous Chinese search engine,
is better at Chinese-language searches than Google, whereas Google is
better at English-language Internet searches. Most of China's university
students prefer to use Google, and because this generation of students
will one day be China's leadership, Google's withdrawal from China
in the face of difficulties would constitute a large setback for the up-
and-coming educated Chinese elite and, ultimately, for the world itself.
The final resolution of the Google issue will be an important bellwether
for freedom of expression in China.

THE CHINA THREAT

Mao's old ideas about "people's war," or fighting off a land invasion
of China by a foreign force such as Japan or the Soviet Union, are
largely regarded as passé and irrelevant by a significant majority of
China's military establishment today. Ever since the technological performance of the United States military in Iraq during the first Gulf War,
Chinese strategic thinkers have conceptualized more modern types of
warfare, which they have labeled "limited wars under high-tech conditions." With this new emphasis on military technology have come
new ideas about how to resist foreign interference in what China
regards as its internal territorial matters, namely the Taiwan issue. In
2000 RAND Corporation researchers Michael D. Swaine and Ashley
J. Tellis pointed out in their now-classic study of China's strategic
intentions in the twenty-first century that:

Beijing has also embarked on a serious effort to acquire capabilities that could increase the risks accruing to any U.S. attempts at armed diplomacy or outright intervention. These efforts have focused principally on improving China's ability to detect, track, and target U.S. carrier battle groups by multiple means as far away as possible from the Mainland. This includes developing air- and ground-launched cruise missile systems for standoff attack, sea denial capabilities centered on subsurface platforms as well as anti-surface attack and mine warfare systems, and information attack capabilities, centered on anti-satellite warfare, electronic warfare, and deception and denial operations. (126)

Does this mean that China is now preparing for war with the United States at some future date? Perhaps. (It would, in fact, be surprising if China did *not* envision possible wars or battles with the United States in at least some of its war-planning scenarios. All major militaries have these scenarios.)

In Chinese studies in the West and particularly in the United States, there exists something of a dichotomy between Sinophiles on the one hand and Sinophobes or on the other. The former supposedly lap up at face value the Pablum the Party and its newspaper (the *People's Daily*) dish out to them.

Sinophobes, on the other hand, are now legion, as an online search of the offerings of any major booksellers will indicate. They tend to be suspicious of Chinese motives, be wary of Chinese nationalism, and see the devil in every Chinese detail. At this, the end of the first decade of the twenty-first century, China threat books and blogs are a dime a dozen. Such authors think they see in China another incipient Soviet Union or Nazi Germany and write alarmist diatribes predicting doom and destruction for the free world unless the United States wakes up quickly to the threat of the restive dragon.

Most China threat books are sensationalist and irrelevant, but a few do stand out for the depth of their research, knowledge, rigorous scholarship, and fully demonstrated competency with the written and spoken Chinese language. Among such are those by Arthur Waldron, Ralph D. Sawyer, and Michael Pillsbury.

Every year the U.S. Department of Defense, as required by law, issues a report on the military capabilities of the People's Republic of China, and every year Beijing issues a retort claiming that U.S. estimates of China's military might and intentions are distorted and inflated. The *People's Daily*, the official newspaper of the Communist Party, reports dutifully on this in Chinese and English in both its printed and electronic editions.

Some Sinophobes are constantly dinning into the ears of the American and Western publics that war between China and the United States is inevitable, but in this they are not necessarily any more accurate than all of the Cold War prophets of doom who insisted that a great and final war between the Soviet Union and the free world was a future certainty. There are very few if any certainties in history and in human experience, other than the mortality of us all. War with China does not *have* to happen, in spite of what they fear. Perhaps China will, like the Soviet Union before it, eventually collapse. Perhaps China and the United States will learn to tolerate each other, if not have a great deal of affection for each other. Perhaps something else entirely, which we cannot fully imagine now, will happen. The twenty-first century in China will be interesting.

PROSPECTS FOR CHINESE DEMOCRACY

The Chinese government claims that China is democratic already, but this is largely untrue. The Chinese people have little direct say in how they are governed, especially at the national level, and there are no meaningful elections in the country. The Chinese word for "democracy," *minzhu*, means literally "people as sovereign." But today the Party, and not the people, is sovereign in China. It could be said in Chinese that China today is a *dangzhu* ("Party as sovereign") society, not a democratic society. (The Chinese people have never yet been fully sovereign over their own country.) Just as the emperors of imperial times were sovereign over China and ruled with Neo-Confucian ideology, so the Chinese Communists today are sovereign over China and rule with their own state orthodoxy. And they, like the emperors of yore, brook no serious challenges to either their rule or their ideology.

Like their predecessors the emperors of imperial China, the Chinese Communists today insist that ideology trumps democracy. That is, they maintain that politically correct ideological assessment of the basic needs and desires of the people obviates the need for national elections and parliamentary democracy. For the emperors of the late imperial age, this ideology or state orthodoxy was Confucian thought as interpreted and annotated by the Southern Song Neo-Confucian thinker Zhu Xi (1130–1200). For the Chinese Communists, state orthodoxy today is a convoluted comingling of thought systems that might be called Marxism-Leninism-Mao Zedong Thought as refined by Deng Xiaoping, focused by Jiang Zemin, and maybe even tweaked a bit by Hu Jintao. But it is often simply called "socialism with Chinese characteristics" for short. Today the ideology-over-democracy notion is summed up in Jiang Zemin's "Three Represents" theory, first propounded in 2002, which holds that the Party (and thus not the Chinese public itself) represents the best interests of "advanced social productive forces" (the economy), China's culture, and "the fundamental interests of the majority" (the popular consensus).

Actually, the view that correct ideology makes democracy and democratic institutions unnecessary was also shared by the former Soviet Union. Both the Soviet and the Chinese Communist political systems "utilized ideology to buttress the legitimacy of the system, and held that leaders embodied the correct ideology, leaving no room for private, individual interests or for organized opposition to the state" (Lieberthal 1995, 157).

Will China someday have a democratic form of government? Prior to the Tiananmen crackdown, some Western observers were optimistic about the prospects for democracy in China. Merle Goldman's 1993 book *Sowing the Seeds of Democracy in China*, for example, covered the democratic thought of the group around Hu Yaobang, the democratically minded general secretary of the Party until his death in the spring of 1987. But now, for the time being or at least ever since Tiananmen, the Chinese Communists seem to have ruled out any possibility of allowing the emergence of a multiparty democratic system in China. On 9 March 2009 Wu Bangguo, China's second-highest ranking Communist Party member, iterated tersely that China would never implement democratic reforms. Wu represented the Party's conclusion that a multiparty political system, an independent judiciary, and the separation of powers were unworkable for China. "Without a single Communist Party in control, [China] would be torn by strife and incapable of accomplishing anything," he stated flatly (*NYT*, 9 March 2009).

The Chinese Communist Party today is not as fearful of a violent overthrow of its rule as it is of what it calls "peaceful evolution" (*heping yanbian*) away from its one-party dictatorial rule. The Chinese Communists fear that economic development, rising standards of living, and the influences of Western (and perhaps South Korean) culture will combine to make the Communist Party less appealing to the Chinese people and lead to the formation of other, more democratically minded parties and a multiparty democratic political system. This is in fact what may well happen in the long run, but exactly how long that long run will be is anybody's guess. Meanwhile the Party maintains a hyper-vigilant, almost paranoid defensive stance against "peaceful evolution" and regularly inveighs against it in public propaganda campaigns and in political harangues by Party spokespersons.

But enlightened intellectuals and Party members already know that democracy is the wave of the future for China. Zhao Ziyang, the high Communist Party official who was cashiered and put under house arrest for the rest of his life for opposing Deng Xiaoping's bloody Tiananmen Massacre on June 4, 1989, forcefully came to this realization during the last two decades of his life. His comments on parliamentary democracy in his recently discovered political memoirs are courageously forthright, trenchant, and prescient:

> I once believed that people were the masters of their own affairs not in the parliamentary democracies of the developed nations in the West, but only in the Soviet and socialist nations' systems with a people's congress, making the latter system more advanced and a better-realized form of democracy.
>
> This, in fact, is not the case. The democratic systems of our socialist nations are all just superficial; they are not systems in which the people are in charge, but rather are ruled by a few or even a single person ...
>
> In fact, it is the Western parliamentary democratic system that has demonstrated the most vitality. This system is currently the best one available. It is able to manifest the spirit of democracy and meet the demands of a modern society, and it is a relatively mature system ...
>
> In the past few decades, the newly emerging nations with their fast-paced development have illustrated more clearly the trend to converge on a parliamentary democratic system. I am certain this is not by chance. Why is there not even one developed nation practicing any other system? This shows that if a country wants to modernize, to realize a modern market economy, it must practice parliamentary democracy as its political system ...
>
> Given current conditions in China, we must establish that the final goal of political reform is the realization of this advanced political system. (Zhao 2009, 269–70)

During the course of their Meiji Restoration in the late nineteenth century, the Japanese had already realized the universal applicability of Western-style parliamentary democracy. In the words of Taguchi Ikichi (1855–1905), an influential Meiji-era economist and essayist, "We study physics, psychology, economics, and the other sciences not because the West discovered them, but because they are the universal truth. We seek to establish constitutional government in our country [Japan] not because it is a Western form of government, but because it conforms with man's own nature" (Pyle 1969, 90). The large majority of bright young Chinese students also now believe that parliamentary democracy is the world's best form of government, and they quietly and privately tell North American students and professors that they too will someday have an open democratic political system, but that they are concerned about the possible disruptiveness that a rush into democratization might cause in China. Therefore they are content with a slow and incremental progression toward authentic democratization.

China may well be a democratic country one day. It is perhaps something of a naïve American article of faith that democratic countries are necessarily friendly, peace-loving countries. But a fully democratic China could turn out to be even more restively anti-American (and anti-Japanese) than it is right now. The Chinese Communists are acutely aware that any mass passions, be they political, nationalistic, or religious, are potentially destabilizing politically and socially. That is why the Chinese government manages periodic outbursts of nationalistic fervor quite adroitly, as during the Sino-American spy plane collision incident off the coast of Hainan Island in the spring of 2001 or the vandalous anti-Japanese protest marches in Shanghai over the content of newly revised Japanese history textbooks in the spring of 2005. The Chinese government's formula for managing such periodic outbursts of public nationalistic fervor seems to be "validate, facilitate, deescalate." In other words, the state first acknowledges the legitimate public outrage at whatever indignity, real or imagined, China has suffered. Then the state may facilitate protests, for example by busing angry students to protest sites or allowing incendiary comments on Internet sites to remain a few hours (or even days) longer than normal. Finally the state deescalates the matter by encouraging the public and the students to return to their jobs and classes and work hard to make China strong and great again.

Will democratization be the nostrum for all, or even most, of China's ills? Will democratization really transform the Chinese dragon into a fuzzy and loveable panda doll? Is China indeed ready for democracy? What would China be like without the restraining hand of the Communist Party on Chinese nationalism, which sometimes borders on irrational xenophobia? Zealous Chinese and Western ideologues who hope and agitate for the quick democratization of China might do well to contemplate such questions carefully and soberly. An even more urgent question than whether the Chinese people will eventually tire of the Chinese Communist Party and cast it aside, whether peacefully or violently, is this: Who and what will replace the Party if and when they do? The bedraggled Republic of China, eloigned to Taiwan since 1949, is not currently an alternative, if it ever was. The "ROChinese," or the Blue-leaning people of Taiwan, are not real mainland Chinese and have no idea how to govern mainland China. The Falun Gong is a religious group and not a government in waiting or exile. Perhaps the biggest difficulty for China so far in the twentieth-first century is that the Chinese Communists win through simple default, for want of a better or more viable alternative.

But this will not always be the case. The Chinese writer Lin Yutang once wrote during the height of the Cold War in 1966 that "The Chinese people have always outlived their tyrants" (Lin 1966, opposite xvi). The twenty-first century in China will be interesting.

11

A Prosperous and Confused Island: Taiwan since 1945

Chiang Kai-shek's Nationalist government assumed control over Taiwan soon after the Japanese surrender in early September 1945, and there was a brief euphoria and honeymoon period on the island over its restoration to Chinese rule. The situation quickly soured, however, as the realities and difficulties of everyday governance of Taiwan began to sink in for Nationalist Chinese and native Taiwanese alike. In a nutshell, the problem was that native Taiwanese quickly came to see mainland Chinese as oppressors, while mainlanders despised the islanders for being culturally and linguistically Japanese and suspected them of harboring fond memories of Japanese colonial rule.

Like its Communist alter ego on the mainland, Taiwan's KMT government was, from 1949 to the mid-1980s, a dictatorship. Chiang Kai-shek was no democrat, and he ruled Taiwan during this time with terror, high-handed oppression, and tacit U.S. support. During the Cold War Chiang was, in the estimation of the United States, preferable to Mao and the Chinese Communists on the mainland. Soon after the arrival of mainland troops in Taiwan, the island's population grew disappointed and disillusioned with the mainlanders, the majority of whom seemed uncouth and uneducated; most of them had not even known about running water or electricity prior to their arrival. Worse yet, most mainlanders harbored a sense of hostility, resentment, and suspicion toward the Taiwanese because they had been under Japanese rule for 50 years. Tensions eventually flared up between the two groups, and even though the native Taiwanese vastly outnumbered the mainlanders (85% to 15%), the mainlanders had political power and the firepower of the armed forces to give them the advantage in any intercommunal confrontation on the island.

THE FEBRUARY 28 INCIDENT

The mainland Chinese troops were not universally welcomed in Taiwan, and tensions between native Taiwanese and mainlanders began to increase, culminating with a reign of terror on the island that began on February 28, 1947. On that day widespread protests against the Kuomintang government's harshness and excesses broke out. Unnerved by these protests, Chiang Kai-shek unleashed a massive, violent crackdown. Before it was all over more than 20,000 Taiwanese, including many nonviolent intellectuals, had been murdered. The Kuomintang government then swept all record and discussion of this violence under a rug of guarded secrecy, and it was not until the late 1980s that the people of Taiwan began to talk openly, instead of in whispers, about the February 28 Incident. The incident and the long period of terrified silence that followed it seriously diminished the moral stature and legitimacy of the Nationalist government in the eyes of Taiwan's native population. The mainland Chinese who arrived in Taiwan after August 1945 were, at least initially, largely welcomed as liberators and fellow countrymen, but after the February 28 Incident they were reviled as oppressors even worse than the Japanese. "The dogs have gone, the pigs have come" was how many Taiwanese characterized the transition from Japanese to Nationalist Chinese rule.

By early 1947 Taiwan was a powder keg waiting to explode. The fateful spark came on February 27, when an elderly woman selling contraband cigarettes on the streets of Taipei was roughed up by Nationalist agents from the Tobacco and Alcohol Monopoly Bureau. When she resisted and protested a crowd gathered, and in response the agents panicked and fired their pistols wildly into the crowd, leaving one person dead. When news of the incident spread throughout the city the next morning there were protests and riots, and mainland Chinese agents of the Monopoly Bureau were beaten to death.

Rioting quickly spread to other Taiwanese cities, and within a day or two many mainlanders were in hiding, frightened at the specter of widespread ethnic violence on the island. The newly appointed Nationalist leader of Taiwan was concerned enough about the precarious situation to send urgent appeals to Nanjing for military assistance, and when Nationalist military forces arrived in response in early March there was a general bloodbath throughout much of the island. Order was restored through sheer brute force and terror. The violence poisoned intercommunal relations between mainlanders and islanders for decades, and ethnic harmony on the island has been a hotly emotional issue ever since.

George H. Kerr, an American who lived in Japan and Taiwan before World War II, was an Assistant Naval Attaché assigned to Taiwan at the war's end, and in 1947, as a Foreign Service Staff officer and Vice-Consul, he was an eyewitness to the February 28 massacres in Taiwan. His book *Formosa Betrayed*, first published in 1966, is a classic for its portrayal of the Kuomintang's brutality in Taiwan, and his chapter "The March Massacre" contains vivid eyewitness accounts of the violence following February 28 in Taipei:

> Nationalist Army trucks rolled slowly along the road before our house, and from them a hail of machine-gun fire was directed at random into the darkness, ripping through windows and walls and ricocheting in the black alleyways . . .
>
> From an upper window we watched Nationalist soldiers in action in the alleys across the way. We saw Formosans bayoneted in the street without provocation. A man was robbed before our eyes—and then cut down and run through. Another ran into the street in pursuit of soldiers dragging a girl away from his house, and we saw him too cut down.
>
> This sickening spectacle was only the smallest sample of the slaughter then taking place throughout the city, only what could be seen from one window on the upper floor of one rather isolated house. The city was full of troops. (Kerr, 292–93)

Uneducated Nationalists seemed to have had it in for Taiwan's intellectual and economic elite. "The ignorant warlord mistrusts the 'clever' intellectual," Kerr observed (Kerr, 300).

> Tan Gim, Columbia University graduate, banker, and head of a large trust company was taken from a sickbed and done away with. The *Min Pao* editor, Lin Mou-sheng, another Columbia University graduate and former professor of the English and German languages, was dragged naked into the night and not heard of again. Gan Kin-en,

owner and director of important mining interests, was seized and killed. (Kerr, 298)

Students were also regarded with suspicion by Nationalist ruffians and liquidated in large numbers:

> We saw students tied together, being driven to the execution grounds, usually along the river banks and ditches about Taipei, or at the waterfront in Keelung. One foreigner counted more than thirty young bodies—in student uniforms—lying along the roadside east of Taipei; they had had their noses and ears slit or hacked off, and many had been castrated. Two students were beheaded near my front gate. Bodies lay unclaimed on the roadside embankment near the Mission compound. (Kerr, 300–01)

Mainlander violence against native Taiwanese was at times startlingly petty and vindictive and was perpetrated out of spite or to settle old scores:

> At Keelung a minor employee of the Taiwan Navigation Company (an accountant) was taken out to the street in front of the offices and there shot before his assembled office colleagues; he had offended the Manager—an influential mainland Chinese—late in 1945 when he laughed and criticized the Manager's blundering attempts to drive an automobile. (Kerr, 304)

The exact number of people murdered in the February 28 bloodbath may never be known precisely, but according to Kerr it is at least in the several thousands:

> Formosan leaders in exile charge that more than 10,000 were slaughtered in the month of March. I must assume that there could not have been less than 5000 and I am inclined to accept the higher figure. If we add to this the thousands who have been seized and done away with since March, 1947, on the pretext that they were involved in the affair, the number may reach the 20,000 figure often given by Formosan writers. (Kerr, 310)

LAND REFORM

The Nationalist government on Taiwan quickly took steps to improve its image and public relations in the wake of the February 28 disaster. In 1948 the Joint Commission on Rural Reconstruction, composed of Chinese and American members, began planning for the implementation of Sun Yat-sen's long-delayed land reform program. Land reform was the Nationalist government's forced redistribution of farmland to the farmers who actually farmed it.

Land reform program had three stages. During the first stage, which began in 1949, the Rent Reduction Act was implemented. This specified that the maximum any landlord could charge farmers was 37.5 percent of their yield. This single act was very popular among the island's farmers, but the government followed it up in 1951 with the second stage: the sale of public lands (mostly confiscated from Japanese officials at war's end) on easy terms and at no interest to working farmers. (The government made certain that city-dwellers or former landlords were not allowed to buy the land.) The third stage of the land reform program, called the Land to the Tiller Act, began in 1953 and required all wealthy landowning elite families to sell their land, beyond what they needed for their own sustenance, to the state at specified prices. The state then sold this land, again at easy terms and no interest, to tenant farmers. (Fortunately for the Nationalists, they were not dependent on rich landowning families in Taiwan for support, so they could afford to confiscate and redistribute their land with little fear of consequences. A small number of Taiwan's economic and cultural elite families were unhappy with the land reforms, but they were largely ignored.)

Many Nationalists were well aware that they had lost the mainland to the Chinese Communists because of Nationalist neglect of the countryside. In Taiwan, their last bastion, they were determined that relations with farmers would be better. Land reform was enormously popular in Taiwan and considerably improved relations between the Nationalist government and the island's agricultural population. In its wake millions of Taiwanese farmers gained title to their own land. Farmers' income more than doubled over the next few years, and agricultural productivity soared. Land reform was achieved without the bloodshed that occurred on the mainland, and it deprived what few communists there really were in Taiwan of an issue.

THE WHITE TERROR

Safely beyond the reach of the Chinese Communists on the mainland and hiding behind the skirts of the U.S. military, Chiang Kai-shek insisted until his death in 1975 that his military and government would one day return to the mainland in triumph and cleanse it of communist occupation. He stubbornly regarded his as the sole legitimate government of all of China and the Communists on the mainland as mere "communist bandits" (*gongfei*) who would one day be exterminated. Generations of soldiers in Taiwan were inducted into the Nationalist armed forces and indoctrinated with this unrealistic hope. Until around 1987, political and military slogans about one day returning to the mainland and defeating the Communists were plastered everywhere: on government buildings, street signs, school walls, and even mailboxes. Chiang Kai-shek suspended plans for participatory democracy in Taiwan indefinitely because of the "national emergency" involving "Communist bandit insurgency" on the mainland. The ragtag remnants of his central government and various provincial governments ran the entire show, and the tiny number of officials from Taiwan he allowed to be elected into his government and rubber-stamp legislature made little significant difference in the formulation of government policy. Chiang ruled Taiwan with an iron fist and promptly clapped anyone who criticized him or his government in jail. His government controlled all newspapers, television stations, and radio broadcasts and encouraged people to inform anonymously on "Communist troublemakers" (*feidie*, literally "bandit agents"). Government signs in public buses gave people the telephone numbers to call to inform on suspected Communist troublemakers. "Everyone is responsible for informing on bandit agents" (*Jianju feidie, renren you ze*). Fear in the populace and paranoia in the government characterized the bad old days under Chiang's rule.

The Nationalists were in paranoid shock after they relocated to Taiwan in 1949 and 1950, and many of them tended to see communists behind every door and under every rock. Chiang Kai-shek's son Chiang Ching-kuo (later the President of the Republic of China on Taiwan from 1978 to 1988) was put in charge of the Nationalists' internal security apparatus on the island, and his agents were ruthless and greatly feared. During Taiwan's long period of White Terror (1949–1987), when martial law was in force, the Nationalist government arrested large numbers of suspected communists, sometimes on the flimsiest of evidence, and brutally and summarily executed many of them. Thousands more were arrested, tortured, and sentenced to long terms in prison on charges of criticizing the government, sedition, advocating Taiwan independence, or functioning as communist agents. The majority of these victims were innocent, and several of them were prominent members of Taiwan's society, including female dance instructor Ts'ai Jui-yueh, female radio broadcaster and performer Ts'ui Hsiao-p'ing, writer Poyang, English grammar textbook author K'o Ch'i-hua, Presbyterian Church leader Kao Chun-ming, and writer/gadfly/comedian/politician Lee Ao. A majority of these victims were mainlanders.

In Taiwan during the White Terror there were several prisons for the thousands of dissidents found guilty of "political crimes," or expressing political opinions that differed from those of the Kuomintang. Many of the most prominent dissidents were eventually imprisoned for years on Green Island (about 30 kilometers east of Taiwan) in an infamous brainwashing and torture concentration camp run by the Kuomintang. Several high-profile political dissidents, including the famous mainland Chinese writer Poyang (Kuo I-tung), spent years languishing on Green Island. Happily, the political prisoner camp there is today an open museum and a monument to human rights.

Poyang (1920–2008) was imprisoned in the late 1960s by Chiang Ching-kuo for his Chinese-language translation of one segment of the newspaper comic strip "Popeye the Sailor." In the frames in question, Popeye had ended up on a small island and was addressing his subjects there as "Fellows." Poyang translated "Fellows" into Chinese as "Military and civilian compatriots of the entire nation" (*quanguo junmin tongbaomen*), a favorite phrase Chiang Kai-shek used at the beginnings of his speeches. Poyang claims in his memoirs that he meant nothing at all by this translation and did not intend to insult or hurt the feelings of Chiang Kai-shek. Chiang Kai-shek's son Chiang Ching-kuo, however, was furious, and it was not long before Poyang was arrested by the island's feared internal security forces and tortured into confessing to charges of being a communist agent, if not a full-fledged member of the Communist Party. In his memoirs Poyang recalls his 1967 arrest and coerced confession in horrifying detail.

> "Dear Poyang," he [interrogator Liu Chan-hua] said. "Whether to arrest you or not is for us to decide. But whether or not you can walk out that door [to freedom] is for you to decide. If only you come clean, you may leave immediately. Bandit agents the likes of you can never comprehend the lofty and noble sentiments of those of us who are true believers in the Three Principles of the People. We treat people with sincerity. If only you are willing to cooperate, I pledge on my honor that . . . from now on, nobody will ever dare touch you again!"
>
> My two hands were swollen. I said that I was willing to come clean and cooperate, but that I had truly never participated in any subversive organizations.
>
> "Yesterday you confessed to joining the Communist Party, and today you are contravening even yesterday's words!"

Liu Chan-hua put down his ballpoint pen, took up a yardstick, and brandished it menacingly, coming very close on several occasions to piercing my eyeballs. My two hands were burning. Then, quicker than lightning, the yardstick landed with a resounding whack on my right cheek. A fiery flash of pain made me feel like he was using a red-hot iron. As I cried out my left cheek was lashed with the yardstick, and I said, "You beat people?!" With this he struck my right cheek even harder, this time with his fist. My glasses flew off my face and I lost my balance, collapsing onto my cot as I fell out of my chair, which went flying. He then kicked my left knee with the sharp point of his leather shoe, and as I struggled to make it back to my feet he kicked me hard in my right knee. It seemed like I heard the sound of bones breaking, and the fierce pain in both knees made me cry out in pain. As I rolled around on the floor I got another brutal kick, this time in the sternum. I crawled over to a corner of the room wailing in pain and feeling like a stray dog that was about to be beaten to death under a hail of blows. As I struggled to draw my knees in towards my chest I was kicked directly in my right ear. I held my head and was unable to restrain my cries.

"Now you listen here," Liu Chan-hua said. "If you're flogged to death, we'll just say you killed yourself out of fear for your crimes, and that'll be the end of that. You've overestimated yourself."

Suddenly he grabbed me by the hair, and then his fists rained down on my face and chest. I struggled to block his blows with my hands, but he kicked me in my exposed lower abdomen with his leather shoes. I crashed my forehead on the floor but was not willing to die. And even if I did die, it would not have stopped him from beating me. After all, an agent would not be an agent if he cared whether a criminal lived or died. I feared his kickings would give me a brain concussion or make an invalid out of me.

"I'll confess! I'll confess," I cried. "Don't beat me any more."

"Alright. Sit back down in your place."

It took all of three or four minutes for me to crawl from the corner to the edge of the table. I was wet all over and could not manage the fete of standing up. I was shaking like a withered and fallen leaf blown into a corner by a strong wind. Perspiration, fresh blood, and tears covered my face. I gasped for breath and wiped my face with my hand, and only then did I know my face was covered with mud. Liu Chan-hua kindly helped me up and into my chair.

"Out with it!" He took up his pad and ballpoint pen again. I don't know where he threw the yardstick.

"I ... I ... " I thought to myself that I longed to know what he wanted to hear me confess. What sort of participation in which subversive organization would satisfy him? As I groped about mentally for a clue to his intentions I saw the two characters for "Democratic Alliance"

[*Minmeng*] at the beginning of my file, and it seemed like I had found a small clue. With this I sobbed and said, "I participated in the Chinese Democratic Alliance [*Zhongguo minzhu tongmeng*]"

"There now," Liu Chan-hua said with a friendly smile. "Dear Poyang, if you had said this earlier, how could we have had our misunderstanding just now? Actually, we have all your materials at hand. We just wanted you to confess on your own." (Poyang 1996, 267–69)

Poyang remained a political prisoner on Green Island until 1978, when pressure from Amnesty International finally secured his release. After his return to freedom he continued with a distinguished writing career. During the 1990s Poyang began to write in Taiwan's newspapers about his years as a political prisoner, and his erstwhile tormentor, Liu Chan-hua, was so upset about it all that he threatened to sue Poyang for defamation. But Liu Chan-hua's day had passed. In 1996 Chiang Ching-kuo's younger brother, retired Kuomintang general Chiang Wei-kuo (1916–1997), publicly apologized to Poyang on behalf of his deceased brother for how the Nationalist government had mistreated him. Poyang died on Taiwan in 2008, and his passing was widely noted and mourned on the island. His ashes were scattered off the shore of Green Island.

Incredibly, many countries supported Chiang's fiction of being the only legitimate government of all China, of which Taiwan was a part, until well into the 1960s and 1970s. Britain, never a fan of Chiang Kai-shek's government, had recognized the People's Republic immediately after its founding, but most other major countries continued to recognize the Nationalists. In 1964 France extended diplomatic recognition to the People's Republic of China regime on the mainland, and in response Chiang Kai-shek quickly severed diplomatic relations between France and his Republic of China on Taiwan. Canada recognized the People's Republic in 1970, followed by Japan in September 1971. The next month, Chiang Kai-shek's Republic of China on Taiwan withdrew from the United Nations. Chiang Kai-shek was enraged that the PRC was allowed into the United Nations and angrily predicted that the UN would soon collapse as a result. By the mid-1970s most of the industrialized democracies of the world had, with the exception of the United States, faced up to reality, broken off relations with Chiang's Nationalist regime on Taiwan, and recognized the People's Republic of China and *its* claim to be the only legal government of China, of which Taiwan was a part. In the early 1970s the Americans made tentative overtures to the Chinese Communists, and anyone who could sense the directions of the political winds of the time could tell that the United States would eventually recognize the PRC. Chiang Kai-shek did not live to see the final break with the Americans. He died a deeply frustrated and disappointed man in 1975, probably knowing that his government would end up forsaking his dream of recovering the mainland.

On December 15, 1978, President Jimmy Carter finally announced the United States' break with Taiwan and pending normalization of relations with mainland China, which would be effective on January 1, 1979. The abrupt, unceremonious break with Taiwan led to widespread anger and fear in Taiwan. Anti-American riots broke out, and some Americans were beaten for their country's "betrayal" of Taiwan. A mob of protesters went to the Chiang Kai-shek Airport to throw eggs at the U.S. envoys who had flown to the island to speak with Chiang Ching-kuo about the derecognition.

Taiwan was essentially a police state from 1949 until Chiang Kai-shek's death in 1975. During the 1950s Taiwan's White Terror continued internally, and the island was in something of a constant state of alert for a counter-attack against the mainland, which never did happen. The United States did not support Chiang Kai-shek's military ambitions and even actively opposed them for a while during the decade. Chiang Kai-shek stubbornly held the islands of Quemoy and Matsu off the shore of mainland China, despite U.S. misgivings. By the early 1960s, in the wake of the disastrous Great Leap Forward on the mainland, Chiang once again made plans for attacking the mainland, but these came to nothing.

THE KAOHSIUNG INCIDENT

After the death of Chiang Kai-shek in 1975 there were a few brief years of relative openness, and it appeared for a time that more popular elections were in the offing and that there would be broader tolerance for dissent. By the late 1970s, however, these hopes were dashed. The Kuomintang would not loosen its stranglehold on political power without direct popular action and political rallies and protests.

In the summer of 1979 political dissidents Shih Ming-teh and Huang Hsin-chieh began publishing *Formosa* (*Meilidao*), a magazine critical of the Kuomintang government. The government tolerated its publication and distribution, but rogue right-wing opponents, possibly the "Iron Blood Patriots" or the "Anti-Communist Heroes," damaged some of the magazine's twelve offices throughout the island, and on one occasion a *Formosa* staffer was beaten by thugs. Others were constantly tagged and harassed by Kuomintang agents, and their telephone lines were tapped. Activists associated with the magazine planned a rally for December 10, 1979, in observance of International Human Rights Day. This was one of a series of rallies that were to climax on December 16, the anniversary of the U.S. announcement of its impending break of diplomatic relations with the Republic of China on Taiwan and recognition of the Communist regime on the mainland. The Kuomintang permitted the rally but prohibited protest marching. But the march went ahead anyway, with clashes between rally participants (who numbered between 10,000 and 30,000) and police ensuing and each side blaming the other for inciting the ensuing violence. Police with shields and riot helmets fired tear gas canisters into the crowd. Many rally participants and the police officers attempting to control and contain the rally were seriously injured in the subsequent melee, but fortunately nobody was killed.

Official accounts of the incident as well as historical writings based on them claim that the police had been instructed not to retaliate even if they were beaten. There are, however, also reports and indications that there were Kuomintang or gangland *agents provocateurs* in the crowd who stirred up much of the trouble. The Kuomintang-controlled media on the island portrayed the rally as a violent and seditious riot at which the police displayed extraordinary restraint, even to the point of allowing themselves to be beaten without defending themselves. Television news reports featured prominent politicians and entertainers visiting injured policemen in hospitals.

Meanwhile, a full 48 hours after the incident, the Kuomintang began arresting several leaders and organizers behind the rally. Shih Ming-teh eluded capture for a few weeks. The apprehension, show trial, conviction, and sentencing of the "Kaohsiung Eight" became an international media spectacle, and the Kuomintang government did its best through its Government Information Office, headed by Director-General James Soong (Song Chuyu), to control and contain the public relations damage for the Kuomintang government internationally.

The Reverend Dr. Kao Chun-ming, General Secretary of the Presbyterian Church in Taiwan, was imprisoned for several years for his role in sheltering Shih Ming-teh. In his memoirs, Reverend Kao recalls his difficult decision to harbor Shih Ming-teh from the Kuomintang authorities:

On 23 December 1979, Shih Ming-teh escaped into the night as the Kuomintang's dragnet was spread. After this all of Taiwan was on the lookout for him, and a reward of 500,000 NT for information leading to his arrest was put up. In a few days this reward was raised to a million NT, and then to two million, and then 2.5 million NT. Everyone was jittery and fearful of their own shadows.

One day, perhaps 15 December, the publication manager of the Bible Society, one Rev. Chao Chen-erh, came to see me at the General Assembly. He closed my office door and said quietly, "Shih Ming-teh is desperate and has nobody to turn to. I hope you can find a way to help him."

I did not immediately respond to his entreaty. I told Rev. Chao, "Let me think about it." If it were merely my own personal destiny at stake here, this would not have mattered much. But I was also responsible for more than eight hundred Presbyterian churches and 160,000 believers throughout Taiwan. I paced back and forth in my office for more than ten minutes, thinking and praying.

Shih Jui-yun, my assistant, reminded me, "If Shih Ming-teh is arrested again, this time he will be sentenced to death." My heart skipped a beat. The situation is indeed serious, I thought to myself. Shih Ming-teh was not facing any ordinary punishment. He was facing death.

In Christian faith there is an inescapable responsibility to love and protect those in the midst of affliction and suffering. All other Christian duties are relatively secondary to this. Jesus said, "Greater love hath no man than this, that a man lay down his life for his friends." Of all the types of love, the most important is the ability to forsake one's own life for others or for friends. What is more, Shih Ming-teh had been designated by Amnesty International as a prisoner of conscience. He had been using non-violent means in pursuit of political ideals and had been struggling mightily for Taiwan for many years. All the more reason to help him, I concluded.

I said to Reverend Chao and Shih Jui-yun, "Alright." (Gao 2001, 271–72)

With Reverend Kao's help, Shih Ming-teh eluded Kuomintang capture for a few weeks. His American wife, Linda Arrigo (Ai Linda), whom James Soong (Song Chuyu) once compared to Mikhail Borodin (a Soviet Comintern agent who attempted with varying degrees of success to spread communism in Mexico, the United States, the United Kingdom, and China), was deported in mid-December. Linda later returned in the 1990s and today still lives in Taiwan. Meanwhile her arch-critic, James Soong, has largely faded into obscurity.

For a few years, until the full truth about the incident was known, majority public opinion in Taiwan believed that entire incident had been instigated by seditious rabble-rousers and troublemakers.

Leaders of the protest were labeled as insurgents and traitors, and for a while this vilification campaign seems to have worked.

The Kaohsiung Incident (also known as the *Formosa* Incident) turned out to be a major watershed event in the democratization of Taiwan. Several of the imprisoned "Kaohsiung Eight" were to emerge over the next two decades as important leaders in Taiwan. Among them were Annette Lu (Lü Hsiu-lien), who was elected vice president in 2000 and reelected in 2004, and Chen Chu, a woman who was elected mayor of Kaohsiung in 2006. Even more importantly, the lawyers who came to their defense were to emerge in the early twenty-first century as major political figures in Taiwan, among them Chen Shui-bian, Su Tseng-chang, and Frank Hsieh (Hsieh Ch'ang-t'ing).

UNSOLVED POLITICAL MURDERS OF THE 1980S

In addition to open state oppression of the island's political and ideological dissidents, during the last 10 years of martial law there were also some high-profile extrajudicial murders of political dissidents, murders that remain partially or completely unsolved today. The dark shadows of these political murders have left scars on Taiwan's public political psyche to this very day, and their perpetrators remain eerily at large.

The first of these were the Lin family murders of 1980. In February of that year Lin Yi-hsiung, one of the "Kaohsiung Eight" and a vocal Taiwanese dissident and provincial assemblyman who had been charged with sedition and imprisoned for his participation in the Kaohsiung Incident in December 1979, told his wife during a visit from her how his Kuomintang captors had tortured him in an attempt to get him to confess to trumped-up charges. On February 27, 1980, Lin's mother attempted to contact an Amnesty International office in Japan about her son's mistreatment. The next day, on the symbolically important date of February 28, an assassin armed with a knife broke into Lin Yi-hsiung's home on Hsin-yi Road in Taipei and there slashed Lin's mother and twin seven-year-old daughters to death. A third daughter named Huan-chün, then nine years old, managed to survive the murders in spite of having received multiple stab wounds. All of this happened in spite of the Kuomintang's claim to have been watching over Lin Yi-hsiung's home 24 hours a day. A misinformation campaign concocted by the Kuomintang claimed that a mysterious bearded foreigner had committed the murder, but today Huan-chun (now Judy Huan-chün Linton), who works in a Christian ministry, adamantly denies ever having claimed or thought any such thing. An open media statement from her in 2008 says it all:

> I was the sole surviving eyewitness of the murders that took place in my home. I alone saw the assassin. Yet in an effort to divert attention away from the KMT, the KMT controlled media of that time began to circulate a description of a "man with a bushy beard." Though I never once mentioned the assassin as having any beard, every media reporting repeated over and over again this image of a heavily bearded man. Eventually, a bearded foreigner was exiled from Taiwan. The assassin in my home did not have a beard and was not a foreigner.
>
> Fast forward to the year 2003. Just four years ago, 24 years since the murders of my family members, I accepted an interview with TVBS Magazine. I appeared on the cover of the magazine and was their main story for that issue. In large captions, the headline of the article stated: "Judy Lin says, 'I have forgiven the bearded murderer.'" Though I never once used the word "bearded," 24 years later, some one from the KMT still wants to make sure that the murderer is not associated with the KMT.
>
> Several months after that interview, the reporter who penned the article saw me on the street and came running up to me. She wished to ask for my forgiveness. She said it was the decision of her superiors to put words in my mouth, but she still felt responsible. All I could do was smile, expressed [sic] my forgiveness, and pray to God for ultimate justice. (http://www.taiwandc.org/judylinton-Mar2008.htm)

Because nobody wanted to occupy or own a house in which such grisly murders had taken place, the Presbyterian Church in Taiwan bought the home and converted it into the Gikong (I-kuang) Presbyterian Church, which today has a small congregation and additionally functions as a historical site or shrine related to Taiwan's struggles for democratization. Lin Yi-hsiung himself is still alive and has now withdrawn from political life, having chosen instead to work in a nonpolitical capacity for environmental and political reforms. He is very widely admired and respected in Taiwan and is perhaps the closest thing the island has to an elder statesman or national hero.

The murderer of the Lin family members is still at large. According to investigative journalist David E. Kaplan, a shadowy group called the "Iron Blood Patriots" was behind the murder, and behind the group was likely Chiang Hsiao-wu (Alex Chiang, 1945–1991), the no-good, ne'er-do-well second son of President Chiang Ching-kuo and grandson of Chiang Kai-shek himself. Although Chiang Hsiao-wu was, according to Kaplan, "a friend of gangsters and spies," his alleged role in the murders will likely never be clarified. Regardless of who was ultimately responsible for the Lin family murders, a climate of terror and intimidation prevailed in Taiwan for months afterward, as Kuomintang goon squads roamed the island unchecked and unchallenged (Kaplan 1992, 305–306).

The next political murder to shake the island occurred in the summer of 1981, when the body of Chen Wen-chen was found in Taipei early one morning on the campus of National Taiwan University, Taiwan's premier institution of higher learning. Chen Wen-chen, a native of Taiwan, had earned a Ph.D. in statistics at the University of Michigan and landed a tenure track position at Carnegie-Mellon University in Pittsburgh, Pennsylvania. While he was visiting family and friends in Taiwan that year, three Kuomintang members from Taiwan's infamous Garrison Command (*Jingbei zongbu*) showed up at his brother's house and interrogated him for 13 grueling hours about his activities in the United States, which included a quite minimal amount of association with critics of the Kuomintang regime. Chen was, however, by no means a fanatic or an extremist, and there were many Taiwanese critics of the Kuomintang in the United States who had a higher profile than he did. Nonetheless, for some reason Chen Wen-chen's case seemed to stick in the craw of some of his Kuomintang tormenters. The Garrison Command later claimed to have escorted Chen back to his brother's apartment, but he never did return there. The next morning he was found dead, with a fresh one-hundred New Taiwan Dollar bill stuffed into one of his shoes, reflecting an old Chinese superstition that held that if executioners left the deceased with some money, his remains would be properly handled and he would not come back as a ghost to haunt them.

Nobody knows who the murderer of Chen Wen-chen was, but it seems likely that it was someone in the Garrison Command. The case remains unsolved today, and his murderers are still at large and living outside the law. The U.S. government pursued active interest in the case because it involved Kuomintang spying on Chen on American soil. After some investigation the AIT (American Institute in Taiwan, America's quasi-embassy in Taiwan after its recognition of the People's Republic of China regime on the mainland) concluded that out-of-control vigilante gangs, and in particular the Iron Blood Patriots, were likely behind the murder. The group seems to have colluded with sympathetic elements within the Garrison Command to kidnap and murder Chen while on his way home to his brother's apartment. The Taiwan Garrison Command did not like being implicated in the murder, and its commander, General Wang Ching-hsu, publicly speculated that Chen had committed suicide out of feelings of guilt for his supposed crimes. But the public in Taiwan was not fooled, and its sympathies were clearly with the Chens:

> As details of the Chen case emerged, sympathy for the Chen family swept Taiwan. Virtually no one believed the Garrison Command's version of events. Realizing they had a public relations disaster on their hands, KMT officials appointed a special task force to investigate Chen's death. At the same time, hard-liners in the government turned to another overused tactic, cracking down on the press. Warnings went out to newspapers that while they could report on the case, they had best avoid speculation on the cause of death. AIT officials learned that James Soong, the ham-handed director of the Government Information Office, personally telephoned the Hong Kong bureau chief of a foreign wire service to advise him to have his reporters back off the story. (Kaplan 1992, 309)

The thug or thugs who murdered Chen Wen-chen will live on in history in anonymous ignominy, but the professor himself is well remembered as a martyr in Taiwan's struggle for democratization and human rights. Today the Professor Chen Wen-chen Memorial Foundation awards scholarships to college and university students in North America and promotes studies on Taiwanese history, culture, and language. It operates a website at http://www.cwcmf.net.

The most spectacular and high-profile political murder of the 1980s was the carefully planned assassination of Chinese-American muckraking author Henry Liu (Liu I-liang), who was killed on American soil in California by Taiwan-based organized crime thugs operating in collusion with rogue elements and officials in the Kuomintang and the Kuomintang government.

Henry Liu was born in mainland China and fled to Taiwan with the Nationalists in 1949, but by the late 1960s he had grown disillusioned with them and became a prominent critic of the Kuomintang. He emigrated to the United States and became an American citizen, and there he seems to have believed that his U.S. citizenship made him impervious to the Kuomintang's wrath. He eventually turned his writing skills to a biography of Chiang Ching-kuo (1910–1988), Chiang Kai-shek's son and president of the Republic of China in Taiwan from 1978 until his death from old age and diabetes in 1988. Henry Liu was more of a freelance scandal digger than a serious historian or biographer, and his book on Chiang Ching-kuo is an amateurish hatchet job. Nonetheless, Henry Liu's biting style and spicy tone raised some eyebrows in Taipei, and eventually Admiral Wang Hsi-ling, a high-ranking rogue intelligence official in the Kuomintang's state security apparatus, decided along with several other like-minded Kuomintang party members that Henry Liu should be killed, both for his defamatory biography and for his supposedly increasing coziness with the communist regime in Beijing. They may also have intended, by murdering Henry Liu, to convey a warning to other people whose actions they strongly disliked.

Accordingly, Wang Hsi-ling invited Ch'en Ch'i-li (1943–2007) to a dinner appointment on August 2, 1984. Ch'en Ch'i-li was head of the Bamboo Union, a criminal gang founded in Taiwan in 1957 and that in 2008 was named by *Foreign Policy* magazine as one of the three most dangerous gangs in the world. Ch'en happily accepted the assignment to travel to the United States, locate Henry Liu, and kill him. On September 14, after a farewell dinner hosted by Admiral Wang, Ch'en Ch'i-li flew to the United States on his assassin's errand. On October 15, Ch'en Ch'i-li, accompanied by Wu Tun and Tung Kui-sen, found Henry Liu at home in his garage in Daly City, California. One of them shot him to death.

This time, Kuomintang hardliners had gone too far. The murder was a news sensation in the United States, and the U.S. government was aroused and angered that such a brazen political murder had occurred on its soil. (The FBI had strategically placed listening devices and possessed concrete evidence pertaining to the murder.) Congressman Steven Solarz conducted Congressional hearings into the case and demanded the extradition of killers Ch'en Ch'i-li and Wu Tun to stand trial in the United States. The Kuomintang declined to do this, on the pretext that the extradition treaty between the United States and the Republic of China had been rendered null and void by Washington's recognition of the Beijing regime on the mainland in 1979.

But the Kuomintang government was clearly vexed and distressed by the incident and tried hard to make amends with Washington over it. President Chiang Ching-kuo blew his stack at an important meeting of high-ranking Kuomintang leaders and announced to them that all contacts between high government officials and gangsters were to cease at once. He launched a major campaign against organized crime on the island and allowed FBI investigators to come to Taiwan to interrogate Admiral Wang Hsi-ling and subject him to a polygraph test, which Wang failed. Sensing that the Reagan administration did not want to punish Taiwan severely for the murder, President Chiang Ching-kuo made amends by secretly having his government make two deposits of one million American dollars each to Oliver North's secret Swiss bank account for funding the "Contras," who were then fighting the leftist Sandinista government in Nicaragua. President Chiang also strictly forbade any further covert operations in the United States. (Taylor 2000, 385–94)

In Taiwan in April 1985 Ch'en Ch'i-li, Wang Hsi-ling, and Wu Tun were tried in Kuomintang military court, found guilty of murder, and sentenced to "life" imprisonment, but everybody knew they would be out before long. And indeed they were; in 1991 all three murderers were released, ostensibly as part of a general amnesty to mark the occasion of the 80th anniversary of the founding of the Republic of China in 1911. Ch'en Ch'i-li then became a businessman in Taiwan for a time but in the mid-1990s fled to a life of self-imposed exile in Cambodia. After he died of pancreatic cancer in Hong Kong in 2007 his body was shipped back to Taiwan, where gangster Wu Tun helped organize and conduct his funeral. Meanwhile, in 1986 Tung Kuei-sun wound up being extradited from a third country to the United States, where he stood trial, was convicted, and sentenced to 25 years to life imprisonment. He met his end in 1991 at the hands of fellow inmates at a federal prison in Pennsylvania.

We will perhaps never know who ordered the murder of Henry Liu, but there are persistent reports that the man behind it all was, once again, President Chiang Ching-kuo's wayward son Chiang Hsiao-wu (Jiang Xiaowu/Alex Chiang). Chiang Ching-kuo himself seems to have believed that his son Alex was involved in some way:

> At the minimum, however, Ching-kuo came to believe that Alex's "love of intrigue," his life style, his unsavory friends, and his reckless comments had at the least led indirectly to the murder. Almost certainly Ching-kuo himself knew nothing of the plan to kill Henry Liu, but nevertheless he also bore responsibility. . . . The prominent political murders in 1980 and 1981 were also very possibly or even probably related. (Taylor 2000, 390)

DEMOCRATIZATION

Life dragged on in Taiwan during the long White Terror, with the occasional anti-Nationalist riot to break up the monotony, but eventually it improved both economically and politically. Taiwan was emerging as a wealthy and fairly industrialized island by the early 1980s, and during this time there appeared some faint but hopeful signals that Taiwan might become more democratic. Chiang Ching-kuo must be given a portion of the credit for fostering the transition to genuine democracy in Taiwan. He took a significant step toward the reconciliation of the island's mainlander and native populations by appointing Lee Teng-hui, a native Taiwanese with a Ph.D. in agricultural economics from Cornell, as his vice president. He also eased up on many of his father's more draconian policies and perceptibly toned down the back-to-the-mainland rhetoric, although he continued to excoriate the Chinese Communists during his entire tenure as president. In a Chinese speech competition for nonnative speakers sponsored by his government in 1984 in the Dr. Sun Yat-sen Memorial Hall in Taipei, the themes required for the speeches included "upright anti-Communist heroes (*fangong yishi*) fleeing in droves to freedom in Taiwan" and "the demarcation between the Three Principles of the People and communism." That same year Chiang Ching-kuo insultingly referred to the Chinese Communist party as the "Chinese Communist bandit party" (*Zhonggong feidang*) in a televised speech he delivered to an enormous crowd assembled in Taipei for the October 10 National Day celebrations. He had little tolerance for talk of Taiwan independence, but by the mid-1980s he seems to have begun to understand that his father's claim to be the sole legitimate government of all of China was unrealistic. His own purpose seems to have been more toward making the Republic of China on Taiwan as good as it could be and having it serve as an attractive alternative to continued Communist administration of the mainland. To this day, the Chiang Ching-kuo Foundation remains dedicated to promoting Chinese culture and fostering interest in it all over the world.

During the 1980s President Chiang Ching-kuo seems to have had something of a change of heart regarding the legacy of his rule over Taiwan. He took credible measures to reduce corruption in government, and he wanted to be thought of as a man of the people. He frequently traveled around Taiwan and loved to be photographed with groups of ordinary people. During the 1980s local restaurants throughout the island featured pictures of President Chiang patronizing their establishments. As he aged and mellowed he also grew more tolerant of non-Kuomintang political organization. In 1985 he announced that the next president of the Republic of China on Taiwan would not be a member of his family.

Until the late 1980s the formation of political parties was technically illegal, so critics and opponents of the Kuomintang government were referred to collectively as *Dangwai*, or "outside the [Nationalist] Party." Sensing an imminent change of political direction in the air, by the mid-1980s *Dangwai* people and movements became bolder and more assertive, especially after several of them were successful in the local elections the Kuomintang allowed. Many *Dangwai* activists who had been involved in the publication of *Formosa* magazine and the Kaohsiung Incident were now widely regarded as heroes and inspirations.

In 1986 it was plain that major changes were on the horizon, and a trickle of travelers ventured out of Taiwan for the mainland. That same year, in September, many *Dangwai* politicians met informally at a famous hotel in Taipei. During their meeting a bold and daring motion was made to form a political party, and it carried. This was the birth of the Democratic Progressive Party (DPP), which was destined to play a major role in Taiwan's democratization. Fortunately for the DPP founders, they had read the political climate in Taiwan correctly. The next year President Chiang Ching-kuo lifted martial law on the island and allowed many people in Taiwan to visit their families on the mainland.

Chiang Ching-kuo passed away in January of 1988 and was succeeded as president by Lee Teng-hui. Everyone knew momentous changes were coming. In 1990 the Wild Lily student movement demanded direct popular election of Taiwan's president and vice president. President Lee approved of this, and in 1996 Taiwan held its first-ever fully open and democratic presidential election. Lee won it and served a final term of four years as president, and during this term he came out more and more in favor of "Taiwanization," or the strong assertion of the island's differences with the mainland.

After Chiang Ching-kuo died in 1988, the Kuomintang began allowing democratic reforms. The transition from essentially one-party rule to authentic democracy was brief but intense and highly confrontational. Fistfights and even gang fights frequently broke out on the floor of Taiwan's legislature, right under a gigantic portrait of Sun Yat-sen, as members of the DPP, Kuomintang, and other parties struggled to learn how to disagree with one another in a peaceful and civilized manner. One rogue politician with a Ph.D. in philosophy from a German university was in the habit of snatching the microphone away from rival lawmakers, and once a woman legislator walked up to the podium where another woman legislator was speaking and slapped her right in the face, in full view of television cameras. The former one-party rule by mainlander Kuomintang members had fostered such a black-and-white paradigm of good versus evil in Taiwan that people had difficulty imagining that someone could oppose the government and yet remain loyal to the nation. The concept of loyal opposition was new to Taiwan, and for a while it showed. By the late 1990s, however, the people of Taiwan had become more democratically mature, and the fisticuffs tapered off significantly.

In the spring of 1995, President Lee delivered a speech to a gathering of alumni at his graduate alma mater, Cornell University in New York, where he had earned a Ph.D. in agricultural economics. Ironically, the mainland Chinese government, in spite of its long record of haranguing the United States for interfering in China's internal affairs, tried to pressure the U.S. government into refusing to grant Lee a visa. Their reasoning was that Lee, as president of a government that neither the United States nor China recognized as legitimate, should not be allowed to travel abroad because his travel in his official capacity as "president" of the "Republic of China" might lend him some air of legitimacy and implied official recognition. If Lee wanted to go abroad later as a private citizen, after he had stepped down from his position as president, the mainland would have no objection to that. When the U.S. government refused to bow to Chinese pressure and issued President Lee a travel visa over Beijing's objections, denunciations of the U.S. government and President Lee were broadcast nationally on Chinese television and radio, and angry diatribes against Taiwan and the United States were plastered all over public buildings and college campuses. Matters worsened somewhat when the government claimed to discern hints of Taiwanese independence in his speech and lodged the usual and very predictable accusations of U.S. behind-the-scenes complicity in the entire affair. The government's anti-American and anti–Lee Teng-hui propaganda appeared on bulletin boards and blackboards all over the campus of Nanjing University in mainland China. A few people angrily confronted American students about this and wanted to argue about it, but the vast majority of Chinese students on the campus found the entire matter a laughable tempest in a teacup and paid it no mind. They had come to expect these paranoid antics by the government, it seemed, and they were largely cynical and dismissive of them. The mainland government, however, took the entire affair very seriously and indefinitely suspended national unification talks with Taiwan in protest of Lee's visit to the United States. This turned out to be a mistake on the mainland's part because it further increased resentment and suspicion across the Taiwan Strait and interrupted a once-fruitful dialogue between the two governments.

In 1996 Taiwan held its first openly democratic and popular election for the president of the Republic of China. Prior to this time, the president was appointed by the government; even Lee Teng-hui's elevation to the presidency upon the death of Chiang Ching-kuo was the result of succession, not election. Lee Teng-hui had vowed to hold an open and democratic election for the presidency, and in 1996 this became a reality. The Communist leaders of mainland China, always fearful of direct democratic elections, watched nervously as the people of Taiwan excitedly participated for the first time in all of Chinese history in a genuinely democratic and popular election of a national leader. The free speech of the campaign unnerved the Communist rulers and led them to fear that widespread sentiment in favor of Taiwan's formal independence might be given popular and legitimate expression in the election. Mainland Chinese news broadcasters, failing utterly to understand the momentous significance of the democratic nature of the election, warned Taiwan not to harbor ambitions of formally breaking away from China based on its "excuse" of having "changed the manner of selecting its president." Lee, for his part, publicly stated during the campaign that the mainland was "crazy in the head" (a phrase he spoke in Japanese) over the election and his visit to Cornell the year before.

Highly distressed by all of this and suspicious that Lee was secretly scheming for independence, the mainland launched a crude campaign of intimidation aimed squarely at Taiwan's voting public. Mainland Chinese warships plied the waters near Taiwan and "test fired" several missiles in the general direction of the island. Their purpose was to create panic and fear in Taiwan and goad the island's population into backing away from their pending election of Lee Teng-hui. This clumsy demonstration of brute force showed just how little the mainland rulers really knew and understood Taiwan's people, and their actions produced the opposite effect. Support for Lee actually *increased* during this time, especially after he traveled to the Pescadores (a group of islands midway between Taiwan and the mainland) and defiantly shook his fist at the mainland, proclaiming that nobody was frightened of Chinese Communist scare tactics.

U.S. President Bill Clinton jumped into the fray by sending two carrier battle groups from the U.S. Seventh Fleet (stationed in Japan) into the waters off Taiwan in a show of force against the mainland vessels attempting to intimidate the island. This action enraged the Chinese leadership, and soon the inevitable accusations of U.S. connivance in Taiwan's elections were flying. In the end, however, the Chinese warships backed off and returned to port, and the situation blew over. Hotheads in the mainland nursed a growing grudge against the United States for its influence in the region, while in Taiwan some advocates of Taiwanese independence began to believe, perhaps unrealistically, that the action proved that the United States would never stand idly by and allow the mainland Chinese military to invade or seriously menace their island.

Tensions between the mainland and Taiwan were once again heightened in mid-1999, when President Lee announced in an interview broadcast over German radio that he and his government would now conduct talks and contacts with the Communist government on the mainland only on the basis of government-to-government relations. In doing so Lee was simply emphasizing the obvious facts that two governments on either side of the Taiwan Strait did in fact exist and that the Republic of China had been a reality since 1912. To the mainland, this was an ominous step closer to a formal declaration of independence. Given the mainland's recent belligerent mood and saber rattling, Lee's "one country, two governments" formulation was precipitous and ill-advised. It only increased suspicion and heightened tensions in the Taiwan Strait, across which fundamental misunderstanding existed in both directions.

Tensions flared up once again in February 2000, when the mainland Chinese government issued a white paper making new threats to Taiwan. Like mainland China's saber rattling in early 1996, these new threats occurred on the eve of democratic presidential elections on Taiwan and were obviously intended to intimidate and bully the island's voting population into selecting a candidate pleasing to Beijing. The Chinese Communists were clearly unnerved by the possibility of a pro-independence candidate winning the election and taking Taiwan even farther down the road of formal independence. The three candidates running were Lien Chan (President Lee's vice president); Chen Shui-bian, a native Taiwanese and member of the DPP who had declared that Taiwan already *was* a sovereign state and did not need to declare it formally; and James Soong, a former member of the Kuomintang who now ran as an independent and generally favored closer ties with the mainland. Of these three candidates, James Soong was obviously the most suitable as far as Beijing was concerned, and Lien Chan, even though he had been Lee Teng-hui's vice president, was certainly more acceptable than the pro-independence choice Chen Shuibian. Chen Shuibian won the election with 39 percent of the popular vote. James Soong finished right behind him with 37 percent; and Lien Chan came in a distant third at 23 percent. The remaining 1 percent of the vote went to minor also-rans.

James Soong and Lien Chan both favored eventual reunification of Taiwan with mainland China. Meanwhile, they would pursue a status quo ante policy, neither rejecting unification nor taking concrete steps toward it. It was just this go-slow, status quo approach to unification that was troubling Beijing in early 2000. The Chinese Communists did not want to wait forever for the unification of China, and they could not understand why Taiwan rejected Deng Xiaoping's "one country, two systems" approach for China, which seemed to them to be working nicely enough for Hong Kong.

The previous blustering from the mainland had consistently emphasized that Taiwan would be invaded if one of two situations developed: a formal declaration of independence or foreign invasion of the island. In February 2000 a third condition was added: indefinite postponement of unification. Taiwan loomed very large in Jiang Zemin's thinking about his historical legacy. Mao and Deng both made great contributions to China: Mao had liberated China from Chiang Kai-shek and foreign imperialists, and Deng had stopped Mao's ruinous mass movements and brought relative prosperity by opening China to trade and contact with the outside world. Jiang was the third major leader of the People's Republic of China; what would his historical contributions be? Jiang noted with satisfaction that the return of Hong Kong in mid-1997 and Macao in late 1999 had both occurred during his rule. The reunification of China would be his legacy, along with the continuation of Deng Xiaoping's policies. Only Taiwan remained beyond Beijing's grasp, and Jiang longed to bring the island back to the motherland during his rule. Taiwan's continued resistance to Beijing's overtures was a source of frustration and vexation for Jiang Zemin and China's other Communist leaders as the year 2000 dawned in China and around the world.

THE PRESIDENCY OF CHEN SHUI-BIAN

As president, Chen Shui-bian grew increasingly open about his wish for Taiwan to formalize its de facto independence, but in this he was opposed by the Kuomintang majority in the island's legislature, and he and his vice president, Annette Lu, were demonized by the Chinese Communists and their media on the mainland. Chen and Lu ran for reelection in 2004 against the Kuomintang's Lien Chan and James Soong, narrowly winning the vote. Up until the last few days of the campaign it appeared that Lien and Soong would win the presidency handily, but on March 19, 2004, there occurred a bizarre shooting incident that likely tipped the scales in the favor of Chen and Lu. On that day in the city of Tainan, the president and vice president were traveling in an open Jeep vehicle when both were grazed by bullets. Their injuries proved only superficial, and they were both released from hospital the same day. Whether or not this was a staged incident (*kurouji*) engineered to elicit sympathy votes for Chen and Lu is still a controversial and divisive question in Taiwan, and what a person thinks about it seems largely predetermined by his or her political sympathies. Whatever the realities of the incident, Chen and Lu won the vote by 30,000 votes and served four more years as president and vice president.

Allegations against Chen and his family about financial wrongdoing and money laundering emerged during Chen's second term. In response, in the late summer and fall of 2006 Shih Ming-teh, one of the "Kaohsiung Eight," launched a popular campaign to oust Chen from the presidency or pressure him into stepping down. (Ironically enough, Chen Shui-bian had once been Shih Ming-teh's defense attorney in the aftermath of the Kaohsiung Incident.) Shih's followers wore the color red to symbolize their anger and to emphasize his contention that his followers were united mainly by their frustration at Chen's alleged corruption. The "Red Shirt" movement held marches throughout Taiwan for a time, but it ran out of steam by the end of the year without succeeding in toppling Chen.

The entire movement was divisive and unnerving for the island. People driving red cars in southern Taiwan had their vehicles vandalized, and barbed wire barricades and jack-booted troops armed with M-16 machine guns surrounded the Presidential Palace to protect it. The movement brought to the surface some latent-foreign feelings. The specter of increased ethnic tensions also loomed.

President Chen badly mismanaged Taiwan's economy, and this plus widespread public suspicion that he or his family members had indeed been involved in illegal financial transactions doomed the election chances for Frank Hsieh and Su Tseng-chang, who ran on the Democratic Progressive Party's presidential ticket. They were defeated in the March 2008 presidential elections by the Kuomintang candidates Ma Ying-jeou and Vincent Siew, who are now the President and Vice President of the Republic of China on Taiwan. Ma and Siew have dramatically decreased tensions with mainland China, and with their Kuomintang super-majority in the island's legislature they now rule the island without much effective opposition or criticism.

Former president Chen Shui-bian was arrested in November 2008 and remains in prison as of this writing. He and his sympathizers suspect that his confinement and prosecution are part of a political payback campaign waged against him by the Kuomintang, and there have been some troubling indications that he and others implicated in his case have been denied some measure of due process. Nevertheless, members of his family have pled guilty to financial wrongdoing. The ultimate fate of Chen himself remains to be seen.

GREEN AND BLUE

Partisan politics in Taiwan today are sometimes badly polarizing and stridently Manichaean, especially during national elections. Since Taiwan's democratization in the 1990s, a duality of "Blue" versus "Green" has emerged, with "Blue" symbolizing the people and parties (mainly the Kuomintang or Nationalists) who generally favor some sort of eventual accommodation or unification with mainland China, and "Green" representing people and parties (mainly the DPP, or Democratic Progressive Party) who identify with the island's majority ethnic group and topolect and hope for an eventual separation from the mainland, amicable or otherwise. The Green and Blue camps sometimes demonize each other in the most puerile of terms, with Blues insisting that Greens are traitors to China and lackeys of the Americans and Greens swearing just as adamantly that the Blues are traitors to Taiwan and allies with the Communists on the mainland. Foreigners who allow themselves to be swept up in the maelstrom of Taiwan politics usually sympathize with the Greens, and their subjective blogosphere invective sometimes reflects an undercurrent of animosity toward mainland Chinese. (Some mainland Chinese and their first- and second-generation descendants in Taiwan today have their own prejudices toward the ethnic majority in Taiwan, but these animosities do not often find expression on the English-language Internet.)

TAIWAN'S PATH OF DARKNESS

Politics in Taiwan are already difficult and strident enough, but compounding the island's complexities even further is the widespread problem of organized crime, known in Mandarin Chinese as *heidao*, the "black way" or the "path of darkness." The ubiquitous extent and influence of organized crime on the island was perhaps no more apparent than during the widespread media coverage of the 2007 funeral for Ch'en Ch'i-li, the crime gang boss behind the murder of Henry Liu.

Ch'en's funeral was attended by men in black shirts, retired state security officials, and miscellaneous Taiwan establishment glitterati, including celebrities and business fat cats. Most astonishing of all, however, was the presence at the funeral of several politicians, among them Legislative Speaker Wang Jin-pyng of the KMT (Kuomintang) and Legislator Ko Chien-ming of the Democratic Progressive Party (DPP). In a scathing editorial entitled "Gangsters, gangsters everywhere," the English-language, Green-leaning *Taipei Times* on November 9, 2007, lit into the two lawmakers for their attendance:

In the course of mourning Chen, the sight of a string of celebrities, ne'er-do-well politicians and retired security agency officials lining up to pay their dues played itself out. Of the former, pop singer Jay Chou was the most conspicuous, and he has gutted his reputation—and raised questions about who he owes and how much—by paying his respects. Chou should be ashamed, but we are not sure if he has the depth of character to feel it.

But it is the politicians—and their seniority—that should be of enduring concern. How astonished and enraged Americans would be if House of Representatives Speaker Nancy Pelosi joined the organizing committee for the funeral of a notorious mafia boss. Yet that is exactly what has happened here: Legislative Speaker Wang Jin-pyng of the KMT blessed Chen by having his name added to the list of honorary funeral officials. Again, one might ask, what does Wang owe, and to whom?

The KMT, it seems, can't get by without cavorting with criminals.

But this is not a partisan cancer. Even more despicable is the presence on the honorary list of Democratic Progressive Party (DPP) legislative caucus convener Ko Chien-ming, who warrants expulsion from the party.

… This easy association with criminality continues to plague the legislature, too, with an attempt to restrict candidates for public office to people with no criminal record or a minor criminal record being defeated in recent days.

Both parties have acted shamefully and shamelessly on this matter. President Chen Shui-bian, as chairman of the DPP, deserves censure for not intervening to ensure that DPP support for the changes did not eventuate.

And Wang Jin-pyng deserves an equally strong rebuke for blithely dismissing this debacle as being unworthy of any concern …

It is all too easy to say "a pox on all their houses" or some such, but the fact is that all of this behavior is tolerated by a large number of voters who will put any lowlife into office as long as it is not someone from the opposition. Thus continues this collapsible morality in the face of criminal connections to the political, security, and entertainment establishments.

According to a high-ranking law enforcement official in Taiwan, the reach and influence of organized crime on the island has recently reached crisis proportions (Chin 2003, 13–14).

In November 1996 Taoyuan County Magistrate Liu Pang-yu was murdered along with several other people, including his bodyguards, in a mafia-style hit. The murders remain unsolved today. Newspaper headlines screamed the story to the public, and the subsequent feeling of dread and dismay throughout the island was palpable. Taiwan's justice minister became famous for revealing that around one third of Taiwan's 800+ city and county councilors were tainted by organized crime backgrounds or contacts and for his warning that if efforts at "sweeping away organized crime" (*saohei*) were not thorough, Taiwan would become another Sicily.

Things have not dramatically improved since 1996. According to a recent study of organized crime in Taiwan, "Hardly a day goes by without news reports about politicians, businessmen, and gangsters being involved in financial scandal, bid rigging, corruption, vote buying, violent confrontation, or fraud" (Chin 2003, 14). A corrupt triangular nexus among politicians, gangsters, and businessmen has developed in Taiwan, with each corner of the triangle giving benefits to, and receiving benefits from, the two other corners. The result of this baleful triangulation is the moral confounding of Taiwanese society:

> A relationship between the upperworld and the underworld has evolved into an integration of the two worlds into one and the development of public figures who are at the same time gangsters, entrepreneurs, and politicians in the fullest sense. An influential legislator who is also the convener of the judicial committee of the legislature could also be one of the richest entrepreneurs in the country and the one who proclaimed himself to be the "spiritual leader" of a powerful gang and listed as a hoodlum by the authorities. A county magistrate who was imprisoned as a hoodlum could also be the owner of a major construction company and other big businesses and considered by his constituents as the best county executive in Taiwan. The integration of the upperworld and the underworld in Taiwan results in the development of a morally confusing society where politicians are talking and acting like gangsters and gangsters are talking and acting like politicians. (Chin 2003, 19)

Although voter participation rates in Taiwan are quite high, the ubiquitous tentacles of organized crime and shady moneymen in Taiwanese politics have given some people in Taiwan, particularly intellectuals, considerable pause and moral qualms about voting. There is little wonder that so many mainland Chinese are so cynical about Taiwan's democratic process. Further, a large majority of American leaders and policy makers would quite likely rethink their view of Taiwan as a viable emergent democracy if they knew the extent to which criminal gangs manipulate the island's democratic institutions. These gangs constitute a significant threat to the island's newfound democracy and international security and are a blight, nay a tumor, on Taiwan's body politic.

TAIWANESE SOCIETY

Taiwan's society is another story. Taiwan has been called an island of corruption and covetousness, but in terms of public and personal safety and violent crime rates it is superior to almost any Western country. Random mass murders, shootings in post offices or schools, and poison gas attacks in subways are unknown. It is quite safe to walk in Taipei after dark, and unless one gets involved in drugs, commercial sex, or gambling there is very little reason to fear the organized criminal gangs on the island. Health care delivery is efficient, inexpensive, and socially just.

For all of its problems and setbacks and its current economic slump, Taiwan is a more livable and loveable society than mainland China is today or the island itself once was before its democratization. Taiwan has a much more modern feel to it, and this is not limited to its material prosperity. Now that the bad old days of the White Terror and one-party Kuomintang rule are gone, the tiresome and ubiquitous political slogans against communism on the mainland have disappeared, and so have most statues of dictator Chiang Kai-shek. There is no more censorship of domestic or foreign news media, and there are dozens of television channels from which to choose. (There were only three until the late 1980s.) The people of Taiwan are, by and large, well-mannered and speak quietly in public. Public restrooms in Taiwan are much cleaner than they once were, and vehicular traffic is relatively orderly. (Sometime between 1985 and 2005 drivers in Taiwan learned not to honk their horns indiscriminately.) Users of Taipei's ultramodern rapid transit subway system actually line up for subway cars and escalators, and smoking is now strictly prohibited in public places in Taipei. The written language in Taiwan is beautiful and aesthetically coherent because it retains the traditional, complex characters. Dogs are liked in large Taiwan cities and are treated relatively well. The Taiwanese topolect is openly and freely spoken in public now, and gone forever are the signs that used to exhort the Taiwanese, "Be proper and upstanding Chinese people—speak Mandarin!" Forming a political party in Taiwan is not an illegal or seditious act, and Internet users in Taiwan can write virtually anything they want about their government and fear neither censure nor censorship nor recrimination. The island feels modern, open, free, and relaxed, quite possibly because it is democratic.

THE POLITICS AND IDEOLOGY OF TAIWAN HISTORY

In Taiwan today, Taiwan history is a polarized field, with Green voices predominating, at least in the more popular histories of Taiwan commonly available in bookstores. The arguments for and against Taiwan's historical independence from China are manifold and convoluted. A popular argument posits in crudely racial or genetic terms the non-Chinese identity of the majority of Taiwan's people today, maintaining that historical patterns of intermarriage between Han Chinese and the island's aboriginal populations have produced a population ethnically distinct from that on the mainland. (This argument presupposes, of course, that the essential core of Chineseness is genetic or phenotypic, an assumption fallacious on its face and unworthy of serious comment.)

Others argue that Taiwan was never ruled by Qing China, which is of course a distortion of historical facts. More sophisticated historians and history buff activists argue that the Qing never ruled over *all* of Taiwan; only the western plains region of the island settled by Han Chinese were ruled by the Qing government, they observe, whereas the aboriginal regions in the mountains areas and the eastern coastal areas were largely left to their own devices and rule. This argument usually includes some description of Qing Taiwan's society as particularly turbulent and prone to rebellion. But according to a highly authoritative history of seventeenth- and eighteenth-century Taiwan, Qing Taiwan's society was neither exceptionally turbulent nor its government exceptionally corrupt, and the Qing "ruled Taiwan with the same repertoire of policies it applied to other regional societies" (Shepherd 1993, 3).

Others maintain that Taiwan during the Qing dynasty was not part of China but of the Manchu empire. This contention, however, is questionable because it does not *ipso facto* negate the very real geopolitical and administrative union of Taiwan with Fujian province on the mainland in the 1680s; the Qing dynasty *was* China's government at the time, and the ethnicity of the ruling dynastic house that accomplished this union of Taiwan with mainland China is irrelevant.

Still others concede that although China may have had sovereignty over Taiwan, this sovereignty ended in 1895 when China ceded the island to Japan in accordance with the terms of the Treaty of Shimonoseki. (This argument assumes, of course, that Taiwan was the Qing's to give away in the first place.) Blue historians counter by arguing that the Treaty of Shimonoseki was part of the nineteenth-century era of unequal treaties and imperialist victimization of China and was, therefore, legally illegitimate. Any subsequent developments flowing from the Treaty of Shimonoseki are fruits of the poison tree and are irrelevant, Blue historians maintain, at least as far as the ultimate fate of Taiwan is concerned. Many Green historians, on the other hand, affirm the legality of the Treaty of Shimonoseki and then point out that Japan in the San Francisco Peace Treaty, signed in 1951 and effective as of April 1952, renounced all claims and title to Taiwan but did not specify which country or regime would gain sovereignty over the island. Blue historians counter that the Cairo Declaration, issued by the United States, Great Britain, and the Republic of China in 1943, and thus predating the San Francisco Peace Treaty by several years, contains a provision that Taiwan would be retroceded to China after the defeat of Japan. Green historians respond that the Cairo Declaration was just that: a *declaration* and not a legally binding treaty.

And so the debate goes, on and on, around and around, with no definitive resolution in sight. In some ways the debate is dishonest or at least not genuine, since many of its principals already have conclusions and positions firmly in mind prior to considering historical evidence and arguments. Many of the contours of this debate are actually quite compelling and interesting, but ultimately the historical debate over the international disposition of Taiwan is largely irrelevant. This is because the most ingeniously constructed and eloquently presented historical arguments will never convince Beijing to quit its territorial claims to Taiwan. Most people who take a clear-eyed view of Taiwan's past and present do know this. So what are historian-activists who agitate and argue for Taiwan independence really doing? Their hearts may be in the right place, and they may be striving for the moral high ground, but the fate of Taiwan is not really very much of a moral issue. Taiwan's fate is first and foremost a *political* issue, although in the worst-case scenarios it might also become a military issue.

TAIWAN'S FATE

What will become of the new and flourishing democracy on Taiwan? This is one of the major international questions for the first decades of the twenty-first century. In Taiwan today there is a widespread sense of helpless fatalism or impending, resigned acceptance of whatever the island's ultimate fate turns out to be. Perhaps only a minority will want to stand and fight in the face of an invasion from the mainland. People who three decades ago were "recapture the mainland" true believers and ardent Cold Warriors are now soberly defeatist or capitulationist in their attitudes. There seems to be little sense among Taiwan's youth today that their island democracy is worth fighting and dying for. Therefore they may lose it.

Despite the fondest wishes of Taiwan independence advocates and Republic of China boosters alike, Taiwan's fate will not be decided by the people of Taiwan alone. It will be decided partially in Taipei, perhaps, but certainly in Beijing as well, and perhaps also in the corridors of power in Tokyo, Washington, New York, and Brussels. Taiwan has often felt swept along in the strong political currents flowing through the Taiwan Strait—currents it cannot control and does not always fully understand. Taiwan's helplessness in the rough neighborhood in which it lives often elicits sympathy from outside observers and expatriate residents alike, but for the island's own good, sympathy must not trump reality. If foreign sympathy implies hopes for concrete outside support for formal independence, it weakens the island's security rather than fortifying it. In their naïve political ineptness, people who advocate the formalization of Taiwan's current de facto independence seem to assume that they can heedlessly pursue their headlong course and that the United States will, in the end, come to the island's rescue when the chips are down. Independence advocates on the Internet do not fully understand that they are playing an exceedingly dangerous game, one that could very quickly draw China and the United States into a war over Taiwan's fate and destroy the very democracy on the island they seek to defend.

Many Green-leaning supporters seem to live in their own world, and it is not unreasonable to state that many of them do not really understand the rest of East Asia, much less the realities of the broader international community. Advocates of formalizing Taiwan's independence seem to assume that if one has a full and nuanced understanding of the domestic political climate on the island, one has understood the Taiwan problem. This is not so; at most, they have understood exactly one *half* of the Taiwan problem. The other half is the other side of the Taiwan Strait: the communist People's Republic of China on the mainland and its unflagging resolve to bring Taiwan back into China's embrace—even a death embrace, if push comes to shove. Mainland China simply will not allow Taiwan to go its own way, and op-ed pieces in the pages of the *Taipei Times* belittling the rationality or sanity of the mainland Chinese ruling authorities do not alter or attenuate this adamantine fact.

Taiwan grossly underestimates the mainland's determination and commitment to bring Taiwan back into its grasp, by force if necessary. The mainland rulers are well aware of, and distressed by, public opinion in Taiwan that favors independence for the island. But public opinion on Taiwan will not alter their plans to absorb the island because they have an even more awesome consideration in mind: the momentum of history. Since its first unification under the Qin in 221 B.C., China has placed an enormous premium on national unity. At the end of the twentieth century, Hong Kong and Macao returned to Chinese sovereignty, and Taiwan is now the last piece of historically Chinese territory left for the People's Republic to recover. As much as the government of the People's Republic of China would like to, it cannot proclaim at the end of the first decade of the twenty-first century that its great enterprise of achieving complete national unity is accomplished. Much to its frustration, the mainland government cannot even point to a timetable for an orderly transition to national unification; that remains an elusive goal. Taiwan's continuing independence from the People's Republic is a painful thorn in the side for all mainland Chinese patriots. The mainland will not let Taiwan go without a tooth-and-nail fight, and it seems that if the people of Taiwan truly desire independence from the mainland, they must admit that they are in fact cutting off their historical ties with mainland China and then prepare themselves for a very long and disruptive battle with mainland invaders. They must neither underestimate the determination and military ability of the People's Republic to resist their moves toward independence nor naively expect the United States or other countries to rush to their rescue in their hour of need. The United States might elect to stay out of the fight and wait to see what comes of it. U.S. intervention in a battle across the Taiwan Strait could very well lead to a larger war between China and the United States, which would mean tremendous losses for both sides, but especially for China. China's economic development would be ruined and set back 30 years or more, and mass starvation would likely break out in China after the disruption of its transportation and communication infrastructure. The United States would probably prevail in any armed conflict with China not involving a ground war, but the cost in blood and treasure for such a victory might ultimately prove higher than the American public is willing to tolerate.

Mainland China, for its part, badly overestimates Taiwan's desires for reunification with the motherland. In Taiwan today a majority of the population would favor formalizing independence for their island if it could be achieved without provoking an armed attack from the mainland. Taiwan today has good reason for not being enthusiastic about unification with the mainland in the near future. Already in the 1990s, Taiwan was light-years ahead of the mainland in terms of prosperity, democracy, respect for human rights, and freedom of expression. The island does struggle with some measure of corruption and organized crime, but the overwhelming majority of its people would be quite unwilling to trade their newfound democracy, freedom, and prosperity for any form of mainland-style authoritarian government that might take harsh moves to improve social stability. An invasion of Taiwan by the Chinese mainland would post an enormous quandary to the United States, which heartily approves of Taiwan's recent democratization and prosperity and yet greatly desires harmonious diplomatic relations with China, the world's most populous state and potentially America's largest market. The U.S. Seventh Fleet is stationed in Japan, and the question for the Americans would be whether to intervene.

Over the past decade and a half there has emerged in books on China's growing military might a consensus that of all the irritants in relations between China and the United States, only the Taiwan question could lead to war between the two giant countries. One such book, published in 2007, is *A War Like No Other: The Truth About China's Challenge to America*, by Richard C. Bush, who has been involved in Taiwan and mainland China issues for two decades in the U.S. government and is now a scholar at the Brookings Institution, and Michael E. O'Hanlon, a national security expert at the Brookings Institution. Bush and O'Hanlon warn repeatedly that conflict between mainland China and Taiwan could go careening out of control, especially if the United States becomes involved in it, and lead very quickly to a direct military confrontation between two nuclear states.

> War between China and Taiwan is a distinct possibility. Such a war could easily drag in the United States, pitting the world's only superpower against its main rising power and thus leading to the first serious conflict in history between nuclear weapons states.
>
> It seems inconceivable, in this day and age, that the United States and China could really wind up in a war. Their mutual interests in cooperating are so strong, their economies are so intertwined, the dangers of war are so enormous, and the number of other problems for them to worry about is so great that it would seem the height of foolishness for the two huge powers ever to come to blows.
>
> There is much truth to this. Indeed, as we have argued in chapter three, most of the reasons why China and the United States could theoretically fight do not in the end hold water. But the Taiwan problem is different . . . the way that a China-Taiwan crisis could begin and escalate would hold the inherent potential for escalation to direct superpower war. (Bush and O'Hanlon, 99)

Avoiding such a war is in the interests of Taiwan, mainland China, and the United States. But if a war starts, it will because mainland China starts it; neither Taiwan nor the United States will strike the first blow. Mainland China will be viewed worldwide as the aggressor and will be condemned both in history and in international public opinion.

Mainland China needs to understand that Taiwan does not find immediate reunification attractive because it finds the undemocratic, authoritarian colossus across the Taiwan Strait repulsive. The people of Taiwan have now tasted freedom and democracy, and they are not going to turn or look back. Many public opinion polls conducted in Taiwan over the past few years have shown that absent any military threat from the mainland, a majority of Taiwan's population would opt for formalizing and openly, joyously affirming its present independence from mainland Chinese control. In such an event, Taiwan's current status as an abnormal and largely unrecognized independent state that hesitates to provoke Beijing with too much talk or action as a sovereign entity would become an oddity or curiosity in the history books, where it belongs.

Taiwan was clearly and unambiguously an integral part of Chinese territory from 1683 to 1895, but time and experience since the late nineteenth century have given the people of Taiwan a very real sense of distance and separateness from the mainland. If mainland China truly longs for reunification with Taiwan, the best thing it can do is to stop threatening Taiwan and start democratizing itself. The longer mainland China postpones its democratization, the more difficult peaceful reunification will be. And for peaceful reunification to be viable and enduring, the people of Taiwan must be openly and democratically consulted about it. Reunification accomplished in any other way will smack of brutal annexation and will poison mainlander/Taiwanese intercommunal relations in a way that may well make February 28, 1947, and its decades-long repercussions look sedate by comparison.

Notable People in the History of China

Amherst, Lord (1773–1857): British diplomat who attempted unsuccessfully in 1816 to obtain diplomatic and trade concessions from the Qing dynasty.

An Lushan (703–757): General in eighth-century Tang China whose rebellion shook the Tang to its very foundations and began a long period of decline for the dynasty.

Arrigo, Linda Gail (Ai Linda; 1949–): American human rights campaigner and researcher. After graduating from the Taipei American School in 1966, she made political activism and academic research her life's work. For her involvement in the Kaohsiung Incident, the Kuomintang deported her as a foreign political subversive on Human Rights Day (December 10), 1979. She was not allowed to return to the island until after its democratization in the 1990s. An unflaggingly energetic figure, Arrigo today continues living and working in Taiwan and is involved in an endless string of causes, now particularly environmental ones. Today she is openly critical of her ex-husband, Shih Ming-teh. Arrigo is very widely respected and thanked in Taiwan for her human rights work on the island.

Cai Yuanpei (1868–1940): Early twentieth-century Chinese intellectual, educated in Germany and France, who transformed Peking University into a serious academic institution and an intellectually alive environment.

Ch'en Ch'i-li (Chen Qili; 1943–2007): China-born Bamboo Union gangster in Taiwan. The fascist wing of the Kuomintang chose Ch'en and his underlings to murder Chinese-American dissident writer Henry Liu at his home in California in 1984. Ch'en was sentenced to a prison term in Taiwan for the murder but was soon released by the Kuomintang. He fled Taiwan in the mid 1990s for Cambodia and died there in 2007. A high Kuomintang official in Taiwan attended his funeral that same year.

Chen Duxiu (1879–1942): Early twentieth-century Chinese intellectual educated in Japan and France who lampooned Confucianism in the pages of his magazine *New Youth*; cofounder of the Chinese Communist Party.

Chen Shui-bian (1951–): Victorious candidate in Taiwan's March 2000 election, ending 50 years of Nationalist rule over the island; member of Taiwan's Democratic Progressive party and advocate of Taiwanese independence; therefore of grave concern to mainland China. Reelected to the presidency in 2004 after an apparent shooting failed to kill him. Later disgraced and imprisoned on corruption charges relating to his terms in office and his family's financial crimes.

Chen Wen-chen (Chen Wencheng; 1950–1981): Taiwanese-American professor of statistics at Carnegie-Mellon University. Chen was murdered in Taiwan by rogue elements of the Kuomintang's Garrison Command in 1981, and his body was dumped on the campus of National Taiwan University. His murderers are still at large, and his unsolved case symbolizes the White Terror policies the Kuomintang previously used to rule Taiwan.

Chiang Ching-kuo (1908–1988): Son of Chiang Kai-shek and president of the Republic of China on Taiwan from the late 1970s through the late 1980s; lifted martial law, ameliorated many of his father's excesses, and began the democratization of Taiwan.

Chiang Kai-shek (1887–1975): Virulent anti-Communist and virtual dictator of Nationalist China from 1926 until his death in 1975; the defeated remnants of his government and military fled to Taiwan after losing the civil war on the mainland to the Chinese Communists.

Chinggis Khan (1167?–1227): Mongol conqueror during late twelfth and early thirteenth centuries; subjugated much of Central Asia but left China unconquered.

Chu Hsi: *See* Zhu Xi.

Cixi, Empress Dowager (1834–1908): Powerful Manchu imperial clan woman and the real authority behind the throne from 1862 until her death in 1908; her encouragement of the Boxers led to catastrophe for China.

Confucius (551–479 B.C.): Eastern Zhou philosopher and the dominant figure in Chinese intellectual history; taught a this-worldly philosophy emphasizing familial and social harmony and the importance of benevolence, or human-heartedness.

Deng Xiaoping (1904–1997): Second major leader of the People's Republic of China from 1977 until his death in 1997; reversed many of Mao's ruinous policies, liberalized the Chinese economy, opened China to the outside world, and apparently ordered the Tiananmen Square Massacre of June 4, 1989.

Duke of Zhou (fl. twelfth century B.C.): Brother of Zhou dynasty King Wu and regent to King Wu's young son and successor; tutored the young heir and surprised many people by relinquishing his political power when the heir reached his majority; regarded by Confucius as the epitome of morality, loyalty, and virtue.

Elgin, Lord (1811–1863): Former governor-general of Canada; led two expeditionary forces, one against Canton and Tianjin in 1857 and 1858 when he bullied the Qing into signing the Treaty of Tianjin, and another in 1860 when he fought his way into Beijing, burned the Manchu Summer Palace, and forced the Qing to sign the Convention of Peking.

Elliot, Charles (fl. 1830s): British official, appointed superintendent of trade in 1836; responsible in part for the outbreak of the Opium War between Britain and China.

Empress Wu (625–705): Woman emperor during Tang dynasty, which she interrupted and renamed Zhou; reigned from 684 until 705, when she was finally deposed; her reign was in many ways quite successful.

Genghis Khan: *See* Chinggis Khan.

Gongsun Long (320?–250? B.C.): Logician-philosopher; best known for frivolous argumentation and meticulous parsing of analytical categories—"A white horse is not a horse" is one of his better-known statements.

Guangxu (1871–1908): Qing emperor from 1875 to 1908; supported many of Kang Youwei's reforms but was ultimately cloistered by the Empress Dowager Cixi, his aunt; perhaps murdered in 1908 by Cixi just prior to her own death.

Han Fei (d. 233 B.C.): Theorist and major figure in Legalist thought; advocated harsh governance and argued against the applicability of ancient institutions to current situations.

Han Wudi (156–87 B.C.): Han dynasty emperor who reigned from 141 to 87 B.C.; greatly expanded Han territory and waged relentless warfare against the Xiongnu.

Han Yu (768–824): Late Tang Confucian scholar often credited with beginning the Neo-Confucian movement; somewhat anti-Buddhist in thought but retained some attachment to the religion.

Henry Pu Yi: *See* Pu Yi.

Hong Xiuquan (1814–1864): Apparently mentally unstable leader of the Taiping Rebellion, a pseudo-Christian military uprising in nineteenth-century China that nearly succeeded in toppling the Qing dynasty.

Hu Jintao (1942–): Native of Jiangsu; hydraulic engineer by profession. Currently China's strongman, Hu Jintao holds the triumvirate of political power in China: Presidency of the People's Republic of China, General Secretary of the Party, and, especially important, Chairman of the Central Military Commission. Hu is widely thought of as a pragmatist and moderate and has thus far in his reign made no signal contributions, theoretical or otherwise, to communist rule in China.

Hu Shi (1891–1962): Chinese intellectual educated at Cornell and Columbia in the early twentieth century; influential May Fourth thinker who espoused the thought of John Dewey and opposed communism; energetic advocate of the plain language movement.

Hu Yaobang (1915–1989): Originally a fellow moderate and trusted confederate of Deng Xiaoping; replaced Hua Guofeng as CCP chairman in 1981, only to be dismissed from this post in 1987 by Deng Xiaoping, who disapproved of his bourgeois liberalism and support of student demands for increased democratization; mourning after his death of a heart attack in April 1989 led to student demonstrations and eventually the Tiananmen Square movement during the spring of 1989.

Hua Guofeng (1920–): One-time designated heir of Mao Zedong; briefly chairman of the CCP after Mao's death; ordered the arrest of the Gang of Four; elbowed out of power and relegated into obscurity by Deng Xiaoping.

Huang Chao (d. 884): Late Tang rebel leader who captured Canton (Guangzhou) in 879 and slaughtered thousands of Christian, Jewish, and Muslim merchants there, perhaps blaming them for China's famines and other troubles.

Hurley, Patrick (1883–1963): American diplomat who attempted unsuccessfully right after World War II to get the Chinese Nationalists and Communists to enter into a peace agreement.

Jan Wong: *See* Wong, Jan.

Jiang Zemin (1926–): Third major leader of the People's Republic of China from 1997; handpicked successor of Deng Xiaoping; unoriginal intellect and continuator of Deng Xiaoping's policies; voiced approval of Tiananmen Square Massacre. Replaced by Hu Jintao in early 2000s as China's strongman.

Kang Youwei (1858–1927): Late Qing idealist and would-be reformer; unsuccessfully launched comprehensive reform movement in 1898; subsequently fled to Japan, where he energetically advocated constitutional monarchy for China under the Manchu emperors.

Kangxi (1654?–1722): One of the two great Manchu emperors (r. 1662–1722); consolidated the Qing conquest of China, conquered and incorporated Taiwan into Chinese territory, and secured the submission of the Outer Mongols in the 1690s.

Kao Chun-ming, Rev. (Gao Junming; 1929–): Native of Taiwan and veteran democracy activist and human rights campaigner. The Japanese imprisoned Kao in a labor camp in Japan during World War II, forcing him to manufacture munitions for the Japanese military. After the war Kao became a minister in the Presbyterian Church in Taiwan and eventually rose to the rank of General Secretary of the church, a capacity in which he served from 1970 to 1989. Kao was imprisoned for four years in the 1980s for his role in harboring the fugitive Shih Ming-teh in the wake of the Kaohsiung Incident. Kao is widely respected in Taiwan today but does have a few critics and detractors.

Kerr, George H. (1911–1992): American diplomat who lived in Japan and Taiwan for five or six years just prior to the outbreak of war between Japan and the United States in 1941. After the war Kerr was an eyewitness to the February 28, 1947, massacres in Taiwan. His book, *Formosa Betrayed*, published in 1965, is a classic indictment of Kuomintang brutality. (It was banned in Taiwan until the island's democratization.) Kerr is very well thought of in Taiwan.

Khubilai Khan (1215–1294): Mongol conqueror and grandson of Chinggis Khan (Genghis Khan); emperor to the Chinese and Grand Khan of the Mongol world empire; sent his younger brother Hulegu to conquer Persia and Mesopotamia, while he attacked and ultimately conquered all of China by 1279; "the most powerful man since Adam" according to Marco Polo.

King Wen (fl. twelfth century B.C.): Early Western Zhou ruler who led his people in revolution against late Shang tyranny; traditionally credited with discerning Heaven's will that a change of dynasty take place.

King Wu (fl. twelfth century B.C.; r. 1111–1104 B.C.): Early Western Zhou ruler, son of King Wen, who finished his father's revolution by overthrowing the Shang and establishing a new dynasty.

Lao-tzu: *See* Laozi.

Laozi (fl. sixth century B.C.): Legendary, or semi-legendary, founder of Taoism; traditional accounts credit him with writing out the text of the *Tao-te ching* sometime during the sixth century B.C.

Lee Teng-hui (1923–): Democratically elected Nationalist party president of the Republic of China on Taiwan from 1996 to May 2000; his seeming tacit support of Taiwanese independence soured his government's relations with the leaders of mainland China, who energetically renounced him during the 1990s.

Li Dazhao (1888–1927): Librarian at Beida who subscribed to Marxism during the May Fourth era (young Mao Zedong was one of his assistants); cofounder of the CCP; might have been the leading figure in the Chinese Communist movement if he had not been captured and executed by the warlord Zhang Zuolin in 1927.

Li Hongzhang (1823–1901): Helped Zeng Guofan quell the Taiping Rebellion and then advocated selective reforms in China; often called upon to deal with foreign problems, Li was China's virtual foreign minister until his death in 1901.

Li Peng (1928–): Premier of China who, in 1989, declared martial law during the Tiananmen Square demonstrations; greatly disliked by the protesting students of the time.

Li Yuan (565–635): Sui dynasty general who rebelled against the excess of that dynasty and became the founding emperor of the Tang dynasty.

Li Zicheng (1605–1645): Chinese peasant rebel who captured Beijing in April 1644 and toppled the Ming dynasty.

Lien Chan (1936–). Nationalist party candidate for the presidency of Taiwan in March 2000; lost to Chen Shui-pien.

Lin Biao (1907–1971): Chinese military commander who joined the Communist movement early; eventually rebelled against Mao; apparently killed in the early 1970s while trying to flee to the Soviet Union.

Lin Yi-hsiung (Lin Yixiong; 1941–): Native of Yilan County in Taiwan; prominent dissident politician and democratization proponent during the Kuomintang's White Terror over Taiwan. On the symbolically important date of February 28, 1980, rogue Kuomintang assassins murdered Lin's mother and twin daughters for attempting to divulge his torture to Amnesty International. The murderers are still at large, and the case has never been solved. The Lin Family Murders helped galvanize Taiwan's democratization movement and today remain potent symbols of rule by the political party that once resorted to such brutality to guarantee its power. Lin has now largely withdrawn from politics and is widely revered throughout the island as a heroic elder statesman.

Lin Zexu (1785–1850): Imperial commissioner during the 1830s who cracked down on opium trafficking in southern China; British reactions to his policies led to the Opium War.

Liu Bang (247–195 B.C.): Founding emperor of Han dynasty; ordinary commoner who alleviated most of the Qin's excesses and abuses.

Liu, Henry (Liu Yi-liang; 1932–1984): Chinese-American writer and author of a Chinese-language biography critical of Taiwan president Chiang Ching-kuo. Liu was murdered by Kuomintang assassins at his home in California in 1984. His murder was a news sensation in Taiwan and was widely regarded as one of the most brazen instances of gangster-Kuomintang collusion in the Kuomintang's history.

Lu Xun (1881–1936): Prominent left-wing Chinese writer prolific during the early decades of the twentieth century.

Macartney, Lord (1737–1806): Late eighteenth-century British diplomat who attempted unsuccessfully to wring diplomatic concessions from the Qianlong emperor.

Mao Zedong (1893–1976): Dominant personality and preeminent leader of the Chinese Communist movement from the 1930s until his death; before 1949 did much to liberate China from foreign domination and Nationalist tyranny, but afterward his influence in China seems to have been largely negative.

Marco Polo (1254?–1324?): Venetian merchant who traveled to Mongolia and China; claimed to be in Khubilai Khan's government.

Marshall, George C. (1880–1959): American diplomat who tried unsuccessfully in 1946 and early 1947 to get the Chinese Communists and Nationalists to come to a peace agreement.

Mencius (c. 380–289 B.C.): Confucian philosopher who taught that human nature is innately good and that *ren* inheres in human hearts.

Mo Di: *See* Mozi.

Möngke Khan (1209–1259): Grandson of Chinggis Khan and Kha-ghan (grand leader) of the Mongol world empire from 1251 until his death; began the final conquest of the Southern Song but died before completing it.

Mozi (ca. 470–391 B.C.): Chinese religious philosopher who taught that all people should love each other universally or equally.

Napier, Lord William John (d. 1834): Briton who brusquely confronted the Qing authorities in Canton in 1834 but failed to wring any concessions from them.

Nurhachi (1559–1626): Manchu leader who unified the Manchu tribes and began the "great enterprise" of building a conquest dynasty to topple the Ming; his successors continued his work and conquered Ming China in 1644.

Ögödei Khan (1185–1241): Mongol conqueror, son of Chinggis Khan; planned to depopulate northern China and turn it into pasturelands for Mongol horses.

Patten, Chris (1944–): Last British governor of Hong Kong; infuriated the Chinese Communists in 1995 when he introduced democratic institutions and held free and open elections for the colony's Legislative Council.

Peng Dehuai (1898–1974): Pugnacious military commander in the Chinese Communist movement who fought valiantly in the Korean War and later censured Mao at the Lushan meeting in the late 1950s for the disastrous effects of the Great Leap Forward; later imprisoned; his reputation has been posthumously rehabilitated.

Poyang (1920–2008): The penname of Kuo I-tung (Guo Yidong), a native of He'nan province. Poyang went to Taiwan with the Nationalists in 1949. He was never one of them, however, and criticized the Kuomintang relentlessly in books and articles. He was sentenced to many years of imprisonment on Green Island, the Kuomintang's prison island off the east coast of Taiwan. He was eventually released from prison under pressure from Amnesty International and died a widely revered cultural hero in Taiwan in 2008. His ashes were scattered around Green Island.

Pu Yi (1906–1967): Last Qing emperor; a child when the Qing ended, the Japanese eventually installed him as their puppet ruler in Manchukuo.

Qianlong (1711–1799): Qing emperor (r. 1736–1796); one of the Qing's two great monarchs; during his reign, the Qing reached its height and also began its decline.

Qin Gui (1090–1155): Infamous imperial chief counsellor during the 1140s who apparently favored a more capitulationist line against the Jurchens, who were then under attack by the Southern Song patriot general Yue Fei; almost universally reviled in China as a traitor for recalling Yue Fei from his campaign against the Jurchens and throwing him into prison, where he died.

Qin Shihuang (259–209 B.C.): Harsh Legalist ruler of the Qin dynasty who proclaimed himself emperor (*huangdi*) and unified all China in 221 B.C., thus ending feudalism and beginning imperial China; traditionally excoriated for his brutality and despotism, but his enduring contribution was to establish the historical precedent for unity, political and otherwise, in China; contrary to popular opinion, he probably had nothing to do with the building and positioning of the Great Wall of China.

Shih Ming-teh (Shi Mingde; 1941–): Taiwanese political activist and democratization campaigner. He was a prominent figure in the Kaohsiung Incident and spent 25 years in Kuomintang prisons as a political dissident. More recently he has been critical of Taiwan's president Chen Shui-bian and in 2006 led an unsuccessful popular protest movement to depose him. In the mercurial and fluid world of Taiwanese politics today, Shih is a highly polarizing figure, loved and hated with equal parts passion.

Shun (early cultural hero): Legendary figure credited with perfecting bureaucratic organization and establishing the basics of China's criminal code; struggled with a great flood in China during his reign.

Sima Qian (145?–90? B.C.): Former Han Confucian historian, castrated by Han Wudi for temerity; his great historical work *Shiji*, which covers Chinese history from the earliest times up to Wudi's reign, became a model for most subsequent historical writing.

Song Taizong (r. 976–997): Second Song emperor; twice failed to prevail against the Kitans on the battlefield.

Song Taizu: *See* Zhao Kuangyin.

Song Zhenzong (r. 997–1022): Timid Northern Song emperor who concluded the Shanyuan Treaty with the Kitans in 1005.

Soong, James (1942–): Independent candidate for the presidency of Taiwan in March 2000; finished slightly behind Chen Shui-bian of the Democratic Progressive party. Later a failed candidate for mayoralty of Taipei City and now a washed-up politician.

Soong, Meiling (Madame Chiang Kai-shek) (1897–): American-educated Chinese woman and tireless anti-Communist.

Stilwell, Joseph (1883–1946): Acerbic American general in China during the 1940s who criticized Chiang Kai-shek's military tactics and his refusal to fight alongside the Chinese Communists against the Japanese; recalled in 1944.

Su Song (1020–1101): Prolific Northern Song scientist and inventor who tinkered with mechanical clocks and dabbled in cartography, which he used to address a border dispute with the Kitans.

Sui Yangdi (r. 605–617): Second Sui dynasty emperor, infamous for his harshness, extravagance, and failed military expeditions against Korea; overthrown by Li Yuan, the founder of the Tang.

Sun-tzu: *See* Sunzi.

Sun Yat-sen (1866–1925): Western-educated medical doctor and the father of modern China; worked for revolutionary action against the Manchus and was president of the Republic of China after the abdication of the Manchus in 1912; ultimately turned to the Bolshevik Russians after Western nations refused to aid him; cooperated with the

Chinese Communists in the early 1920s; died in 1925 on the eve of the Northern Expedition.

Sunzi (d. 320 B.C.): Eastern Zhou military strategist; author of *The Art of War,* a manual of strategy.

Tang Taizong (597–649): Second Tang emperor and the dominant personality of the early Tang period; subjugated the Turks in the early seventh century and ruled over them as Khan and over the Chinese as emperor.

Tang Xuanzong (685–762): Mid Tang emperor (r. 712–756) who ruled over the dynasty at its height and helped precipitate its decline by turning over too much military authority to General An Lushan, a relative of his favorite concubine.

Wang Dan (1969?–): Tiananmen Square student leader sentenced to four years in prison for his role in the Tiananmen protest movement; persecuted by the Chinese Communist government and sentenced to prison again in 1996.

Wang Jingwei (1883–1944): Left-wing Nationalist politician who led the Wuhan regime in the mid-1920s; later regarded as a traitor to China because he headed up a Japanese puppet regime in Nanjing.

Wang Mang (45 B.C.–A.D. 23): Confucian literalist who usurped the Han throne from 9 to 23 A.D., during which time he renamed the dynasty Xin.

Wang Shouren (1472–1529): Ming dynasty neo-Confucian philosopher who disagreed with Zhu Xi's rationalistic dualism and taught that the monastic truth of the universe inhered in the hearts or minds of people.

Wang Yangming: *See* Wang Shouren.

Wen Wang: *See* King Wen.

Wong, Jan (1952–): Canadian student and journalist who lived in late Maoist China and was an eyewitness to the Tiananmen Square Massacre.

Wu Bangguo (1941–): Native of Anhui; second highest-ranking member of the Chinese Communist Party; head of China's rubber-stamp National People's Congress. No friend of democratization in China, Wu is perhaps most famous (or infamous) for his statements in 2007 that "Hong Kong will have as much power as Beijing wants it to and nothing more" and in 2009 that "Without a single Communist Party in control, China would be torn by strife and incapable of accomplishing anything."

Wu Peifu (1874–1939): Northern Chinese warlord who fancied himself a scholar and a gentleman; defeated during the Northern Expedition; infamous for machine-gunning strikers in Beijing in 1923.

Wu Wang: *See* King Wu.

Wuer Kaixi (b. 1960s?): Student leader during the 1989 Tiananmen Square student movement; a fiery Uighur who offended Li Peng with his forthrightness.

Xiang Yu (232–202 B.C.): Aristocrat and rival of Liu Bang for power after the fall of the Qin dynasty in 206 B.C.; dramatically committed suicide when Liu Bang triumphed over him; his story is a favorite theme for operatic performances.

Xuanzong: *See* Tang Xuanzong.

Xunzi (ca. 300–237 B.C.): Confucian philosopher who taught that human nature is innately predisposed toward evil and that goodness (*ren*) is the result of conscious, concerted effort and submission to *li*, or conventions of correct behavior.

Yang Guifei (719–756): Tang dynasty beauty who stole the heart of Tang emperor Xuanzong (r. 712–756); sometimes blamed for contributing to the decline of the Tang dynasty.

Yao (early cultural hero): Legendary figure credited with perfecting a calendar and choosing a competent minister rather than his son as his successor.

Yongle (1360–1424): Third Ming emperor (r. 1403–1425) who transferred the Ming capital from Nanjing to Beijing.

Yu (the Great) (early cultural hero): Legendary figure credited with quelling the floodwaters in antiquity.

Yuan Shikai (1859–1916): Late Qing militarist who sided with Sun Yat-sen's early Chinese republic, only to betray it and try to become emperor of his own dynasty.

Yue Fei (1103–1141): Southern Song Chinese patriot and general who fought against the Jurchens during the twelfth century; executed by Qin Gui; one of the most celebrated patriots in Chinese history.

Zeng Guofan (1811–1872): Chinese general who fought for the Qing dynasty against the Taiping Rebellion of the nineteenth century and ultimately quelled it in 1864.

Zhang Xueliang (1898–2001): Manchurian warlord general who in the mid-1930s refused to continue the fight against the Chinese Communists during the Japanese invasion of China; kidnapped Chiang Kai-shek in late 1936 near Xi'an; under Chiang Kai-shek's house arrest from this time until the 1980s. Became a Christian later in life and died a centenarian in Hawaii in 2001.

Zhao Kuangyin (927–976): Founding emperor of Song dynasty; concentrated more military and political power into the emperor's hands.

Zhao Ziyang (1919–2005): General secretary of the CCP and a moderate who favored reform and was sympathetic with the demands of students demonstrating in Tiananmen Square in 1989; arrested after Tiananmen Square Massacre and kept under house arrest; nemesis of Jiang Zemin.

Zhou, Duke of: *See* Duke of Zhou.

Zhou Enlai (1898–1976): Prominent leader of the Chinese Communist movement from its early years until his death; suave and multilingual, Zhou blunted some of the most harmful of Mao's Cultural Revolution excesses; second only to Mao in prestige and influence; today his memory is arguably more revered than Mao's.

Zhu De (1886–1976): Commander of the Red Army from the early days of the Chinese Communist movement until his death.

Zhu Rongji (1928–): Native of Hu'nan; China's Premier from 1998 to 2003. Zhu is infamous in Taiwan for his red-faced, finger-wagging attempt to lecture the Taiwanese voting public in 2000, instructing them to vote for the candidate Beijing liked best or face the consequences. Zhu's unartful boorishness badly backfired, and since his blunder Beijing has learned not to comment on Taiwan's democratic process, lest there be more electoral results unpalatable to the Chinese Communists.

Zhu Xi (1130–1200): Southern Song philosopher and one of the major figures in configuring and synthesizing neo-Confucianism; developed a rationalistic cosmological dualism.

Zhu Yuanzhang (1328–1398): Founding emperor of the Ming dynasty who gathered unprecedented amounts of political power into his own hands, thus making the position of emperor much more powerful than previously and instituting Ming despotism; he and Liu Bang were the only commoners who ever founded major dynasties in Chinese history.

Zhuangzi (ca. 369–ca. 286 B.C.): Taoist philosopher who employed parody and parable to explain Taoist teachings.

Zou Rong (1882–1905): Chinese racist who authored the anti-Manchu tract *The Revolutionary Army.*

Zuo Zongtang (1812–1885): Chinese general who helped Zeng Guofan and Li Hongzhang quell the Taiping Rebellion.

Chinese Dynasties

Pre-Imperial China	
Xia	2205?–1766? B.C. (unverified)
Shang	1766?–1122? B.C.
Zhou	1122?–256 B.C.
Western Zhou	1122?–771 B.C.
Eastern Zhou	771–256 B.C.

Early Imperial China	
Qin	221–206 B.C.
Han	202 B.C.–A.D. 220 (with Xin usurpation)
Former or Western Han	202 B.C.–A.D. 9 (capital: Chang'an)

Xin usurpation	A.D.9–23
Later or Eastern Han	A.D.25–220 (capital: Loyang)
Period of Division	220–589
Three Kingdoms	220–280
Western Jin	280–317
North-South Division	317–589 (Southern Chinese capital: Nanjing)

Middle Imperial China	
Sui	589–618 (capital: Chang'an)
Tang	618–907 (capital: Chang'an)
Five Dynasties	907–960
Song	960–1279
Northern Song	960–1127 (capital: Kaifeng/Bianliang)
Southern Song	1127–1279 (capital: Hangzhou/Lin'an)
Yuan	1279–1368 (capital: Beijing)

Late Imperial China	
Ming	1368–1644 (capital: Nanjing to 1403; then Beijing)
Qing	1644–1912 (capital: Beijing)

Glossary of Selected Terms

Analects: The text of many of Confucius's most important sayings.

APCs: Agricultural producers' cooperatives; a communal form of agricultural organization that was attempted unsuccessfully during the 1950s.

Beida: Chinese abbreviation of Peking University (*Beijing Daxue*).

Beiping: Name for Beijing (formerly spelled Peking) from the late 1920s through 1949.

boddhisatvas: Merciful beings who were thought, on the brink of *nirvana*, to have turned their attention and compassion back toward the world of the living and were thus able to help all who called on them in faith.

CCP: Chinese Communist Party.

DPP: Democratic Progressive Party of Taiwan, a democratic opposition party founded in the 1980s that has somewhat favored Taiwan independence in the past; its presidential candidate, Chen Shui-bian, won Taiwan's presidential election in March 2000.

Falun Gong: Popular religious movement in China during the 1990s and beyond that seems to combine elements of Buddhism and Taoism with a regimen of physical exercises. Falun Gong practitioners insist that their movement is not a religion and emphasize its uniqueness from Buddhism and Taoism.

huangdi: "August Sovereign," the title by which Chinese emperors were known since Qin Shihuang's reign.

Jinshi: The highest degree in the imperial civil service examinations, somewhat equivalent to a doctoral degree.

junzi: In Confucianism, an "evolved man" or "consummate man" who embodied the Confucian virtues; sometimes translated "gentleman."

Juren: Second highest degree in the imperial civil service examinations; roughly equivalent to a master's degree.

kaozheng: Careful philological textual scholarship developed and practiced during Qing times.

Khaghan: Mongolian title meaning Supreme Khan.

Khan: Mongolian leadership title; sometimes used interchangeably with Khaghan.

KMT: Abbreviation for Kuomintang (now usually spelled Guomindang), the Nationalist Party of China; politically conservative and anti-Communist.

kowtow: A gesture of extreme ritual obeisance and submission that involved groveling on the knees and elbows and knocking the forehead audibly on the floor.

Kuomintang (Now usually spelled Guomindang): the Nationalist Party of China; politically conservative and anti-Communist.

Legalism: A school of thought in ancient China that valued law and state power above all else.

li **(in Confucianism):** Ritual or ceremony as narrowly defined, and conventions of propriety as broadly conceived.

li **(in Neo-Confucianism):** "Principles," the nonmaterial realities of the universe.

Mahayana Buddhism: A variety of Buddhism, somewhat reminiscent of a savior religion; emphasizes calling upon *boddhisatvas* in faith.

nirvana: In Buddhism, the state of desireless, and therefore painless, bliss; liberation from desire and the suffering it causes, including reincarnation.

PLA: People's Liberation Army of Communist China.

PRC: People's Republic of China, the official national title of mainland China since 1949.

qi: In neo-Confucianism, the material reality of the universe.

ren: The highest virtue or quality aspired after in Confucianism; sometimes translated "humanity" or "human-heartedness" or "benevolence."

shanyu: Leader of the Xiongnu, or Huns, an ancient pastoral nomadic people who menaced Han China.

Shengyuan: The lowest degree in the imperial civil service examinations; roughly equivalent to a bachelor's degree.

sutra: Buddhist scriptures, often translated from Sanskrit into Chinese.

taiji: In Neo-Confucianism, the Supreme Ultimate of the universe; the ultimate cosmological reality.

tao: In Taoism, the profound and mystical Way of the universe, which is ultimately beyond expression and intellection.

Tao-te ching: The classic and authoritative work of Taoism.

TRA: Taiwan Relations Act, passed by the U.S. Congress and signed into law in 1979, which states that mainland Chinese aggression on Taiwan would be a matter of "grave concern" to the U.S. government.

Xiucai: Colloquial term for the *Shengyuan* degree.

Works Cited

Andrade, Tonio. 2008. *How Taiwan Became Chinese: Dutch, Spanish, and Han Colonization in the Seventeenth Century*. New York: Columbia University Press.

Arrigo, Linda Gail, and Lynn Miles, eds. 2008. *A Borrowed Voice: Taiwan Human Rights through International Networks, 1960–1980*. Taipei: Social Empowerment Alliance.

Bao, Ruo-wang (Jean Pasqualini), and Rudolph Chelminski. 1973. *Prisoner of Mao*. New York: Penguin.

Becker, Jasper. 1996. *Hungry Ghosts: Mao's Secret Famine*. New York: Henry Holt and Company.

Bernstein, Richard. 1982. *From the Center of the Earth: The Search for the Truth About China*. Boston: Little, Brown.

Bernstein, Richard, and Ross H. Munro. 1997. *The Coming Conflict with China*. New York: Knopf.

de Bary, William, et al., eds. 1960. *Sources of Chinese Tradition*, vol. 1. New York: Columbia University Press.

Boyang (as told to Zhou Bisi). 1966. *Boyang huiyilu*. Taipei: Yuanliu.

Bush, Richard C., and Michael E. O'Hanlon. 2007. *A War Like No Other: The Truth About China's Challenge to America*. Hoboken, New Jersey: John Wiley & Sons.

Chan, Wing-tsit. 1963. *A Sourcebook in Chinese Philosophy*. Princeton: Princeton University Press.

Chang, Gordon G. 2001. *The Coming Collapse of China*. New York: Random House.

Chang, Hsin-pao. 1964. *Commissioner Lin and the Opium War*. Cambridge, Mass.: Harvard University Press.

Chang, Iris. 1997. *The Rape of Nanking: The Forgotten Holocaust of World War II*. New York: Basic Books.

Chang, Jung. 1991. *Wild Swans: Three Daughters of China*. New York: Anchor Books/Doubleday.

Chang, Jung, and Jon Halliday. 2006. *Mao: The Unknown Story*. New York: Anchor Books.

Chen, Guidi, and Wu Chuntao. 2006. *Will the Boat Sink the Water? The Life of China's Peasants*. New York: PublicAffairs.

Cheng, Nien. 1986. *Life and Death in Shanghai*. New York: Grove Press.

Chin, Ko-lin. 2003. *Heijin: Organized Crime, Business, and Politics in Taiwan*. Armonk, New York: M. E. Sharpe.

Chong, Denise. 2009. *Egg on Mao: The Story of an Ordinary Man Who Defaced an Icon and Unmasked a Dictatorship*. Toronto: Random House Canada.

Davidson, James Wheeler. 1896. A big baby republic: History of its rise and its quick undoing. *Inter Ocean* 5.

Davidson, James Wheeler. 1903. *The Island of Formosa, Past and Present*. London: Macmillan & Company.

Dietrich, Craig. 1998. *People's China: A Brief History*, 3d ed. New York: Oxford University Press.

Dreyer, June Teufel. 2004. *China's Political System: Modernization and Tradition*, 4th ed. Boston: Allyn and Bacon.

Economy, Elizabeth. 2004. *The River Runs Black: The Environmental Challenge to China's Future*. Ithaca: Cornell University Press.

Fenby, Jonathan. 2004. *Chiang Kai-shek: China's Generalissimo and the Nation He Lost*. New York: Carroll & Graf Publishers.

Fenby, Jonathan. 2009. *The Penguin History of Modern China: The Fall and Rise of a Great Power, 1850–2009*. London: Penguin.

Gao Junming (Kao Chun-ming) and Gao Li Lizhen (Kao Li Li-chen). 2001. *Shizijia zhi lu: Gao Junming Mushi huiyilu*. Taipei: Wang Chunfeng.

Graff, David, and Robin Higham, eds. 2002. *A Military History of China*. Boulder, Colorado: Westview Press.

Hébert, Jacques, and Pierre E. Trudeau. 1961. *Deux innocents en Chine rouge*. Montréal: Editions de l'homme; distributeur exclusif: Agence de distribution populaire enrg.

Hsü, Immanuel C. Y. 1990. *The Rise of Modern China*, 4th ed. Oxford: Oxford University Press.

Hsü, Immanuel C. Y. 2000. *The Rise of Modern China*, 6th ed. Oxford: Oxford University Press.

Hudson, Valerie M., and Andea M. den Boer. 2005. *Bare Branches: The Security Implications of Asia's Surplus Male Population*. Cambridge, Mass.: The MIT Press.

Hunter, Edward. 1951. *Brain-washing in Red China: The Calculated Destruction of Men's Minds*. New York: The Vanguard Press, Inc.

Huntington, Samuel P. 1996. *The Clash of Civilizations and the Remaking of World Order*. New York: Simon & Schuster.

Jacobs, Andrew. 2009. Seeking justice, Chinese land in Secret Jails. *New York Times* 8 (March).

Jagchid, Sechin, and Van Jay Symons. 1989. *Peace, War, and Trade Along the Great Wall: Nomadic-Chinese Interaction Through Two Millennia*. Bloomington: Indiana University Press.

Jones, Kristin. 2006. "China's Hidden Unrest." Committee to Protect Journalists Special Report (May 1). http://cpj.org/reports/2006/05/china-06.php.

Kaplan, David E. 1992. *Fires of the Dragon: Politics, Murder, and the Kuomintang*. New York: Atheneum.

Keliher, Macabe, trans. 2003. *Out of China, or Yu Yonghe's Tales of Formosa*. Taipei: SMC Publishing Inc.

Keliher, Macabe, trans. 2004. *Small Sea Travel Diaries: Yu Yonghe's Records of Taiwan*. Taipei: SMC Publishing Inc.

Kerr, George H. 2007. *Formosa Betrayed*. Upland, California: Taiwan Publishing Co. (First published in Great Britain in 1966.)

Khazanov, A. M. 1983. *Nomads and the Outside World*. Cambridge: Cambridge University Press.

Kim, Mike. 2005. *Escaping North Korea: Defiance and Hope in the World's Most Repressive Country*. Lanham, Maryland: Rowman & Littlefield.

Lee, Kuan Yew. 1996. Speech. The 1996 Architect of the New Century Dinner, hosted by The Nixon Center. Washington, D.C., November 24.

Li, Zhisui. 1994. *The Private Life of Chairman Mao*. New York: Random House.

Liang, Heng, and Judith Shapiro. 1983. *Son of the Revolution*. New York: Vintage Books/Random House.

Lieberthal, Kenneth. 1995. *Governing China: From Revolution through Reform*. New York: W. W. Norton.

Lin, Mohan, and Wei Wei, eds. 1999. *Women tuoqi nazhong Zhongguoren: "jingying" zai haiwai*. Gansu: Gansu Renmin Chubanshe.

Lin, Yutang, ed. 1942. *The Wisdom of China and India*. New York: Random House.

Lin, Yutang. 1975. *My Country and My People*. Taipei: Mei Ya Publications.

Mao, Zedong (Mao Tse-tung). 1976. *Quotations from Chairman Mao Tsetung*. Peking/Beijing: Foreign Languages Press.

Mateo, José Eugenio Borao. 2001. *Spaniards in Taiwan, Vol. I: 1582–1641*. Taipei: SMC Publishing Inc.

Mateo, José Eugenio Borao. 2002. *Spaniards in Taiwan, Vol. II: 1642–1682.* Taipei: SMC Publications, Inc.

Mateo, José Eugenio Borao. 2010. *The Spanish Experience in Taiwan, 1626–1642: The Baroque Ending of a Renaissance Endeavour.* Seattle: University of Washington Press.

Meisner, Maurice. 2007. *Mao Zedong: A Politilcal and Intellectual Portrait.* Cambridge: Polity Press.

Menges, Constantine C. 2005. *China: The Gathering Threat.* Nashville, Tennessee: Nelson Current.

Mote, Frederick W. 1971. *Intellectual Foundations of China.* New York: Alfred A. Knopf.

Nathan, Andrew J., and Perry Link, eds. 2001. *The Tiananmen Papers: The Chinese Leadership's Decision to Use Force Against their Own People—In their Own Words.* New York: PublicAffairs.

National Geographic. *Atlas of China.* Washington, D.C.: National Geographic.

Paine, S. C. M. 2003. *The Sino-Japanese War of 1894–1895: Perceptions, Power, and Primacy.* Cambridge: Cambridge University Press.

Pei, Minxin. 2007. "Corruption Threatens China's Future." *Carnegie Endowment for International Peace Policy Brief* 55 (October): 1–8. http://www.carnegieendowment.org/publications/index.cfm?fa=view&id=19628.

Polo, Marco (Manuel Komroff, translator). 1982. *The Travels of Marco Polo the Venetian.* New York and London: Liveright.

Pyle, Kenneth B. 1969. *The New Generation in Meiji Japan: Problems of Cultural Identity, 1885–1895.* Stanford: Stanford University Press.

Rickett, Allyn, and Adele Rickett. 1981. *Prisoners of Liberation*, New Edition. San Francisco: China Books. (First published by Cameron Associates, Inc. in 1957.)

Roy, Denny. 2003. *Taiwan: A Political History.* Ithaca: Cornell University Press.

Rubinstein, Murray A. 2007. *Taiwan: A New History,* Expanded Edition. Armonk, New York: M. E. Sharpe.

Schurmann, Franz, and Orville Schell. 1967. *Communist China: Revolutionary Reconstruction and International Confrontation, 1949 to the Present.* New York: Vintage Books.

Schwartz, Benjamin I. 1985. *The World of Thought in Ancient China.* Cambridge, Mass.: Belknap Press of Harvard University Press.

Shapiro, Judith. 2001. *Mao's War Against Nature: Politics and the Environment in Revolutionary China.* Cambridge: Cambridge University Press.

Shen, Tong, with Marianne Yen. 1990. *Almost a Revolution.* Boston: Houghton Mifflin.

Shepherd, John Robert. 1993. *Statecraft and Political Economy on the Taiwan Frontier, 1600–1800.* Stanford: Stanford University Press.

Short, Philip. 2000. *Mao: A Life*. New York: Henry Holt, 2000.

Sommer, Matthew H. 2000. *Sex, Law, and Society in Late Imperial China*. Stanford: Stanford University Press.

Spence, Jonathan D. 1969. *To Change China: Western Advisors in China, 1620–1960*. Boston: Little, Brown.

Spence, Jonathan D. 1999. *Mao Zedong*. New York: Viking.

Swayne, Michael D., and Ashley J. Tellis. 2000. *Interpreting China's Grand Strategy: Past, Present, and Future*. Santa Monica: RAND.

Taylor, Jay. 2000. *The Generalissimo's Son: Chiang Ching-kuo and the Revolutions in China and Taiwan*. Cambridge, Massachusetts: Harvard University Press.

Taylor, Jay. 2009. *The Generalissimo: Chiang Kai-shek and the Struggle for Modern China*. Cambridge, Mass.: The Belknap Press of Harvard University Press.

Temple, Robert. 1986. *The Genius of China: 3,000 Years of Science, Discovery, and Invention*. New York: Simon and Schuster.

Teng, Emma. 2004. *Taiwan's Imagined Geography: Chinese Colonial Travel Writing and Pictures, 1683–1895*. Cambridge, Mass.: Harvard University Asia Center / Harvard University Press.

Trudeau, Pierre, and Jacques Hébert. 1968. *Two Innocents in Red China*. Toronto and New York: Oxford University Press.

Trudeau, Pierre, and Jacques Hébert. 2007. *Two Innocents in Red China*. Vancouver: Douglas & McIntyre.

Tsou, Jung (Zou Rong). 1968. *The Revolutionary Army: A Chinese Nationalist Tract of 1903*. Edited and translated by John Lust. The Hague: Mouton.

Waldron, Arthur. 1990. *The Great Wall of China: From History to Myth*. Cambridge: Cambridge University Press.

Waley, Arthur. 1958. *The Way and Its Power: A Study of the Tao te ching and Its Place in Chinese Thought*. New York: Grove Press.

Watson, Burton, translator. 1963. *Mo Tzu: Basic Writings*. New York: Columbia University Press.

Watson, Burton, translator. 1993. *Records of the Grand Historian: Han Dynasty II*, rev. ed. Hong Kong: Columbia University Press.

Wei, William. 2002. " 'Political Power Grows Out of the Barrel of a Gun': Mao and the Red Army." In *A Military History of China*, edited by David Graff and Robin Higham, 229–48. Boulder, Colorado: Westview Press.

Wong, Edward. 2009. "At least 74 Miners Are Killed in China Blast." *New York Times*, 22 (February).

Wong, Jan. 1996. *Red China Blues: My Long March from Mao to Now*. Toronto: Doubleday / Anchor Books.

Wright, David Curtis. 2001. *The History of China*. Westport, Connecticut: Greenwood Press.

Wright, David Curtis. 2002. "The Screed of a Humbled Empire: The *Xin Tangshu*'s Prolegomena on the Turks." *Acta Orientalia* 55(4): 379–89.

Wright, David Curtis. 2006. "Trudeau's Great Leap: A new translation of his Chinese travel diaries prompts both admiration and concern." Review article of *Hongse Zhongguo di liangwei tianzhenhan* (*Two Innocents in Red China*). In *Literary Review of Canada* 14(9) (November): 27–28.

Wu, Harry, and Carolyn Wakeman. 1994. *Bitter Winds: A Memoir of My Years in China's Gulag*. New York: John Wiley & Sons Inc.

Wu, Ningkun. 1993. *A Single Tear: A Family's Persecution, Love, and Endurance in Communist China*. New York: Atlantic Monthly Press.

Yardley, Jim. 2007. "Beneath booming cities, China's future is drying up." *New York Times* 28 (September).

York, Geoffrey. 2009. "A canary in the Chinese coal mine." *Globe and Mail* (March 31).

Yu, Mok. C., and J. Frank Harrison, eds. 1990. *Voices from Tiananmen Square: Beijing Spring and the Democracy Movement*. Montreal: Black Rose Books.

Zhai, Zhenhua. 1992. *Red Flower of China: An Autobiography*. New York: Soho.

Zhang, Liang, comp.; Andrew J. Nathan and Perry Link, eds. 2001. *The Tiananmen Papers*. New York: Public Affairs.

Bibliographic Essay

PRINT SOURCES

The best single-volume general history of China is Jacques Gernet, *A History of Chinese Civilization*, 2d ed. (Cambridge: Cambridge University Press, 1996). Also useful, though less detailed and informative, is John K. Fairbank and Edwin O. Reischauer, *China: Tradition and Transformation*, rev. ed. (Boston: Houghton Mifflin, 1989). The volumes of *The Cambridge History of China* (Cambridge: Cambridge University Press, various years) are tremendous assets for examining specific dynasties or periods of twentieth-century Chinese history in more detail. F. W. Mote's recent *Imperial China, 900–1800* (Cambridge, Mass.: Harvard University Press, 1999), a magisterial work of over 1,100 pages, will remain for decades the authoritative treatment of the Song, Yuan, Ming, and Qing dynasties.

F. W. Mote, *Intellectual Foundations of China*, 2d ed. (New York: McGraw Hill, 1989), is a concise and informative introduction to China's intellectual history. More detailed and comparative is Benjamin Schwartz, *The World of Thought in Ancient China* (Cambridge, Mass.: Harvard University Press, 1985). Yu-lan Fung's classic two-volume *A History of Chinese Philosophy*, 2d ed. (Princeton: Princeton University Press, 1963), is now somewhat dated but is still an essential standard work. Translated excerpts from Chinese philosophers and other influential thinkers are included in William Theodore de Bary et al., *Sources of Chinese Tradition*, vols. 1, 2 (New York: Columbia University Press, 1960), and in Wing Tsit-chan, *A Source Book in Chinese Philosophy* (Princeton: Princeton University Press, 1963).

The best historical survey of Sino-nomadic relations remains *The Perilous Frontier: Nomadic Empires and China* (Oxford: Basil Blackwell, 1989), by Thomas J. Barfield, an anthropologist. Hopefully a historian will eventually produce a more detailed and less theoretical survey of this topic. René Grousset's old masterwork *Empire of the Steppes: A History of Central Asia* (New Brunswick, N.J.: Rutgers University Press, 1970; translated from the French by Naomi Walford) is detailed and still very useful.

Volumes of Joseph Needham's monumental *Science and Civilisation in China*, a work that will contain a projected 25 volumes, have been published by Cambridge University Press since the 1950s. A one-volume distillation of some of Needham's most important findings is Robert Temple, *The Genius of China: 3,000 Years of Science, Discovery, and Invention* (New York: Simon and Schuster, 1986). Also useful is the five-volume abridgment of Needham's work by Colin A. Ronan, *The Shorter Science and Civilisation in China* (Cambridge: Cambridge University Press, 1985–1995).

"Modern" Chinese history is usually thought to have begun around 1800 or so, with some acknowledgement of major developments during the Qing. Jonathan Spence, *The Search for Modern China*, 2d ed. (New York: W. W. Norton, 1999), is a very readable survey of modern Chinese history by an eminent historian at Yale. Slightly less readable but certainly more packed with information is Immanuel Chung-yueh Hsü, *The Rise of Modern China*, 6th ed. (Oxford: Oxford University Press, 1999). Surveys of the People's Republic of China since 1949, with some examination of the Chinese Communists' rise to power since the 1920s, are Craig Dietrich, *People's China: A Brief History*, 3d ed. (New York: Oxford University Press, 1998), a readable and concise treatment, and Maurice Meisner, *Mao's China and After: A History of the People's Republic*, 3d ed. (New York: Free Press, 1999), a much denser work with a heavier theoretical and political science approach. Kenneth Lieberthal, *Governing China: From Revolution Through Reform* (New York: W. W. Norton, 1995), is a comprehensive survey of government in China from imperial times to the present, with emphasis on twentieth-century developments and the challenges China's Communist regime will face in the future. Also useful is June Tuefel Dreyer, *China's Political System: Modernization and Tradition*, 4th edition (2004).

Important interpretive and first-hand studies of mainland Chinese history are coming out at an accelerating rate. *Will the Boat Sink the Water? The Life of China's Peasants* (2006), by Chen Guidi and Wu Chuntao, contains accurate and compelling accounts of misery today in rural China. Denise Chong, *Egg on Mao: The Story of an Ordinary Man Who Defaced an Icon and Unmasked a Dictatorship* (2009) is an account of the indefatigable Lu Decheng and his years in prison for defacing Mao's portrait in Tiananmen Square in 1989. Important studies of China's environment include Elizabeth Economy, *The River Runs Black: The Environmental Challenge to China's Future* (2004) and Judith Shapiro, *Mao's War Against Nature: Politics and the Environment in Revolutionary China* (2001). *A Military History of China*, edited by David Graff and Robin Higham (2002), is a pioneering study of Chinese military history from early times to the present. *Bare Branches: The Security Implications of Asia's Surplus Male Population* (2005) draws attention to China's looming demographic crises.

To date there is, incredibly, no full-length English-language biography of Mao Zedong by a competent Sinologist. Until one appears, works by journalists will have to suffice. The most distinguished of this lot is Philip Short's long *Mao: A Life* (2001). Mao's physician wrote memoirs which pertain largely to Mao: Li Zhisui, *The Private Life of Chairman Mao* (1994). Professional Sinologists skirmish with full-length biographical treatments of Mao but end up with frustratingly short books. Among these are Jonathan Spence's Penguin volume *Mao Zedong* (1999) and especially Maurice Meisner's brief masterpiece *Mao Zedong: A Political and Intellectual Portrait* (2007), which is the single best biography of Mao currently available, short or long. Jung Chang and Jon Halliday, *Mao: The Unknown Story* (2006), is a two-dimensional hack job on a three-dimensional subject and is not to be taken seriously. (See my review, "Mao: The Inadequate Story." *Journal of Military and Strategic Studies* 9, no. 1 [Fall 2006].)

There is now a good biography of Chiang Kai-shek by a competent scholar who reads Chinese and utilizes Chinese materials: Jay Taylor, *The Generalissimo: Chiang Kai-shek and the Struggle for Modern China* (2009). (Previous to Taylor there was Jonathan Fenby's *Chiang Kai-shek: China's Generalissimo and the Nation He Lost* (2004), another work by a journalist.) Jay Taylor has also produced a first-rate biography of Chiang Ching-kuo, the son of Chiang Kai-shek: *The Generalissimo's Son: Chiang Ching-kuo and the Revolutions in China and Taiwan* (2000).

Taiwan: A New History (Armonk, N.Y.: M. E. Sharpe, 1999), edited by Murray A. Rubinstein, is a multi-authored survey of Taiwan's history. John Robert Shepherd, *Statecraft and Political Economy on the Taiwan*

Frontier, 1600–1800 (Stanford, Calif.: Stanford University Press, 1993), is an authoritative treatment of the island's premodern history. Important new treatments of Taiwan's transition from authoritarian Nationalist rule to full-fledged democracy include Shelley Rigger, *Politics in Taiwan: Voting For Democracy* (Routledge, 1999), and Linda Chao and Ramon H. Myers, *The First Chinese Democracy: Political Life in the Republic of China on Taiwan* (Baltimore: Johns Hopkins University Press, 1999).

More recently, the usual floodtide of books of uneven quality on the perennial topic of "crisis" or "relations" across the Taiwan Strait continues unabated. But a great many of these works are of evanescent value as historical studies and pertain more to political science. Over the past decade there has been a small avalanche of important new books on Taiwan history. Tonio Andrade's *How Taiwan Became Chinese: Dutch, Spanish, and Han Colonization in the Seventeenth Century* (2008) is an in-depth consideration of the century that made Taiwan a distinct society. Emma Teng's *Taiwan's Imagined Geography: Chinese Colonial Travel Writing and Pictures, 1683–1895* (2004) is a study of how mainland Chinese opinion about the island and its people evolved over three centuries. José Eugenio Borao Mateo's *The Spanish Experience in Taiwan, 1626–1642: The Baroque Ending of a Renaissance Endeavour* (2010) is an examination of a badly neglected period and topic in Taiwan's history. Denny Roy's *Taiwan: A Political History* (2003) is useful and informative. In 2007 an expanded edition of Murray A. Rubinstein's edited volume on Taiwan history was published. Most serious English-language studies on Taiwan history are published by foreign or Taiwanese academic presses.

Books and blogs written by foreign political junkies and amateur history buffs are a dime a dozen in Taiwan. Their books, especially if they are published by commercial presses in Taiwan, are of limited value because they are not peer-reviewed and because of their half-baked conclusions, shrilly partisan perspectives, and the ideological axes they seek to grind. They represent a typical scenario or pattern for the development of a foreign amateur autodidact who eventually comes to fancy himself an authority on all things Taiwanese, especially politics and history: Foreign white guy comes to Taiwan planning to teach English for a while, falls in love with and marries a local girl, absorbs her political views and ethnic prejudices like a sponge (setting aside his own natural objectivity and neutrality in the process), goes native after a few years, and ends up running an angry and biased pro-Green website or blog.

There are, however, a few outstanding exceptions to this general rule. Linda Gail Arrigo and Lynn Miles, important participants in modern Taiwanese history, have put together an extremely valuable compilation of primary historical documents: *A Borrowed Voice: Taiwan Human Rights Through International Networks, 1960–1980* (2008). Volumes I and II of José Eugenio Borao Mateo's *Spaniards in Taiwan* (2001 and 2002) are rich treasure troves of primary historical documents in both the Spanish originals and modern English translations. Macabe Keliher's translations of the writings of the Qing literatus Yu Yonghe on Taiwan are readable, informative, and engaging.

NONPRINT SOURCES

There are several important online newspapers for keeping up with China. The *New York Times* (America's newspaper of record) and *The Globe and Mail* (Canada's newspaper of record) often have good, informative articles on China. *The South China Morning Post* is also a very good newspaper, one based in Hong Kong, but unfortunately it requires readers to pay for all but a few articles.

The online edition of the *People's Daily* is the official propaganda arm of the Chinese Communist Party and is, therefore, hardly an objective and unbiased news source. It is, however, valuable for conveying what the Party wants its readers to think and conclude about the news being reported. Unfortunately, the *People's Daily* is often written in clumsy, awkward English. Many English-language newspapers in East Asia have learned the vital importance of having native Anglophone editors, but the *People's Daily* is not yet one of them.

The *Taipei Times* is a Green-leaning English-language newspaper that offers good coverage of Taiwan, especially Taiwanese politics. It is written in intelligent English and sometimes features engaging human interest stories. The *China Post* is, despite its confusing title, also an English-language newspaper in Taiwan. It has a Blue editorial stance overall, although it is not as ideologically Blue as the *Taipei Times* is Green.

There are many blogs about Taiwan, but the majority of them, even by PhDs, are shallow and surprisingly poorly written. The best Taiwan blog is Michael Turton's *The View from Taiwan*. Turton is, like almost all foreigners who blog about Taiwan, stridently Green and pro-independence. He is, however, very well informed about the island and is something of an Internet institution for Taiwan and has been for many years. If a Taiwan-related blog does not make his list of such blogs, it is likely not worth reading.

Good Internet resources for Chinese history, as opposed to current events, are harder to find. Many websites are either too simple or shallow for a curious, intelligent reader or else too technical and detailed. A few surveys of Chinese history published more than 75 years ago are available online because they are no longer copyrighted, but they are of course badly out of date. A good place to start reading is *A Visual Sourcebook of Chinese Civilization*, available at http://depts.washington.edu/chinaciv/. There are many valuable research tools available online, but these typically make extensive use of Chinese characters and are primarily for scholars who already know Chinese.

Index

About the Author

DAVID CURTIS WRIGHT is Associate Professor in the Department of History and Executive Research Fellow at the Centre for Military and Strategic Studies at the University of Calgary in Calgary, Alberta, Canada. He earned his PhD in East Asian Studies at Princeton University.

Other Titles in the Greenwood Histories of the Modern Nations

Frank W. Thackeray and John E. Findling, Series Editors

The History of Afghanistan
Meredith L. Runion

The History of Argentina
Daniel K. Lewis

The History of Australia
Frank G. Clarke

The History of the Baltic States
Kevin O'Connor

The History of Brazil
Robert M. Levine

The History of Bulgaria
Frederick B. Chary

The History of Cambodia
Justin Corfield

The History of Canada
Scott W. See

The History of Central America
Thomas Pearcy

The History of the Central
Asian Republics
Peter L. Roudik

The History of Chile
John L. Rector

The History of China,
Second Edition
David Curtis Wright

The History of Congo
Didier Gondola

The History of Cuba
Clifford L. Staten

The History of the Czech
Republic and Slovakia
William M. Mahoney

The History of Egypt
Glenn E. Perry

The History of El Salvador
Christopher M. White

The History of Ethiopia
Saheed Adejumobi

The History of Finland
Jason Lavery

The History of France
W. Scott Haine

The History of Germany
Eleanor L. Turk

The History of Ghana
Roger S. Gocking

The History of Great Britain
Anne Baltz Rodrick

The History of Haiti
Steeve Coupeau

The History of Holland
Mark T. Hooker

The History of Honduras
Thomas M. Leonard

The History of India
John McLeod

The History of Indonesia
Steven Drakeley

The History of Iran
Elton L. Daniel

The History of Iraq
Courtney Hunt

The History of Ireland
Daniel Webster Hollis III

The History of Israel
Arnold Blumberg

The History of Italy
Charles L. Killinger

The History of Japan, Second Edition
Louis G. Perez

The History of Korea
Djun Kil Kim

The History of Kuwait
Michael S. Casey

The History of Mexico, Second Edition
Burton Kirkwood

The History of New Zealand
Tom Brooking

The History of Nicaragua
Clifford L. Staten

The History of Nigeria
Toyin Falola

The History of Pakistan
Iftikhar H. Malik

The History of Panama
Robert C. Harding

The History of Peru
Daniel Masterson

The History of the Philippines
Kathleen M. Nadeau

The History of Poland
M.B. Biskupski

The History of Portugal
James M. Anderson

The History of Puerto Rico
Lisa Pierce Flores

The History of Russia, Second Edition
Charles E. Ziegler

The History of Saudi Arabia
Wayne H. Bowen

The History of Serbia
John K. Cox

The History of Singapore
Jean E. Abshire

The History of South Africa
Roger B. Beck

The History of Spain
Peter Pierson

The History of Sri Lanka
Patrick Peebles

The History of Sweden
Byron J. Nordstrom

The History of Thailand
Patit Paban Mishra

The History of Turkey
Douglas A. Howard

The History of Ukraine
Paul Kubicek

The History of Venezuela
H. Micheal Tarver and Julia C. Frederick

The History of Vietnam
Justin Corfield